The Revival of the

The Revival
of the
Democratic Intellect

Scotland's University Traditions
and the Crisis in Modern Thought

Andrew Lockhart Walker

Polygon
EDINBURGH

First published by
Polygon
22 George Square
Edinburgh

Typeset in Linotron Sabon
Printed and bound in Great Britain by
The Short Run Press Ltd., Exeter

A CIP record for this title is available

ISBN 0 7486 61883

The publisher acknowledges subsidy from

towards the publication of this volume

For Shelley and Rowan

Contents

Preface

In January 1992 a committee of the University of Edinburgh decided to freeze the Chair of Scottish History as a contribution to the university's efforts to reduce its financial deficit. It did so at a time when the demand for greater constitutional autonomy had reached a peak in Scotland. There was of course an outcry in the media by a wide cross-section of opinion, and this compelled a partial withdrawal by the university, though the chair was still not to be filled till the autumn of 1993. But how could such a decision have been reached, apparently without qualms, at a time of exciting developments in Scottish historiography and in a university which was at the heart of the Scottish Enlightenment, a university of which Thomas Jefferson had said in the eighteenth century that there was no place like it in the world for science? How could the University of Edinburgh be so utterly out of touch with Scottish opinion?

This book is an attempt, at least in part, to answer that question. A number of letters to the press spoke of excessive anglicization, of a majority of the staff at the University of Edinburgh being English and thus trained in a higher education tradition very different from that of Scotland. For them Scottish history was a minor subject very suitable for making economies. There has been a growing unease in Scotland as more and more areas of the nation's culture have been handed over to English direction, especially in the arts. There was George Rosie's television programme *The Englishing of Scotland*; politicians like Jim Sillars have spoken of "cultural genocide"; while books like Michael Hechter's *Internal Colonialism: the Celtic fringe in British national development* speak of cultural colonization and a deliberate policy of "inferiorisation" of things Scottish.

Nowhere did this anglicization process begin earlier than in the

universities, and nowhere, it can safely be said, is it likely to have
a more powerful influence on the national psyche and the national
self-image, since a large number of the nation's most aspiring and
ambitious young people pass through the universities. It is not too
much to say, as things stand, that Scotland's cultural soul is at stake.
Yet a number of authors, mainly historians and educationalists, have
recently sought to deny that there has been a process of anglicization
at work in our universities. There has been no thorough, detailed
attempt to make out the case since George Elder Davie's two seminal
books in a philosophical mode *The Democratic Intellect* and *The
Crisis of the Democratic Intellect*, which have in fact been treated
rather frivolously by the authors referred to.

I must immediately enter a strong caveat to the reader. I am no
philosopher, nor yet a historian, nor even an educationalist. I am a
retired academic linguist who has spent half-a-lifetime in English and
Scottish universities, and who has become increasingly worried as
he watched the quite evident takeover of Scotland's universities, first
by English staff with their different epistemological approach, and
now by English students to the exclusion of Scottish applicants. The
great Scottish tradition of a broad, general education has been all
but wiped out, especially the philosophical questioning at the heart
of it. Yet there has never been a time when it was more important
to teach students to ask questions, in view of the vast, planet-wide
problems that face us all.

So my intention is straightforward, even if technically unskilled. I
wish to demonstrate, as simply as I can, that Scotland's universities
have been hijacked by an intellectually alien tradition, and that it is
very necessary and not impossible to restore our own tradition, that
of the democratic intellect. This whole area of thought on the future
of Scotland's higher education requires very careful consideration,
yet there is very little evidence that people in politics and higher
education are paying anything more than superficial attention to it.
My perforce modest hope for this book is that it will provoke some
of these people to pay much more serious attention to the fundamental problems facing our universities, and encourage better scholars
than I to fill in the gaps I have left and develop further this vitally
important but strangely neglected area of our national cultural heritage. If action is not taken soon Scotland will lose, irretrievably,
that great educational tradition that goes back to Columba and has
been the very soul of this nation.

So this book is a work of advocacy. It attempts to persuade the
reader to visualize the problems of Scotland's universities in a particular way. For different reasons this perspective has been muffled
and hidden, except in the work of George Davie, though it is clearly

evident in the historical record. It is therefore necessary to go back to square one, to *partir de loin* in the French manner. The first chapter is a rapid overview of the development of universities up until the foundation of the first universities in Scotland. Chapter 2 covers the development of Scotland's universities until the nineteenth century. Chapter 3 does the same for England' universities, i.e. Oxford and Cambridge, for purposes of comparison and contrast. Chapter 4 documents the wholesale reforms imposed on the Scottish universities during the nineteenth century and the effect those reforms had on traditional epistemological approaches and teaching methods. Chapter 5 shows the widespread influence of traditional Scottish university teaching throughout the world. Chapter 6 deals with the efforts of the new universities in the 1960s to try and restore something of the tradition of a general, philosophical education on the Scottish model. Chapters 7 and 8 attempt to delineate, in a very amateurish way, the fundamental philosophical and scientific doctrines that lie behind the evolution of thought in the universities. Chapter 9 outlines the Scottish philosophical contribution and seeks to bring out the consistent, anti-dualistic, ethical, common sensethread that runs right through it from John the Scot (Scotus Erigena) to Alasdair MacIntyre. Chapters 10 and 11 seek to show the nature and reality of the democratic intellect in the past practice of Scotland's universities. Chapter 12 documents the hyper-specialization which, in the opinion of many thinkers, is destroying our universities. Chapters 13 and 14 show how the wholesale anglicization of Scotland's universities has weakened them. Finally Chapters 15, 16 and 17 attempt to convince the reader that, despite the present deplorable situation, our universities can restore, in a modern form, the great tradition of the democratic intellect and thereby make a major contribution to preparing today's young people to tackle the gigantic environmental problems and problems of human development that now face us. The 'Envoi' offers reasons for hope.

I had a problem of presentation. First, I wanted to avoid academic aridity as much as possible and secondly, to bring out the breadth and intensity of the public debate on these questions over the years, since it had been largely forgotten, overlooked or hushed up. After various experiments I concluded that the best thing was to let the protagonists speak for themselves. I have therefore used much quotation from monographs, periodicals and ephemera. I do not claim to have succeeded in making the subject live, but I hope that I may have eased the reader's task in tackling a long book.

Finally, I owe warm thanks to Linda Youngson of Stirling University Library, who helped me get started and was always ready with bibliographical assistance; to my daughter Shelley for an important suggestion and for her constant encouragement in very difficult circumstances; to my son Ruaraidh for his skill and stamina in a lengthy word-processing rescue operation; and to Cairns Craig but for whose challenging suggestion this book would probably never have been written. Special thanks are due also to the editors and contributors of the *Times Educational Supplement for Scotland* and *The Times Higher Education Supplement* for their assiduous mapping and thoughtful analysis of the changing higher education scene in Great Britain.

ANDREW LOCKHART WALKER

1

Precursors

"We are dwarfs perched on the shoulders of giants"
Bernard of Chartres

In the Preface I said it was necessary to go back to square one. In the case of Scotland's universities this means taking a look at the development of the idea of a university in the years preceding 1411, when Scotland's first university, St. Andrews, was founded. This is necessary because, as G. S. Osborne explains, Scotland's universities "have had the responsibility of preserving the cultural and intellectual life of the country, and this was – and still is – based on a concept of liberal education far older than the oldest of the British universities." The earnest Scottish student was well known on the Continent long before the establishment of any Scottish university, and the "design of the Scottish ordinary degree courses in Arts can be seen to have evolved directly from the seven liberal arts of classical times as they were interpreted by the universities of Western Europe."[1]

The story begins in Athens, Alexandria and Rome. Education at Athens, in its voluntary, free-wheeling style, was very like that in the universities of Bologna and Paris in the twelfth century, though it was of much greater importance to the ancient world than Paris was to Europe. From the beginning of the Roman Empire it received endowments, partly public, partly private, and with them more definite organization. There were three principal chairs – rhetoric, politics and philosophy – the first of which was considered the most important. The chief source of income, however, was students' fees, including those of what we should today call mature students. Rival teachers competed for students, and the arrival of a ship at the Piraeus was met by a rush, not of vendors but of students touting for their own particular sophist. Athens survived until the second century A.D., and was recognized as the centre of the most accomplished scholarship.

Its greatest rival was Alexandria, which was the first centre of learning to give distinct form and organization to a "university" as we understand the word. The great library, the Serapeum, was founded in 298 B.C., contained 700,000 volumes, and was only finally destroyed by fire in A.D. 640. The studium generale, or Museum, was founded by Ptolemy, lasted 600 years, and provided a carefully organised and endowed education, which was also more practical than at Athens. There were taught philosophy, mathematics and what we would today call physics, and also medicine, law and astronomy. One of the great names connected with it was Plotinus, the philosopher and mystic, who died in 205 A.D. For, despite the attractions and reputation of Athens, the palm for philosophical thought passed to Alexandria from the first century onwards. It was seen as the progressive university of its day; its great specialism was medicine.

It was during the lifetime of Quintilian, who died in 118 A.D., that the Roman university began. He was a great teacher, and his *Oratorical Institutions* is a pedagogical work which expounds the best Hellenic and Roman teaching of his day. It began under Vespasian and Hadrian, for the promotion of higher education was deliberate imperial policy: "By means of endowment and organization, men who might otherwise have employed themselves in misleading youth and disturbing the social order were brought into the service of the imperial idea."[2] The students were young, entering at 14 (as later in Scotland), and they studied the trivium and quadrivium, as at Athens and Alexandria. Strong public support was forthcoming for education; teachers were held in high respect and enjoyed, as Gibbon puts it, "many lucrative and honourable privileges".

The compendium of studies later to be known as the trivium and quadrivium dated from the time of Isocrates and were influenced by Aristotle among others. They were: grammar, rhetoric and dialectic – the trivium; and music, arithmetic, geometry and astronomy – the quadrivium. Dialectic included logic, metaphysics and ethics. The seven liberal arts were studied solely in the interests of general culture and with no professional aims, with the exception of rhetoric, which aimed to prepare young people for public life. At Alexandria there was specialist training in medicine, at Rome professional education for lawyers. But the "arts" training came first. "It is imperative", says Laurie, "to keep this in view, if we would understand the higher schools of the Greeks and Romans and the subsequent character of medieval education."[3] It is also important to know that for a great teacher like Quintilian formal studies such as logic and rhetoric were to be undertaken "with a view to the solid substance of philosophy, science and art. The realities of life, not the form of words or trick of phrase or felicity of construction, were to be the preparation for the good orator." (This neatly encapsulates the fundamental difference between the Scottish universities and Oxbridge in the nineteenth century if one replaces the word "orator" by "professional").

By the middle of the second century, however, "philosophy had become an intellectual game, personal morality a matter of convention and prudence, and rhetoric an artifice. Words took the place of things, forms of realities".[4] The condition seems familiar in our day – it is known as decadence. "It is a curious but, I think, undeniable fact", says Laurie, "that from the time education became an object of solicitude to the civil power, genuine philosophic ardour and literary productivity began to decline, and a marked and steady decline of the scientific spirit was visible . . . philosophy had become void through the absence of ethical purpose".[5] As Sidonius Apollinaris (died in 488) said: "Young men no longer study, professors no longer have pupils; knowledge languishes and dies."[6]

At this point the early Christian monastic schools take over. With the fall of Rome and the advent of the Dark Ages learning disappeared from Europe, except in Ireland and South-West Scotland. The Irish or Scoti cultivated Greek and Latin literature when other parts of the "civilized" world had ceased to do so, and "they were much given to dialectic disputation".[7] Scholarship was very much alive among them and a genuine speculative spirit. These celebrated schools, says Laurie (to whom I am heavily indebted in this chapter), must have been founded at the beginning of the sixth century, and he quotes Döllinger: "While almost the whole of Europe was desolated by war, peaceful Ireland, free from the invasions of external foes, opened to lovers of learning and piety a welcome asylum."[8] From these schools the Scots monks bore learning and founded monasteries in Scotland, England, France, Germany, Switzerland. The evidence of this peaceful invasion is still there today in such places as Strasbourg, St. Gallen, Munich and Vienna.

The monastic system established by Columba in Iona was highly important from the educational point of view, because it was the type of early Christian culture which did so much for centuries to mould the intelligence and character of the Scottish people.[9] All the monasteries set up by Columba and his disciples were in fact educational seminaries and youths were sent to them to receive a general education, and not only to be trained as monks. Education was indeed Columba's greatest service to Scotland; he was the first in the line of great Scottish educators. "By the schools he established up and down the country of his adoption, he laid the foundations of its national system of education."[10] Even then young people were

attracted from England and Ireland to receive a general education.
This great Scottish tradition of a general education goes back a very
long way.

Laurie tells a delightful anecdote in illustration of this theme which
is worth retailing.[11] During the reign of Charlemagne (742–814)
two Scots, Claud Clement and John Melrose, turned up in the
market-place at Aix-la-Chapelle and called out their educational
wares like a town-crier: "Si quis sapentiae cupidus est, veniat ad
nos, et accipiat eam, nam venalis est apud nos" (If anyone wants
knowledge, let him come to us and get it, for we have it to sell). Market forces were clearly already at work in Charlemagne's empire.
Charlemagne sent for them and asked what they wanted for their
knowledge, and they replied that their price was "a place to teach
it, pupils to learn it, and needful food and raiment". Already here
there is more than a hint of what was much later to be known as
the "democratic intellect" – a spirit of egalitarian simplicity, of high
thinking and low living. Charlemagne, to his credit, accepted their
offer. He set up a school in his palace under Clement, and settled
Melrose as the superintendent of a schola at Pavia. They clearly
did very well out of their marketing skills! This was the origin of
the Palatine School for members of the court and their children.
Charlemagne also set up important schools at Bologna and Paris.
It is quite likely that these four schools helped to lay the foundations of the university movement three centuries later. The idea of
a studium generale may have grown from Charlemagne's practice
of concentrating eminent teachers at important centres. There were
also episcopal and cathedral schools, as at Orléans, where a law
university was set up three centuries later, but it was the monastic
schools which played the most important role in education.

The hand of the Scots is prominent in all these developments. For
example, Laurie tells us that "it was not in all schools, but only in
the more advanced, and especially those under the influence of the
Irish or Scots school of monks, that such authors as Virgil were
tolerated".[12] In these schools the sons of serf and nobleman might
often be found sitting side by side – again an early example of the
democratic intellect. It was in the Irish monasteries and St. Gallen –
another 'Scots' establishment – that Greek received most attention.

The downside was that the humanities could not develop alongside faith, alone necessary for salvation. Science was impossible,
since it depends on free investigation; and so was philosophy, since
it must be free to follow wherever thought takes it. But the time was
now fast approaching when the speculative 'Scots' mind was to start
asking metaphysical questions. Clement, whom we have met, introduced the freer and more speculative theology of the Celtic church

into the Palace School, and John Scotus Erigena, known as John the Scot, was appointed to the school under Charles le Chauve.[13] This was a big step forward in liberalizing thought. King Alfred of England also set up a palace school and called on Scotus to help him. This was the first of many innovative Scottish interventions in English education, especially higher education, as we shall see in the sequel.

John Scotus Erigena was the greatest thinker in the 500 years from the sixth century to the middle of the eleventh century. He defended the rights of reason against the authority of the fathers at a time when the intellectual asceticism of medieval Christianity shunned speculative investigation. The 1926 edition of the *Encyclopedia Britannica* says of him that he is the most interesting figure among medieval writers: "The freedom of his speculation and the boldness with which he works out his logical and dialectical system of the universe altogether prevent us from classing him along with the scholastics properly so called. With him philosophy isn't in the service of theology; philosophy, or reason, is first." The highest faculty of man is reason, *intellectus* or *intellectualis visio*, and it is that *which is not content with the individual or particular but grasps the whole and thereof comprehends the parts. In this supreme effort of reason thought and being are at one, the opposition of being and thought is overcome.* Erigena said: "Authority is derived from reason, not reason from authority; and where the former is not confined by the latter, if it is valueless."

Here we see – it is not fanciful to believe – the auspicious beginnings of three major characteristics of the Scottish epistemological approach in the universities :

1 The belief in reason, the "philosophical itch to dispute all things";

2 The instinct for universality and interconnectedness in thought, so strongly evident during the Scottish Enlightenment; and

3 The determination to overcome Cartesian dualism in the Scottish school of commonsense philosophy.

So the universities may be regarded as a natural development of the monastic and cathedral schools, but there were very few men even remotely approaching the calibre of John Scotus Erigena. There was a general stagnation as the first millennium, expected to be the end of the world, approached. The next crucial impulse came from the Mohammedan, Arab world, from the great schools at Baghdad, Babylon, Alexandria, Cairo, Cordoba, Granada and Seville, where profound, original study of the liberal arts was carried on and where Christian and Jewish teachers and students were

welcome. The Saracens restored what Laurie calls the "university
life of the Greeks".[14] The Mohammedan courts were host to such
great figures as Avicenna and Averrhoes.

Why did the first universities arise when they did? Because of the
sheer growth and accumulation of knowledge on the subjects essential to the welfare of society it became necessary to specialize, and
because, as we have seen with John Scotus Erigena, reason and
knowledge more and more took on a lay flavour. The result was that
from the very start the universities specialized: Salernum in medicine,
Bologna in law, and Paris in philosophy and theology. This specialization attracted large numbers of upwardly mobile young people
anxious to get on in medicine, the law or the church. Whereas the
arts schools in monasteries and cathedrals came under ecclesiastical rules, these specialized schools were open to all (*studia publica*
or *generalia*) for the free pursuit of professional studies. These are
the two distinguishing features of the new university or studium
generale. Laurie defines it as "a privileged, higher, specialized and
self-governing school open to all the world, free from monastic or
canonical rule, its privileges including the right of promotion".[15]

These specialized studies, however, were always preceded by an
Arts course – the trivium at least, i.e. grammar, rhetoric and dialectic. These were at first obtained outside the universities, in the
cathedral or monastic schools, but very soon became an integral
part of university teaching. At Salernum, for example, a three-year
course in arts was necessary as preliminary to a five-year course in
medicine. This is a tradition that the Scottish universities faithfully
followed right down to near the end of the nineteenth century. We
will suggest much later that it should be restored, in modified form
to suit our times, to repair a dangerous gap in the general education
of today's students. This is because the English three-year, and even
the Scottish four-year, honours course, are clearly too short to give
students a good general education, followed by specialist training,
in today's hugely expanded universe of knowledge as compared
with the eleventh century.

So Salernum was the first university, in 1060, to give specialized
instruction and to have a collegiate constitution, but it was Paris
and Bologna that set the pattern for all subsequent European universities. And it must be stressed that their primary purpose was a
professional, practical one: their aim was to minister to the needs
of society by the improvement of medicine, law and, to a lesser
extent, theology. This, too, was an example followed by the Scottish
universities, especially in the eighteenth and nineteenth centuries,
in contradistinction to Oxford and Cambridge.

Bologna was first given formal recognition as a university (meaning a community) by Frederick I in 1158. This status was confirmed by the Pope in 1254, at which time Bologna already had 10,000 students. It was to have 20,000 at the time of Roger Bacon. It was a lay community but retained the intellectual and moral preoccupations of its monkish origins. The large numbers of non-Italian students were divided into "nations", modelled on trade guilds or orders of chivalry, and these were free and very democratic self-governing societies. Here was born the office of Rector, still preserved in Scotland's older universities. Professors as scholars exercised power along with the students, but as professors they had no additional prerogatives. This is a tradition we have lost, but which we should perhaps restore. This model of a largely student-run university was followed by Glasgow University when it was founded. Study was very strictly organized in a system of lectures, repetitions and disputations, again a model closely followed in Scotland's universities.

The University of Paris arose directly out of the Notre Dame Arts School and is closely connected with the romantically tragic figure of Peter Abelard, who was one of the greatest university teachers who has ever lived. He was the next great champion of free speculation and inquiry following John Scotus Erigena. He set up a school of dialectic at Melun, and then became head of the Paris Arts School in 1113. When tragedy struck – and the story is too well known to need repeating – he became a Benedictine monk and withdrew to St. Denis where 3000 students from all over Europe asked him to teach. Jealousy and accusations of heresy still pursued him, so he withdrew to the forest six miles from Nogent-sur-Seine and built an oratory with reeds and thatch. He called it Paraclete, that is, the consolation. Again the students followed him, living in tents and mud huts, and rebuilt his oratory in stone. Still he was persecuted by the doctors of the church as a heretic. Here we see, for the very first time, and in France, the close relationship between the university and freedom of inquiry. The image of the persecuted philosopher, in the forest, surrounded by students in the simplest and poorest university imaginable, is a universal symbol of what we would today call academic freedom. It exercised a very powerful influence in Scotland's universities, for there could be no more inspiring example of what was much later to be called the "democratic intellect". It was Abelard's genius as a philosopher that finally converted the Arts school of Paris into a universitas, into a great specialized theological and philosophical school; and this central, seminal position of philosophy was to become perhaps the most distinguishing feature of the Scottish universities. The great historic

irony of Abelard's career was that twenty of his pupils became
cardinals and 50 bishops or archbishops. There is no teacher like
an enthusiastic and courageous radical.

Paris, unlike Bologna, was not run by the students; it was an
'universitas magistrorum' where the teaching staff were in control. It rapidly acquired a European reputation and spread from
the cathedral into buildings all over what is today known as the
Quartier Latin. Provision was made for free maintenance for poor
scholars – another tradition followed in Scotland, though not at
Oxford or Cambridge. It is indeed a curious and welcome paradox
that the great power and influence of the University of Paris lay in
its sheer material poverty. "What rendered the University of Paris
especially powerful was its poverty."[16] The university, the faculties,
the nations, were all of them poor. The university did not have a
building of its own and relied on friendly monastic orders for places
to meet. "Thus", says Laurie, "its existence and power assumed a
purely spiritual character[17] and was rendered permanently independent of the temporal authority". So knowledge could be distinct
from power: "Both the liberal university tradition and the scientific
tradition had this common origin in the prehistory of the medieval
university, because science is only possible when knowledge has
been freed from political expediency."[18]

Throughout the Middle Ages the University of Paris was looked up
to as the leading university in Europe, and the main reason for this
was its cultivation of philosophy. Philosophy was then understood,
as also later in the Scottish universities, in a much wider sense than
today. It included the analysis of both mind and matter, so that, for
example, physics or natural philosophy was a part of philosophy.
So a course in philosophy provided a very broad cultural training,
and, unlike the other main subjects of specialized university study,
namely medicine and law, it was free of all professional ambitions.
The Scottish universities remained true to this valuable tradition,
with its concomitant breadth of culture and understanding, until
deliberate government policy, in a sustained campaign throughout
the nineteenth century, finally put an end to it. We now begin to
see, as universities disintegrate into dozens, or even hundreds, of
highly specialized departments and sub-departments with no common language, how valuable that tradition was, and how necessary
it is to renew it if students are to have an integrated view of the
world and its appalling problems, and be able to ask the right
questions.

For that, Laurie points out, "the asking of endless questions",[19]
was the result of the growth, fostered by the church, of specialist
schools of learning with republican constitutions. They finally led

the thought of Europe and initiated the scientific spirit of inquiry, "that virile independence of mind which it is one of the chief objects of universities to promote."[20]

Today, when the universities seem to have lost their way, it is vital to get back to these first principles, particularly in the universities of Scotland where they held sway for so long.

2

The Scottish University Tradition

"It has been shown that, from a very early period, schools of various kinds existed over the greater portion of Scotland, and that, in the more important towns, there was more or less complete provision for advanced education."[1] To give just one example, Ayr Burgh School was founded in 1233, that is 150 years before Winchester, England's oldest public school, and 82 years before Robert the Bruce was crowned king of Scotland at a national parliament held in St. John's Church in Ayr in 1315.

So where did the young Scots go, who wanted a higher education, before St. Andrews was founded in 1411? A few went to Oxford and Cambridge, which began their careers as full universities in the thirteenth century, but the great majority went to universities on the Continent, mostly in France. They formed part of the famous wandering scholars of the Middle Ages, a practice that still exists in Germany. Indeed, the number of Scottish students in Paris in the fourteenth century was so great as to attract the attention of the authorities, and the Bishop of Moray found it necessary to found a Scots college in Paris in 1326. The words Collège des Ecossais can still be seen on a frontage in the Rue Cardinal Lemoine. Other Scots colleges were set up at Oxford: Balliol College founded by Sir John de Balliol in 1293; Douai 1576; Ratisbon (Bavaria) 1515 in the Scots monastery of St. James, founded at the beginning of the twelfth century; Rome, 1600; Madrid, 1627; Valladolid, l770, still functioning; Montpellier, founded by Patrick Geddes in 1924 after failing to resuscitate the Collège des Ecossais in Paris – it is still flourishing.

It is hardly surprising that the authorities were forced to take note of the Scots since the students led a pretty wild life in Paris. "This life, curiously compounded of hardship and kindliness, was doubtless useful in teaching them to face and overcome difficulties, but the freedom of it and the self-reliance it fostered, almost necessarily created a habit of mind impatient of restraint and strict discipline when they reached the precincts of the university."[2] This independent life of the students, with the universities having no responsibility for them, no status *in loco parentis*, was ever after to be the normal practice at Scottish universities, as different as could well be imagined from the cloistered, cosseted life of students at Oxford and Cambridge, with proctors and bulldogs hemming them in. An amusing example of this six centuries later is given by the late John Mackintosh MP:

> Professor Grierson, who once held the Chair of English at Edinburgh, used to commence lecturing each year by trying for five minutes to be heard above the uproar. When he failed he would shriek: 'Send for the police!' A group of burly constables who had been waiting outside rushed in, seized the leading troublemakers and threw them outside on the pavement, after which there was some semblance of order.[3]

The students were treated like any ordinary members of the public; they had no special penalties to face and no special immunities.

Since Scotland was a very poor country the number of young men who could afford to study abroad in this way must have been limited, though numerous enough as we have seen. Many of those who had profited from the "advanced education available in the more important towns" would have been unable to do it. "The astonishing thing", says Sir James Irvine,[4] a former Principal of the University of Edinburgh, "is that a small, poor and sparsely populated country produced scholars in suffiency to justify the bold educational experiment made by the little band of Masters and Doctors who, in 1410, commenced lectures in St. Andrews". The university received its charter from Bishop Henry Wardlaw on 27 February 1411. Even more astonishing, of course, was the fact that by the end of the century there were two more universities in Scotland: Glasgow, set up by Bishop William Turnbull in 1451, and Aberdeen, founded by Bishop Elphinstone in 1494. The demand was quite clearly there, so that by the end of fifteenth century, and before the creation of Edinburgh nearly a century later, Scotland already had one more university than England.

In its early period Scottish university education benefited from the talents of a few very able and very wise men, Bishop Elphinstone being one of the first for he held the view that "Scotland's greatest educational need was the provision of trained university teachers, and that more purposes could be served by a university than merely guaranteeing a succession of recruits for the Church".[5] One

of the greatest of these men was Andrew Melville who, like so
many able Scots of the period, taught in the universities of Europe.
Aberdeen's first Principal had been a professor in the University of
Paris; Melville had been a student at Paris, a regent (i.e. lecturer)
at Poitiers, and a Professor at Geneva. On his return from Geneva
he reorganized the University of Glasgow so that within a few
years "there was no place in Europe comparable to Glasgow for
a plentiful and good cheap market of all kinds of languages, arts
and sciences".[6] These references to what can only be described as
academic market forces should not worry the contemporary reader
too much. They reflect the fact that Scotland's universities followed
the medieval tradition of being "largely vocational schools . . . The
universities, overwhelmingly orientated towards the professional
needs of society, became increasingly reflective of the establishment
which they served."[7] It turned out to be a healthy tradition, as we
shall see in the eighteenth and nineteenth centuries especially, since
it meant that the distinction between the academic and the vocational, between the gentlemen and the players, was never as strong
in Scotland as in England, where it did great damage by creating
deep-rooted and restrictive elitist instincts throughout the education
system.

   In Scotland it was otherwise. "From the beginning the Scottish universities have been among the most democratic in the world – duke's
son and cook's son sat on the same student benches and shared the
same fare at the common table."[8] The most important feature of all
was the "ouverture aux talents": "From the humblest of Scottish
homes there was now a direct connection through the schools to
the class-rooms of the College, and the ladder of learning – rudely
fashioned and with uneven steps – had become a reality."[9] There
was to be no such ladder of learning in England till four centuries
later. Here was born the reality of the 'lad o' pairts' – no myth or
legend, as some contemporary scholars have sought to show. True,
it became the Scots' favourite image of their educational tradition,
but that is entirely to their credit. It is surely infinitely preferable
to the shibboleths of such contemporary pundits as Sir Christopher
Ball, who calls for the reduction of Scottish university courses to
three years instead of four, and for students of "imaginative and
creative minds to devote themselves to . . . the more immediate and
pressing issues of making and selling".[10] Or Dr. John Ashworth,
Director of the London School of Economics, who also calls for the
reduction of Scottish university courses to three years, and makes
much play with fashionable jargon terms like 'quality assurance'.[11]
The records give convincing proof that the longing for learning was
and is something real in Scotland, shared by rich and poor alike.

The three earliest universities had many points in common. They were all based more or less completely on the medieval universities of the Continent. Indeed, the older Scottish universities are now the only true continuators of the medieval organization, for they recognize the following elements as constituting the 'university': 1) the students; 2) the graduates (or *magistri non regentes*; 3) the professors (or *magistri regentes*); 4) the Rector; and 5) the Chancellor.[12] Papal authority was required to give them as learned communities self-government, immunity from taxation, power to give degrees and the freedom to teach. Owing to the poverty of Scotland and the selfishness of the nobility the only support they could count on was that given them by church dignitaries who took an interest in them. Their development was greatly hindered by international struggles. Indeed, in 1560 they were to be all but wiped out at the time of the Reformation. One of the reasons that so many young Scots went to France rather than England for a university education was that during the split in the Papacy Paris and Scotland supported Pope Clement in Avignon, whereas England supported Pope Urban in Rome. So young Scots were not welcome at Oxford and Cambridge.

Indeed, it would not be an exaggeration to say that no other country underwent an ordeal so prolonged and so destructive of the social peace necessary for the progress of the universities. During the latter part of the sixteenth century and the whole of the seventeenth century, every twenty years there would be a change in the religious authority in power: stern and moderate Presbyterian, spurious and genuine episcopacy. "At each stage a fresh Commission would adapt the conditions in the universities to the wishes of the Church for the time in the ascendant. Confusion and the destruction of discipline was inevitable and steady progress impossible."[13]

Yet, already before the Reformation, in 1496, the first compulsory Education Act recorded in history was passed in Scotland. And Hume Brown could say, in his *Life of Buchanan*, another in the line of great Scottish educators: "There is excellent reason for believing that, with the exception of the Netherlands, no country in Europe was better provided than Scotland with schools for what was then primary and secondary education."[14] Morgan shows how the early Celtic Church of Columba and his followers, and then the Roman Catholic Church, created schools all over Scotland, both within the monasteries, abbeys, priories and in neighbouring burghs, and even controlled schools in distant towns and parishes. Thus there were abbey schools in Dunfermline, Arbroath, Cambuskenneth, Paisley, Melrose and Kinross, and outside schools at Dundee (to which William Wallace went), the Canongate School, the Royal

High School, Haddington, Stirling, Abernethy, Roxburgh, Perth, etc. "In this manner, before the end of the fifteenth century, all the principal towns in Scotland, and many that have since fallen into obscurity, had grammar schools in which the Latin language was taught."[15] Morgan refers also to universities, saying that we should "gratefully acknowledge that it was to the Roman Church that we owe the great universities which have always continued so natural in their character and have afforded during the centuries the opportunities of a liberal education to the poorest of the people".[16]

The democratic intellect again. Have all our educational historians been wrong about this, as some contemporary authors would have it? The fifteenth century in Scotland was a time of great literary achievement, which, as Hume Brown tells us, "no country except Italy surpassed or even equalled".[17] Yet much of that literature – prose, poetry and historical writing – was written in the language of the people and was addressed to them, as witness Sir David Lyndsay:

> Whairfor to coilyearis, carters and to cuikis,
> To Jok and Tam my ryme shall be direckit,
> With cunning men howbeit it will be lackit[18]

Whatever the critics thought, it is clear the colliers, carters and cooks could read and appreciate literature. Yet Scotland had only 250,000 inhabitants. This popular love of literature was to be the seedbed for the genius of Robert Burns three centuries later.

It is not therefore so surprising that three universities should have been set up in the fifteenth century. A well-educated populace needed local institutions of higher education, rather than having to travel to the Continent. It is an extraordinary fact that at the end of the fourteenth century nine out of twenty-one students in the 'English' nation at the University of Paris (which was composed of the British Isles, Germany and Scandinavia) should have been Scots; all of them became bishops in Scotland.

How then was teaching and learning conducted in the Scottish universities? "The business of instruction was not confined to a special body of privileged professors. The university was governed, the university was taught, by the graduates at large. Professor, master, doctor, were originally synonymous. Every graduate had an equal right of teaching publicly in the university the subjects competent to his faculty and to the rank of his degree; nay, every graduate incurred the obligation of teaching publicly . . . for such was the condition involved in the grant of the degree itself."[19] Thus Sir William Hamilton, one of Scotland's greatest professors of philosophy, in the eighteenth century, speaking of Glasgow University in its early years. Its Charter was modelled on that of Bologna, the student-run university, but it also imitated Louvain, because Louvain's Rector was a Scotsman, John Lichlin.

The teachers were called Regents and would take a class through the four years of the Arts degree, *in all subjects*. The degree courses, based on the classical trivium: grammar, rhetoric, dialectic; and the quadrivium: astronomy, music, mathematics, natural philosophy thus consisted of seven different classes, taught for four years by the same man. So the teachers had to be something of a walking encyclopedia, and they had pastoral duties to the students as well. A Master of Arts on graduating was obliged to teach for two years, but then escaped. For many years no salary was attached to the post, and the regents were dependent on the students' fees, which were very small, and indeed were waived altogether for poor students (as they were at Paris). Scotland being such a poor country, there was a great lack of printed books, so much time was taken up by the dictation, or 'diting', of notes. Morgan calls this "a cramping system that still lingers in some of the excessive note-taking of today". His view is that little real advance of knowledge was possible as long as teaching was tethered to textual exposition.[20]

Laurie, on the other hand, says that, though intellectual activity had to limit itself to dictation and exposition of the definitions and propositions of the recognised authorities, this was not a fruitless exercise. No doubt these discussions gave rise to much dialectical absurdity as well as subtlety, but it would be wrong to despise this as some do, quite lacking a sense of historical perspective. "For such dialectic, even in its crudest form, was in marked and significant contrast to the dead conformity of the Church preceding the universities, and familiarized the minds of the students to a quasi-independence in speculation . . . When Thomas Aquinas had written and Duns Scotus speculated theology tended to pass more and more into metaphysics. Scotus Erigena had at last triumphed."[21]

The want of books also gave great opportunities to regents who were good teachers. It compelled students to do much memory-work and to reflect on the lessons dictated to them, and was thus a very effective producer of mental discipline. This was further developed by the oral side of the students' work, which was highly organized in the form of 'disputations'. These come directly down from the Greeks, and especially from Aristotle. "The practice was coeval with the Scottish universities, and it appeared to suit the temperament of the people for it increased as time went on and may have helped to develop what is often regarded as a feature of the Scottish character – 'the scholastick itch of disputing all things'."[22] At fixed times students would come together in a group to debate a thesis set beforehand on the basis of the work done in class. Some of the students would have been told to 'impugn', i.e. attack, the thesis, others to 'prepugn' or defend it. There can be no question that this exercise developed the students' dialectical skills. Indeed, one wonders whether this long-lasting pedagogic practice (it was still going strong in the nineteenth century) has had anything to do with the superior debating skills of the students of Glasgow University who have so often won the Observer Mace for debating. The main test on graduation was a public disputation on a lengthy thesis based on the student's four-year course. In the forenoon each student defended his thesis; and in the afternoon warded off the arguments of those who attacked it. All this was in Latin, and the candidate must on no account show resentment when refuted.

Much must have depended, as always, on the teaching skills of the regent, but the method of teaching, so far as it went, was admirable. Indeed, some of the more modern teaching methods in today's universities are harking back to these rhetorical skills, which must have produced very articulate students. An interesting sidelight is thrown on the work of the regents by one author who says that the Scottish universities followed quasi-professional courses, keeping literary culture to a minimum, and were scarcely influenced by the social ideal of the gentleman prevalent at Oxford and Cambridge, with the exception perhaps of St. Andrews. They concentrated on subjects like logic and metaphysics "in a more professional, perhaps more rigid mould than was the case in England. There was all the difference in the world between the haphazard appearance of an English student's notebook and a Scots student's, the one deriving from an informal tutorial system, the other, systematically laid out, following the dictates of a lecturer, the 'regent' . . . The students' notebooks of the Restoration period reveal an impressive concern to come to grips with the problems presented by the 'new philosophy', and the range of reference was much wider than any English equivalent during the period."[23] The 'new philosophy' was the ideas of Descartes, Gassendi, Hobbes, Boyle and Bacon.

So the abolition of regenting was not an unmixed blessing. It severed the close teaching relationship between master and student, so that one of its first effects was to lead to irregularity of studies and to a great decline in the numbers graduating in Arts, since students now went only to classes that met their needs. Only at Aberdeen's two separate colleges did this not happen, they being the very last to abolish regenting.[24] The method did not, however, go far enough for Andrew Melville when he took over at Glasgow in 1577 and cleared the decks with his *Nova Erectio*. He was the right man at the right moment and his six years at Glasgow marked an epoch in Scottish higher education. His first aim was to abolish the regenting system which in his view made scholarship worthy of a university impossible. He allowed an assistant to carry on in the old way while he trained a selected group of young men for teaching under the new system, where a teacher specialized in one subject. This involved an exacting six year course in which he undertook all the teaching with the assistance of his nephew James Melville. Scottish higher education owes a very great debt to Andrew Melville, for it was he who first created the idea of the specialist teacher. His Nova Erectio was well ahead of its time and "it contained the most progressive and enlightened ideas regarding university teaching and administration to be found at the period in Europe. It ushered in an epoch of great reform in all the Scottish universities."[25]

The one great weakness of his proposals, many maintained, was in dropping metaphysics and relegating philosophy to a subordinate place in the curriculum. These had been at the heart of Scottish university teaching from the beginning. It will be remembered that the University of Paris was renowned as a great specialist school of philosophy, and that it had a very great influence on the curricula of Scotland's ancient universities. So throughout the centuries the prominence given to philosophical studies was a feature of the Scottish university curriculum. At Edinburgh, up to the Second World War, philosophy was the one subject that had to be studied by every MA candidate. The historian of Europe's medieval universities Hastings Randall lays great stress on this feature of Scottish university education and merits quotation at some length: "The consequences of the retention of the old medieval curriculum in the Scotch universities, and the subsequent evolution of distinct chairs of philosophy out of it, have been of the utmost importance, not only in the history of Scotch education, but in the history of British and even European thought. Scotland gained from an education at once stimulating and practical, however grave its deficiencies on the score of sound preparation and classical discipline; while to the seemingly accidental circumstance that the Scotch universities provided philosophers not merely with chairs, but with classes to teach, Europe probably owes in no small measure the development of an important School of Philosophy. Between the time of Francis Hutcheson and John Stewart Mill, a majority of the philosophers who wrote in the English language were professors, or at least alumni, of Scotch universities."[26] This is a question of central importance in the development of Scottish universities both in the past and in the future. We shall return to it at length in a subsequent chapter.

Melville's ideal of replacing regents with specialist subject teachers, the forerunners of the professoriate, took a long time to implement in full. It was to be only at the beginning of the eighteenth century that opinion would move strongly in favour of specialization of teaching and the harnessing of each regent to a particular subject. Thus regenting was only finally abolished at Edinburgh in 1708; Glasgow in 1727; St. Andrews in 1747; Marischal College, Aberdeen in 1753; and King's College, Aberdeen not till 1798 (Aberdeen had two universities for centuries). This, however, was well ahead of other universities. Morgan notes[27]: "The widening of the intellectual horizon, and the progress of science in all directions owing to the rise of the inductive philosophy, made the 'ambulatory' system no longer suitable." This again is a matter of great moment in the development of the universities and of Western thought as a whole. It has now reached its apogee with the extreme specialization and fragmentation of knowledge. We shall discuss its effects on the universities in a later chapter.

A few years before Andrew Melville returned to Glasgow occurred the most important event in the whole history of Scottish education. This was the publication of the *First Book of Discipline* in 1560, a document which enshrines the essential spirit of democratic intellectualism despite, or perhaps because of, the auspices under which it was written. Its authors were the 'six Johns', but there is no doubt that its principal author was John Knox. It was in effect the constitution for the governance of the newly created Presbyterian Church and it was laid before the Church's General Assembly in 1560. The chapter on schools and universities must be one of the greatest manifestos on education ever written. It proposed that there should be:

1 In the country parishes elementary schools open to all children from 5 or 6 to 8 years of age;
2 In "towns of any repute" grammar schools where town children would learn the rudiments and then, together with country children, Latin grammar from 8 to 12;
3 In important towns high schools where selected pupils of 12 to 16 would learn the other classical languages, along with logic and rhetoric.

The best scholars, able to pass the entrance qualification, would then advance to university to study for eight years (a three year 'Arts' course, including mathematics and moral and natural philosophy, then five years of professional study in medicine, the law or theology). They would receive a bursary if necessary, for there were to be bursaries for the 'clever poor': seventy-two for St. Andrews and forty-eight each for Glasgow and Aberdeen. Only people entirely lacking a sense of historical perspective could fail to see what a progressive proposal this was for the period. It was a continuation of the tradition at Paris and Bologna and was to continue right down to the twentieth century. And there would be ten 'superintendents' "appointit to visit scholles for the tryall of their exercise, proffit and continewance." HMIs in short. Interestingly, too, it proposed that there be a different teacher for each subject at the universities some seventeen years before Andrew Melville. Both were a century ahead of their time.

This plan has been, and continues to be today, of the greatest importance in Scottish education. It proposed a system covering the whole nation, and was by far the most comprehensive national education scheme in Europe. It saw education as the right of all children, and, appreciating as they did its enormous value, it was to be compulsory. Girls are not mentioned, but in fact the parish schools were co-educational from the start. It placed great stress on the moral and spiritual culture of the child. It preserved the family and community influence (most Scottish students still live at home). There was to be a national organization of the universities, without snobbery or special privileges for the rich. As James Scotland says[28]: "In the event more poor boys got to the universities in Scotland than in any other country before the late nineteenth century development in the United States." This in a small, desperately poor country.

The scheme was highly practical; indeed one could say that it was largely a rationalization of what already to a considerable extent existed. All it required was money, but of course it didn't get it; the rapacity of the nobles saw to that by plundering the wealth of the Church. But it has shone like an inspiring beacon of advanced educational thought through the centuries and still does now. Its fundamental ideas have still not been fully implemented, so we can still learn from it. These ideas were that Scotland should have a complete national system of education forming a highway from the primary school to the university; and that there should be close coordination between the different grades: primary school, secondary school and university. The condition of admission to the university should be a favourable report from the schoolmaster. Education must be compulsory and a boy should continue at school till the special talent is discovered by which he can best serve the community. Education is not the privilege of a class but the common need and right of all, and there should be free scope for the upward movement of ability at every level of society. Finally the poor but clever student should be maintained by the State.

The epilogue of the chapter on schools and universities of the First Book of Discipline reads as follows: "If God shall grant quietness

and give your Wisdoms grace to set forward letters in the sort
prescribed, ye shall leave wisdom and learning to your posterity,
a treasure more to be esteemed than any earthly treasures ye are
able to provide for them; which, without wisdom, are more able
to be their ruin than help or comfort." These words have a powerful resonance today as we look around at our greedy consumerist
societies, the starvation and destitution in the Third World, and
our incredible despoliation of the biosphere. Carlyle, in his rectorial address at the University of Edinburgh, said: "Knox was heard
by Scotland, the people heard him and believed him to the marrow of their bones; they took all his doctrine to heart and they
defied principalities and powers to move them from it."[29] One
cannot, alas, say as much for those who direct educational affairs
in Scotland today.

It can truly be said that most of the progress in Scottish education has consisted in advancing towards Knox's ideals, and Hume
Brown even says that the First Book of Discipline is the most
important document in Scottish history. Its proposals and guiding
spirit have moulded the Scottish character and instincts, in relation
to education, for more than four centuries. Of course the reality,
because of lack of resources, never fulfilled these noble aspirations,
but their enormous, lasting influence gives the lie to those who
today, for whatever reason, dismiss the idea of the 'lad o' pairts' as
a romantic myth and that of the democratic intellect as the eccentric
brainchild of George Elder Davie.

Some scholars seem at a loss to explain how there could be such
sophisticated educational thinking and modern, advanced teaching
in Scotland's universities. Speaking of the fifteenth century, one of
them says: "The cultural climate in Scotland in the fifteenth century
was curiously and inexplicably rich, fostering native writers and
poets who have not ceased to be read. It is difficult to account for
this resurgence of culture in a country which was in so many ways
still disordered, primitive and poor ... " Proceeding, he exclaims
how astonishing it is that they (Scotland's universities) "should
have continued to produce scholars of such quality that, at least in
the eighteenth century ... they cast Oxford and Cambridge into
the shade ... The progress made in mathematical and scientific
studies was the more impressive when contrasted with the state of
affairs at the English universities ... It is not easy to explain the
exuberance of Scottish culture at this time. It must surely reflect
the excellence of the parish and high schools fostered by legislation in 1646 and 1696." He gets it in one. It was precisely those
embodiments of the democratic intellect, those rungs on the ladder
for the 'lad o'pairts', that provided the well-educated youngsters

the universities so thrived on. They served to create, as he puts it, a society that was "literate, mobile and, if spiritually authoritarian, socially democratic". It was probably also, he suspects, due to "the vitality of urban life sustained by an interchange between academic and mercantile society not to be found at Oxford and Cambridge." At any rate the climate of the Scottish universities in the eighteenth century was secular and liberal, the prevailing tone being set by the moral philosophers with David Hume, Adam Smith and Thomas Reid in the van. They even tended to support the French Revolution, with the celebrated lawyer John Millar presiding over a dinner to celebrate the event, and Professor John (Jolly Jack Phosphorus) Anderson (whom we shall meet again) presenting the French with his shock-absorbing gun carriage and balloons to carry messages. St. Andrews, *horribile dictu*, even presented a medical degree to Jean-Paul Marat!

Our author was impressed by the fact that the Scottish professor was more likely to be a specialist than the tutor who was responsible for teaching all subjects at Oxford and Cambridge. He concludes by saying that the conditions provided fertile ground for the ideas of Bacon, Newton and Locke – indeed Newtonian physics were taught in Scotland before they were taught at his own university, Cambridge. There was also a lively interchange with the celebrated universities of Holland, especially Leyden and Utrecht, so that in the eighteenth century "the universities of Scotland, except St. Andrews, became more adventurous and dynamic, while their counterparts in England were suffocating under the weight of tradition."[30]

Green also provides some figures which make an interesting comparative social comment on the features of the Scottish universities he has been discussing. Between 1740 and 1839 13% of the students at Glasgow University came from the families of the nobility and landed gentry, by comparison with 35% at Cambridge between 1752 and 1849; 11% at Glasgow came from industry and commerce, as compared with 8% at Cambridge. Whereas there were virtually no working-class children at Cambridge, at Glasgow one third, i.e. 33⅓, came from labouring families. That non-existent democratic intellect again! Glasgow was particularly dynamic and had scholars of European reputation: R. C. Jacob in Classics, and Edward Caird who later became the Master of Balliol College, Oxford. Above all there was William Thompson, Lord Kelvin, who became professor of natural philosophy in 1846, a chair he held for 53 years. He set up the very first chair in experimental natural philosophy (i.e. physics) in 1855, and the BSc degree was established in 1872.

Two centuries earlier the gradual abolition of regenting had enabled men like James Gregory, who came to Edinburgh from St. Andrews as professor of mathematics, to concentrate on specialized mathematical teaching and research. His *Optica Promota* of 1663 is remarkable for its description of the first reflecting telescope. He was the first to introduce the work of Kepler, Galileo and Descartes to a Scottish university, and he was responsible for the first observatory in Britain, at least two years before the establishment of the Royal Observatory at Greenwich. Sadly, he died in the prime of life in 1675, "having anticipated his friend and correspondent Isaac Newton in the solution of some of the most abstruse problems of mathematics and physics."[31]

Thus by about 1730 the Scottish universities had succeeded in developing a wide range of subjects taught for the most part by specialist teachers who were alive to the latest developments in their field, yet (and this is central to an understanding of the Scottish university tradition) "still retaining a sense of the inherent unity of the education system in which they were comprehended."[32] The view was generally held that the proliferation of academic centres in Scotland – five, including Marischal College in Aberdeen – was an inherent part of the notion of an educated community. The remarkable thing is how widely these new ideas and teaching methods were distributed and the peaks of intellectual distinction reached by men heavily involved in teaching large numbers of young students. "What must never be forgotten is that the belief that education and intellectual achievement should have breadth of involvement as well as height of virtuosity was the great gift to Scotland of the Renaissance and the Reformation ... an inheritance furthermore that would ensure that the Scottish form of the Enlightenment would be protected against the kind of brittle elitism that too often predominated elsewhere."[33] These attitudes were prevalent at all levels of education. As R. H. Campbell points out, "By the modest standards of what was being achieved elsewhere, the record, in lowland rural Scotland art least, is undeniable, whether tested by the extent of the provision or by the standard of instruction. Many of those who made the greatest contribution to the intellectual achievements of the Enlightenment in Scotland were themselves the product of that education system."[34]

What were the values, the principles of action, that led to these remarkable educational achievements in a small, poor country with a fiercely turbulent history? One was certainly a collectivist attitude imposed on them by that history; here Scotland has similarities with other small peoples. "It is interesting to note that of all the European peoples who seem to excel in educational achievement, the

Jews, the Scots, the Czechs (who have the highest rate of university education in Europe) and the Finns, seem to have developed their 'love of learning' as oppressed national or religious minorities."[35]

But collectivism is also a mode of status allocation, and status in Scotland has usually come from identification with public rather than private ventures. Thus the great individual benefactions in Scotland have been made to education, as in the case of Andrew Carnegie, and, unlike England, have been made to the public system. There were many smaller benefactions to support poor university students – up to one third of the students at one university in the 1840s.[36] The aim of this generosity was also to make education publicly accessible as a matter of social policy. So higher education in Scotland, as Andrew McPherson makes clear, was highly collectivist in all three dictionary senses of that term: an assertion of nationality; a mode of status allocation; a type of social policy.

The accent throughout the centuries in Scotland's universities has been facilitating access in three senses: geographically, numerically and socially, i.e. availability to different social classes. It was justified by reference to the traditional model, that of John Knox in the *First Book of Discipline*; to principle, i.e. the ideal of individual upward social mobility; and to expedience, in that it favoured general economic prosperity. As the (Argyll) Education Commission was later to show (in 1868), this policy paid off handsomely. One in 205 of the Scottish population went to public secondary schools, and one in 1000 went to university. The corresponding figures in England were one in 1300 and one in 5,800. The Argyll Commission Report explained the thinking behind these figures. "The theory of our school system as originally conceived was to supply *every member of the community* with the means of obtaining for his children not only the elements of education, but such instruction as would fit him to pass to the Burgh school, and thence to university, or directly to the university from the parish school. The connexion between the parochial and Burgh schools and the university is therefore an essential element in our scheme of National Education."[37]

No such ladder of educational opportunity existed in England. McPherson makes the point: "Scotland's emphasis, relative to England, on contest mobility (i.e. more young people are given a chance for longer) is attributable to a value that has been consciously and consistently held over a considerable period of time."[38] As a result, in the 1860s something over 20% of students in Scottish universities had manual origins; Aberdeen had as many as 33%. McPherson calls this an 'open doors' policy. It is interesting to compare these figures with the situation today. Nor are they surprising when one knows what was being done in the schools. The Glasgow presbytery in 1700 proposed that pupils in 'English schools' should be taught "to write weel and to read write (i.e. handwriting as well as print); and to count also; some of the plainest and usefulest parts of Geometry and Geography; and music, at least the common tunes; and History, especially of our own Church and State." Those who went on to grammar schools were to go through this course beforehand. Able children went to a four or five year public Latin school, where they did Greek and Hebrew in their fifth year. In addition, they studied Greek and Roman antiquities, a compendium of trades and sciences, and the Janua and Atrium of the great seventeenth century Czech educationist Comenius. They also had to acquire some knowledge of geography "both by the globe and plain chart . . . which was very profitable for schools and helpful to the understanding of history and reading it with pleasure; also some elements of chronology, all which may be rendered easie and delightful by Tables, draughts and pictures."

D. J. Withrington, from whom this information is taken,[39] says this is remarkable because "this desire to widen and make relevant the curriculum was supposed only to have happened in the later eighteenth century. Yet here we have doubts about the classical languages even before the Union. The newer subjects, including navigation and mensuration, should be taught to the classical scholars as well." Only today, with the publication of the Howie Report on the upper classes in secondary school, but with a divisive academic/vocational split, are we cautiously approaching ideas which were the subject of discussion and practical application all but three centuries ago. For example, Ayr Burgh School in 1746 transformed itself into a school which had three sections: Classical; English subjects; Arithmetic, book-keeping, geometry, navigation, surveying, algebra, other parts of mathematics and parts of natural philosophy. It was an exceptionally comprehensive curriculum in a single publicly-run institution which included all post-elementary schooling: Classical, English and 'scientific'.

This first hint that a narrow, purely classical education, as at the English public schools and Oxford, was not the best education in a country beginning to feel the throes of the industrial revolution, was to become a major leitmotif of the higher education commissions and debates that took up most of the nineteenth century from 1826 onwards. On this subject our national poet laid about him in his usual inimitable style:

> A set o' dull, conceited hashes,
> That tease their brains wi' college classes,
> They gang in stirks and come oot asses,

> Plain truth to speak,
> And syne they think to climb Parnassus
> By dint o' Greek.

A telling criticism of the purely classical curriculum. Francis Jeffrey, advocate, co-founder of the *Edinburgh Review*, wielded a more skillfully forensic rapier:

> I admit, on the whole, the justice of the reproach levelled against our general national instruction, namely, that though we have a greater number of all ranks who possess considerable information, there are fewer who are completely learned – that our knowledge, in short, though more general, is more superficial than with our neighbours in England. That is quite true, and our system of education leads to it; but I think it is a great good on the whole; for many of those who leave college very imperfectly instructed, supply the defects by their own study afterwards, in a manner they could not have done, but for that superficial training and initiation by their teachers.[40]

Lyon Playfair was to make a telling, and by implication similar, point near the end of the great debate in 1876: "Oxford and Cambridge have exalted the preparatory pedagogium, or Arts Faculty, to be the end instead of the beginning of the universities and thus have cut themselves off from the professions."[41] This, of course, made them odd man out in Europe and cut them off also from the medieval tradition.

So the great educational battle was joined, with Scotch critics and Edinburgh reviewers on one side and affronted Oxbridge dons on the other. The issue at stake: a general education before professional specialization, and democratic intellectualism, as in Scotland's universities, versus a refined, narrow, elitist, classical or mathematical education at Oxford and Cambridge. Utility versus knowledge for its own sake. Breadth versus cultivation of the intellect. The 'open door' policy versus finishing-school for the sons of the rich and influential. Secular, liberal education versus ecclesiastical domination. Sir William Hamilton versus William Whewell.

However, before we can enjoy this debate we must take a straight look at the opposition in the blue corner: Oxford and Cambridge.

3

Oxford and Cambridge

John Perry, Professor of Mechanics and Mathematics at the Royal College of Science, had this to say about Oxford: "Oxford is hard, unspiritual and idolatrous, and the absence of scientific method is evident everywhere. Oxford is like a technical school, training these better men for the higher posts in the Church, in the Civil Services, in journalism, at the Bar, and in boys' schools. And it is found that the successful men have dwarfed imaginations and no power to think for themselves outside their narrow professional grooves ... She has always held herself aloof from manufacturers and commerce. It is almost incomprehensible that a university aiming at breadth of culture should scorn those things that keep England in her high position."[1]

This is an image of Oxford that is still recognizable today, despite the changes forced on her by contemporary developments. What is very interesting is to learn when these attitudes began. They began, according to Hugh Kearney,[2] with the growth of the Court in London and the rise of London as a centre of social life. There was a flood of young men into Oxford and Cambridge in the latter half of the sixteenth century, just as John Knox was writing his famous manifesto on schools and universities in Scotland. But the reasons for the rapid growth of the student body at Oxford and Cambridge were as different from Knox's prescriptions as could well be. The basic reason was the quest for status. This was not simply a matter of snobbery, since it affected every aspect of life. The great majority of Englishmen were excluded from the quality of gentlemen, and their life chances and those of their children were consequently impaired. So the rise of the gentry was the process by which the self-made men of the fifteenth century rose in social status. There were three ways of doing this: through the Army or the Court or – and this was the easiest and cheapest route – a couple of years at the university. "Thus the expansion of the universities and the appearance of the English gentleman were two facets of the one development."[3] The desire for social advancement was the principal reason for the increase in numbers at Oxford and Cambridge.

Furthermore, the two universities retained and developed their main function in the Middle Ages, which was to produce learned clergy. This was to continue to be their main function down to the late nineteenth century It was precisely because they were the training grounds for the parish clergy that the government showed such an interest in them. Religious orthodoxy was equated with political loyalty, so that it was vital that Oxford and Cambridge (England's only universities, it should be remembered) "should be a loyal and sound source of loyal and sound clergy."[4] The Chancellors of both universities were prominent politicians, and fellowships and college headships were frequently obtained through government patronage. The aim was that the gentry should form an educated elite solidly supporting the Church. The goal of the education dispensed was service to the state with obedience as the prime virtue. These goals are in essence the same as those of J. R. Seeley and Jowett three centuries later. In his Cambridge inaugural Seeley said, "Our university is and must be a great seminary of politicians". So Oxford and Cambridge were, in the sixteenth century, and in the nineteenth century, as they are still today, an essential part of the English establishment. It is an interesting fact that already, at that time, there were complaints in Scotland at attempts to introduce English methods into the Scottish universities. Robert Baillie, a celebrated professor of theology at Glasgow, criticized Dr. Porter, a professor at St. Andrews during the 1630s, for the reason that "he had no sooner settled himself into his chair while he began to recommend the English method of studie".[5] The presumption that "anglicization and civilization are readily interchangeable terms"[6] has a long history.

Cromwell attempted to create, in Scotland as in England, a gentry-dominated society in Church and State. Baillie called Cromwell's Scottish advisers "our three complying gentlemen", and said "the colleges were expected to become seminaries for a complaisant clergy". Kearney says that the universities were expected to carry out the same conservative social function as in England, as opposed to Hugh Trevor-Roper's thesis that Cromwell was the saviour of the Scottish universities by bringing the values of the English country gentry into Scottish intellectual life. In fact, Oxford resisted the pressure towards more 'modern' or more useful studies. As we have seen, Newton and Descartes were taught in Scottish universities before they were in England. This intellectual conservatism reflected Tory attitudes: Convocation banned books by George Buchanan – the great Scottish scholar and Latinist – John Milton and Thomas Hobbes because of their common belief that civil society derived from the people.[7] This, of course, has been the foundation stone of Scottish constitutional belief since the Declaration of Arbroath in 1320.

Kearney's conclusions are that Oxford and Cambridge strengthened the division between the leisured class and the agricultural population. They constituted an elite. They perpetuated the medieval division of society into the clergy and the laity. A scholar was a clerical scholar, so that the criteria of orthodoxy were constantly threatening. The result was that university scholarship was guided scholarship. Oxford and Cambridge were a ready-made instrument for political centralization, because the gentry from all over England and Wales were exposed to the same system of elitist values, thus arousing the anger of the excluded majority. This was clearly one of the major reasons for the Civil War. They stood for the 'eternal verities', both social and intellectual, as Newman, Jowett and others right on into the twentieth century were to do.[8]

In a comparative postscript on the situation in the nineteenth century Kearney shows that the same gentlemanly values were still very much to the fore, if in slightly altered form. It was the done thing to go to Oxford and Cambridge, and a matter of social degradation to go to a 'provincial' university. The criterion of the gentleman is now membership of certain professions: the established Church, law, medicine, the army, the higher civil service, the Indian civil service, banking, the 'city', and politics. Entrance to these was governed by a public school education and an Oxbridge degree. The one-on-one tutorial was as much a social as an intellectual occasion. Certain colleges had great social cachet, King's at Cambridge, for example. Still the very narrow degree courses – Classical at Oxford, pure mathematics at Cambridge – continued, with the pretention that a Greats man could 'get up' any subject without difficulty. Bertrand Russell summed it up with his remark on Montagu Butler, Master of Trinity: "Straight out of Thackeray's *Book of Snobs* !"

That Russell's comment is not the *boutade* of a maverick is shown by the following quotations: "There is nothing I less wish than to see Oxford turned into a German or a London university", said Jowett whose *Plato's Republic* is a classical defence of elites. Macaulay: "If the Ptolemaic system were taught at Cambridge instead of the Newtonian, the senior wrangler would, nevertheless, be in general a superior man to the wooden spoon . . . "He goes on: "If alchemy

were taught, the young man who showed most activity in the pursuit of the philosopher's stone would generally turn out a superior
man." This is the Oxbridge accolade: the 'fine mind' who would
be good at anything, including conspicuous uselessness. Finally Sir
Charles Trevelyan, the reformer of the civil service:

> Who are so successful in carrying off the prizes at competing
> scholarships, fellowships, etc. as the most expensively edu-
> cated young men? Almost invariably the sons of gentlemen,
> or those who, by force of cultivation, good training and good
> society, have acquired the feelings and habits of gentlemen.
> The tendency of the measure will, I am confident, be decidedly
> aristocratic, but it will be so in a good sense by securing for
> the public service those who are, in a true sense, the best.

It is hardly surprising that, as we shall see, Scottish students found
it so hard to get into Trevelyan's civil service.

Green sums it up: "For the universities to prosper, they had
to win favour from the established order. At all stages of their
history their studies have been more or less closely correlated to
the national needs. They represented the training-schools for the
established order."[9] Henry VIII's break with Rome placed them
completely at the mercy of the crown, and it took effective measures to ensure that they toed the line. The practice of visitations
by royal officials, which started under Thomas Cromwell, was to
be followed on many subsequent occasions to ensure compliance
with the royal wishes. "High Tory in feeling"[10] and maintaining an
essentially clerical personnel, excluding non-Anglicans (who went
to Glasgow and Edinburgh) from membership, so that they were
"little more than breeding-grounds for the gentry and aristocracy",
the older universities "slumbered through the eighteenth century
while in the Scots universities intellectual life flourished".[11] As institutions Oxford and Cambridge were in some danger of petrifaction,
says Green.

Sir Charles Grant Robertson, Fellow of all Souls, Hon. Fellow of
Hertford College, Oxford, and Vice-Chancellor of the University of
Birmingham 1919–38, says the situation at Oxford and Cambridge
was quite hopeless. They were expensive, catered to the aristocracy and gentry, operated religious lists excluding Dissenters and
Roman Catholics, and many colleges had ceased to be humanist in
method and purpose. There was no science or modern languages,
no advanced or postgraduate work, and the amount of research was
negligible. The teaching, such as it was, was purely conventional.
"Oxford and Cambridge trained, in a conventional way, the gentry
for the public life of politics or for the position of landowners in
the country, and were the central seminaries for ordinands to the

ministry of the Church of England . . . In a word (they) had come
to be the endowed preserve of a class . . . they were not in the
mainstream of the national life . . . "[12] Oxford and Cambridge were
'imperial' universities.

A contemporary updating of this description is given by another
Oxford man.

> It is the cultivated norm, corresponding to the type of author-
> ity in society which is sanctioned by custom and tradition
> which is historically most characteristic of Oxford, at least
> since the Reformation. An educational system of this kind
> is one designed to cultivate the pupil for the style of life of
> the dominant stratum of society, which means, in the case of
> Oxford up to the middle of the twentieth century, the amateur,
> gentlemanly administrator of imperial Britain. And again . . .
> the curriculum of such a system is derived from the cultural
> norms and standards of the dominant stratum."[13]

Another contemporary scholar puts it rather more bluntly. Terry
Eagleton, when appointed professor of English literature at Oxford,
said: "I have always found Oxford an uncomfortable place for a
radical to be, but also a necessary place. The place that fashions
the ruling class. You can't just leave it to them."

S. S. Laurie, who was the first professor of education at
Edinburgh, in 1876, nearly 20 years before chairs of education were
set up in England,[14] makes a very severe judgment of this Oxbridge
educational system. He points out that they had restricted themselves until quite recently to the role of schools of arts interpreted
in the narrowest sense, whereas in the medieval universities –
a tradition continued by the Scottish universities – 'Arts' meant
all departments of knowledge not specifically professional, i.e.
language, rhetoric, logic, psychology, metaphysics, politics, physics, natural history, geometry, music, astronomy and so on. He
then says:

> An university, properly understood, is the home of the arts and
> sciences. It exists to teach them and it equally exists to pro-
> mote them. In the English universities (he means Oxford and
> Cambridge) the culture and discipline of the general student
> has been the almost exclusive aim. To speak of 'culture' as the
> aim of college and university life is to throw a mere phrase at
> the head of the public. Culture can never be a conscious end to
> a man without unmanning him. Still more must it emasculate
> a university where it is achieved by not more than one in 500.
> And when we do find it in its supremest and most precious
> form, we cannot say we like it. It is always narrow, and must,
> from the psychological nature of the case, be egotistical. That

indeed is a poor result of the highest education – a man who
thinks himself supreme or precious and who spends his life
in turning pretty phrases when not engaged in admiration of
his own exclusive intellectual possessions."[15]

This is an absolutely fundamental difference between the ancient
Scottish universities and Oxford and Cambridge. The former, as
we have seen, continued the classical and medieval tradition of
being specialist institutions for the teaching of medicine, the law,
philosophy and theology, but these specialist studies were preceded
by a three or four year 'Arts' course. This general education was
an essential prerequisite for specialist education. At Oxbridge, on
the other hand, there was no specialist – in the sense of professional – education until the later nineteenth century. There was
detailed training in the classics at Oxford and in pure mathematics
at Cambridge. The tensions between the two burst into the open at
the beginning of the nineteenth century, with the *Edinburgh Review*
in the van of a general attack on Oxbridge dilettantism.

Sir William Hamilton, the philosopher, did not pull his punches:
"The Academy of Oxford is therefore not one public university,
but merely a collection of private schools, and the professions are
sacrificed to the paltry ends of a few contemptible corporations."
Another hotly contested issue relating to the nature of a liberal
education was that of generalism and specialization. The Edinburgh
reviewers made no bones abut their opposition to the Oxbridge
pattern which, contrary to the general view that a liberal education
should embody a certain width of curriculum, was quite deliberately a very narrow one: "exactness within a narrow range", as Sir
John Seeley described it; "the thin clear stream of excellence", as
Sir Eric Ashby was to say in the twentieth century. It aimed not
at width but at "high specialized excellence and polish."[16] They
condemned this trenchantly: "The epithet of scholar is reserved for
him who writes on the Aeolic reduplication . . . and is familiar with
Sylburgills his method of arranging defectives . . . his object is not
to reason, to imagine or to invent; but to conjugate, decline and
derive . . . Would he ever dream that such men as Adam Smith and
Lavoisier were equal in dignity or understanding to, or of the same
utility as, Bentley and Hayne?" Adam Smith himself condemned
them as the "sanctuaries in which exploded systems and obsolete
prejudices found shelter and protection". With entertaining acerbity
Lord Chesterfield had written to his son: "What do you think of
being a Greek professor at one of our universities? It is a very pretty
sinecure, and requires very little knowledge (much less than I hope
you have already) of that language."[17] In the 1820s Darwin found
Christ's College, Cambridge, "intellectually sterile".

The exclusiveness of Oxford and Cambridge were even more strongly attacked than the narrowness of the education they provided. But the cause of reform "was too closely associated with the criticism of established order for it to make much headway. The Church of England feared for its monopoly . . . the university Tories looked to their defences, and cemented the alliance with the established order in Church and State."[18] Still today, when all such religious bars have long been done away with, Oxford and Cambridge are very exclusive places. "I cannot remember meeting a local during seven years at Oxford, at high table, or in the common rooms, let alone in the lecture room or study."[19]

The battle went on from 1809 to 1845. In 1810 Oxford struck back. "The habit of discrimination, the power of stating a question distinctly, and of arguing with perspicuity, are of much greater importance than the hasty acquisition of miscellaneous knowledge."[20] The implied accusation here is that the broad preliminary arts course at Scottish universities, covering both the arts and sciences and with a strong emphasis on philosophy, makes students into 'smatterers' or 'sciolists'. Inevitably the standards in classics and mathematics were behind those of Oxford and Cambridge, but we have seen that the *Edinburgh Review* condemned the Oxbridge approach as too narrow, lacking in critical spirit and ignoring major concerns like science. Whereupon William Whewell weighed into the argument in 1837: "The critical system seems to me to be properly addressed not to students who are undergoing education, but to philosophers who have already been completely educated. Nor can I believe that to put young men in such a position, at a period of their lives when they ought to be quietly forming their minds for future action, can have any other result than to fill them with a shallow conceit of their own importance (and) to accustom them to deliver hasty judgments."[21]

Many issues were raised: that the value of knowledge lies in its utility;[22] the uselessness of classical education and the slight regard paid to science and political economy;[23] knowledge is good for its own sake.[24] Here the main bone of contention is liberal classics versus practical vocationalism. It is still with us today, albeit in altered form. In the 1830s it was Cambridge's turn. Sir William Hamilton attacked pure mathematics at Cambridge, while William Whewell defended it. Between them, Hamilton, Copleston and Whewell clearly delineate the difference between the Scottish universities and Oxbridge on the respective merits of the classics, mathematics and philosophy. Hamilton also strongly attacked the wealth and power of the colleges in comparison with the weakness of the universities as such and the professors – the exact opposite of the situation in

Scotland. The quality of the college tutors was also doubtful since they were not appointed purely on their academic ability; much of the teaching was poor.

Around the same time, in 1840, another common criticism was voiced by a young American from Yale who had spent five years at Trinity College, Cambridge: "On the whole we may say that, admitting the present examinations as fixed parts, the private tutorial is the best mode of preparing for them. It is dear – but England is a dear country, and everything connected with an English university education is expensive."[25]

These and other issues were to be debated throughout the century as reform finally got under way at Oxford and Cambridge in the 1850s, and some of the greatest names in English higher education, science and philosophy took part. For example, John Stuart Mill, when he gave his inaugural address at St. Andrews in 1867, said that there should be public facilities for the study of law, medicine and engineering, and that it might be an advantage if they were in the same localities as the universities and under the same general supervision. But, he continued, "they are needed only by a comparatively few . . . and even those few do not require them until after their education, in the ordinary sense, has been completed." The use they will make of them "depends less on the manner in which they are taught their profession than upon what sort of minds they bring to it – what kind of intelligence, and of conscience, the general system of education has developed in them." There could hardly be a better argument for the traditional Scottish system of a general arts course followed by professional study. Mark Pattison had a slightly different slant on the same issue: "There is no reason why every class of vocation in which intelligence and refinement are applicable . . . should not have a corresponding 'Faculty' arranged for it in the university where an appropriate training – not practical and professional, but theoretical and scientific – might be had."[26] In 1876 Pattison makes his view even more explicit: "A university should be in possession of all science and all knowledge, but it is as science and knowledge, not as a money-bringing pursuit, that it possesses it. There is an old saying. 'A university is founded upon Arts' . . . its fabric of the special sciences is raised upon the liberal studies."[27]

Again almost a definition of what the Scottish universities had been doing for a very long time. In 1874 T. H. Huxley, one of the greatest and most admirable of English educators, expressed views very similar to those of Pattison. He said it could be doubted whether universities were the places for technical schools of engineering, or applied chemistry, or agriculture. "But there can surely be little question that instruction in the brands of science which lie at the foundation of these arts, of a far more advanced and special character than could, with any propriety, be included in the Arts curriculum, ought to be obtainable by means of a duly organized Faculty of Science in every university." He also made a lapidary statement that expressed the very heart of what the Scottish universities had always tried to do and which ran counter to Whewell's view that students should be quietly and uncritically assiduous: "A criticism of life is the essence of culture."

This great debate on the universities in England waxed particularly strongly between 1852 and 1882. One of the major contributors was of course Newman whose collection of lectures *The Idea of a University* has played a key role in thinking about higher education in England. In the first paragraph of his preface he defines the university as a "place of teaching universal knowledge. This implies that its object is, on the one hand, intellectual not moral: and on the other that it is the diffusion and extension of knowledge rather than its advancement. If its object were scientific and philosophical discovery, I do not see why a university should have students; if religious training I do not see how it can be the seat of literature and science." The emphasis on the distinction between teaching and research is one that still troubles higher education today. Teaching is just as important now as it was to Newman, but teaching supposedly prevents scholars from getting on with their research, and if they do not do good research the prospects of promotion are dim. The contradiction has still not been solved, and the implementation of plans to divide universities into research and teaching institutions, with the title of centre of excellence going to the research institutions, will but exacerbate it.

   The weakness of Newman's position was that the goal of his liberal education was the gentleman of 'delicate taste' and 'candid, equitable and dispassionate mind'. He was aware of this: "Some persons may be tempted to complain that I have servilely followed the English idea of a university . . . and that an academic system, formed upon my model, will result in nothing better or higher than in the production of that antiquated variety of human nature . . . called 'a gentleman'." His rather feeble reply to this anticipated charge was that the aim was "training them to fill their respective posts in life better and of making them more intelligent, capable and active members of society". The first phrase reflects perfectly the attitudes of Victorian Oxbridge; the latter was followed by the Scottish universities, but, as Francis Jeffrey pointed out, [28] it applied to an incomparably wider section of society.

Another weak point of his argument was "if a liberal education be good, it must necessarily be useful too" since "it prepares (the student) to fill any post with credit". All that need be said about this argument is that Britain's rulers and controllers of all major aspects of British life for the past century have mostly been educated at Oxbridge with precisely such assumptions of superiority. A cursory glance at 20th century British history shows how inefficient they have been. Here Newman was crossing swords with that intellectual gad-fly, the *Edinburgh Review*, which had said:

> When a university has been doing useless things for a long time, it appears at the first degrading to them to be useful . . . and yet what other measure is there of dignity in intellectual labour but usefulness? And what ought the term university to mean, but a place where every science is taught which is liberal, and at the same useful to mankind? . . . Looking always to real utility as our guide, we should see, with equal pleasure, a studious and inquisitive mind arranging the productions of nature, investigating the qualities of bodies, or mastering the difficulties of the learned languages. We should not care whether he was chemist, naturalist or scholar, because we know it to be as necessary that matter should be studied . . . as that taste should be gratified and imagination inflamed."

Newman's answer was a rather empty generalisation: "Intellectual culture is its own end; for what has its end in itself, has its use in itself also." Again we come up against the strong contrast between the Scottish universities, which followed the medieval tradition of university education for the professions, whereas Oxford and Cambridge had been sidetracked by the sixteenth century drive for status and prestige into becoming finishing-schools for the rich, the ambitious and the pretentious. They have never lost that image, as the television series *The Glittering Prizes* showed in the 1970s along with many others.

Newman, however, did not have it all his own way in England. The scientist Herbert Spencer totally reversed Newman's priorities. For him the highest form of knowledge was that which served "those activities which directly minister to self-preservation, " so that vocational and professional studies are of prime importance, science being the most important of all. These views appeared extreme in the 1850s. Indeed, Spencer himself noted that they were "regarded by nine out of ten people as monstrous". Yet they were the same as the views expressed by R. L. Edgworth and Sidney Smith in 1810. It was a view which John Stuart Mill could not accept, as we saw in his inaugural address at St. Andrews in 1867. Law, medicine and engineering, he maintained, "are no part of

what every generation owes to the next"; they are not something
"on which its civilization and worth principally depend". He considered that the classical languages were still best "for stimulation
and discipline for the inquiring intellect". He did not agree with
Whewell's view that the classics were received truths that could
not be questioned; they were a means of learning to think and
speculate, which for Mill were the key purposes of the university.
But, unlike Newman, he accepted the sciences, seeing no conflict
between them and the arts. Mark Pattison's position was the same
as Mill's, except that he went further in his acceptance of science,
agreeing with T. H. Huxley who maintained that what Mill said of
the arts could with equal validity be said of the sciences. Indeed,
to prove it, he took a passage from Mill's inaugural, replacing the
word 'arts' with the word 'sciences.'[29]

It was Pattison, in his famous book *Suggestions on Academic
Organization*, who came nearest to the position as it existed at the
Scottish universities. The universities had a dual role in providing
both specialized knowledge for the professions and what he called a
'general or humane' education. He deplored the old Oxford liberal
education as a sham and welcomed the shift to specialized studies.
He wanted specialized faculties, including science, regretting the
fact that they had hitherto been excluded from the education of the
upper classes. He spoke of training for vocations and careers, but
in the form of theoretical and scientific training, as we have seen.
The position taken up by Huxley and Pattison was influenced by
the German concept of the university as a place for scholarship
and research. So, like the Scots, they wanted a strong professoriate
engaging in original research.

Benjamin Jowett, however, like Newman, harked back to the
older Oxford tradition of the university as a place for teaching and
education rather than research. He was all for the colleges and the
tutorial system, preparing students for the Church and the civil service and imperial administration. Pattison deplored the university
being turned into a super public school; he disliked the 'college
spirit'. He summed up the conflict between himself and Jowett as
consisting "in a difference upon a fundamental question of university politics – viz. Science and Learning versus School-keeping". It
was Jowett who won the battle, however.

Finally Matthew Arnold stepped into the fray. He took advantage of Huxley's rectorial address to make a major defence of the
literary-type liberal education. He disagreed with Huxley that an
exclusively scientific education would be as culturally valuable as
an exclusively literary one. He agreed with Newman on the distinction between education as instrumental or as an end in itself;

but he now introduced a new idea into the debate. Science produces exact knowledge, but not knowledge that can be related to
man's sense of beauty or to those other instincts which are a part
of human nature. Since it is a fundamental desire of the mind
to relate newly acquired knowledge to these innate instincts, the
study alone of forms of scientific knowledge which do not admit
of this relation is merely "weariness and dissatisfaction". This is
a very perceptive and subtle defence of the old liberal education.
In many ways, too, Arnold seems to have been proved right or
at least partly right since, despite the inroads that logical positivism and utilitarianism have made into academic thinking, and
despite the superior financial rewards, prestige and 'usefulness' of
the sciences, it is literature, sociology and history, whose subject
matter most closely relates to "the constitution of human nature",
that attract students in increasing numbers. However, the enormous
government-sponsored growth of business studies has given a big
boost to the middle-class philistinism and utilitarianism that were
Arnold's main targets. Also, with the advent of ecology, 'green'
politics, the Friends of the Earth, and Greenpeace, it is no longer
true to say that scientific knowledge cannot be related to man's
sense of beauty or sense of conduct. This is an important marker
for the future course of our universities.

While this battle for the intellectual soul of Oxbridge was going
on, developments were also taking place on the social and administrative front. It has been said that many of the problems of
contemporary English education derive from arrangements made
in the mid-Victorian period. We see constantly in the media the
appeal that expensive, private education still has, its obvious class
basis, its aristocratic, elitist tradition, its gentlemanly pretensions
and outright snobbery.[30] The most important effect of the reforms
gradually brought about in Oxford and Cambridge by government
pressure from the 1850s onward was to make them utterly inac-
cessible to poor people. They became more socially exclusive than
ever before; once again they were used by the parvenu bourgeoisie
to gain status and influence. The introduction of open competition
for entry to the universities was so one-sided in its effects that "from
1850 to 1900 the poor boy of parts had no chance of getting to
either Oxford or Cambridge unless he happened to be in a place
towards which the colleges recognized a special duty or where the
schools had been strong enough to hold to their time-honoured
privileges."[31] The idea that working-class children should have the
opportunity of going to Oxford or Cambridge was no part of the
intentions of those who introduced the reforms, since their aim was

to sweep away clerical restrictions and privileges and to create truly national universities: "So far as the working-class was concerned, for one exclusive monopoly was substituted another, even harder to break."[32] Before the nineteenth century there were only nine 'public' schools in England, but during the century there was a great expansion in their numbers, and after 1860 they were even more exclusive than before 1860. Just as in the sixteenth century, there was a sudden, quite unprecedented expansion in the early 1860s, "the mass entrance of new wealth into the citadels of clerical and aristocratic privilege".[33]

The social mores of this exclusive society were as different as they could well be from the freedom prevailing at Scottish universities. The colleges were surrounded by walls, gates and ditches to keep gown well away from town. There was an elaborate code of discipline – compulsory chapel and college lectures, dinners in hall and college, including punishments: admonitions, rustication, expulsion, prohibitions, literary tasks. Dons, chaplains, tutors, were responsible for student conduct, and the streets were policed by proctors and their 'bulldog' assistants. Curfews were established and all dinner and supper parties in lodgings or in the town had to be notified in advance to the authorities. College tutors received all bills run up by students. The university assumed police power in the town, treated prostitutes in a high-handed way, and took powers of inquisition into prisoners in the university prison that were completely at variance with common law.[34]

Generally speaking, there were two types of don: the amiable type, fond of good food, convivial wine parties, and gambling; the distant priggish type, usually a pedantic, rather morose scholar, arrogant and humourless. In both cases their scholarship was very narrow. Unsurprisingly, teaching was not very good, and indeed became virtually a formality in the early Victorian period. More and more, especially at Cambridge, teaching passed into the hands of the private coaches; these were the most important teachers at the university all students were forced to use them. Lectures, which didn't even cover the examination syllabus, were neglected. A coach's reputation was measured by his ability to cram and drill a student intensely to get a high place in the examinations. "His labours were given a market price and evaluated in commercial terms. A well-paid coach had to be competitive, sure of his technique, well organized and willing to work six hard tutorial hours every day."[35] It sounds remarkably like the *juku*, the Japanese crammer's class to which so many Japanese youngsters go in the evening after school to fit them for Japan's intensively competitive education system.

But surely the most eloquent condemnation of the college system is in Whewell's remark that "the pupil values what he has to himself, what he pays for himself, and what is given to him in a familiar and companionable tone". Thirty years later it was said in the *Cambridge Review* that an undergraduate went to a private tutor because he was recognized as an individual. Nor was any sort of independence encouraged in the student when it came to the examinations. The formula which produced success was: set problems, set books, set solutions. Some there were who decried the system, for example V. H. Stanton, who subsequently became Regius Professor of Divinity at Cambridge. He recommended that tutors engage in some teaching and encourage the best students in general intellectual interests in order to counteract over-specialization.

There were few such voices, however. The narrow spirit and manner in which Cambridge students pursued their mathematical studies continued. So deeply rooted was the disdain of commerce and industry that many dons considered that almost no subject that could be turned to the benefit of business deserved recognition. Naturally enough, the leaders of commerce and industry returned the resentment; they preferred people trained in the works and believed college life ruined a man for a business career. They were not particularly interested in specialized university training for graduates in business. Even where scientific skills were required, they preferred a theoretical, broad and less practical education. Their emphasis was on vaguely humanistic qualities, or on logic, clarity of thought, intellectual independence and general mental discipline.[36] Precisely the qualities developed by the broader, more general education given at the Scottish universities.

> It is the extraordinary similarity of Oxford and Cambridge that is most striking. In size, in antiquity, wealth, influence, educational pattern, academic organization and status they are almost identical ... they constitute an entirely distinct species, a distinct genus, even a distinct Family of the Order of Institutions of Higher Education.[37]

For many children, parents and schoolmasters Oxbridge is the apex of the social system. If going to Oxbridge is a family tradition through the generations (Eton and King's, Winchester and New College, Cheltenham Ladies and Lady Margaret Hall), then this educational itinerary has become part of the national order of things. There is a general belief that Oxbridge is the ladder to wealth, power and influence, and there is plenty of evidence to support this view. British Cabinets, the Civil Service, the Diplomatic Service are stuffed with Oxbridge graduates; until quite recently the BBC was the Oxbridge accent; the Sunday papers coruscate with

Oxbridge wit, taste and cattiness. The Oxbridge colleges are full of titled persons. For numerous snobbish parents there is no possible social alternative to Oxbridge. Similarly, English schoolmasters want their pupils to read in the Bodleian and drink wine in the same room with scholars of world-wide renown.

To get in there is the scholarship examination. The sixth form specialist master is not a teacher, he is a coach and prepares his pupils as for a Boat Race. The Oxbridge admissions system demands specialist tuition, so teaching becomes hectic and pressurised, in other words cramming. Its effect on the school curriculum is devastating. It pursues the most specialized attainments (Greek and Latin verse, for example) all breadth of culture is thrown overboard. The two cultures problem, of which C. P. Snow spoke, is largely the fault of Oxford and Cambridge.[38] Many undergraduates, as a result of the narrow obstacle race, later fall into inertia and boredom. It is still quite generally the case that students who do not obtain admission to Oxbridge, but must content themselves with Sussex, Durham or Edinburgh, look upon themselves as failures. And of course the Scholarship Examination is totally unfair. The advantages enjoyed by applicants from Eton or Manchester Grammar School are obvious. The fears of the dons of a century before have been fully realised: "Could it have been the intention of the pious and charitable donors of the scholarship funds that these should ever be used merely to give recognition to expert and well-paid handling of good raw materials?"[39] Such was the end result of opening the college scholarships to public competition.

Specialization is basic to this whole approach to learning; indeed it is almost certainly an Oxbridge invention. It clamps a mould on many young people whose natural attitude of mind is wide-ranging, curious and discursive, so that many undergraduates fall victim to a mood of disenchantment with their studies. Another three years of what they had already done so intensively in sixth form is just too much. This is the result of Sir John Seeley's "exactness within a narrow range". It is the precise opposite of the Scottish universities' approach to learning; and indeed we may ask whether the widely recognized innovativeness of the Scots is not in large measure due to non-specialization, to lateral thinking?

Despite this intensive specialization external examiners find little difference between the examination papers of First Class graduates at Oxbridge and at other universities. Yet an Oxbridge First is automatically accorded superior ranking. The specialization becomes even narrower and more intense in research for an Oxbridge DPhil or PhD, which has the very highest reputation in the academic world at large, yet "it can be a very unlearned, very narrow little fact-grub indeed".[40] To this must be added the academic inbreeding which arises from Oxbridge reluctance to appoint staff from each other, let alone from other universities. This has very serious effects for Oxbridge and for other universities. This charmed circle, so difficult to break into, exacerbates the envy and resentment widespread in other universities. "It is a medium which breeds intrigue, self-seeking and intellectual cynicism."[41]

Then there is the social and cultural life of Oxbridge with its constant round of parties and pleasures; the cliques which form around sporting or social or academic interests, and who find each other again in London in such professions as teaching, publishing, journalism, broadcasting and advertising, in a world which must seem a simple extension of Oxbridge. Such a life "does not breed missionary zeal. The preservationist atmosphere, the traditions, the ceremonies, the legacy of the past to be loyally guarded and bequeathed unharmed to posterity – all these crush any capacity for imaginative social action. There are rebels but they are eventually checked and frustrated."[42] There are liberals but their liberalism is very old-fashioned and unradical.

Most dons see Oxbridge as a breeding-ground for the academic elite, while accepting that it is also a finishing-school for gentlemen. Since they also prefer specialization to what they see as superficiality, Honours degree syllabuses are aimed at the most outstanding undergraduates rather than the rank and file. This bad practice has been copied throughout the universities of Great Britain, like so many other bad Oxbridge habits. Despite all these negative features and many others that could be mentioned, Oxford and Cambridge are placed at the top of the pecking order of higher education institutions. This exalted position is mainly due to their age and descent. However, they also get the pick of the brightest schoolchildren who put them as their first choice and work very hard, in specialist sixth forms, under teachers who have years of practice, to get there. Inevitably, therefore, they get a much higher proportion of highly talented youngsters than other universities – whom they then proceed to turn into the decorous mediocrities we see on our television screens.

The staff situation is much the same. At the beginning of the nineteenth century, as we have seen, there was no original science and scholarship at Oxbridge. Yet today they can boast of first-rate research schools in most subjects. How did this happen? Quite simply, their great prestige has enabled them to tempt the finest scholars from other universities to take up chairs. As we have seen, they can also cream off the best students, not only from Britain but from all over the Commonwealth. So, given the money from the State to finance research centres, Oxford and Cambridge could scarcely fail to become great centres of scholarship.[43] Consequently, British universities all have a large complement of Oxbridge-trained staff who inevitably practice what they were taught, for good or ill. It is not surprising that a leading British politician said a few years ago: "Oxford and Cambridge are the canker at the heart of British education." Halsey and Trow[44] phrase it differently: "Once established, the provincial universities tended everywhere to shift the scope and balance of their studies to resemble as closely as possible the norms set by Oxford and Cambridge. But they lacked the wealth, the independence of cultural tradition, the social status and the political connections to offer a serious challenge to the entrenched position of the ancient foundations." Or to put it quite bluntly: even in higher education the English disease is snobbery.

Halsey and Trow, who everywhere talk about Britain when what they mean is England, summarise in eight points the English idea of a university:

1 It should be ancient;
2 It should draw students not from its own locality, but from the nation and internationally;
3 Studies should be carefully selected to fit into and maintain the established life and character of the university;
4 Those who enter should be offered 'education' and not merely 'training';
5 Students should live in a small-scale community affording close contact of teachers with taught in a shared domestic life;
6 There should be a high staff-student ratio for individualized teaching;
7 A university should be autonomous, which tends to mean richly and independently endowed;
8 The internal affairs of the ideal university should be governed by a democracy of its own academic members.

This is a handy modern definition of Oxbridge, provided it is read critically and in conjunction with *Camford Observed* by Rose and Ziman. One wonders, for example, how the 'education' tallies with the narrow, over-specialized training in a short three-year degree which Oxbridge in fact provides; or how universities which have been closely linked to political power throughout their history can be described as 'autonomous'. But let that pass. One can see in this 'English idea of a university' how, supported by the Establishment, Oxford and Cambridge have worked for not far short of two centuries now to make all British universities over into their image. This has done great damage to the Scottish universities in particular, and with that we shall deal in the next chapter.

But before we do we must hear the views of three Scots with detailed experience of Oxford, all of them from the University of Glasgow, which has to this day remained faithful, despite all difficulties, to some of Scotland's higher education traditions. The first is A. D. Lindsay, who was Master of Balliol College and then became Vice-chancellor of Keele University where he attempted to introduce innovations that were inspired by his Scottish educational background.

Lindsay, who spent many years at Oxford and loved the place, was nonetheless opposed to certain of its ideals. He disliked the emphasis put on quality or excellence rather than the imparting of information, and also Oxford's contempt for anything 'vocational'. In his view the education there given was aimed at meeting the requirements of the Civil Service – the Jowett ideal – and was not derived from educational or philosophical theory: it had no theoretical underpinning. This attitude of excellence, the competition between the colleges to head the examination lists, resulted in contempt for the less able who would lead to a lowering of standards – Kingsley Amis's 'more means worse'. It led to concentrating study on peak figures, top writers. There was very little in the way of professional and utilitarian studies, and an attitude of scorn for the social and physical sciences. He agreed with the Oxford view of the primacy of teaching over research, but he did not like the cult of 'quality', the Oxford 'exquisites'. He was in open conflict with Oxford on the orientation of intellectual interests. There was nothing wrong with seeking distinction, but it should not be made the primary aim of university life. He was, as a result, accused by many in Oxford of committing *la trahison des clercs*, of being willing to trade away Oxford's liberal traditions – though they hadn't existed for very long, we should remember – for a nasty mess of socialistic, bureaucratic, dubiously religious and dangerously authoritarian aims of his own.[45] The answer to which was that Balliol was known to inculcate a sense of 'calling' in its students.

The other two Scots were Snell Exhibitioners from Glasgow University to Balliol, which was, we recall, founded by a Scot in the Middle Ages. They have just graduated and express their feelings about Oxford in an entertaining article in the Times Higher Education Supplement.[46] Their voice is young and uninhibited but it should be listened to since it reflects very accurately the feelings of almost all young Scots. They begin uncompromisingly:

> In the nineteenth century Oxford provided most of the colonial bureaucrats who, armed with the necessary faith in their own racial and intellectual supremacy, given them by their education, cold-bloodedly administered the subjugation,

brutalization and murder of countless Africans, Asians and Caribbeans. Today, a large proportion of Oxford's graduates annually take up positions in the City – the major centre of European financial oppression – in an endorsement of human exploitation no less objectionable for being distanced from its victims.

The impact of 'English imperialism' on Scotland, they say, was a long and gradual process, though it began to gather pace around the time of the Enlightenment, with such institutions as the Select Society encouraging Englishmen to come to Scotland to teach the natives how to speak English. But the acquisition of an English education "often required a sojourn in the South, usually followed by resettlement in either Glasgow or Edinburgh, the twin metropolitan foci of England's internal colonization". Oxford was instrumental in this internal colonial movement, "training and anglicizing many of the young Scots intellectuals who would become its agents". The Snell Foundation, from which they had benefited as Glasgow graduates, is a typical example of this. "One cannot go on crossing social, cultural and national borders and to expect one's original identity to remain unfragmented." They give some amusing examples of the phenomenon. They are often asked if, after their studies end, they will 'go back', – something, they point out, only ever asked of foreign students. One of them studied "the national literature" for four years at Glasgow in a department staffed mainly by Oxbridge-trained academics; he did not have to study, discuss or write on any Scottish authors except Henryson and Dunbar, who were valued as "Scottish Chaucerians". And this was after five years of secondary schooling "in which virtually the only concession to Scottish literature was being given Macbeth rather than Hamlet as an examination test".

Is it simply canny mistrust of things English that leads us to disfavour Oxford, they ask. Are we being anachronistic? The answer is unfortunately no because "what John Snell did for Scottish Oxonians the British Council is now doing for the nationals of the underdeveloped countries". They receive a scholarship to Britain, get a thoroughly English education, go back to influential positions in their own countries – and help to create a sustainable British niche in foreign markets. "Oxford is not the only university servicing the seedy politics of international commercial competition. But where better to get a thoroughly British (read English) education – that is to say, an education which at worst encourages or at best fails to question the social injustice such a politics underpins." The lamentable consequence of Oxford's dominant ethos, "that consortium of individual careerism, protective hierarchicalism and rampant status-quo-ism" is the eagerness with which so many of its graduates take morally questionable occupations. The ethos is further reflected in the arrogance, smugness and snobbery which still pervade its senior common rooms, "shot through with cold, nasty and bloody-minded talk". as Raymond Williams once bluntly said at Cambridge.

The authors end with a brief 'blether' in Scots with a Scottish cashier at the Oxford Co-op, and conclude "the ready recognition and easy casualness of the encounter testify to the sense of community, identity and solidarity (of the Scots). There are, the event seems to insist, social networks, less formal, stronger and more human than the Oxford Union, Balliol and the old school tie."[47]

Any reader tempted to dismiss these sentiments would do well to remember that the authors are two very able young men who have spent four years at Glasgow University and three years at Balliol, arguably Oxford's best college.

The last word in this chapter, however, must go to Charles Kingsley who, in his celebrated novel *Alton Locke*, published in 1850, had this to say:

> They gave us what they had, those medieval founders: whatever narrowness of mind or superstition defiled their gift was not their fault, but the fault of the whole age. The best they knew they imparted freely, and God will reward them for it. To monopolise these institutions for the rich, as is done now, is to violate both the spirit and the letter of the foundations. The letter is kept – the spirit is thrown away ... It is not merely that we are bad churchmen that you exclude us, else you would be crowding your colleges, now, with the talented poor of the agricultural districts, who, as you say, remain faithful to the church of their fathers. But are there six labourers' sons educating in the universities at this moment? No! the real reason for our exclusion, churchmen or not, is because we are poor.

The same exclusion was responsible for the most powerfully resonant and evocative title in all English fiction: *Jude the Obscure*.

4

"The Decay of Ane Universitie"

It will be clear to the reader from the two preceding chapters that the ancient universities of Scotland and those of England were as the poles opposed. In almost every respect the former were superior to the latter throughout the eighteenth century, when they produced the geniuses of the Scottish Enlightenment, and when the latter, as Gibbon put it, were sunk in sloth and port. Then, and throughout most of the nineteenth century, the Scottish universities were producing the men who created and sustained the industrial revolution, while Oxbridge eschewed anything remotely industrial or commercial. The Scottish universities had been imbued with the spirit of the democratic intellect since at least *The First Book of Discipline* in 1560, whereas Oxford and Cambridge were the very pinnacle of elitism and fashionable snobbery both in their social life and in their colleges.

It should be noted too that it was the Scottish universities which were, as they still tenuously are, the true inheritors of the medieval tradition, and that they remained close to the principles and practices developed since the foundation of the universities of Bologna and Paris. That is the tradition whereby universities existed to train people for the professions, having first given them a broad all-round education in a three or four year 'Arts' course. Oxford and Cambridge, on the other hand, broke with that tradition, retaining only the Arts part, very narrowly defined: classics at Oxford, mathematics at Cambridge. It is no wonder so many authors use terms like finishing-schools for the aristocratic and wealthy to describe them. They were and are the odd man out in Europe.

The reader might therefore suppose, in all innocence, that if either had anything to learn from the other, it was surely the English universities; and that, in view of their great wealth, they might have hoped to develop the system which had served Scotland so well to heights of achievement which the Scottish universities in their poverty could not have hoped to emulate. But no! Beginning in 1826 there was, throughout the nineteenth century, a determined, prolonged and cumulative effort to get the Scottish universities "to resemble as closely as possible the norms set by Oxford and Cambridge".[1]

Matthew Arnold in the mid–nineteenth century described the Scottish university tradition as being Hebraic rather than Hellenic, speculative rather than genteel, professional rather

> than amateur. The Scotch . . . as the state of their universities shows, have at present little notion of *la grande culture* . . . Instead of guarding, like the Germans, the *wissenschaftliche Geist* of their universities, they turn them into mere school-classes . . . Accordingly the Scotch middle class is in *la grande culture* not ahead of the English. But so far as intellectual culture has an industrial value, makes a man's business work better and helps him to get on in the world, the Scotch middle class has thoroughly appreciated it and sedulously employed it, both for itself and for the class whose labour it uses; and here is their superiority to the English and the reason of the success of Scotch skilled labourers and Scotch men of business everywhere.

Again, noted by a great nineteenth century English cultural guru, another difference between the Scottish democratic intellect and the cultural elitism of Oxford and Cambridge.

Thus the Scottish universities inherited a very particular tradition and a particular function to fulfil – an education that was cheap, popular and to a great extent professional in character; and the whole Scottish system was more easily understood by the visiting European than by products of Oxford and Cambridge. This last point is very important in understanding what was to follow. The same points are made, though in a different perspective, by L. J. Saunders.[2] He points out that it would be unfair to restrict a comparison between the ancient English and Scottish universities to their classical scholarship. There was greater enthusiasm for education, inspired by strong professional ambition and by the widespread popular interest in academic distinction and opportunity. Country teachers, families, parish authorities took pride in the number of students they could send to college. Furthermore, "the intellectual independence of the more mature students responded to an active teaching in philosophy and science that was not yet conspicuous at Oxford and Cambridge. The critical approach was indeed marked in the Scottish intellectual inheritance from the

eighteenth century Enlightenment and the philosophical tradition
was now spreading out into exposition and research in the physical
and natural sciences . . . " This is a far cry from the assiduous devotion to classical grammar and syntax demanded by a Whewell, and
one hopes that today few would argue that the Oxbridge approach
to teaching and learning was superior to the traditional Scottish
approach. It should never be forgotten that the greatest explosion
of all-round creative genius ever witnessed in the British Isles took
place in Scotland in the latter half of the eighteenth century and the
first quarter of the nineteenth. The modern sciences of economics,
sociology and geology were created then; chemistry was revolutionized; agricultural methods and banking practice were transformed;
James Watt's steam engine drove the industrial revolution, and so
on. It was said that Watt's workshop was "a kind of academy
whither all the notabilities of Glasgow repaired to discuss the nicest
questions in art, science and literature". Watt's post was that of
mathematical instrument maker, and today he would probably be a
senior lab technician. In his usual acerbic style Voltaire said that if
you wanted to learn about anything from epic poetry to gardening,
your had to go to Scotland to learn it. David Hume, not to be out-
done even by a Voltaire, summed it all up: "The same age, which
produced great philosophers, and politicians, renowned generals
and great poets, usually abounds with skillful weavers and ship-
carpenters. We cannot reasonably expect, that a piece of woollen
cloth will be brought to perfection in a nation, which is ignorant
of astronomy, or where ethics are neglected."[3] Hume's clever, and
withal pawky, dialectical acumen gives the perfect definition of the
Scottish Enlightenment and of yet another aspect of the democratic
intellect. This is light years away from the narrow concentration
on construing Latin and Greek in the protected, socially isolated
hothouses that were Oxbridge colleges.

   The men who collectively created this intellectual miracle were
for the most part educated in Scotland's universities. So one has to
ask: how could anyone, in his right mind, hard upon the heels of
the Scottish Enlightenment, have set on foot in 1826 moves which,
some sixty years later, were to end by the complete subversion
of the Scottish universities through the introduction of Oxbridge
norms which were utterly foreign to the whole Scottish intellectual
tradition? It is all the more puzzling because, at precisely the same
time, many learned Scots were migrating to London as politicians,
philosophers, doctors, journalists and publishers. They were seen
to have a common intellectual approach deriving from the Scottish
context of instruction and the bracing tradition of intellectual zest
and freedom of Scottish students. The activity and influence of these

men "suggested to the advocates of a new metropolitan university that the example of Edinburgh might be more instructive to them than that of the historic English foundations".[4] Thus was University College, London, founded in 1826. It followed the example of the Scottish universities and was largely set up by Scotsmen. The same was to be true of Owen's College established later in the century at Manchester.

Again one must ask: why and how were the Scottish universities, whose example stimulated the development of modern universities in England from the 1820s onward, brought to undermine their own traditional values and adhere increasingly to those of Oxbridge? Here a valuable clue is provided by G. S. Osborne who says that in the century following the Act of Union Scotland became increasingly anglicized – one thinks of David Hume going to elocution classes to improve his English! – *except in education* which was becoming more and more unlike English education.

> There was something unstable about this Scottish attempt to have it both ways, and to combine social dependence on England with educational independence . . . Consequently by 1830 a severe crisis had arisen in Scotland on the question of how far the universities were to subordinate themselves to the southern system, or were to retain their independent initiative and time-honoured ties with the Continent."[5]

The first step towards easing the crisis was the Universities Commission of 1826, the members of which were mainly Scottish aristocrats who had been educated at Oxford and Cambridge. Thus, as already pointed out, they did not really understand or appreciate the Scottish system; their approach could not but be an anglicizing one. Oblivious of the democratic merits of Scotland's open door system and of Jeffrey's concern for "the many self-taught, late-taught, home-taught",[6] the Commissioners' aims were to raise the standard of university scholarship in Scotland. All the Scottish universities were poor and, in contrast to Oxford and Cambridge, had few endowments. There were many small bursaries to help poor students because the desire for knowledge was widespread, but few fellowships for scholars. Even for those who intended to embrace the learned professions the Commissioners found there was "little motive for paying almost exclusive attention to the ancient languages or for their seeking to acquire that profound acquaintance with all the difficulties of Latin and Greek which is in England venerated as the undoubted evidence of learning". The point of course is that Scottish university aims were quite different: "to disseminate that measure of Literature and Science which is generally valued and to do this in the most efficient manner".[7] Again the distinction between the democratic intellect and elitism. The Commissioners wanted to make the classics the basis of advanced literary, philosophical and scientific study, considering that this was the best possible intellectual training for young men. The example of English education was familiar and increasingly potent. So a Hellenic tradition was to be introduced to a people whose educational tradition, inspired by the Reformation and the Enlightenment, "emphasised equality of opportunity rather than a refined excellence; whose higher education had been long associated with the professions and with practice; whose contemporary enthusiasm was for science as applied to a wide range of human affairs".[8]

The Commissioners therefore proposed to abolish the Junior Classes at Scottish universities – what we would today call access classes. They also wanted to institute an MA after the BA, and the examinations for both these degrees were to be conducted as at Oxford and Cambridge. How some contemporary authors[9] can, in the face of such facts, accuse George Elder Davie of nationalist rhetoric when he speaks of the anglicization of Scotland's universities, is at best wilfully perverse. Even worse, the Commissioners wanted to institute an entrance examination, which would of course at one stroke abolish the open-door policy and exclude some 30% of entrants, mostly from the poorest classes of the population.[10] Their view was that, entry to the Scottish universities being cheap, many young people were thereby encouraged to undertake higher education for whom it would be a blind alley. As we have seen, the Scottish universities dispensed many small bursaries to help the poor. Indeed, in the two Aberdeen universities (King's and Marischal) one in three students received a small bursary. It appeared to the Commissioners "that some of these persons are at last left in the most distressing of all situations, disqualified for the occupations in which they might otherwise have been employed and unable to turn to any account the education which they have received".[11] The character of the instruction received must be lowered by the presence of such students. So bursaries should be given to encourage more advanced university studies and as a reward for established merit. In other words, hewers of wood and drawers of water, obscure Judes, need not apply for higher education because more means worse – the cry of the conservative English upper middle classes down the generations, totally at variance with Scottish educational traditions.

Why did the Commission quite openly call for the transformation of Scotland's universities into Oxbridge look-alikes? It may be useful at this point to quote at some length from the memoirs of an Edinburgh professional man:[12]

England is rapidly conquering Scotland. What the two tyrants, the long-shanked Edward I and bluff King Hal, tried in vain, Steam and Telegraph are fast accomplishing. The facilities of communication are bringing the upper classes in Scotland into closer proximity with England, and the natural result has followed. The larger and wealthier nation has infected the smaller and poorer nation, and every Scot who has aristocratic tastes and the means of gratifying them adopts English ways and manners. Not only the noblemen but the rich merchants and manufacturers must send their sons to an English public school and an English university, and their daughters to an English boarding establishment.

But, forty years ago, the custom had not come into full force, many people of great wealth and station throughout the country sent their children to Edinburgh to be educated – their boys to the Academy and their girls to ladies' boarding schools. Edinburgh, therefore, was the Promised Land of education, the great goal which every ambitious schoolmaster in the country kept in view. Consequently, it contained the very best teachers of what is called Secondary Education. Some of these were men of the highest gifts and scholarship; and if they had possessed that invaluable passport to success, the art of getting on – if they had, at every opportunity, pushed themselves into notice, looked preternaturally wise and heavy, and courted and flattered the great and influential – they might have been professors. But they preferred to remain in a comparatively humble position rather than barter their dignity and self-respect.

How very true that still rings today! The custom might not have come into full force forty years before these words were written, but it had in fact begun some seventy years earlier, It began in 1824, to be precise, just two years before the Universities Commission held its first session, with the opening of the Edinburgh Academy. Sir Walter Scott gave a speech and Lord Cockburn hailed the occasion with legal precision as "an important day for education in Scotland in reference to the middle and upper classes."[13] Fees at the Academy were six times higher than for the High School to which Scott, Cockburn, Francis Jeffery and Lord Brougham (later to become Lord Chancellor) had all gone and, it may be supposed, received a pretty good education. It should be noted that the education at the High Schools and Academies (such as Perth Academy) was not at all equivalent to that given at English public schools. They were expensive and crowded with pupils from different backgrounds and of varied interests. But the anglicizing itch described in the above

extract had already begun to affect the upper professional classes
who inhabited the New Town and the West End of Edinburgh and
who "felt the need of a school where boys might be taught classics
in the English style and so prepared for the Southern universities
and an official or professional career of wider scope than in Scotland".[14] Because of its high fees Edinburgh Academy was able to
pay high salaries to its teachers and so was able to select them from
English as well as Scottish universities. It is symptomatic of the
estrangement of such schools from Scottish traditions that to this
day, nearly 170 years later, there are only seven such schools in the
whole of Scotland. The irony is that our Edinburgh professional
man thought Edinburgh Academy was a good thing, rather than
the slippery slope leading to the English public schools. This was
a common illusion at the time: "The object was purely patriotic
one: to bring Scottish educational standards into line with those of
England, so that young Scots would not have to sent abroad to be
educated in England to give them the same sort of start in life as their
English contemporaries."[15] A perfect definition of the anglicization
some authors claim never existed.

The young people for whom this type of school was intended
were a tiny minority of the population, but it was a section which
at that time exercised even greater power and influence than it
does now because of the lack of democracy in political life. They
were the sort of young people destined to run the empire, and
they needed this English public-school type education in order to
compete effectively in the examinations for the Indian Civil Service.
These examinations were set by Oxford and Cambridge trained
people and they of course favoured applicants trained in the same
way, that is narrow, intensive study of the classics or mathematics.
The first Scottish applicants had no chance at all, coming from
a quite different tradition. "Students from the English universities
must possess an immense advantage in all public examinations,
owing partly to the fact of their more thorough, long-continued
training in certain departments of . . . learning; partly also from
the fact that the examiners upon whom the fate of the competitors
depends, are chiefly more conversant with English methods, and,
by the very questions they put as well as their way of putting
them, give a decided advantage to the English candidates.[16] So, for
a small minority of a small minority the whole Scottish university
tradition, which had served the country so well, was put under
immediate threat. If the Oxbridge-oriented aristocratic Commissioners got their way, the "success of Scotch skilled labourers and
Scotch men of business everywhere" and "their superiority to the
English", noted by Matthew Arnold, would also disappear.[17]

There was no possibility of political resistance to such misguided policies, since at that time the Scottish members of parliament were in an even smaller minority than they are now. Though by the Act of Union of 1707 the Scots retained their national systems of religion, law and education, the loss of political and economic independence – the foundation of all civil society – severely undermined the universities. It was felt by the English Establishment and its Scottish supporters, as the vast politico-economic developments of the nineteenth century got under way, that the Scottish system, with its Continental bias and sympathies, was incompatible with the 'British way of life'. The Universities Commission was the first attempt to anglicize the Scottish universities. Only those who are determinedly blind to the actual facts, such as the attempt to set BA and MA examinations on the Oxbridge model, would try to refute this.

There are, admittedly, other aspects that need to be taken into account. The rapid expansion of industry, the enormous increase in population, especially in the cities, in the early nineteenth century, necessitated rapid expansion of education. The situation was radically new and Scotland had to adapt her education to it. One might think that the traditional Scottish open-door policy in the universities was precisely what was needed in such a situation. But – and it is an insurmountable but – Scotland's universities, like the country as a whole, were poor. They desperately needed money for expansion, and "the English were minded to exact some measure of conformity in return for cash payments . . . When politics entered into education, the balance of power inevitably shifted to the South".[18] As Osborne[19] points out: "It is necessary to bring these problems of the English connection into the open because Scotland displays in her education many of the usual symptoms of dependence".

The practical terms of the seesaw struggle throughout the century for the soul of Scotland's universities were as follows: should they continue, as before, to take students early, put them through a four-year course of general education, including classics and sciences and compulsory philosophy, after which they would take up their specialist or professional training? Or should they do as desired by the growing and influential group of Scots, usually Oxbridge educated, who looked up to England as the model in most departments of life: abolish general education and philosophy as a central part of it; raise the university entrance age to 18 as in England, extend the secondary school course, and get the Scottish universities to provide only advanced, specialist education? This sixty-year-long struggle between the anglicisers and the defenders

of the Scottish university system can be briefly summarized. There
were four set pieces:
  1 The appointment, in 1826, of a Royal Commission to
    investigate the whole organization and curriculum of all Scot-
    land's universities. The Commission reported in 1831 but its
    recommendations were postponed;
  2 A second Royal Commission was appointed in 1858, reported
    in 1863, and a Universities (Scotland) Act was passed;
  3 The controversy continued and a third Royal Commission was
    appointed in 1876 and reported in 1878;
  4 Finally, the General Report of the Commissioners under
    the Universities (Scotland) Act of 1889 was passed (though
    published only in 1900) and it controlled the work of the
    universities for 75 years.
In 1826 the charge laid against the Scottish system by the Commissioners was that it was too superficial and did not go into as much
depth as in England. To which the reply was "it is a great good on
the whole because it enables relatively large numbers of people to
get . . . that knowledge which tends to liberalize and make intelligent the mass of our population, more than anything else.[20] In his
memoirs Henry Brougham refers to a dinner in his honour, saying
that in reply to a speech
    I seized the opportunity to declare my decided approbation of
    the Scotch system of education, as contrasted with the English.
    I said that I had never known any scheme so well adapted for
    forming and finishing a learned course, as that pursued in the
    old High School of Edinburgh, and in the University. For that
    was the system so invaluable in a free State – a system which
    cultivated and cherished higher objects than mere learning,
    which inculcated a nobler ambition than the mere acquisition
    of prosody and dead languages. My English friends will cry
    aloud against this doctrine which they designate a rank heresy.
    Nevertheless, such was my opinion in 1825, and such it still
    is after a lapse of 40 years[21]
The issues at stake will stand repeating. They were:
  1 The age of admission to university, which the reformers
    thought was too low;
  2 The qualifications of the applicants – the reformers thought
    there should be an entrance examination, as at Oxford and
    Cambridge;
  3 The 'junior classes', already mentioned, which the reformers
    thought were superficial and should be abolished;
  4 The relationship of the general or ordinary degree, which all
    students had to sit, to more specialized qualifications. The

reformers simply wanted to abolish the Ordinary Degree, for centuries the necessary preliminary to professional study. As a consequence they wanted to improve general education in schools and thus to lengthen the secondary school course.[22]

Scottish opinion was shocked by the appointment of the Royal Commission, and the sharpness of Sir William Hamilton's animadversions against Oxford was no doubt due to this. There was stubborn resistance to the proposals of what Osborne calls the 'anglicizing faction', as can be seen from the multiplicity of commissions and reports and from the sixty-three-year-long timetable. The recommendations of the 1831 Report were quite simply postponed because of this resistance. "The perennial dilemma remained: whether to retain the traditional broad curriculum based on philosophy or to adopt English goals of specialist excellence for an elite."[23] However, similar Royal Commissions reported on Oxford and Cambridge and the respective university acts of 1854 and 1856 revived the impetus in Scotland. The second Royal Commission of 1858 simply took up again the Rosebery Commission's report of 1831 and largely remodelled the Scottish universities along the lines it suggested. "Stimulated no doubt by the success of the Oxford honours schools and the Cambridge triposes, the Commissioners followed the recommendations of the Rosebery Commission by instituting graduation with honours."[24] Thus was a very un-Scottish concept of specialization introduced into Scotland's universities. Not the traditional professional specialization in medicine, law or theology/philosophy after a general arts course – the legacy of Bologna and Paris – but narrow specialization in any subject on the Oxbridge model. Having got their toe in the door, so to speak, the Commissioners waited, in the face of much controversy, until the next Universities (Scotland) Act was passed in 1878. This time they went the whole hog. They set "graduation with honours on a proper footing by discontinuing the obligation on candidates to go through the whole curriculum for the ordinary degree before proceeding to specialization".[25]

Seldom can such bland words have heralded such a mighty change in the whole approach to knowledge of a nation's universities. We are suffering very severely today from the ultimate effects of this narrow approach, as is recognized by many authors. Nor was it simply that the defenders of the Scottish system were digging their heels in and refusing to listen to reason. They were as aware as anyone else that Scottish society and the Scottish economy were changing very rapidly, and that the universities would have to produce specialists in many industrial areas if the challenge of, for example,

German industry was to be met. They had, after all, been teaching science long before Oxford and Cambridge, and furnishing the men who made the industrial revolution. The *aggiornamento* of the Scottish universities need not have taken the form it did. They need not have been pressed into the Oxbridge mould. They could have learned much from Germany and France, as they had in the past. Indeed some Scots, "with an inspired vision",[26] wanted to set up postgraduate schools for specialization, and "had the English been prepared to pay for the system of Scottish postgraduate schools . . . much of the distinctive structure and curriculum of the Scottish universities could have remained and the resultant system would have resembled the American more closely than the English". What a marvellous opportunity for fundamental educational innovation was there missed, and deliberately missed! Those who argue that blaming anglicization is dangerous and can lead to looking for an English conspiracy[27] would do better to provide an explanation of such blatant actions as that instead of indulging in empty general remarks like "restricted range of appropriate research strategies" and "the conceptual categories here are decidedly crude".

Thus, by the Act of 1878, the broad general Arts course for all students, containing elements from the languages, science and philosophy, was abolished and students could specialize from the day they arrived at the university. Worse still, the general degree was made an *alternative* to the honours degree, in other words for weaker students who were thereby made to feel their weakness. This was the introduction of the approach so typical of English education, i.e. selection and elitism. The Commission of 1876 set the unambiguous goal of the assimilation of the Scottish system to the English one, and the reorganization of the relations between school and university also in conformity with the English model. Such was the continuing resistance of the Scots, however, that this could not be implemented immediately. It was, however, made clear that no government would in future have any sympathy with any independent or Continental-style development of the Scottish universities, and that they would not give the financial support the English colleges were receiving until they assimilated their academic system very closely with the English one. It was not till 13 years later, by the Act of 1889, that the defenders of the Scottish system finally gave in. They broke away from a system that had evolved over centuries, which had a close kinship with continental methods and a world-wide reputation, in favour of what George Davie calls "a piece-meal, opportunistic policy designed to conciliate the English rather than impress the world". The 1889 Act was a decisive watershed.

The long-term effects of these momentous decisions can be glimpsed from comments made quite recently in an academic journal.[28] The writer points out that Honours graduates score higher in intelligence tests than Ordinary graduates, and suggests that this intellectual selection is an odd way of justifying the continued existence of the Ordinary degree. "Odd, too, is the implicit equation of specialization with intellectual excellence and of general education with intellectual mediocrity." He then says that in Davie's view, without the Ordinary degree the Scottish higher education system "would be reduced to little more than a North British examination board". But those who support the Ordinary degree fail to realize that the changes made in 1892 and 1908 following the 1889 Act and which established ordinary degrees in more or less their present form, "largely destroyed a long tradition of Scottish liberal or general education" for which the previous generation of academics had fought so hard. The Ordinary Degree was no longer a general educational preparation for subsequent professional specialisation, but had been downgraded to a *pis-aller* for also-rans. Elitism wearing the cloak of "raising standards" and "excellence" had destroyed a tradition that had endured and evolved since the Middle Ages and whose aim was "to liberalize and make intelligent the mass of our population, more than anything else".[29] The author's conclusion is of the utmost importance for the future of higher education in Britain, but especially in Scotland. "This lost tradition is highly relevant to such contemporary problems as . . . the need for general and recurrent education and the expanding demand for mass higher education. Curiously, many who now face these problems in England are feeling their way towards a model for higher education which resembles the very nineteenth century Scottish university model that the English displaced with the turn of the century reforms." As we see, the author is quite clear about who were the authors of these very harmful changes.

He is not alone in this. Hanham[30] has a whole chapter on the problem of anglicization. The Scots, he says, were acutely aware of the need to protect their characteristic institutions, "lest they simply be replaced by English ones". He stresses that this was an internal Scottish debate, not "a dialogue between England and Scotland". Pressure for anglicization had begun to be felt about the middle of the eighteenth century. "Wealthy Scots had begun to feel that a Scottish education would put their children at a disadvantage in the struggle for life and began to send their children to English schools where they might learn to pass as Englishmen." Without the English type of public school education it was difficult for Scottish students to do justice to themselves at Oxford or Cambridge. Hanham makes the important point that, at Scottish schools and universities, far more emphasis was placed on the general understanding of classical texts than on textual learning or Latin and Greek composition. This had also been true of Paris in the Middle Ages. and is consonant with a philosophy-based approach to learning. Understanding of intellectual content was seen as more important than philology and language manipulation. As Professor George Jardine, Professor of Logic at Glasgow in the early nineteenth century, had said: "The Scots believe it to be of greater consequence to the student to receive instruction in the elements of science both physical and mental, than to acquire even the most accurate knowledge of the ancient tongues when all that is most valuable in them may . . . be obtained without so great a sacrifice of time and labour."[31]

But the pull of Oxbridge exerted great pressure on the Scottish universities. They were expected to fulfil their traditional function of teaching everyone who aspired to a university education, while preparing some to go on to Oxbridge, and endeavouring to compete with Oxbridge by keeping their best students in Scotland. It was, says Hanham, the introduction of open competitive examinations[32] for the Indian and Higher Civil Service that exerted irresistible pressure for the Scottish universities to come into line with 'Oxbridge practice' – confirming the argument presented above. Hanham, who does not fully understand the Scottish educational situation and seems to think there is a strong case for anglicization, nonetheless admits that by changing to English norms something valuable was lost: "the distinctive national point of view which put more emphasis on making education freely available to all and on a 'philosophical' approach to learning than on examination achievements". Professor J. S. Blackie realized that people who wanted to anglicize the schools for patriotic reasons could well end up believing that anglicization was a good thing in itself. That is precisely what happened. That remarkable Scot James McCosh, an evangelical minister and professor of philosophy, who became one of the principal creators, and President, of Princeton University, foretold what would happen in a chapter devoted to Francis Hutcheson, the founder of the Scottish philosophy: "The Scotch were quite competent at that time to educate the nobility of the country, who had not yet fallen into the way of going to the great English schools and colleges, there to lose their national predilections and become separated, as they did in succeeding ages, from the sympathies, social, political and religious, of the middle classes and common people of Scotland, to the great injury . . . of the nation generally."[33]

Hanham quotes Treasurer Leishman of Edinburgh Town Council, speaking in 1911: "It was strange that people should send their boys to England to be taught when they could get such an excellent education here." This, however, had not been the view of *The Times* of 4 December 1856, which had said of Scotland: "The universities are inferior, the schools for the middle and higher classes are inferior, professional education and the professional spirit are not what they are in England." (We shall deal with this 'inferiorisation' later in the book.) Osborne, on the other hand, says that there can be no doubt that tutelage to England resulted in grave educational loss to Scotland. Referring to the Schools Act of 1872, he says: "England was at least a generation behind Scotland in its educational ideals and practice. Yet it was English ideals, English standards, English classification which ruled Scotland.."[34] He adds that the "infelicities (or worse) in the Universities (Scotland) Acts can also be blamed on anglicizing influences . . . " He makes the telling point (of great topical interest) that the devolution of political and administrative control is not tidy or complete. "It is the politician's answer, short of giving Scotland her own parliament, to the problems raised by the existence of two separate value systems." For Knox[35] there is a clear distinction to be made between these value systems: "It would appear that Scotland, which had a national system of education when England was still groping in the dark, has been marking time or even falling behind . . . With 250 years of steady progress in education behind her, Scotland has good reason to cultivate her distinctive tradition." As we have seen, however, she was not allowed to, and the depth of ignorance and insensitivity in these matters of prominent English experts can be illustrated by the following quotation. The writer claims that the English tradition has had the main shaping influence in our society, but concedes: "It has been a very fortunate thing for us that Scotland . . . (has) had such freedom to cultivate a distinctive tradition, British indeed, but having traits all its own."[36]

There have been several hints in the course of this depressing tale that some Scottish educational ideas were at least a century ahead of their time. Some also had great influence abroad while they were being distorted and traduced at home. This is a fascinating theme which we shall now explore.

5

Scotland's Academic Diaspora

The Carnegie-Mellon Bagpipe Syndrome
As Scotland's great university traditions were thus being undermined, James McCosh, evangelical minister, prolific writer on
philosophy and theology, and Professor of Philosophy at Queen's
University, Belfast, set off across the Atlantic in 1866 for a lecture
tour of America from which he was destined never to return. He
is, according to the American scholar J. David Hoeveler Jnr., to
whom I am greatly indebted, our best vehicle for answering the
question: what happened to the Scottish intellectual tradition as
it confronted the new direction of ideas in the middle and late
nineteenth century?[1]

James McCosh went to both Glasgow and Edinburgh universities, became a minister, walked out of the Church of Scotland
with Thomas Chalmers in 1843, and was the product of the battle
between Scottish Moderation, represented by the university philosophers led by Sir William Hamilton and the national ministry of the
Church of Scotland, on the one hand, and Scottish evangelicalism
on the other. This battle resulted in the Disruption of 1843. The
evangelicals decried the Enlightenment and its social effects, for
"Enlightenment ideas were not in pursuit of a Utopian future; they
were intended to preserve the status quo and the best values of the
age of North Britain".[2]

McCosh tried to merge these two traditions, as can be seen in his
writings on philosophy, ethics and evolution, and also in his reorganization of Princeton College. Princeton in the McCosh years,
says Hoeveler, reflected, in its style and character, both of these
Scottish cultural traditions. For it is a fact that the Scottish philosophy, the philosophy of common sense, had a dominant position
in American academic thought in the early and middle nineteenth

century. The Scots had a much greater influence in America than any other group of Enlightenment spokesmen.[3] As Hoeveler says, "the Scottish thinkers were familiar to five generations of American college students. Indeed they dominated American academic thought for almost a century".[4] This is well illustrated by the fact that the New Jersey presbyterian college, which ultimately became Princeton University, was led by two Scots, John Witherspoon in the late eighteenth century (he arrived in 1768), and James McCosh in the nineteenth century.

John Witherspoon, who became President of the College of New Jersey, Princeton in 1768, was described by McCosh as "the energetic man who actually introduced Scottish thought to the new world".[5] James Madison, perhaps the most philosophical of all the framers of the American constitution, acknowledged his debt to the study of moral philosophy under Witherspoon:

> The increased attention paid to the study of the nature and constitution of the human mind, and the improvements which had been introduced into this fundamental department of knowledge by the philosophical inquiries of his own country-men, constituted a marked and most important feature of Dr. Witherspoon's reforms. Mr. Madison formed a taste for these inquiries, which entered deeply ... into the character and habits of his mind and gave to his political writings in after life a profound and philosophic cast, which distinguished them eminently and favourably from the productions of the ablest of his contemporaries.[6]

Witherspoon, who was an enthusiastic advocate of the Scottish philosophy, said, in his moral philosophy: "Some late writers have advanced, with great apparent reason, that there are certain first principles or dictates of common-sense, which are either simple perceptions or seen with intuitive evidence. These are the foundation of all reasoning and, without them, the reason is a word without a meaning. They can no more be proved than you can prove an axiom of mathematical science." It was from this time that the Scottish philosophy became the most important philosophical influence in America. It is intriguing to find very similar ideas being promoted by one of the finest and most imaginative of modern writers on science: "The processes of rational thought are not ends in themselves but must be perceived in the larger context of human good; the nature and direction of rational and analytical endeavours should be determined in significant part by their ultimate human implications as revealed through intuitive thinking."[7]

Witherspoon flung himself into the struggle for American independence and he was elected a representative in Congress for the

State of New Jersey in 1776. He is one of the names – the most
honoured of all names in the United States – attached to the Declaration of Independence and his portrait hangs in Independence
Hall. McCosh says, with evident pride: "I rather think that – if
we except Washington, Franklin and perhaps half-a-dozen others –
none had so important an influence as Witherspoon in guiding the
American Revolution . . . Scotland did not allow him, what would
have been for her good, to become a leader of men; and Scotland's
loss became America's gain."[8] Nor was Witherspoon alone in his
exiled glory. What a roll-call one could make of great Scots who
had to go abroad to give of their best. One could even start with
John Paul Jones, who gave the English so much trouble on the high
seas in the American War of Independence.

John Witherspoon's secure niche in American constitutional
history is not totally surprising when one recalls the Scottish constitutional tradition, enshrined in the Declaration of Arbroath of
1320, that the King rules by popular will and for the good of the
people. Witherspoon's influence can be measured by the fact that
no less than 16% of the representatives at America's Constitutional
Convention were Princeton graduates.

McCosh, a century later, was determined to establish at Princeton
the basic principles of the Scottish university teaching style, and
this was made clear in his inaugural address: "I hold that in study,
while the true end is the elevation of the faculties, they never will
be improved by what is in itself useless, or found to be profitless,
in the future of life."[9] He called for a standard broad programme
in the freshman and sophomore years, followed by several elective
courses in the last two years – this being the major accomplishment
of his term of office. He was, however, opposed to what Charles
William Eliot, a great educational reformer who became President
of Harvard in 1869, described as "a broad elective system", on the
grounds that this would allow students to study only the ancient
languages or only the sciences. He and Eliot debated this in 1885.
McCosh affirmed that students are too young to know what they
want and may lay misguided emphasis on one division of learning,
the result being a product that is "narrow, partial, malformed".
Here McCosh was being true to the system under which he had studied at Glasgow. There, after a first year in the preparatory classes
(which, we remember, our nineteenth century anglicizing reformers
abolished), he had studied Greek, Latin, logic, metaphysics, moral
philosophy, mathematics and natural philosophy, or physics. It is
a matter of fact that his most excellent work was in the last two.[10]

McCosh and his Scottish accent were much loved at Princeton.
Hoeveler quotes an amusing and instructive dictum: "But, mon,

is he alive? He is said to be a man of ability and a high scholar. I am anxious to know whether he is also a lively teacher".[11] By all accounts McCosh was a great teacher and a powerful personality who believed that "the rooting of good principles in students depends much on the philosophy they are taught".[12] A student view was that the distinctive characteristic of Princeton college life was "the particular habit of philosophical enquiry . . . so apparent that it colors discussions over beer and even in tobacco smoke".[13] As McCosh's successor, Winthrop Daniel, put it, at Princeton the philosophic temper was "pervasive and universal. This is one of our many inheritances from Dr. McCosh".[14]

The American university emerged in those years with the breaking-up of the old rigid curriculum; the introduction of new, modern subjects; the rise of professional academics specialized in their training and dedicated to the advancement of knowledge. In a striking phrase, Hoeveler says that the liberalization of Princeton "reflects the long reach of the Scottish Enlightenment and the moral fervour of the Free Church of Scotland". For McCosh, who, as we have seen, had marched out with Thomas Chalmers in the Disruption of 1843 which split the Kirk, was a curious mixture: he embodied the liberal spirit of learning and also evangelical commitment; he was a devoted Christian who had none of the difficulty that beset Bishop Wilberforce in accepting Darwin's theories of evolution;[15] he believed in scientific studies, and also in revivalism.

He was above all an 'intuitive realist', part of the long tradition of Scottish philosophical opposition to dualism. He fought a great battle of the books with John Stuart Mill over Sir William Hamilton's ideas. He thought Mill's moral theories wrong and dangerous – an empirical ethics linked to the happiness principle which substituted association for judgment. This whole philosophical debate was a very big issue in mid-nineteenth century America. Most interestingly of all, he defended till the end of his life the arch-sceptic David Hume's "attempt to introduce the experimental method of reasoning into moral subjects". Hume was McCosh's greatest challenge. He would have agreed with the principal protagonist of the Scottish common-sense philosophy, Thomas Reid, when he asked: "What are we to think when we find intelligent minds asserting that there is no heat in fire or no colour in the rainbow; when men of acumen seek to disprove the existence of a material world, and assert that we ourselves are all ideas in a mind without substance? I say, when we consider such extravagances of many of the most acute writers on this subject, we may be apt to think the whole to be only a dream of fanciful men who have entangled themselves in cobwebs spun out of their own brain."[16]

McCosh undoubtedly made a great contribution to the pro-
nounced moral atmosphere at American universities at that time.
On his death in 1894 the *New York Times* said: "To him more
than any other man in its history, Princeton owes the reputation
which it has today as a broad, unsectarian, progressive institution of
learning." It has to be said, however, that McCosh would not have
liked the exclusive, top-drawer Ivy League establishment Princeton
became after his death.

Nor was it only at Princeton that Scottish influence was strong.
Just a few years after McCosh's death Andrew Carnegie founded
Carnegie-Mellon University in Pittsburgh. In 1989 that university
offered a BA in bagpipe-playing, eliciting a stock joke in the col-
umns of the *Times Higher Education Supplement*. A letter to the
editor complained about this and referred to Carnegie-Mellon's
"enlightened decision. *Ceol mor*, the classical music of the Highland
bagpipe, has a strong claim to being Scotland's greatest contribution to the arts, and it is not so much surprising that an American
university should offer such a degree as scandalous that no Scottish
university has yet had the wit to do the same."[17]

The same comment could be made about all the other Scottish
university methods and ideas that were introduced into America's
universities as they were being eliminated by anglicizing pressures at
home. For instance, the role of general education in the first degree.
An American scholar points to "the unique role of general education
as a component of nearly all US first degree courses".[18] Then there
was, and is, the American version of the Scottish open-door policy – some 3300 separate higher educational institutions at different
levels and with different teaching styles and other academic characteristics, but made into one system by the unit-credit scheme which
permits student transfer. Trow contrasts this with European elitism
whose slogan is "Nothing, if not the best", whereas America's (and
eighteenth- and nineteenth-century Scotland's) is "Something is better than nothing". "We have not been able", says Trow, "to afford
the luxury of high academic standards across all our degree-granting
institutions. The result is the diversity of standards and functions
in our colleges and universities that we find so familiar and that
Europeans find so strange. So long as the governing assumption of
a system of higher education is that only a minority can work at the
required standard, that system is constrained both in its size and in
the functions that it can perform for its students and for the larger
society. Such a system may perform the functions of elite selection,
preparation and certification ... But it cannot penetrate as deeply
or as broadly into the life of society as American higher education
has."[19] Though stated at greater length, this is precisely the message

that Francis Jeffrey put to the Universities Commission of 1826 in Scotland,

Trow draws from this American experience of mass higher education conclusions which are valid far beyond the US borders. It broadens the perspectives of students, giving them an appreciation of other cultures, making them more tolerant of cultural differences and weakening the prejudices characteristic of uneducated people. People who have been to college view issues on a longer time-scale than the less well educated. Governments, administrations, industry and commerce need people who can take the long view. But perhaps most important is the heuristic effect of higher education. People who have been to college learn how to learn other skills – again as Francis Jeffrey said. It is impossible to overestimate the importance of this. Even a little higher education creates a surge in adult education. Trow says that the generous provision for education for adults in the USA engenders and distributes more widely the habit of 'life-long learning' than is true of most other countries. The truth of these arguments is movingly illustrated in a passage from Saul Bellow's *The Adventures of Augie March* :

> Normally Simon and I would have gone to work after high school, but jobs weren't to be had anyway, and the public college was full of students in our condition, because of the unemployment, getting a city-sponsored introduction to higher notions and an accidental break into Shakespeare and other great masters along with the science and math levelled at the Civil Service exams. In the nature of the case it couldn't be avoided; and if you were going to prepare impoverished young folks for difficult functions, or if merely you were going to keep them out of trouble by having them read books, there were going to be some remarkable results born out of the mass. I knew a skinny, sickly Mexican too poor for socks and stained all over, body and clothes, who could crack any equation on the board; and also Bohunk wizards at the Greeks, demon-brained physicists, historians bred under pushcarts, and many hard-grain poor boys who were going to starve and work themselves bitterly eight years or so to become doctors, engineers, scholars and experts.[20]

Trow concludes that the presence of more mature, part-time and working students has confounded the prediction of a decline in enrolments after 1979. There seems, he says, no limit to this development; a large segment of American higher education seems ready to provide some useful educational service to all non-traditional students. This was one of the main aims of the Scottish universities in the eighteenth and nineteenth centuries, and had they been allowed to follow their own traditional open-door policy, I believe there can be little doubt they would have arrived long ago at the mass higher education policy which now exists in the United States and which we are at long last now trying to create in Britain. After all, as James Scotland says: "In the event more poor boys got to the universities in Scotland than in any other country before the late nineteenth century developments in the United States."[21]

As a final illustration of the influence of Scottish university approaches to knowledge on American higher education, we may quote the 'mission statement' of two contemporary American universities. Many of these, it has to be said, are trivial, but some stress an element that was basic to the Scottish approach. For example, Indiana University's statement in 1981 says that "institutes of higher education have a responsibility for an honest and ethical academic atmosphere. As part of that effort, each discipline must arrange for its students to consider and ponder the moral questions of the field. Whether this will be done by integrating ethics into all courses or by the introduction of specific ethics courses remains to be seen and must be answered soon. Our graduates should develop during their time here a keen sense of professional responsibility in these complex and changing times." Similarly, the University of Cincinnati in 1977 had this to say: "As a moral community, the University is concerned with choices and values, behaviour and actions, judgments and decisions as to what is equitable, worthy and just."[22]

As to the British universities – including, alas, those of Scotland – the editor of the *Times Higher Education Supplement* in 1984 said that fundamental questions about the purpose of universities are "habitually avoided". The American Carnegie Commission on Higher Education (interesting how that name keeps cropping up in connection with higher education) in a report in 1968 stated: "The American nation needs and expects from higher education . . . quality of result and equality of access." A full 16 years later, in 1984, Keith Joseph, then Secretary of State for Education and Science, was saying that the "keynotes" of Government policy in higher education are "quality and cost-effectiveness". The difference is marked. A second difference is that in Great Britain discussion rarely touches on questions of intellectual content, though questions are sometimes raised about excessive specialization and the overwhelming emphasis on the honours degree. There is not the faintest echo of "the clamorous American debate about the nature of a liberal education and the flight from the humanities".[23] A third difference is of course the contrast between the 'more means worse' tradition in England and the open-door policy in the USA. This is clear from a Carnegie Commission statement of 1971 which recommends "universal access for those who want to enter institutions of higher education and are able to make reasonable progress after enrollment, and can benefit from enrollment". Indeed, college has become almost 'compulsory' in the USA: "As more and more college-age youngsters go on to college, not to be or to have been a college student becomes increasingly a lasting stigma, and a grave handicap in all the activities and pursuits of adult life."[24]

So what might be called the 'Carnegie-Mellon Bagpipe Syndrome' is equally true of matters of vast moral import. As the world heads deeper and deeper into great planetary problems that demand value choices, our universities will be forced – if they are not to become irrelevant – once again to teach the ethics of social living, indeed an ethic of the biosphere. The wheel is turning full circle with a vengeance. Can Scotland's universities take up again where they were forced to leave off in 1889?

Canada: The Infusion of the Scottish Tradition

In laying the cornerstone of the university that was to bear his name, Lord Dalhousie said in 1820 that "the object and intention of this important work" was "the instruction of youth in the higher classics and in all philosophical studies; it is formed in imitation of the University of Edinburgh". This was not the first time that mention had been made of the relevance of the Scottish university system to the Canadian situation. In 1815 John Strachan, an Aberdeen graduate, had said the Scottish reliance on the lecture as the principal means of instruction had practical advantages for Canada. He was at that time deeply involved in the discussions leading to the foundation of McGill University, and in a letter to the members of the legislature of Lower Canada he strongly urged the acceptance of the Scottish model. His argument was entirely practical. "Oxford and Cambridge were well adapted to a rich ... country like England, but they were not an appropriate model for Canada, a colony which could afford neither professors who lectured once a week nor the fellowship which allowed tutorial instruction." Even before this in 1808 Thomas McCulloch, a presbyterian minister, had begun to conduct a grammar school in his own house at Pictou in Nova Scotia, and in 1815 he established the Pictou Academy. The curriculum followed the Scottish pattern: Latin, Greek, logic, moral philosophy, mathematics, political economy and rhetoric (i.e. exercises in analysis and composition). In 1838, after 30 years of experience of teaching Canadian youngsters, McCulloch, on the point of assuming the presidency of Dalhousie College, rejected the proposal that the classics receive special attention:

That he who teaches these languages in Dalhousie College
should know his business well, its respectability requires. But
that boys should in Halifax or elsewhere spend six or seven
years upon Latin and Greek and then four more in college
partly occupied with the same languages is a waste of human
life adapted neither to the circumstances or the prosperity of
Nova Scotia . . . If Dalhousie College acquire usefulness and
eminence it will not be by an imitation of Oxford, but as an
institution of science and practical intelligence.

This was the basic Scottish point of view, a view held both by emigrants like Strachan and native born Canadians like J. W. Dawson
and G. M. Grant who went to Scotland for their university education. "Such men were particularly influential in the nineteenth-
century development of Dalhousie, McGill, Queen's and Toronto,
the four institutions which above all others set the pattern for
Canadian higher education in the first 50 years of the twentieth
century.[25]

Australia: The critical approach

John Anderson was another Scottish university teacher who emi-
grated, this time to Australia in the 1920s. He had entered the
University of Glasgow in 1911 and graduated in 1917 with first
class honours in Mathematics and Physics and Philosophy. He
was destined to make his mark in philosophy, and he created
a school of thought in Australia which strongly mirrored Scottish preoccupations. He believed, and got his students to believe,
that "philosophy is not simply another specialism, but that it is,
in some sense, the most important of all subjects, in the sense
that it gives one a necessary key to the understanding of science, human nature, society and art".[26] This had always been the
approach of the Scottish universities; another facet of that tradition is reflected in the work of Anderson from whom we get a
sense of "the relatedness of the different branches of culture, the
idea of a common theoretical or 'critical' approach to the different
fields of intellectual creation and discovery".[27] It is an intellectual
approach which seeks to grasp the systematic interconnections of
things, their relationship to a wider context. "The most important side of any department of knowledge is the side in which it
comes into touch with every other department. To insist on this is
the true function of humanism", wrote John Burnett, Professor of
Greek at St. Andrews.[28] In other words for Anderson as for generations of Scottish scholars, moral and social criticism, a view of
the nature and foundations of culture, were an essential object of
philosophy.

Anderson asked a question which is very relevant in this age of the specialist with little general education: is a child the heir of all the ages, or just job-fodder?[29] For him the answer was clear, and he therefore opposed vocational training which he saw as having no educational value. This might seem to contradict the traditional Scottish approach, but of course it does not since all students had to go through an arts course before undertaking professional training. Since criticism was at the heart of his position he was also opposed to 'moralism', i.e. to religion in education, since it asks for uncritical acceptance; for Anderson the very essence of education was coming to understand. All knowledge is of ordering things in space and time: there is no transcendence. Genuine knowledge is systematic, studying not particulars but qualities, seeing things as obeying regular laws; true learning is the discovery of connections, often between things which seem remote from one another. Education is critical, hypotheses are used and discarded. Education means seeing through pretensions of all kinds, through doctrines that serve as a smokescreen. Education is finding a way of life built round principles of understanding and criticism; it is therefore a social activity. The main thing the teacher has to hand on is thinking.

It goes without saying that from such a standpoint the universities have a vital role to play. Anderson would be utterly appalled at the position our universities find themselves in today, since he believed that universities must be protected from the demands of 'society'. This is a stand diametrically opposite to that of, for example, Sir William Hamilton, who thought government had a right to exert control over universities. On the other hand, the society we live in today is far more intrusively controlled by government than was the case in Hamilton's day. Anderson was opposed to practicalist and conformist tendencies in universities; and who, looking at the present position in Britain's universities, could deny that he has a very strong point there? "The aim of education is to give an account of things, to find out the reason why, and thus put knowledge in the place of opinion." This is Anderson's definition of education in his paper *Socrates as an Educator*.[30] It would not go down well with those who have put our universities in the hands of accountants and bureaucrats, who have abolished tenure and thus put academic freedom, in its true sense as defined by Anderson, under severe threat.

Finally, we come to the two characteristics of the Scottish tradition that perhaps most typify it: breadth of general culture and opposition to narrow specialization. In his paper on *University Reform*,[31] Anderson says that there is much to be said for the view "that the standard in all 'technical' faculties would be improved if all; students had to begin by taking a degree in arts or pure science; and it may be added that it would operate strongly for the advancement of science if all science students had a more thorough cultural training". He believed that social orientation was one of the conditions of culture, in the sense of a general grasp of the scientific, artistic and social activities of mankind; and the direction of one's work in relation to these. The advancement of such culture, and that alone, is what can be seriously be meant by university reform.

Finally, he considered that a further important requirement of reform was an increased measure of control of universities by those who work in them, i.e. university staffs, with delegation of a share of responsibility for the conduct of their studies to the students themselves. It was his view, based on lengthy experience, that the governing bodies of most universities are ill-equipped for the management of educational activities, but there is a reluctance to criticize their policies, especially publicly – what he called the 'employee' complex, so that there is a need for the democratic working of universities. In this he was ahead of his time, though now there are many references to this problem in higher education literature, since centralized control of academic work has never been tighter both from without and from within British universities. Still, it was at a university in his native country, Stirling, that perhaps the first battle was fought to democratize a university, following a celebrated incident involving the Queen. The present writer had the honour to chair the incredibly hard-working committee which, in twenty-nine meetings in three months, produced a scheme which was adopted *nem con* in a massive vote of the university's General Assembly – and then was quickly shelved. (Part of this Report is reproduced as an annexe).

New Zealand: A light at the other end of the world
The first New Zealand university, Otago, was founded in 1869 by Scottish settlers with Edinburgh as their model. As university colleges were formed in other parts of the country, Otago formed their template. Waikato became the country's sixth university, and the North Island's fourth, in 1963. "Superficially the English new universities influenced Waikato's foundation; but underneath the place was as Scottish as the rest. New Zealand has the world's last working Scottish university system."[32]

In New Zealand universities are regional, and students require permission to attend a university other than the one in their area. This is a statutory version of what was standard practice at Scotland's universities until after the Second World War. The first degree is unclassified; in other words it is a modern version of the old Scottish Ordinary degree. With a few exceptions, honours degrees are all postgraduate. Most important of all, access to university study is intended to be democratic.

Oscar Lange's programme *Learning for Life* proposes the abolition of the New Zealand UGC, and that control of higher education should rest with the Ministry of Education. However unpopular such a scheme might be with a John Anderson or academics in New Zealand or Great Britain today, it would not have worried Scottish academics in the nineteenth century. Carter points out that under the present system in New Zealand students are entitled to five years of state-funded fees and modest bursaries – the modest bursary for a large number of students is, as we have seen, a Scottish tradition. Indeed the author says that this "student support system is a logical extension of the nineteenth-century Scottish arrangements, built on the example of the most democratic Scottish university, Aberdeen".[33]

Lange's *Learning for Life* entrenches academic freedom through a recognition of the university's legitimate role as an arena for social criticism. But there are fears about the loss of autonomy among New Zealand's dons, since according to Lange's proposals university teachers would be state servants directly controlled by the Ministry of Education. This would, of course, doom 'donnish dominion', the Oxbridge ideal to which many of New Zealand's university teachers subscribe, having been through it themselves. For them it would be the end of civilization as we know it. "Yet this fake Oxbridge university culture", says Carter, "was set in a Scottish system marked by a different logic. Against Oxbridge celebration of donnish dominion and social closure, the Scottish model urged the widest possible access to university study, and rested fairly easily (in common with almost all European university systems) with firm state support and control".[34] Carter suggests that, probably inadvertently, *Learning for Life* proposes to return the New Zealand university system to its Scottish roots.

Carter concludes that as long as open access to university education in New Zealand remains, even in what he calls the restricted current sense (with enrolment as of right possible in the arts and science, but not in commerce or the professional schools), "the democratic Scottish approach to university education, extinguished in its own country, will continue to flicker at the other end of the world."

6

The Wheel Turns Full Circle

Ultimate worth-whileness

In the nineteenth century the Scottish universities had a very distinctive character of their own: Unlike Oxford and Cambridge they were thoroughly democratic – entrance was literally open to all who cared to join the classes – and they had always taken their educational duties seriously. Students . . . all took the three part General Course – Philosophy, Literature and Mathematics – which was an inheritance from the seventeenth century, and the apex of the national educational system to which Scotland's long intellectual eminence was due. But by the mid–nineteenth century the spirit of university reform was in the air. Members of Scotland's professional classes . . . felt that their children would be unable to compete against English graduates unless the new English university syllabuses and teaching methods were adopted in the Scottish universities; and the educational reformers – with their eyes perhaps more on career values than on educational values – carried the day.[1]

A. D. Lindsay was one of the first students at Glasgow to sit for a specialized "honours" degree on the new English model resulting from the process so succinctly summarized in the above paragraph and which we have previously analyzed in some detail. What struck Lindsay above all about Glasgow at the time was the hordes of immigrants from the Highlands and Ireland for whom tenements were run up "far more rapidly than . . . (any) schools in which their children could be taught". But despite this, Glasgow was later "to give rise to a branch of the Labour movement distinguished by its high ethical idealism".

Lindsay was to become Master of Balliol College, Oxford, and subsequently a socialist Vice-Chancellor of the new Keele University. He loved Oxford but his work at Keele expressed his reaction against certain aspects of the Oxford ideal. "His nature, training and experience all designed him for philosophical reflection upon man and society, for moral and political philosophy."[2] This was, of course, the result of his Glasgow education. He was at odds with the dominant logical positivist school, whose weaknesses have become more and more apparent. As Lindsay put it,[3] it is not the philosopher's job simply to clear up logical puzzles. It is rather to question and to explain the ultimate worth-whileness of our main activities, and to articulate and defend the standards by which we judge the ultimate value of work or conduct in any important field – in the arts, in science, in scholarship, in public or private life. The philosopher asks: do we have objective standards for making such judgments or are all our judgments and decisions ultimately subjective? Philosophy is thus a critical activity. The similarity to the position of John Anderson in Australia is very clear.

Lindsay was opposed to the dominant 'logicizing' tendency in English philosophy. He wanted ethics brought back into philosophy, since the criticism of standards had been one of the main tasks of philosophers since the time of Socrates. It is a task which every civilization, every generation, must learn to do for itself, and if the philosopher does not help the man in the street, who will, he asked? In his view a really adequate philosophy of science must centre on the question, "Why think scientifically?" – for utilitarian or some other ultimate reasons? – just as any adequate moral philosophy must ask the central question "Why be moral?" Philosophy must have an influence on the intellectual community as a whole, and on university education in particular. A modern democratic society without philosophical criticism should be – but alas is not – as obviously a contradiction in terms as a modern industrial society without a scientific technology. This statement goes to the heart of the problems not only of Britain but of the developed world as a whole.

In this perspective two features of Lindsay's thought are important for university education: the intrinsic worth-whileness of certain pursuits; and philosophy's peculiar responsibility, through criticism, for maintaining the standards by which we evaluate such worth-whileness. The main task of universities is to evoke and develop in the student a feeling for the intrinsic worth-whileness of intellectual inquiry, of free research, of free discussion of moral, intellectual and aesthetic questions. A university education is also very important for giving service to a democratic community, since the student's experience of engaging in a worthwhile branch of study should show him/her how it depends on, and interacts with, other aspects of community life.[4] Lindsay was convinced that higher education must be quite explicitly linked with the problems of the community and – very importantly – that university teaching subjects need to be regrouped so as to give students a better introduction to, or a better insight into, the intellectual problems of the contemporary world. Despite Lindsay's long, distinguished association with Oxford, such views brought him into conflict with certain of its ideals. There can be little doubt that it was the great influence of Oxford which prevented his ideas from having wider implementation.

Lindsay was opposed to narrow specialization. He did not agree with the German conception of the university as being mainly a research institution for the production of experts, which has had such a strong influence on British universities. The researchers set up the ideal that the human mind is best trained by severe concentration upon a single subject; but this is simply not valid for the mass of people doing other, equally important, jobs. Lindsay rejected the mentality of the expert, quoting Aristotle who defined a slave as a human tool: too many academics are intellectual tools. Academics speak self-importantly of 'my research' as if it were the justification of a probably very narrow and self-centred life and enshrined the whole spirit of the humanities and the sciences. Many specialisms, in Lindsay's opinion, originated through imitation of Oxbridge by ambitious academics. Talk of intellectual mastery is all too frequently humbug.

Lindsay, unfortunately for him, was fighting a losing battle here. Max Weber had warned that the fundamental struggle, in the adaptation of education to industrialism, was between the cultivated person and the expert, a fight which he saw as determined by the "irresistible expanding bureaucratization of all public and private relations of authority and by the ever-increasing importance of expert and specialized knowledge".[5] Halsey says that the voice of the elitist researcher has probably been the most effective voice for change in the twentieth century English universities. It fostered the single subject honours degree as a method of training students for the academic succession and "led the 'provincial' universities to assimilate to Oxbridge rather than the industrial centres in which they were located. As a result the ideology of the elitist teacher was never seriously challenged." If this was harmful for the English 'provincial universities', how much more harmful was it for the Scottish universities whose centuries-old orientation had always been against early specialization. It was nonetheless imposed on them by the nineteenth-century reforms, by the social-academic *Zeitgeist* of which Max Weber speaks, and by the appointment to posts in Scottish universities of large numbers of Oxbridge-trained academics.

For Lindsay what the nation, what the world needs is not specialists. What they need above all is men and women with an informed sense of moral and political responsibility. They will take up all sorts of different professions, but the first necessity is that they be responsible persons, able to give intellectual leadership wherever they work.[6] A modern democratic society obviously needs people with "scientific minds, knowledge-making minds, discovery-making, invention-making, design-making, plan-making, directive-making, even money-making minds. But our universities should aim at producing such minds with the capacity and the desire to reflect sincerely and effectively upon what they are doing".[7] Lindsay's ideal was a self-understanding society needing intellectual leadership to bring out society's aims and tasks and prospects. How does a university do this in modern conditions, as the ancient Scottish universities had sought to do it by having a four-year 'arts' degree precede professional training? Keele University was set up to find the answer.

The object was to bring out attitudes of mind which would make for a self-understanding society, bearing in mind that, generally speaking, there are: the problem-solvers, the systematisers, and the diviners, and that they need to be combined from time to time. Lindsay was convinced that mastery of a foreign language, say French, and its literary culture does not provide an adequate university education; he supported the concept of joint honours, now more and more widespread. Like Politics, Philosophy and Economics (PPE) which had never, in his view, operated at Oxford as relative study ('combined-seeing') of different aspects of, and approaches to, the main problems of modern democratic societies. A really workmanlike implementation of this relational concept at Keele had to wait till some years after Lindsay's death. Clearly, scientific training at a university is inevitably professional and vocational, thought Lindsay, even though some, T. H. Huxley and Mark Pattison, for example, would disagree, believing that only the theoretical science underlying a particular profession or technology should be taught at university. Lindsay did not reject professional training at university; what he did reject was that the provision of such training should be a university's sole aim. Science students should also be trained to think about their science, its past, its future, its place in society and its practical applications to solve practical and social problems. (Lindsay was no doubt influenced here by that seminal work *The Social Function of Science* by J. D. Bernal.) The srtudent must get this from other courses, i.e. Keele's Subsidiary Courses.

Critical and historical thinking will always be needed, indeed they
are vital to the existence of science itself, as the work of Thomas
Kuhn has shown. Arts students, similarly, need to see what 'work'
in science is like. Hence Keele's Foundation year in which there
were more than 200 lectures. Lindsay wanted students to get a
common intellectual background from the Foundation Year, a basis
for discussion between people of widely separate departments. For
him this was a prerequisite of all university study. The concept is
even more important now, when the intellectual fragmentation of
universities is a matter of deep concern to many university leaders
and teachers throughout the developed world. There is now no common discourse whatsoever, and universities are largely a collection
of entrepreneurs with a common parking problem.

Perhaps the most original feature (ridiculous as it may seem in a
university context) and certainly the one which most unequivocally
shows his Scottish intellectual inheritance, was his insistence on
discussion as the most important element in university teaching. In
the old days the Scots philosophers – Jardine, for example, or Adam
Smith, who was first of all a moral philosopher, or Sir William
Hamilton, or Thomas Reid – would conduct brilliantly illuminating
discussion with their classes. It was, as we know, the favourite
method of Socrates and also of the Puritan sects. In Lindsay's view,
people always learn best from discussion or in books in preparation
for or after discussion. "He believed that the general knowledge
thus acquired has a reality, a positive down-to-earth character that
almost all university teaching fails to achieve; and he was determined that in his new college discussion should be the guiding
principle from start to finish."[8] It is interesting to compare Lindsay's
ideas here with the view of a by no means uncritical Balliol-trained
Scottish professor in the nineteenth century:

> Of these classes ... some are mainly devoted to examina-
> tions (= discussion) others to the delivery of lectures. None is
> exclusively occupied with either; for the oral examinations are
> accompanied by running comments from the professor, and a
> conscientious student is in a constant strain of attention, ready
> himself to construe passages or solve problems, or to take his
> share in answering questions passed to his bench; whereas,
> when a lecture (sometimes read, more frequently spoken from
> notes) occupies one hour, a part at least of another is employed
> in *viva voce* discussion of the subjects treated. The Oral exami-
> nation system is on much the same footing as it was thirty years
> ago. I should deprecate anything that would tend to depreciate
> it, for besides the training in self-confidence and promptitude
> afforded, it enables the examiner, more thoroughly than by

any other means, to sift their knowledge, and brings him into direct personal contact with his pupils."[9]

Lindsay was determined at Keele to implement another aspect of the Scottish educational tradition: the university must be fully co-educational. In his inaugural address to the students he called himself "a sociologically-minded man, a man with a passion to become more understanding; or rather more of a learner about the tasks and trials of organized social life" – thus harking back to the creator of sociology, Adam Ferguson, in the eighteenth century. He was also a firm believer in interdisciplinarity. The tragedy was that many of the original thirteen professors didn't agree with him – not surprising since they came from a totally different background. The same thing was to happen to Tom Cottrell at Stirling, but of that more later. The Foundation Year was by all accounts a pretentious and intellectually sloppy affair, "a very selective encyclopedia dictated by the hobby-horses of the professors".[10] There was hardly a trace of a unifying idea, though the situation improved a year after his death. It was probably too much to expect that specialists on the Oxbridge model could change their spots so quickly. They simply could not see the fast approaching breakdown of the universities into congeries of mutually competing specialisms with no common intellectual language, and the danger of students being sent out into an increasingly perturbed world as highly specialized intellectual tools but with precious little understanding of social, political or moral problems. It took visionaries like A. D. Lindsay and Ortega y Gasset, from whom he learned a great deal, to sense the approaching intellectual chaos.

Interdisciplinarity

A similar attempt was made by Asa Briggs at the new University of Sussex to give greater breadth and interdisciplinarity to the courses of study.[11] "Our curriculum is designed to encourage students, while still undergraduates, to reflect upon the relevance of one branch of study to others from which traditionally it has been divided."[12] As we have seen, this has been a constant theme in the Scottish universities. Nor is this holistic approach only a way of giving students an integrated view of the world and society they live in. It is also the most important element in discovery and innovation. "But the various specialist departments of knowledge rarely proceed for long by their own momentum. It is nearly always at the points of intersection, where the specialist expertise is no longer self-sufficient, that the major breakthrough to a new explanation of some important aspect of the universe or the vision of some new possibility of human progress takes place."[13] Also at Sussex they considered that the main teaching effort should be devoted to students who are just beginning the course rather than to those who are concluding it. This is similar to the Scottish tradition whereby the professor always took the first year class, though it is now not so faithfully observed. At Sussex it was felt that philosophy should play an unusually large part in undergraduate study. "Philosophy concerns itself with the most general and pervasive questions about the logical character of other kinds of inquiry and about the ways in which they fit together. Hence, from the moment you make it a main principle of higher education to get undergraduates to think how their major study is related to others, it seems inevitable that philosophic questions should be raised and desirable that they should be thoroughly investigated."[14] All Arts and Science students therefore have to sit a philosophy paper in the preliminary examination and one in the Finals.

The standard pattern of philosophy in British universities is to present it as a recondite special subject to a small minority of undergraduates. But if philosophy is conceived in the Socratic fashion, that is as the relentless probing of assumptions, there is a strong case for giving it a central role in the teaching of undergraduates. The task of the university teacher is to see to it that students realize that there are profoundly different ways of understanding the world, the flesh and the devil, greatly differing concepts of how society should be run, great differences in moral appreciation, and get them to start thinking about these fundamental problems for themselves. It has to be asked whether the function of university is to apply trained intelligence as keenly to our ultimate convictions as to the study of the cell or the atom, or to avoid such contentious issues. Too many universities today, and indeed the whole administration of our universities at top level, fall into the latter category. "The university teacher is there to bring all faiths and assumptions into the open. S/he is there to challenge, to provoke, to raise doubts and difficulties, to prevent thoughtless acquiescence in current assumptions, to awaken to that sense of the precariousness of human thinking that should inform and enliven advanced study and research, and to do what can be done to awaken in them that critical sympathy for men's diverse conditions that is the stuff of civilized life."[15] The student needs to learn how to pose philosophical questions to him/herself, to question his/her own assumptions and values. Philosophy is essentially an argumentative subject: it was said of the Scots that they had "the philosophic itch to dispute all things".

Asa Briggs, the Vice-Chancellor, thought that Sussex had benefited greatly from its radical approach to the curriculum. "The idea of breaking free from excessive specialization loomed large."[16] Each school was to have a curriculum which would combine in different proportions – varying according to the student's own choice – subjects which would normally, "except in general degrees", be kept apart in existing universities. One wonders why Sussex, in that case, did not go the whole hog and restore the old Scottish practice of a general degree for all students before specialization. For it would seem difficult, despite Briggs' claims, to teach adequately in three years all that Sussex claims for their three-year course. The sentiments expressed are impeccable from the perspective of this book, since he says that specialization and general education were seen as essential parts of a balanced university education. This concept was embodied in a balance of core and contextual studies: the core providing the "specialism in depth" and the contextual studies including "a critical evaluation of concepts and procedures, preferably comparatively, and examination of historical perspectives, and an exploration of issues and problems". The claim is made that a Sussex graduate, whatever his/her School, would be given the kind of education in three years that would make it possible for her/him to compare, to relate and to judge. It would be broader than a single subject or combined subjects course, but those who wanted to go on to research or to academic life would be well grounded in their specialism. In addition to all of which the first two terms would be devoted to foundation studies. The ideas are excellent, but those who have been through a joint honours course, even in a Scottish university, where it lasts four years, know that Sussex were trying to pour more than a quart into a pint pot.

Professor Briggs rightly points out that "the specialist honours courses which now dominate most university curricula – at least for the best students – have no long tradition behind them. They are Victorian or post-Victorian in origin and need far more critical study from both intellectual and social historians than they have so far received".[17] In Arts, Social Sciences and Physical Sciences the same kind of pattern was established and, says Professor Briggs, quoting George Elder Davie, "it had something in common with that 'broadly philosophical and historical approach to the languages and the sciences through grounding in first principles which characterized Scottish education at its best'." The intentions were admirable and soundly based in a realization of the poverty of general education in England's universities, but they were no more able in the end to resist the pull and pressure of Oxbridge specialization and its influence on the sixth form hothouse than Keele had been.[18] Who would be the next challenger?

Approaches and Methods
It was Stirling, the youngest of the Scottish universities, which only opened its doors for business in 1967. What's more, its Chancellor was Lord Robbins who, in the ten meaty volumes of his famous Report in 1963, had argued against specialization and for broader first degrees and praised the Scottish general degree. And its Principal was Tom Cottrell, a chemist of distinction who had been awarded the Royal Society's Gold Medal. Surely this combination would put up a better fight than Keele and Sussex had.

It started well. In an article in *Scotland*, the magazine of the Scottish Council and Industry, Principal Cottrell said that Stirling proposed to revert to some of the better features of nineteenth-century Scottish education; there would be a similar insistence on the study of general intellectual methods and it was intended that no student at Stirling would escape "without having had some grounding beyond that obtained at school in rhetoric, arithmetic and logic. Innovation in subject matter should concern itself not only with defining new fields but with the reappraisal of old ones". Stirling intended to do this, and "one is the area in which social and natural sciences are interdependent". A course entitled *Approaches and Methods* was laid down in the very first report of the Academic Planning Board. There were two lectures on information, eight on logic and eight on rhetoric in the first semester given by a philosopher. The second semester, to be taught by a scientist with long experience of industry, was to deal with statistics, scientific method, invention and discovery, numbers and computers. Texts used would be Grierson, Medawar's *Reith Lectures*, Beveridge's *The Art of Scientific Investigation*, HMSO Annual Digest, Stebbings' *Modern Elementary Logic* and Black's *Critical Thinking*. There might be some study of aesthetics. The late Professor Frank Bradbury explained (18 November 1966) that

> Approaches and Methods explains in two words what we are trying to do: give the students at the outset of their university life an approach to the problem of learning which will be helpful to them, and to acquaint them with methods of work, with words, with numbers in science and in arts. Somewhere we should touch on the two cultures – in a critical rather than adulatory way – because this will help to set the university life and its various streams of activity in their context.

Here again we see reflected the constant drive in the Scottish tradition to look at the whole picture – a holistic view of knowledge. This is reinforced in the 1968–69 Stirling University prospectus:

> After a short initial period of instruction on information retrieval and the use of the library, the first semester of the

course deals in general with the nature of language and its various uses. It introduces the basic ideas of logical appraisal and emphasises the application of logic as an analytical tool for clarifying both technical and ordinary language ... The second semester covers the use of numbers, with an introduction to the computer, social arithmetic, problem analysis; uncertainty and games theory; scientific method, discovery and invention.

In his foreword to the Prospectus Tom Cottrell says: "Two main ideas lie behind the undergraduate courses outlined in the prospectus: one is to encourage a general education at university level, but still some specialization; the other is to allow flexibility in the choice of subjects. The intentions behind the course can quite clearly trace their ancestry back to the trivium and quadrivium of classical and medieval times."

The other long-term aim of Scottish higher education to be open to as many people as possible was reflected in Tom Cottrell's remarks at the university's second graduation ceremony: "The expansion of higher education will be the result of a demand from those who want it rather than from those who want the products of it. Society still needs people to know about, preserve, transmit and question its general culture. Whether it will regard this need as sufficiently strong to justify giving such people a higher status in society as they become generally more available, I very much doubt."[19]

The incipient pessimism of this last sentence was soon to receive confirmation. On 2 May 1976 the THES reported under the title 'Is this beautiful ship drifting off course?' that the *Approaches and Methods* course was found by students to be "boring and a waste of time", according to Harold Perkin in a study of the new universities for the OECD.[20] It had lasted for only three years. The report quotes Professor S. J. Lockerbie of the French Department as saying: "The tutors didn't have enough confidence in themselves as exemplary instances of intellectual method. The tutorials developed into shifty sessions where each tutor tried not to reveal ignorance of the other's field." He thought the experiment might have succeeded if a course tutor, genuinely bilingual in numeracy and literacy, had been recruited specifically to run it. This was a clear result of the fact that the majority of university teachers in Scotland were English or had been trained as specialists in the English manner. Roger Young, the headmaster of George Watson's College, called in to examine Stirling's problems in the wake of the incident involving the Queen in 1972, said that the resources and administration required for such a course "were underestimated and unavailable". Young, three years after the demise of the course, thought it worth reviving and said that sadness at its failure was still felt at Stirling.

According to the THES, "The course taught Stirling what all other new universities have learnt: that as long as universities are based on academic specialization, both staff and students will treat general courses as peripheral and irritating chores". This in the country where general courses had produced towering figures like Adam Smith and David Hume! "It was anguish, " said Professor Jim Trainer of the German Department, "when a student was doing well in his major subject, to have him fail A & M. " As if success in a severely limited specialism was somehow better than failure in general education! The university's Academic Council (Senate in other universities) turned down compulsory breadth: it was the familiar new university story of creeping departmentalism and return to the familiar scenario of fragmented specialization. At the very same time the Council turned down Gaelic studies and abandoned plans for an MLitt in Scottish Studies. Not even St. Andrews and Edinburgh were more anglicized than Stirling: all three had a majority of English students as well as staff due to the 'nationalisation' of the universities. In its obituary on Tom Cottrell on 8 June 1973 the TESS said: "He argued forcefully for general and interdisciplinary studies . . . It was clearly a disappointment to him that the short introductory course on basic skills had to be withdrawn so soon, mainly because of a lack of expertise or willingness in the staff." And also because, as he himself once said, "Good ideas don't attract good students" – a sad comment on the condition of our universities. It was not thus in Peter Abelard's day, nor in Andrew Melville's.

Years later Lord Robbins, Stirling's much respected and liked Chancellor, said that the university system, with its emphasis on early specialization, was designed to produce dons and was not the most suitable system overall. Such early specialization, starting from the stage of O-levels, did not exist anywhere else in the civilized world and did not exist in his youth. There had been no stigma attached to general degrees and the system was better attuned to the needs of society. His Report was just as unsuccessful in promoting general education and broad first degrees as the other attempts we have mentioned. The Oxbridge specialist grip still held all Britain's universities through their alumni who taught in all of them or were in positions of political power, and through their quite unjustified position at the apex of the British university system.

The greater utilitarian truths of breadth
Eight years further on the next Principal of Stirling University but
one, Sir Kenneth Alexander, said that the most important changes
in his thinking about education came when he had moved out of
education to become Chairman of Govan Shipbuilders and later of
the Scottish Development Association. Problem-solving in the 'real
world' can bring you up against what you do not know and yet need
to know, whereas in teaching and single subject based research it
is easy to avoid such confrontations.

> It was at this rather late stage that I came to see the impor-
> tance of breadth in education. Very few real problems can
> be effectively solved by narrow specialism. Most problems
> of significance are caused or contributed to by the quirks of
> human behaviour. Educational change which diminishes the
> role of philosophy and psychology is moving in quite the
> wrong direction.[21]

Sir Kenneth believes that the ancient Scottish universities were much
more 'open door' to talent than were most other European universities, and "we must see the need for an intellectual unity as of much
greater importance than skirmishes between the humanities and the
sciences". All very true, but it is perhaps a pity that Sir Kenneth
had not used his reputation, when Principal of Stirling University,
to push these views harder and even lead a movement of resistance
to what was being done to Scotland's universities. By 1988 it was
too late: intellectual unity had disappeared to be replaced by the
present academic smorgasbord. The truth of one of Alexander's
apophthegms – "the greater utilitarian truths of breadth" – was
now swamped by business studies and ethics had been collapsed
to questions of distribution. The "narrow, exact and examinable"
took precedence over breadth. "In 40 years of academic life I have
seen many examples of empire-building taking precedence over the
search for cognitive unity".[22] The conflict between cognitive unity
and greater relevance – the government's view that higher education's job is to improve economic performance – is "particularly
threatening to what remains of 'Scottishness' in higher education
in Scotland". Being an economist, Alexander is strongly in favour
of relevance, but, he says, "we must not allow a false distinction
to attach a tag of irrelevance to philosophy, ethics, literature and
history".

Alexander was one of the first to see that student loans would
bring pressure to reduce the Scottish four-year course to three. He
makes the very pertinent point that we have not used this fourth
year to good effect, and that the most effective defence is to use
the year to make Scottish higher education more distinctive and

to demonstrate that this distinctiveness brings positive advantages and is not a dispensable luxury. "In Scotland we have already surrendered too much of our higher education to specialist appetites", sending young people out into the world well-equipped to solve problems capable of being displayed on a blackboard but lacking in the width of ability required to tackle the many-faceted problems of work and society. "Striking a balance and avoiding the narrow tunnel vision which is the price paid for over-specialization should be the aim of education at all levels." Sir Kenneth cites an event relating to Keele University which should alert every Scottish academic to the grave threat to Scottish university traditions. In 1981 the vice-chancellor of that university asked the University Grants Committee for the reasons behind the swingeing cuts in Keele's funding. "You are too Scottish", he was told. In other words being Scottish is a very serious disability. Such comments from such a source make it very difficult to suppress the notion of an anti-Scottish conspiracy in higher education. The threat to reduce the four-year Scottish degree pattern to three, which Sir Kenneth was anticipating in 1988, went public in 1991 with calls for its shortening from Sir Christopher Ball and Dr John Ashworth, Director of LSE, both pillars of the English higher education establishment. It was perhaps rather rash to entitle this chapter *The Wheel Turns Full Circle*, since its motion would appear to have been reversed. If the combination of Lord Robbins, Tom Cottrell and Sir Kenneth Alexander could not even slow down the juggernaut of specialization, what hope is left?

Higher Education for All
At this point, 'Red Ted' enters the lists. I use the cognomen deliberately. The English Establishment is remarkably skilful in its attempts to discredit those whose criticisms it fears, ably assisted by the tabloid press. In 1982 Professor E. G. Edwards, Vice-Chancellor of the University of Bradford, published a book calling for mass higher education in Britain.[23] It is one of the finest studies of higher education, vibrant in its intelligence and width of reference, and passionate in its vision of the great future of higher education when it is made available to the whole people. The institutions and individuals already mentioned in this chapter were really only tinkering with the problem. Edwards makes a fundamental analysis of the position and role of higher education in the late twentieth century. It will repay lengthy discussion.

Like Sir Kenneth Alexander, Professor Edwards had some 40 years' experience of higher education, at all levels and in all its sectors. This had convinced him that higher education for all had become a necessary goal, not only for social stability but for the survival of the best of the inheritance of culture and science in the context of new social purposes, and with a greatly diversified content and much wider institutional forms.[24]

Edwards starts by pointing out that higher education has been steadily expanding at an accelerating rate in all advanced countries, indeed by a factor of 20 during the past century. This is due to the rapid changes in society, above all through the application of new knowledge to technology and social organization. "The same changes which bring instability, unemployment and the obsolescence of their skills to manual workers enhance the importance, power and adaptability of the highly educated." Between 1955 and 1970 there was a universal international explosion in student numbers by three times. This was not caused by the Robbins Report in 1963 since it was an international phenomenon. It was powered by student demand, but it was dominated, still, by the professional and managerial classes. The participation rate in higher education of the sons of senior professional families was 80%, while that of the daughters of unskilled labourers was a hundred times lower. This social apartheid existed above all in England – though it also existed in the other main Western European countries – and it remained unchanged until 1970. The gap had widened significantly since then despite – indeed because of – Robbins.[25] The children of the professional classes had been brought up to expect to enter higher education, and lived in conditions which facilitated this ambition, whereas for working-class children – the majority – higher education is an alien world, and their circumstances are not favourable. Besides which higher education "cultivates the image of a rarefied atmosphere where only the exceptionally gifted can survive. At a time when there were about 5000 university students in Britain a leading professor forecast the catastrophic degeneration of standards if the numbers should increase. Today (1982) there are upwards of 500,000 at all levels in higher education."[26] There is simply no evidence that academic standards have anything to do with the numbers entering higher education. "The plain fact is that if you come from a family that is determined that you should enter higher education, you have to be almost moronically stupid to avoid the fate, whereas if you come from a background where higher education is abnormal and strange, you have to be unusually devoted to learning, and possibly unusually gifted, to get in."[27]

The rate of expansion is increasing exponentially as is the size of the educated professional classes. Higher education does not ebb and flow with the numbers in the 18-year-old cohort since most of these are ruled out long before reaching the age of choice. The official projections use future fluctuation in the 18 year age group to restrict expansion of student numbers. This of course has no effect on the expanding number of entrants from the educated classes; all that happens is a further fall in the proportion of working-class students. The end result of this Malthusian approach is that Britain is falling behind the countries of Europe, Japan and America in higher education. So Caroline Benn, in her foreword to the book, asks that "that which was once a privilege for the few shall in· future be agreed as a right for everyone who wants it"; it is not only a plea for an end to elitism, but also the recognition that higher education is a vital form of national investment. The exponential growth of higher education between 1860 and 1960 arose mainly from a new awareness of its potential value among the growing professional and managerial classes; it was a product "of the whole new climate of social, cultural, scientific, economic and industrial winds of change".[28] Thus the concept of higher education can be defined "as the level normally associated in the country concerned at the time concerned with making rather than obeying decisions, with independence rather than dependence, with managing rather than being managed", enabling us "to give a less arbitrary place to the idea of standards of academic and intellectual attainment. The standards of knowledge and ability set in higher education will tend to be just those that are necessary in the field concerned in the country concerned at the time concerned to cope with the existing role of the highly educated".[29] Edwards stresses that the original university disciplines were devoted to professional, social functions – the law, medicine and theology – as we have already shown in previous chapters; and that the cultural professions "perform the vital and central stabilising role of legitimising the autonomy of all the other professions since they assert effective control of the ultimate standards of truth, national taste and communicability".[30] Which is why, as we have seen, in earlier centuries in Scotland, all students had to go through a broad-based arts course.

Because of the elitism and contempt for technology inherent in the traditions of England's two dominant universities which set the national trends, Britain has fallen behind in the knowledge revolution. Those countries which have seized the lead are those which have invested in new industries which have the greatest need of new knowledge, and so they have made a greater investment in higher education. Now the emphasis has passed from material goods to communication and information technology. Here the main raw material is trained brains and the finished product is knowledge. Routine labour passes to the micro-computer and the machines it controls, and the limits to the creative application and employment of the products of an unlimited expansion of higher education begin to disappear, as does the borderline between work and creative leisure.

The all-pervasive rule of the specialist is now becoming counter-productive. In Edwards' view the high scientific abstraction and specialisation of higher education were the product of a particular period of rapid advance of the sciences which "isolated them from each other and from their own origins in the problems of action and purpose".[31] Academics greeted each other with, "What is your subject?" The older concept of the 'universitas', where the common advance of common knowledge was the concern of all decayed into a narrow departmentalism. The key academic concern became the piling-up of more and more facts; the value of a university was, is, measured by the number of research papers published, whatever their real value in human terms. The dominant philosophy of knowledge, the dominant epistemology, was that of positivism, "with its enthronement of facts as the only repository of meaning".[32] As Wittgenstein, the outstanding theoretician of positivism, said in 1918: "The world is the totality of facts." Thus the buzz-phrase was "the pursuit of knowledge for its own sake", without reference to practical application or ethical significance. This latter point was the doctrine of A. J. (Freddy) Ayer, who said no meaning could be attached to any ethical statement, and who became the darling of the media. Understandably, since there seems to be a direct line of descent from his denial of moral values to Mrs Thatcher's statement that "There is no such thing as society" at the National Assembly of the Church of Scotland in 1990. It is also a splendid cover for the excesses of the decaying British state: the sinking of the Belgrano or the wholesale bombing of Iraq with smart weapons, to the hurrahs of the tabloids ("Cold Steel up the Argies").

Edwards, rather optimistically, says that the domination of the curriculum by specialisms will cease to be credible as computers take over, and the human mind and human culture will return to human problems and judgments. It has to be said that there are precious few signs of this ten years after the book was written.

Edwards' central theme is that higher education is essential, in all countries, for those who want to join the decision-makers, the 'movers and shakers', rather than the ranks of those who execute other people's decisions. A degree is essential in the knowledge industries, in the knowledge society; it is the path to independent judgment. Hence the rapid escalation of enrolments in the last forty to fifty years. In this new age the broad theme should be human liberation: "The pursuit of universal human liberation is a safeguard against the subjection of learning to the coteries of chance intellectual privilege, or to the changing course of corrupt political pressure. But this theme is only possible for a universal human culture. It cannot be explored within the narrow circle of a blinkered intellectual elite. Its relevance is to a truly humane society and not to the merely materialistic interests of the masters of an exploitative society."[33] In this context the Robbins Report of 1963 ("Higher education should be available to all those with the necessary ability and attainment and who wish to pursue it") was unable to change anything. "It is rather a formula which describes precisely how social privilege in higher education works."[34] That is, there is a quota of deserving young people. This principle arose along with the development of the meritocratic self-image of higher education, the dominance of specialised, factual knowledge, and the rapid rise of the professional specialist. Robbins' intentions were of the best, as we have seen, but in the end, sadly, none of his major goals was achieved. Even the Open University (Harold Wilson's greatest achievement), with its concept of 'éducation permanente', hardly touched the masses of the people; its students, very often teachers, were largely middle class. Within a decade of their foundation, the CATs (Colleges of Advanced Technology) had become universities – even the polys had the same social intake. The situation had not changed radically since the Barlow report on scientific manpower in 1946: "We attach the greatest importance to the atmosphere of an association of men and women which takes all knowledge as its province . . . such an atmosphere has a great part to play in completing any student's education and preventing him from becoming a narrow and cloistered specialist." The report concluded: " . . . and about one in five of boys and girls, who have intelligence equal to that of the best half of university students, actually reach the universities."[35] This is not merely a great loss to the country but a terrific destruction of human potential, since in modern society only those whose education takes them to the point of understanding and using the role of knowledge can enjoy to the full the increased freedom to determine their own lives which is made possible by cultural and technical progress. Today in Britain market forces have been forced upon the universities and all the talk is of cost centres, cost-benefit analysis, the bottom line and so on. Much of the value of education cannot be measured in this way. The most striking example of this is the social value of the education of women who spend most of their lives bringing up their families. Neither their work nor their education can be economically measured by market mechanisms, but their value to society is arguably the greatest reward for the provision of the education services. It is the most important instrument for the transference of the national culture from one generation to the next. "It is the most important of all educational investments in a civilized human future."[36]

In 1992 it might have seemed that the battle for open access to higher education had been won, since Kenneth Baker, when he was Secretary of State for Education, called for a doubling of the numbers in higher education in Britain, and for the upgrading of the polytechnics to university status (now a fact). However, this should alert us that little has changed, especially as no extra funding was to be allocated; indeed public spending was to be cut yet again in the severe recession Britain underwent in the early 1990s. The higher education for all that Edwards called for would need vastly greater funding and a sea-change in the approach to knowledge. "The mechanical projection of the arid orthodoxies and emasculated professional specialisms of the late twentieth century into the indefinite future . . . would simply be an apologia for the status quo - the operations of the free market – aiming at making it acceptable to the people." The reign of the specialist would continue in its modern, amoral, neutral, positivistic guise. Incapable of more general responsibility, the specialist is impotent on the great issues facing society. "Their cultural archetype is an Oppenheimer, supreme in his mastery of the science needed to create the atom bomb, but unable even to imagine the language in which to argue the necessity for its social control."[37]

Edwards puts forward a "strategy of demands" for the development and reform of higher education, which must include the following interdependent areas:

- the expansion of student enrolments, both absolutely and by the ever-widening participation of the working-class;
- the reform of the curriculum of higher education to make it relevant to the cultural and social potential and the economic and political interests of the majority of the people;
- the application of education throughout all areas of employment and social life to realise the dignity as well as the productivity and creativity of work, and to give vitality to the quality of life and culture of the common people.

These aims, with the possible exception of the first, obviously demand a complete reversal of present trends.[38] There is a strong element of Utopia in them, but the careful research he has done and his social idealism are a much needed stimulus in the cynical, demoralised world of today's university teachers. His driving enthusiasm is fired by a deep conviction that there is no limit to the growth of human creative effort[39]; and that it is being artificially limited by resistance to the surrender of privilege. He points out that in

1982 the State spent about six times the amount of public money on the post-school education of the child of a senior professional as on the child of a labourer. The poor were truly being taxed to educate the children of the rich. Now, in the age of computers which can take over much routine work, only a small fraction of nurses, social workers, welfare and community workers or police workers have the benefit of higher education, but there is no doubt in Edwards' mind that the human complexity of much of their service to society could benefit enormously from the study of the human and social sciences. The same is true, in our post-industrial society, for all those employed in the creation and dissemination of culture and entertainment, not to mention catering and tourism. In short, the service professions need highly-educated generalists. Edwards quotes Milton ("The leisure you have for your studies is by the sweat of other men's brows"), and concludes that there is no basis for elitism: "Educational privilege, like every other kind of privilege, tends to be self-perpetuating."[40]

The reader may by now have detected a rather uncanny similarity between the views expressed by Edwards and the practice of the Scottish universities in the eighteenth and nineteenth centuries. He himself, referring to the fact that, by the later nineteenth century, Oxford and Cambridge had become places of sinecure appointment for clergymen waiting for preferment in their dioceses, notes that a rather different position existed in the Scottish universities, "where the professorial chairs were held by the greatest innovators and discoverers of their age. At that time the Chair of Chemistry at Edinburgh was held by great scientists of the calibre of William Cullen and James Black, while Newtonian physics had been taught there before it was recognised as a fit subject for Cambridge, and Adam Smith had founded the science of economics at Glasgow."[41] It was, he points out, a period when the Scottish universities occupied a pre-eminent place in the intellectual life of Europe. What was more important from a present point of view, it was also a period of extremely rapid growth in student numbers, culminating in a remarkable peak about 1820, and this "was largely concentrated in the Scottish universities where the students considerably outnumbered those in infinitely more populous England. Far from causing a dilution of the intellectual level, this surge in growth coincided with, and was the motive force behind, an unprecedented flowering not only in the new sciences, but in the older disciplines of medicine and philosophy".[42] In other words, more does not mean worse; ordinary people are not too innately stupid for higher education; the diffusion of knowledge to the mass of the people does not lead to vulgarization and corruption; higher education should be made available, useful and meaningful to ordinary people. Sir Cyril Burt and Eysenck are wrong. The social order is not the result of biological natural selection, but of power relations based on wealth and ultimately on force.

In short, Edwards'goals for higher education are those of the Scottish universities in the eighteenth and nineteenth centuries. His book is a bold and deeply thought out reaffirmation of the Scottish 'open door' policy, of the democratic intellect, renewed and revitalised for the twenty-first century.[43]

Edwards' aim is the comprehensive university. At the present time there is a chaotic mix of further and higher educational institutes, together with an absence of any effective links between them. Thus transfer from one to the other is difficult. This freezes what Edwards calls 'social apartheid'; it freezes the two cultures; it freezes the two classes, the professional class and the working class; it freezes two kinds of knowledge: pure knowledge pursued for its own sake by a small intellectual elite, and practical knowledge, which is that of the majority of the people. Yet this need not be so; the example of higher education in the USA, particularly in California, is there to prove it. There the majority of school-leavers proceed to higher education: whether to one of the nine campuses of top research universities in California; or to one of the nineteen campuses of the State University; or to liberal arts colleges; or to one of the one hundred and nine community colleges. In addition to which there are also the graduate schools. There is full transferability between all these institutions, so that someone may begin out of simple curiosity and end up doing a doctorate at Stanford. None of them have that peculiar English concentration of specialist undergraduate training into three years, yet they educate a much higher proportion of their population to doctorate level than do British institutions. They demonstrate yet again that there is no need to sacrifice quality to quantity.

The comprehensive university, prefigured in the Californian system where total access is now not far away, must imply equivalent status and complementary functions in its constituent parts; they should be self-governing, subject to proper accountability for public funds provided, that is all members, academic staff, non-academic staff and students should play an appropriate role in decision-making and financial allocation (that is after all the meaning of the term 'universitas' and that is how they did things at Bologna 800 years ago). There should be no division between academic and vocational training: "What could be more vocational than abstract research to get promotion?"[44] Nor should academic freedom be thought to be in conflict with proper educational planning and resource allocation. There should be constitutional safeguards of the rights of all members of higher education institutions to research and publish freely. "The concept of a university also implies a universality of fields of interest and an integrated development of knowledge in its relation to society. This is more consonant with the comprehensive university that we have in mind than the fragmented assemblies of unconnected specialist departments who have been held together in uneasy and arbitrary balance in the recent past."[45]

In my view one of the most important statements Edwards makes is that any education or training worthy of the name, of anything more than the shortest duration, must link together knowledge, practice and value. There is no subject of study, from theology to theoretical physics, that does not gain a great deal from an appreciation of its input to human practice. Conversely, says Edwards, there is no practical subject, from carpentry to chiropody, which cannot with advantage be made the subject of scientific study and human creative concern. "This essential progression from education to application to human welfare was well expressed by the Scottish philosopher John Macmurray in the precept: 'Knowledge is for action and action is for friendship.'"[46] We look at Macmurray more closely in the next chapter.

Macmurray may offer hope for the future, but it is the logical positivists who still run the show with their view of the world as a "mere collection of facts, all equal to each other, all equally devoid of any other human significance than their mere existence".[47] Edwards sees this separation of facts from human values as deriving from Descartes, who said: "Knowing the force and action of fire, water, air, the stars, the heavens and all other bodies that surround us . . . we could employ them to all uses for which they are appropriate and thus become the masters and possessors of nature."[48] This is indeed the programme science has worked its way through these last three centuries, till now we are deciphering the human genome and finding in the uttermost depths of space the microwave irregularities supposedly caused by the Big Bang. It has also led to nuclear weapons and the "impotent horror of Oppenheimer". We are the masters and possessors of nature like small boys throwing helpless nestlings to the ground. We have destroyed, and are still destroying, aboriginal civilizations from whom we have so much to learn about living harmoniously in the world: "The Indians do not have an EC, or an IMF, or a World Bank, but they know how to deal with all aspects of life. We have never had hunger as the world has, our medicines have no side effects, we have no prisons in our villages, you will never see an abandoned child or a badly-treated old person. The most central part in a person is the spirit. The white man needs to look at his spirit, which is very ill."[49]

Descartes it was, too, with his 'cogito ergo sum', who created the split between mind and matter which has been as powerful a force for moulding our higher education as has the mastery over nature thesis. Is it possible to trace the influence of philosophical trends on the development of higher education? We shall see in the next chapter.

7

Philosophy and Higher Education 1

A Celibacy of the Intellect
In his book on Socrates, I. F. Stone, that grand old man of American
political journalism, says that it is a mistake to separate the philosophical from the practical because in practice people are confronted
by choices and these are determined by their basic philosophical
approach. In other words everyone is a philosopher without knowing it. "You do not understand a society until you have plumbed its
philosophical premises; and these premises determine conduct."[1]

Many quotations might be given to illustrate the changing premises
of philosophy over the centuries, but four may suffice. Michel de
Montaigne in his *Essais* said: "Virtue and philosophy teach us how
to know and make use of all good things, and how to part with
them without concern." Francis Bacon, in the seventeenth century,
condemned what he called "a kind of adoration of the mind . . . by
means whereof men have withdrawn themselves too much from
the contemplation of nature and the observation of experience and
have tumbled up and down in their own reason and conceits".
Newman, in the nineteenth century, condemning the ultimate result
of Bacon's approach, said: "The Philosophy of Utility, you will say,
Gentlemen, has at least done its work; and I grant it – it aimed low,
but it has fulfilled its aim." Finally, in the late twentieth century,
we have Robert M. Pirsig:

> Our current modes of rationality are not moving society
> forward into a better world. They are taking it further from
> that better world. Since the Renaissance these modes have
> worked. As long as the need for food, clothing and shelter is
> dominant they will continue to work. But now that for huge
> masses of people these needs no longer overwhelm everything
> else, the whole structure of reason, handed down to us from

ancient times, is no longer adequate. It begins to be seen for what it really is – emotionally hollow, aesthetically meaningless and spiritually empty. That, today, is where it is at, and will continue to be at for a long time to come."[2]

That may be where it is at, but where did it come from? In his foreword to an important book[3] Reinhold Niebuhr says: "It is his thesis that the modern university has built its curriculum and elaborated its educational procedures upon the basis of an inadequate philosophy. It has assumed that the scientific method and spirit are an adequate guide in the pursuit of knowledge. The difficulty with this assumption is that science as such can have no sense of the meaning of life or of history. It must therefore either seek to develop an 'impartiality' and 'objectivity' which remains 'neutral' to all 'values' and every sense of meaning by which men integrate their individual and collective life; or it must covertly insinuate some faith into a supposedly presuppositionless culture. In the former case a 'liberal' culture lives on, and sometimes falls into, the abyss of nihilism; in the latter case it makes faith in 'nature' or 'reason' or 'democracy' or 'capitalism' the unexamined basis of its structure of meaning." The modern mind, according to Nash, fashioned its model of thinking on the natural sciences "and now we have to reckon with the fact that this model in its classical form is no better fitted to explain (let alone change) the contemporary world than the scholastic scheme was adequate for the intellectual demands of a world built on expanding capitalism".[4] At the time of the Renaissance many scholars failed to see the inadequacy of the forms of thought inherited from the past. Then it was the scholastic metaphysicians, "in our day it is the 'logical positivists'". They do not see the force of A. N. Whitehead's statement that the "stable foundations of physics have broken up . . . and the old foundations of thought are becoming unintelligible", nor that it is equally applicable to psychology, biology, economics and politics.[5] As the poet said: "New occasions teach new duties, time makes ancient good uncouth."

Before 1600 there was general agreement among the greatest writers on education – Quintilian, the early Italian humanists, Rabelais, Montaigne – that "the outcome of all sound teaching is a self-active, living mind". 'Accendere animos' is the aim. Plutarch reminds us that the soul is not a vessel to fill, but a hearth on which to kindle a fire. The great writers were agreed on the intellectual aim, but they were even more agreed on the supreme importance of moral education. We may take Michel de Montaigne (one of whose tutors was John Rutherford from Jedburgh, a most interesting man, who was a friend of George Buchanan) as typical of the Renaissance humanists. "What should boys learn?" "Those things", said Agesilaus, "that they ought to do when they become men". According to Montaigne philosophy is the highest fruit of education – not the philosophy of logical formulae – rather the philosophy that has virtue for its end. "Philosophy instructs us to live, and infancy has there its lessons as well as other ages." "We must learn to measure ourselves aright . . . whoever shall observe himself and not only himself but a whole kingdom, no bigger than the least touch or prick of a pencil in comparison with the whole – that man alone is able to value things according to their true estimate and value". Thus humanistic education is the formation of the mind of youth "omnibus artibus quae ad humanitatem pertinent."

We may put the start of the modern period at 1600, and it is with the rise of the school of Francis Bacon that a new idea enters on the scene, though one author gives the palm to Galileo who, "more than any other man, introduced the change in our manner of thinking that broke with ancient and led to modern science. Galileo, Hooke, Wren all stressed the close connection between scientific discovery and practical application. Robert Boyle, in a letter of October 22, 1646, wrote: "The other humane studies I apply myself to are natural philosophy, the mechanics and husbandry, according to the principles of our new philosophical college, that values no knowledge, but as it hath tendency to use." It can be seen that Boyle and his contemporaries had moved a long way from the Greek attitude to manual labour, for whom it was a very inferior occupation. It amounted to a sea change in thought, and, as Lancelot Hogben has said: "Great formative periods in the record of science have occurred when scientific investigators have been interested in the social uses to which their discoveries are put."[6]

But where, to repeat our question, did this great change come from? And why was it – despite the great discoveries made in China, for example – unique to Western civilization? In three centuries, from the publication of Copernicus's *On the Revolutions of the Celestial Orbs* in 1543 to the death of Dalton in 1843 there was born and grew up a movement which "gathered within itself all that was known of the natural world and developed it to an extent which is credible only because it actually happened".[7] And the developments in the last century-and-a-half have been more extraordinary. What made this possible? In his chapter on the *Origins of Modern Science*, A. N. Whitehead says that it was the "union of passionate interest in the detailed facts with equal devotion to abstract generalization". It would not be relevant to the matter of this book to go into lengthy analysis of why this great change happened when it did, but a quick outline may be given. It was a combination of many things: the scholastic tradition of detailed, logical argument even though from outdated premises; the rationality of the Greeks; the personal energy of Protestantism; Roman law and organization; the learning of Constantinople; the interest of Benedictine monasteries in agriculture. But Greek thought was deductive; geometry was the model of all true thinking. In the Middle Ages the earth was of little interest compared with heaven, this life being but a preparation for the life to come. It was in fact the Reformation which made the break, for it produced a mass movement prepared to question authority and ready to accept revolutionary ideas about nature. As John Macmurray has said: "Luther's conversion put an end to man's preoccupation with himself and as a result he found himself no longer interested in himself, no longer the centre of his own world." Luther laid the spiritual foundations for Galileo and his successors when they relegated the earth to what Sartre's anti-hero in *Les Chemins de la Liberté* was much later to describe as the status of a second-class planet going round a third-rate sun in an odd corner of the stellar universe. As Robert Hooke concluded: "The truth is, the Science of nature has already too long been made only a work of the 'Brain' and the 'Fancy'. It is now high time that it should return to the plainness and soundness of observations on material and obvious things." The dam of medieval scholasticism was burst by Protestantism and the subsequent flood of released mental energies led to the era of liberal individualism, producing in religion the proliferation of Protestant sects, in thought the scientific movement, in politics democracy and in economics capitalism.

It is then by acquiring factual knowledge that man is to be educated. Knowledge takes the place of wisdom, moral precepts the place of moral education.[8] This is the new Realism. The many characteristics of this period are: belief in the power of accumulated knowledge to educate the mind; priority given to the study of external reality and consequently to the study of physical science as opposed to the humanities; the application of the inductive method to instruction. The great leader of this new study was Francis Bacon whose *Advancement of Learning* was published in 1605, followed a few years later by his *Novum Organum*.

The essence of Bacon's teaching was that we know things inductively or, as he puts it, "Nihil est in intellectu quod non prius fuerit in sensu". But the impressions relayed by our senses are not themselves to be trusted. It was therefore necessary to establish a way of verifying sense impressions and to work out the grounds of valid and necessary inference, and then to apply them consistently. "The educational bearing of this is manifest", says Laurie, "for it is clear that if we can tell *how* it is we know, it follows that the method of scientific instruction is settled".[9]

In 1609 Bacon, whom Laurie calls the Philosopher of Realism and the Inductive Method, said "the question between me and the ancients is not of the virtue of their race, but of *the rightness of the way*". For him generalization could only follow in the wake of carefully observed facts: "Men have sought to make a world from their own conceptions and to draw from their own minds all the materials which they employed; but if instead of doing so they had consulted experience and observation they would have facts and not opinions to reason about, and might have ultimately arrived at the knowledge of the laws which govern the material world." Bacon did not invent induction, but, says Laurie, he unquestionably gave the world the logic of induction and formulated the practice of Galileo and the premonitions of Da Vinci. Nor will any flush of insight be accepted as objective truth until it has been verified by the reverse process, that is, deduction "by applying the supreme generalization to the elucidation of lower generalizations and ultimately of individual facts, thereby showing that it truly explains them by containing them".[10] Bacon's great goal was: "The End of our Foundation is the knowledge of the Causes and secret motions of things; and the enlarging of the bonds of Human Empire, to the effecting of all things possible."

Laurie, who makes no secret of the fact that he is a latter-day fan of Bacon, states that Bacon and his school were the founders of the modern movement in education, not as based on reflective psychology, but rather as revealed "by the actual process whereby the truth of things was ascertained. He looked at the *matter of thought*, not at the thinking process".[11] He goes rather over the top, in my view, but this is no bad thing since it will enable us to work out the more clearly the distant consequences of the Baconian world-view for higher education. Citing Comenius – one of the greatest educational innovators – Locke, Spencer, Pestalozzi and others as evidence of this new method of teaching, he says: "Look at the universities of Europe at the present day (i.e. before the First World War). Whence comes their life, their progressiveness, without which there is no life? From Bacon and the Baconian induction and from vernacular literatures, I say without hesitation. It is the *scientific* spirit engaged in every department of human inquiry: physical, historical, philosophical, philological, aesthetic, that keeps, in these days, centres of intellectual energy. With all their deficiencies, the learning of the world and all its higher rational interests were never so adequately represented in the universities as now. They are the true centres of light, and why? *Because they seek scientific results, and follow a scientific method. Method has done it all.* "[12]

I can understand Laurie's pride in being the first Professor of Education at a British university, *mais quand même!* Herbert Spencer pitched it even more strongly: "Accomplishments, the fine Arts, Literature etc. should be wholly subordinate to that instruction and discipline on which investigation rests. As they occupy the leisure part of life, so should they occupy the leisure part of education." For Spencer the knowledge, the discipline of most worth was science, "even in the moral and religious sphere".[13] Spencer's analogy here is very revealing. If the arts are for leisure, then science is for work. This statement was made in the full flood-tide of Victorian capitalism. The similarity of the mechanisms of science and capitalism is striking. They both "rest on the rational prediction of the future, whether of the course of business or the sequence of change in a chemical, physical or biological system. Both are based on an unlimited acquisitiveness, of facts or financial gain."[14] But the most important resemblance between science and capitalism, says Nash, citing Tawney,[15] is the fact that they both represent a break-away from ethical considerations. Modern science eschews final causes in favour of efficient causes: it asks 'how' not 'why'; it deals with means, not ends, so an epistemological separation between science and philosophy was inevitable.

In relation to Spencer's views, Clark Kerr was later to say that even in Newman's day the gentleman "at home in any society" was seen to be at home in none.[16] Science was beginning to take the place of moral philosophy, research the place of teaching. The result of this takeover of the universities by the Baconian and Spencerian epistemological stance in the nineteenth century was that philosophy too became a specialised discipline: "It used to be a stage in education, and is now an area of knowledge."[17] It had been what Pattison called "the summit of a liberal education, the crown of the highest culture", this "sustained effort . . . to frame a complete and reasoned synthesis of the facts of the universe". In France philosophy was the "couronnement des études"; Victor Cousin, in 1844, echoing Montaigne, said that philosophy, by "summarising the humanities, teaches what it really means to be a man".

In the medieval university the three philosophies, i.e. natural, moral and metaphysical, were part of the general Arts course that preceded professional study (though in fact rhetoric was very much a 'business studies' course of the medieval university, a vocational training in skill in writing). They came to be seen as the culmination of the Arts course. Robert Grosseteste (1175–1273), one of the leading teachers at Oxford in the Middle Ages, describes the seven liberal arts as attendants, ministrands on the philosophy of nature and ethics. Most importantly philosophy, especially logic, was taught in an argumentative oral mode, the 'disputations', which made the spotting of fallacies a key skill. This traditional evaluation of the importance of philosophy as the basis for a general education preparatory to professional training, together with the traditional oral approach, continued into the late nineteenth century in Scotland. As we have seen, however, the social function of arts courses at Oxford and Cambridge changed in the sixteenth and seventeenth centuries and became an education for gentlemen; nor was it followed by any professional training. Aristotle, who had been the basis of medieval philosophy, was banished, or rather codified. The manner of teaching philosophy also changed: disputations disappeared, there was no longer a dialogue with the classical authors or with the students; lectures became a soliloquy. Ree calls this "the most stupendous and far-reaching innovation". He says that philosophy emerged as a special subject in France and Germany during the classical period through a transformation of the logic and the three philosophies of the late medieval period from their textual basis in Aristotle and granted autonomy as professors' courses. Philosophy was divorced from science and became the study of human reason. This separated it from humanistic culture, and from empirical information whether scientific or historical. This approach crossed to England in the nineteenth century. It was further accentuated by new developments in the nineteenth century: the growth of prestigious life-time careers for teachers in the arts, which had not existed previously; the growth of research on the German model; and undergraduate specialization at the end of the century. One of the fiercest Scottish blasts against these developments came from Sir William Hamilton:

> The Oxford curriculum now abandons both Philosophy itself and the philosophical treatment of what it professes to teach . . . Yet is philosophy (the science of science – the theory of what we can know and think and do, in a word – the knowledge of ourselves) the object of liberal education, at once of paramount importance in itself, and the requisite condition of every other liberal science. If we are really to know aught else, the human faculties, by which alone this knowledge may be realised, must be studied for themselves, in their extent and in their limitations. To know, we must understand our instrument of knowing."[18]

More than a century-and-a-half later the same problem is still being debated, even more hotly perhaps. "One of the problems of identifying as philosophy both what Plato did and what contemporary philosophers now do is that professional philosophy has been transformed into a technical specialism, one among others: the technique of linguistic analysis."[19] We are seeing the depoliticization of philosophy, whereas Socrates was the gad-fly of the state. As James Kelman put it, speaking of philosophy at Strathclyde University: "The lectures on philosophy were to be attended at all costs . . . it was here you learned to question at the level most likely to frighten authority."[20] This depoliticization is very largely the end result of the gradual development of science as a specialized form of thought in the seventeenth and eighteenth centuries. For Descartes, at the beginning of this major mutation in thought, science and philosophy were hardly beginning to be distinguishable, whereas John Locke at the end of it saw himself as "an under-labourer in clearing the ground a little, and removing some of the rubbish that lies in the way to knowledge" – that is, the work of Newton, Boyle *et al*. For Kant philosophy was a special type of inquiry logically different from science and still capable of internal connection with politics through political philosophy, as in the work of Rousseau and Locke. But the analytical movement's 'revolution in philosophy' soon put an end to such dilettantism: political philosophy was split into political science and the vocabulary of politics, both apolitical. The analytical movement isolated itself from twentieth century Continental philosophy and became an Anglo-American school.

According to this school of thought philosophy is not just simply one specialism among others. "Its specialization reflects specialization in general and the growth of intellectual specialisms in particular."[21] Philosophy has specialized in becoming more and more purely reflective of other intellectual activities: philosophy is self-reflection, the self-awareness of thought. Its modern dominant form is epistemology, theory of knowledge. It is meta-thought: "it seeks to represent and theorize all types of thought and knowledge, including itself, and their interrelations". This schema of knowledge is institutionalized in the educational curriculum in the form of distinctions between areas of knowledge, for example, arts and science, pure science and technology, philosophy and history, history and literary studies, and so on. Thus a philosophy is hidden in the structure of the curriculum.

The shrinking of philosophy's role on the intellectual map is reflected in the ideas of Wittgenstein: "My aim in philosophy is to show the fly the way out of the fly-bottle." "Philosophy can in no way interfere with the actual use of language; it can in the end only describe it ... It leaves everything as it is." In other words, philosophy has no positive contribution to make to our knowledge and understanding of the world. A whole number of modern dogmas derive from this position: analysis must be value-free, attitudes must be liberal and not take sides, we see the end of ideology, and so on. "It is not surprising", says Edgley, "that this apolitical philosophy, which 'leaves everything as it is', should have waxed fat in our recent educational prosperity". (Ten years later it was being cut back in every university in Britain.) A consequence of this strait-jacket on philosophy in a humanistic sense has been the demotion of the arts: "the sciences denote, the arts emote". The arts could carry no weight in a world of thought in which the drive for infallibility has narrowed knowledge to verbal propositions which can either be developed logically or submitted to empirical testing. "The mind became identified with analytical reason, truth with logic and/or verification. The arts could carry no transpersonal significance."[22] At the beginning of this philosophical mutation Descartes speaks of poetry as furnishing "ravishing graces and delights" and "the most agreeable fancies". At what Abbs calls "the clapped-out end of the tradition" A. J. Ayer devoted just ten dismissive sentences to aesthetics in *Language, Truth and Logic*: "Aesthetic words . . . express certain feelings and evoke a certain response . . . There is no sense in attributing objective validity to aesthetic judgments, and no possibility of arguing about questions of values . . . The purpose of aesthetic criticism is not so much to give knowledge as to commu-nicate emotion . . . We conclude, therefore, that there is nothing in aesthetics, any more than there is in ethics, to justify the view that it embodies a unique type of knowledge."

The danger of these facile and utterly reductive views is evident in a world where the whole future of the biosphere, including Homo Sapiens, is dependent on the outcome of arguments about values and about ethics.[23] Cartesian dualism created a "schizophrenia which broke the world into the harsh polarities of objectivity and subjectivity, reason and unreason, cognition and affect, science and the arts".[24] This tradition, now coming under increasing criticism, virtually rejected and epistemologically demoted all the inherited means, both biological and cultural, that men use to make sense of the world in which we live. "Our quite remarkable ability to sequence narratives, to construe analogically, to conceive figura-tively, to consider totally, to think musically, to construct maps and diagrams, to make signs and symbols with our bodies; all of these were relegated to secondary levels, as if possessing no serious intel-lectual importance."[25] But an epistemological revolution is under way, says Abbs, in which current philosophical thinking is seeking to locate the different forms of intelligence, the multiplicity of intel-ligence, and their inherited symbolic practices. On this he quotes the late Louis Armand Reid: "So instead of making knowledge a function of the truth of propositional statements, I think we should turn it on its head and say that truth is a function or attribute of quality, of the mind's living, cognitive apprehension of the world."

"The overall influence of positivism on educational theory has been pernicious, because it is ultimately self-stultifying."[26] This is so because education insinuates itself into the very core of the child's, of the student's, being, so that the philosophy embodied in any educational stance is of great theoretical and practical importance. One must ask, in reference to any given educational scheme, whose educational aims are being put forward? If one chooses a set of aims one is excluding other possible aims, other possible views of the meaning and value of life. Positivism refuses, however, to accept such terms as the 'meaning of life' and is thus unconsciously opting for one view of life as against all others. Positivism, despite its claims, has a metaphysical basis. In Rodger's view the aims of education must be discovered, not chosen – and this, positivism would say, is a meaningless exercise. Ayer has defined positivism in the following terms: "Logical positivism is not a system of philosophy. We deny the possibility of philosophy as a speculative discipline . . . we reject metaphysics . . . as an attempt to gain knowledge of the world by non-scientific means . . . we should conclude that if philosophy is to be a cognitive activity it must be purely critical. It would take the form of trying to elucidate the terms that were used in science or mathematics or everyday language."[27] Despite this denial, much of positivism's influence comes from its assuming the authority of a school of philosophy. As already mentioned, it is the source of a whole complex of attitudes which pervade our entire culture, including the education system at all levels.

There is a difference between positivism and empiricism. The latter believes that in studying the universe the only avenue of information is sense experience. Logical positivism, however, is a dogmatic philosophical position which claims that all valid knowledge about the universe comes through the empirical or scientific methods. It says that metaphysics is embedded in the language people use, and tries to develop language in such a way as to avoid spurious metaphysical puzzles. (Wittgenstein says that all philosophical puzzles are caused by "bewitchment due to language".) He and Bertrand Russell tried to develop such a language, but quickly discovered that any language involves philosophical assumptions, that is "some kind of ontological pre-understanding of the world". It was therefore necessary to look at the social contexts in which language is used. Wittgenstein: "Don't ask for the meaning, ask for the use." And again, "philosophy is about life". Analysis becomes barren if isolated from life. Thus adequate linguistic analysis must include personal context as well as a logical element. It must ask what the person using the language thinks s/he is doing; in other words, it must be analysed against the background of the person's basic beliefs about the world, the flesh and the devil: metaphysics is "always involved in a person's 'pre-understanding' of the nature of the issues with which s/he is concerned".[28]

Aims and ends can only be justified – if one is to avoid circularity – by reference to more fundamental – to ultimate ends, and it is at this level that the really vital questions are encountered. What will be done depends on one's beliefs. As Rodger puts it: "It makes sense to burn a person to death if this is the only way to save him from eternal burning in hell."[29] These fundamental values or principles must be recognized as real since they are seen as binding by human beings. They are self-authenticating; they are apprehended rather than created; and they are thus "the realm of the metaphysical, the non-sensical in positivist terms". Consequently, the resolution of differences between rival views as to what is ultimately valuable – 'ultimately worth-while' in A. D. Lindsay's language – can only occur because there are certain values implicit in the human situation. The positivist view is that all values are relative to a valuer, so that there can be no meaningful goals at all. But if one says "all significant values are relative to the human situation", this is both more accurate and does not insist that values are created by the valuer. The ability to recognize values and respond is an important part of our humanity. All those, including logical positivists, who discuss educational aims and goals, do so on the basis of commonly recognized values. Any educational scheme presupposes a theory of human nature, and all the facts of human biology, history, social organisation and the economy have a massive bearing on the choices we can make. Positivism, on the other hand, has a narrow, negative influence, since it excludes all those areas it finds problematical – ethics, aesthetics, metaphysics, etc. Inconsistently, however, Positivism prescribes the aims of education and is embodied in the methodology of education, as we have seen. It involves a deterministic view of human nature which empties human life of all value and moral considerations.

An example of its effects in education can be seen in the work of B. F. Skinner, whose behaviourist theories have had a wide application, as, for example, in the widespread use of language laboratories. Behaviourism is the psychological application of positivism. By behavioural engineering, using the same sort of reinforcement techniques as were used on pigeons, humans can be trained to become contented citizens. But who is deciding what desirable behaviour is? As Arthur Koestler said on BBC1 on 25 June 1969: "Reductionist psychology and biology are an attempt to remove significance and meaning from human behaviour." And John Davy gave a warning: "The outward-looking world of scientific technology threatens to diverge from real human needs, to become enamoured of its power to manipulate, to control, to impose on and ultimately to ignore that sphere of freedom out of which it was originally born." Science is unable to say anything about the appreciation of good music, but that does not mean that music is not enormously important to the individual and society, as it has been at all stages of civilization.

Positivist attitudes have been inculcated in young people for many years now, and this must affect their life-styles. Is there not bound to be a connection between this constant educational bias and the nihilism that afflicts so many young people; the football riots and deaths; the riots and wholesale violence in British and American cities, supposedly among the most advanced? If we educate the young to believe that there is no meaning to life, can we be surprised at these episodes? Especially when reinforced by nihilistic government behaviour? Are we bringing up generations of neurotics? Dr. Arnold Stocker defines neurosis as an "inner conflict between a false suggestion and a true intuition". The false suggestions of positivism will suppress the true intuitions of personal life and mentally cripple many of our young people. The most important thing in life is to be a whole person; much more important than being a rigidly consistent empiricist. Vision and insight are the property of the individual, not of any theory, dogmatic or otherwise.

This emphasis on empirical, factual, positivistic knowledge leads to a diminution of the functions of academic institutions in society: "Universities have become almost entirely instrumental institutions, losing their semi-spiritual quality."[30] By the 1960s a generation educated in philosophic and scientific indifference to good and evil had entered the universities. "Man has lost the capacity to value. Nihilism may be a necessary in human history. But how are we ever to regain our capacity to believe in anything or to be committed at a level which matters – a level from which a new creativity can come?"[31] Reductionism, says Niblett, is legitimate in much scholarly work. But truth-finding is not the whole of a scholar's life. Living is irreducible.

At this point it may be useful to go back a little and canvass the views of one of the finest thinkers about modern science and education. In his great book,[32] A. N. Whitehead says that science has remained predominantly an anti-rationalist movement, based upon a naive faith. It has borrowed the reasoning it needed from mathematics, and it repudiates philosophy. In other words it has never cared to justify its faith or to explain its meaning.

The Baconian revolution was fully justified; the world needed to spend some centuries contemplating irreducible and stubborn facts.

But the progress of science has now reached a turning-point – as, for example, in the break-up of the solid foundations of physics – and if it is "not to degenerate into a medley of *ad hoc* hypotheses it must become philosophical and must enter upon a thorough criticism of its own foundations."[33] Scientific materialism is fine if it is confined to certain types of facts, abstracted from the complete circumstances in which they fit; here the materialistic assumption expresses the facts to perfection. "But when we pass beyond the abstraction, either by more subtle employment of our senses, or by the request for meanings and for coherence of thoughts, the scheme breaks down at once. The narrow efficiency of the scheme was the very cause of its supreme methodological success."[34] Thus the thoroughly justified historical revolt has gone too far and has excluded philosophy from its proper role of harmonising the various abstractions of methodological thought. "Thought is abstract; and the intolerant use of abstractions is the major vice of the intellect." The faith in natural order which has made possible the growth of science is, in fact, a particular example of a deeper faith. "Thus faith cannot be justified by any inductive generalization. It springs from direct inspection of the nature of things as disclosed in our immediate present experience."[35] Which is precisely the point that Abbs and Rodger were trying to make.

Whitehead discusses the inductive method in a penetrating way, pointing that it is the despair of philosophy. Yet all our activities are based upon it. The experimental method is paying attention to the "irreducible and stubborn facts", while the inductive is the eliciting of general laws from the study of the facts. The rational justification of the inductive method is an unsolved problem bequeathed to us by the seventeenth century, he says, because induction has turned out to be a more complex process than Bacon imagined. His view was that if you were sufficiently careful in the collection of instances the general law would stand out clearly. But that, say Whitehead and other authors, is a very inadequate account of the process which leads to scientific generalisations. The baffling task of applying reason to "the general characteristics of the immediate occasion, as set before us in direct cognition, is a necessary preliminary if we are to justify induction". He stresses that it is impossible to over-emphasise the point that the key to the process of induction is to be found in the right understanding of the immediate occasion of knowledge in its full concreteness. Because otherwise we come up against insoluble difficulties if we substitute for this concrete occasion "a mere abstract in which we only consider material objects in a flux of configurations in time and space".[36]

For Whitehead, induction presupposes metaphysics; that is, it rests upon an antecedent rationalism. You cannot make a rational appeal to history unless your metaphysics has assured you that there is a history to appeal to. Nor can you make conjectures about the future unless you are sure there is to be a future, already subjected to the same forms of determination. Without these ideas, which are difficult, you make a nonsense of induction. "You will observe", says Whitehead, "that I do not hold induction to be in its essence the derivation of general laws. It is the divination of some characteristics of a particular future from known characteristics of a particular past. The wider assumption of general laws holding in all cognisable occasions appears a very unsafe addendum to attach to this limited knowledge!"[37]

The mechanistic theory of nature developed by Galileo, Descartes, Huyghens and Newton worked when put to the pragmatic test. It is the orthodox creed of physical science and it has reigned supreme ever since the seventeenth century. So physicists were no longer interested in philosophy. But despite its efficiency the theory of mechanistic materialism soon became subject to difficulties, and these dogged the history of thought throughout the eighteenth and nineteenth centuries. Yet it has remained the guiding principle of scientific thought, and every university in the world organises itself in accordance with this theory. "And yet – it is quite unbelievable. It is framed in terms of high abstractions, and the paradox only arises because we have mistaken our abstractions for concrete realities."[38] It involves – and here we come back to Descartes – a fundamental duality, with matter on the one hand and mind on the other. "In between lie the concepts of life, organism, function, instantaneous reality, interaction, order of nature, which collectively form the Achilles heel of the whole system."[39]

Whitehead calls this problematic the *Fallacy of Misplaced Concreteness*. It is impossible to think without abstractions, so it is vitally important to be vigilant in critically revising one's modes of abstraction. This is where philosophy has its role to play, where it is essential to the healthy progress of society. For philosophy is the critic of abstractions, and a civilization "which cannot burst through its current abstractions is doomed to sterility after a very limited period of progress. An active school of philosophy is quite as important for the locomotion of ideas as is an active school of railway engineers for the locomotion of fuel".[40] And philosophers demand meaning. Whitehead quotes Henry Sidgwick: "It is the primary aim of philosophy to clarify completely, bring into clear coherence, all departments of rational thought, and this aim cannot be realised by any philosophy that leaves out of its view the

important body of judgments and reasonings which form the subject matter of ethics."[41] Whitehead's conclusion is that it should
be the task of the philosophical schools of this country to bring
together the two streams of thought emanating from Descartes on
the one hand, and on the other hand, from Leibniz (with his theory
"that the entities which are the ultimate actual things are in some
sense procedures of organization") and thereby mould them into an
"expression of the world-picture derived from science and thereby
end the divorce of science from the affirmations of our aesthetic
and ethical experiences".[42]

Logical positivism not only did not pay a blind bit of notice; it
denied that such a task had any meaning. Was S. S. Laurie's paean
of triumph for the success of scientific method in the universities
a quarter of a century earlier to prove correct? Had we 'grown
mechanical', as Carlyle put it, for good? Clark Kerr asks: "Does
the machine have within it the seeds of its own destruction? Or
can it develop an overall rationality?"[43] The omens are not good
since "the organized intellect churns out the solutions to problems
with no thought for their consequences. Thus rising population,
rising levels of destructive capacity are not studied in any way commensurate with their huge significance".[44] Kerr's pessimism can
be seen in the statement : "Intellect has become an instrument of
national purpose, a component part of the 'military-industrial complex'. Many authors have touched on this theme. J. K. Galbraith,
for instance, in *The New Industrial State* : "Higher education is
extensively accommodating to the industrial system." Or Ronald
Barnett, in *The Idea of Higher Education* : "Post-industrial society
is essentially a knowledge-based society .. so higher education is
part of the central framework of modern society . . . (and) has less
and less space to define its own agenda."

There exists a widespread suspicion, indeed, that students in higher
education are being exposed to an implicit reductionism concerning
human nature, behaviour and values over the whole range of academic disciplines. What are the implications for our understanding
of the meaning and purpose of human life? Can dangerous, because
simplistic, reductionist assumptions give way to a more positive
set of values? Can a systematic critique of reductionism restore the
interrelation of disciplines within the map of knowledge and "recreate that lost sense of wholeness to which the idea of a university once
testified?"[45] We have already seen that reductionism (Whitehead's
"intolerant use of abstractions") is the prevailing attitude among
scientists. The analytical procedures used in their various disciplines
become almost without thinking a philosophical belief about biological organisms being "nothing but" the bits into which they have

analyzed them. Thus Francis Crick, the Nobel prize-winner for the unravelling of DNA, said in 1966: "The ultimate aim of the modern movement in biology is in fact to explain *all biology* in terms of physics and chemistry."[46] E. O. Wilson says, without blinking an eye: "It may not be too much to say that sociology and the other social sciences, as well as the humanities, are the last branches of biology waiting to be included in the Modern Synthesis." That such claims can be made and not met with guffaws of ridicule shows the dangerous sleep-walking phase that modern science has got itself into. Even more disturbing, perhaps, is the lack of effective criticism from outside science of these overweening claims.

There are three types of reductionism: methodological; ontological; epistemological. The first has been done for centuries and consists in breaking down a problem into pieces and proceeding by explaining both the lower and the higher levels of organization. It has been immensely effective, and so the use of holistic approaches is only a temporary concession to the incompleteness of our knowledge. The second, i.e, ontological reductionism, consists in saying that biological systems are "nothing but" complex patterns of atoms and molecules. Epistemological reductionism "can be described as the view that if the theories and experimental laws formulated in one field of science (e.g. biology, psychology, sociology) can be shown to be special cases of theories and laws formulated in some other branch of science (e.g. physical chemistry, or biology, or the neuro-sciences) then the former science, the former set of theories and experimental laws, is said to be reduced to the latter." Usually the explanatory theory is drawn from a science at a 'lower' level in the hierarchy of complexity. Thus progress in science is always progress in reduction. Efficient though it is, however, this method is unable to give a full account of man; it has great difficulties in dealing with living organisms and "efforts to reduce ethics to biology inevitably end in failure". But reductionism has the knack of making itself popular and exciting. A particularly good example is the writing of Richard Dawkins, whose *The Selfish Gene* was a best-seller with its thesis that we are 'nothing but' vehicles for our genes, which use us much like tanks in their ceaseless, ruthless drive to expand their numbers at the cost of others. Dawkins' work, for all its modernity and sophistication, takes us right back to Descartes, with whom modern biology began and for whom organisms were also particular types of clockwork.[47]

For Steven Rose, legitimising the Cartesian machine image, which came to dominate science, was the fundamental metaphor legitimising the bourgeois world view of a mechanical nature. The crucially important point is that the machine was taken as a symbol of the living organism and not the reverse. "The bodies of living organisms are indissoluble wholes that lose their essential characteristics when they are taken into pieces. Machines, on the contrary, can be disarticulated to be understood and then put back together." It was not long before the Cartesian model was extended from non-human to human models. The human organism, however, has a mind, self-consciousness. This for the Catholic Descartes was the soul, which belonged to God and so could not be mere mechanism. Hence the idea that there are in nature two kinds of material: matter, which obeys the mechanical laws of physics, and soul, or mind, which twiddles the knobs of the mechanical body. (The metaphorical resemblance to Dawkins' ideas is striking). This was dualism – what Rose calls "the inevitable but fatal dysjunction of Western scientific thought"[48]– which soon developed into a dogma. This dogma played a very important ideological role. It was "a solution to the paradox of mechanism" that enabled religion and reductionist science to put off for two centuries the inevitable battle for ideological supremacy that broke out in the nineteenth century. The human mechanism put in hard graft during the working week, but the immortal soul took over on the Sunday.

Cartesian dualism soon developed into the mechanical materialism of a Lavoisier, for whom living energy was like the burning of a coal fire. Humans are what they eat; genius is a question of phosphorus: there was a determined attempt to account for all bodily processes in physico-chemical terms. Finally, in the nineteenth century, the contradiction between reductionist science and religion was solved with the publication of Darwin's work, and a new stage was reached – or, as Thomas Kuhn would say, a new scientific paradigm began to operate. God is dead, killed by science, and a new, revamped, mechanistic theory takes over: natural selection and physiological reductionism take over. This model is continuously updated – the neo-Darwinian synthesis of the 1930s, elucidation of the genetic code in the 1950s – until today we have the central dogma as presented by Crick: from the DNA to RNA to the protein there is a one-way flow of information between the molecules which gives historical and ontological primacy to the hereditary molecule, i.e. the selfish gene. Everything is contained in the gene. So the biologically determinist writings of a Dawkins present an integrated reductionist world view based on the central dogma of molecular biology and claiming that the gene is ontologically prior to the individual and the individual to society. It is striking too how Dawkins transfers the concepts of modern capitalist society into biology: cost-benefit analysis, investment opportunity costs, game theory, systems engineering. It is social Darwinism all over again.

Descartes' mighty programme, which we quoted at the end of the last chapter, has been fulfilled to an extraordinary degree. We are getting closer and closer to the birth of the universe, and are envisaging its death. We are busy mapping the human genome. Even the brain is yielding its secrets by comparing it with the ultimate machine, the computer; neural networks is one of the most fashionable and well-funded areas of research. Well, what's wrong with reductionism if it has achieved so much? As we have seen, it operates from the philosophical premise of the priority of the molecule over the organism, the priority of the individual over society. "Reductionism cannot accept that phenomena are *simultaneously* both individual and part of a greater unity";[49] it also operates by a phenomenon of "arbitrary agglomeration of distinct phenomena". For instance, if we take the example of aggression, reductionism lumps together war, strikes, football hooliganism, intersexual aggression, the space race and so on. It is seen as the sum of the aggressive properties of the individual member of society, which must somehow be localized in the brain. This takes no account of the possibility that behaviour is an expression of the properties of the system. Then there is the powerful trend which Rose dubs "arbitrary quantification", the belief that any property can be quantified on some linear scale. This leads to 'scientization', for example, if one rat kills mice in half the time it takes another rat, then the first rat is twice as aggressive. Papers get published and grants given for a study of 'muricidal activity'. This is then extrapolated to the human situation and leads to the search for an anti-aggression drug. "Arbitrary quantification is then the ascription of numerical values to qualities which cannot be adequately encapsulated in this sort of way." When the spurious mathematical manipulation of these 'data' is done, it turns out that "practically everything is inherited: radicalism, introversion, aggression, intelligence, even ability to learn French".

The examples Rose gives are drawn from recent heritability studies "but they are strictly empty of scientific content". If, then, the properties of societies derive from the properties of individuals which are themselves genetically inherited, it must be possible to find an adaptive evolutionary theory to explain them. This is sociobiology, which is full of "adaptationist myths" and is an example of global reductionist thinking.[50] So we get the *Beatrix Potter syndrome* – baboon harems, propaganda-making ants, prostitution in humming-birds, a gang rape in mallard ducks. This is all gross oversimplification and prevents us understanding the complex reality of the biological world. It ignores the simultaneity of phenomena, the fact that everything is at the same time biological and social.

There is no uni-directional arrow of causation, we should be looking for correspondences between levels. The organism is not passively affected by its environment; it makes choices. Events have a history. Intelligence has improved in humans because they have improved the environment for thinking.

Is scientific reductionism threatening? It can be, according to the moral philosopher Mary Midgley.[51] It depends on the tone which is used. The fact that we are quarks, if discussed in a quiet way, needn't be menacing. But when people start to say that "the organism is only DNA's way of making more DNA" (E. O. Wilson 1975), or that "we are survival machines – robot machines blindly programmed to preserve the selfish molecules known as genes" (R. Dawkins 1976), we notice that man is turned into a passive machine. "This is not just determinism. It is fatalism and the difference is crucial."[52] Fatalism is dramatic: it says we are helpless, it tells us our purposes don't count. We are pawns on an alien chessboard. These socio-biological *cris de guerre* produce their frightening effect "by inflating the modest concept of evolutionary function into direct competition with ordinary individual purpose, and then proclaiming that it has won the battle . . . We emerge as the pawns of our own protoplasm."[53] The West's powerful myths all go in for machine-worship, especially "vast, quasi-mechanical superprocesses" in which we are but cogs. But biology is not threatening, people are not victims, caught in an iron grip. They use their brains and nervous systems, their eyes and ears; they are not used by them. "Wholes use parts." Illicit reductionism is not a healthy influence, brushing away superstitions. It is, says Mary Midgley, "only making room for a new set of demons, seven times as pernicious as their predecessors". Science, with its twin dogmas – science is without assumptions or presuppositions, and science and philosophy must be completely separate – has riveted on the modern world an exaggerated trust in the power of reasoning which equals the rationalistic orgy of the Middle Ages.

The reader may be getting a little restive by now, wondering what all this has to do with university education. Well, as we saw at the outset of this chapter, you do not understand society – and, we may add, its major institutions – until you have plumbed the philosophical premises that determine conduct. That is what we have tried to do, however inadequately, in this chapter, and we will seek to elucidate their effects on the universities in the next. But we must first deal briefly with administrative reductionism in the universities, to wrap up our treatment of reductionism.

Reality is socially defined, so to understand the state of the socially constructed universe at any given time one must understand the social organization that permits the definers to do their defining.

One should ask not so much 'What?' as 'Says who?'[54] There are three kinds of obstacles to holism, to an interdisciplinary approach: logical, tactical and strategic. The first is the simplest; it includes such things as time-tabling, whose difficulties can always be used to block any novel approach, as can also, of course, the delays and longueurs of typing and replication, though word-processing has perhaps weakened the validity of this particular excuse. The tactical obstacles include what Goodlad calls "the machismo factor", which is a preference for lectures rather than tutorials, thereby eliminating discussion and give-and-take. (We may note in passing that this would not have worked in the traditional Scottish system, where every lecture was followed by discussion.) At this time FTEs (full-time-equivalent students, that is) are so important to departments for financial reasons that every effort is made to avoid interdisciplinary work, where FTEs have to be shared; it is also an administrative drag. Then there is reductionism through the preference for examinations over extended essays, once again avoiding discussion and proper teaching.

The strategic obstacles arise from the fact that people do what is to their advantage. Today, as always and despite the rapidly increasing staff-student ratios, promotion depends on 'research'. This leads to hyper-specialism and pushes the whole educational system over towards specialism, including secondary education.[55] It all stems from the reward system of academics. Holist learning by the students might be encouraged if their teachers were interested in it; in other words if there was at least as much incentive for good teaching as there is for research. The work is just as difficult but it is not as well rewarded. Yet Aristotle said: "Teaching is the highest form of understanding"; A. N. Whitehead said that brilliant teachers were "the unthanked benefactors of humanity"; Donald Kennedy, President of Stanford University, said: "Teaching is the primary task of higher education"; and Michael Severn of Columbia University has said: "The great teacher is an endangered species". When there is such a contradiction between what the genuinely great and good think should, and what they know will, happen in higher education, there has to be something profoundly wrong with its basic philosophical premises. We shall examine this question in the next chapter.

8

Philosophy and Higher Education 2

The Idiot Questioner
I should like to begin with two quotations:

> After four centuries of intellectual endeavour modern man finds that he has exchanged the intellectual idolatry of Scholasticism for the intellectual polytheism of scientific positivism. Its influence in the university has been calamitous because it has meant (as Dr. Wm. Temple said in a sermon to the University of Oxford) that the university 'is a place where a multitude of studies are conducted, with no relationship between them except those of simultaneity and juxtaposition.'[1]
> Astonishing as it may seem, we have no theoretical framework in which we can talk about higher education educationally. Put simply, we have no modern theory of higher education.[2]

There are many books on planning, administration, teaching methodology, the curriculum, but very few on the philosophy of higher education. There is much discussion about British economic needs, or access to higher education; this is the instrumental or functionalist view of higher education. It is of course important but bulks far too large and caters for a narrow set of interests – higher education's contribution to Great Britain Inc. – and neglects the intrinsic character of higher education. Most of the literature on education concentrates on the schools, whose role is quite different from that of institutions of higher education.

We live in a knowledge-based society, and it is higher education which legitimises society's cognitive structures. The values that have marked higher education would include the following: the pursuit of truth and objective knowledge; research; a liberal education; institutional autonomy; academic freedom; an open forum for debate; rationality; development of the student's critical ability and his/her capacity to work and think on her/his own; providing critical comment on society; providing a society's intellectual culture, etc. These ideas could all be covered by the phrase 'liberal education', but this is now no longer in fashion. Newman's 'knowledge for its own sake' has been replaced by knowledge which is technically useful to society, for example the massive growth of business studies, the 'enterprise culture'. The traditional epistemological definition of higher education was that it sought objective knowledge. The thesis was that "each and every problem of social life will yield to intelligent investigation by the psychologist, the economist and biologist."[3] This is progress, man and society are slowly getting better, and presuppositionless science, as their only way of reaching truth, is the main agent of this progress through education.

Understandably, in view of our experience these last 50 years, this thesis is now being seriously questioned: "From a post-modern perspective, the central characteristic of modernism, in a philosophical sense, is . . . that objective truth is assumed to be in principle unobtainable, and that means even our observations about knowledge and truth."[4] It is not only in the popular press that the legitimacy of higher education is being questioned, and this makes the absence of any serious work about the nature of knowledge and the place of education in modern society a very dangerous lacuna indeed. An inquiry into higher education would need to cover the following areas: the values and key aims and concerns of higher education as developed over the centuries; what are the assumptions behind our everyday talk about higher education and the terms we use – lecture, tutorial, academic freedom, research, etc? What is distinct about higher education? Why *higher* ? The epistemological problem: are we teaching 'objective knowledge'? The sociological problem: if higher education is becoming, as Clark Kerr indicated, more and more a part of the power structure of the modern state, what are the consequences of this for academic autonony? Is there an ideology of higher education?

Let us remind ourselves of some of the traditional values of the university by a quick overview. In Plato's Academy the central concept was the criticism of conventional knowledge through dialogue involving the student, who must master the technique of asking and answering questions. It is the Scottish universities which held on longest to this technique. In this process of critical examination of acquired knowledge the philosopher pursues all knowledge, not only some part of it, and the student attains a new life of independence. The dominant features of the medieval universities were a participatory approach to learning, a collaborative form of internal government, institutional autonomy and openness to all comers – it was not necessary to complete a degree; continuation of the dialogue approach in the form of structured discussions called disputations; a general arts course based on the classical trivium and quadrivium, with philosophy playing a key role, in preparation for professional study. We have seen Cardinal Newman's view of "knowledge its own end" as a proper training for gentlemen, giving a connected view or grasp of things. The German philosopher Karl Jaspers saw the university as having four functions: research, teaching, a professional education, and the transmission of culture. He was the first to provide a theory of knowledge, an epistemology for the university. He speaks of the universal validity of knowledge reached through consensus, though its absolute objectivity cannot be guaranteed. The pursuit of knowledge is not simply a narrow enterprise; it is also a demonstration of rationality, of the value and creative power of the human mind. Students must be personally active in academic enquiry; higher education is more than the acquisition of knowledge, it needs a sceptical, questioning attitude of mind. An interdisciplinary approach is necessary, and the search for truth depends on dialogue and discussion. So higher education is a process aiming at the transformation of the whole man. Criticism of self and society is vital. This is an emancipatory concept of education.

As university expansion got under way in the 1960s, social service functions bulked larger. Herbert Marcuse, the German/American thinker, saw higher education as the intellectual infrastructure of modern technological society. It was not a neutral force but a form of societal domination with curricula reflecting the needs of state capitalism – a view not far removed from that of Clark Kerr. The idea that students are initiated to the life of reason, that higher education aims at their all-round development, is just so much kidology. Marcuse's fears would be even more trenchantly expressed today when the dominant values in higher education (at least in Great Britain) are value for money, accountability, planning efficiency, good management, performance indicators, mission statements, selectivity, the establishment of a university pecking order with 'centres of excellence' concentrating on research, a second rank doing a bit of research as well as teaching, and a third rank doing only teaching – as if somehow the 'best' universities do research, while the 'weakest' do only teaching. Such a scheme betrays a woeful lack of thought as to the purposes of higher education.

In seeking to reach a new understanding of what universities should be about in our day, and looking for assistance to epistemology, we find, as shown in Chapter 7, that epistemology took "science to be the epitome of what counts as knowledge"[5] in the logical positivism of Wittgenstein and Ayer. Their successors today are Emil Gellner and Karl Popper. Gellner says that non-scientific forms of thought "contain claims and assertions which *sound* cognitive ... but it is understood that they are not fully serious, not commensurate or continuous with real knowledge."[6] Popper says: "Epistemology I take to be the study of scientific knowledge."[7] But both Kuhn and Feyerabend have stressed the point that science has made progress precisely because it has not been bound by the canons of logic and methodology as laid down by Popper, for example, in his theories about problem-solving.

So what is to be taught? "Is the one-dimensional curriculum about to arrive?"[8] During the past ten years many universities have abandoned more and more subjects unconnected with science, technology, business studies and computers. Or as the THES[9] put it:

STERLING CORPORATESHIRE UNIVERSITY;
BUSINESS IS OUR EDUCATION.

More than 30 departments were axed in the Scottish universities between 1979 and 1989, and philosophy in Britain had lost some 30% of posts by 1990. There was not one philosopher under 30 in Wales and Northern Ireland, and only 57 full-time philosophers under 40 to be found in the whole of Britain.[10]

There is, however, now a considerable amount of evidence to show that science is not the value-free, utterly objective knowledge mode whose claims are always subject to verification. There is the argument, presented by Feyerabend, that Galileo and others made their great scientific advances by non-rational means.[11] Science is now also being shown to be a non-cumulative form of inquiry; as being subject to revolutions whose rival paradigms are pitted against each other.[12] Lyotard adds to this the view that science develops not through consensus, but through conflict and incoherence.[13] Finally there are the views of Jurgen Habermas, who says that science has its own inbuilt "constitutive interest" in technical control.[14] All these are leading to a re-evaluation of the status of scientific knowledge. "It cannot any longer be taken for granted as the disinterested, supremely rational form of knowledge it was traditionally claimed to be."[15] Knowledge acquisition, as Habermas has said, cannot be a value-free process; values are inescapably involved.[16] This is quite simply never mentioned in Britain's universities today.

It would appear that social interaction, personal commitment, the development of the mind and the central role of value judgment are the most important elements in higher education. But there is a fifth which guarantees the validity of the learning and teaching process: it is what Barnet calls 'openness'. When these five criteria are taken together they guarantee that real learning has the character of a conversation. Which is precisely the form of learning particular to the

Scottish universities from the Middle Ages to the nineteenth century. During the earlier period it took the form of 'disputations', while in the nineteenth century these classes were called 'examinations', in which the professor held a dialogue with his students to maintain and advance their understanding. Here attention is addressed not so much to the 'facts' as to the process of gaining knowledge. This form of dialogue, of conversation, imposes four intrinsic ethical demands: truthfulness, sincerity, intelligibility and coherence. One must be ready to expose one's viewpoint to the critical gaze of others. This is Habermas's consensus theory of truth: it involves interaction with others and self-criticism. "If this connection of truth with ethics seems strange, it is because we have lost sight of it in modern society. The Greeks were aware of the connection."[17] Barnet does not seem to know that the Scottish universities were not only aware of the connection, but practiced it until last century. We shall have more to say of this later with reference to the work of the Scottish moral philosophers, John Macmurray and Alasdair McIntyre. The ethical dimension must be brought back into higher education.

A transatlantic view of the crisis in higher education created by the sidelining of the humanities and ethical considerations is provided by Allan Bloom who says[18] that "for modern nations, which have founded themselves on reason in its various uses more than did any nations in the past, a crisis in the university, the home of reason, *is perhaps the profoundest crisis they face.*" (The italics are mine.) For Bloom the university's main task is always to keep the 'permanent' questions at the forefront of its preoccupations; something they have almost ceased trying to do. The university presents no distinct map or tree of knowledge to the student. There is a "democracy of the disciplines ... this democracy is really an anarchy ... out of chaos emerges dispiritedness."[19] There is no way for the student to make a reasonable choice; it is easier to renounce a liberal education and choose a specialism, where at least there's a curriculum. The student receives no encouragement to seek for higher human motivation, no notion that a vision of a more human way of life can gained through his/her studies. S/he is put off by the "multiversity smorgasbord." S/he is given no opportunity to study the origins and development of our modern society – whether it is called liberal democracy or the acquisitive society – from its beginnings in the Age of Enlightenment. They are given no chance to study its scientific dogma: Bacon's assertion that the goal of science is to "ease man's estate"; Descartes' statement that science will make man "master and possessor of nature"; and the common place that science is the conquest of nature. Nor do they become acquainted with the opposition to this dogma from such as Dean Swift, whose 'Voyage to Laputa' in *Gulliver's Travels* is a parody of the Royal Society. These scientists cannot understand poets and so, in Gulliver's view, their science cannot be a science of man. The 'Flying Island' is based on Newtonian physics and demonstrates that applied science can open new roads to political power. The scientists' power is almost unlimited and their responsibilities are nil. They require no virtue; since everything runs itself there is no danger that they will be held responsible for incompetence or vice. "Science, in freeing men, destroys the natural conditions that made them human. Hence, for the first time in history, there is the possibility of tyranny grounded, not on ignorance, but on science."[20] An astonishing early preview of the military-industrial complex!

Nor do the students learn of Rousseau's argument that man's distinguishing feature is freedom, that it is denied by the kind of causation used in science and that therefore "the practical life, the exercise of moral freedom, is higher than the theoretical life, the use of scientific reason." As Rousseau said: "Ancient statesmen speak endlessly of morals and virtue; ours speak only of commerce and money." For him virtue, "the science of simple souls", was the essential concomitant of society, and science undermines virtue. Thus Rousseau called on modern man to hark back to the ancient city, because it was whole and a true community. There are so many illustrations in our day of the dangers Swift and Rousseau were talking about that there is no need to cite examples. The threat is no longer only to human society – which a British Prime Minister has said doesn't exist – but to the entire biosphere.

The present problems in higher education cannot simply be attributed to bad management or administration, lack of money, insufficient attention to the three R's, or any of the other explanations endlessly trotted out by government ministers to indicate that everything would be alright if only we would pull our socks up and do what they say. There is a deep lack of belief in the university's vocation, a lack of support for its traditional role. "The essence of all is not social, political, psychological or economic, but philosophic."[21] The university has abandoned the duty of studying and teaching values, thus undermining the value of its own teaching, and allowing values to be dictated by others, usually for their own purposes. Thus it offers no help to the young entrant looking for a good general education;[22] and professional people – lawyers, doctors, politicians, businessmen "get very little in the way of humane learning." The great universities – which can split the atom, find cures for the most terrible diseases, conduct surveys of whole populations, and produce massive dictionaries of lost languages – "cannot generate a modest program of general education for undergraduate students. This is a parable for our times. Without recognition of important questions of common concern, there cannot be serious liberal education."[23] Otherwise courses have titles like *Man in Nature, Culture and the Individual*; they are composed of bits and pieces; there is no overall view. Bloom's conclusion is that the crisis of liberal education is a "reflection of the crisis at the peaks of learning, an incoherence and incompatibility among the first principles with which we interpret the world, an intellectual crisis of the greatest magnitude, which constitutes the crisis of our civilization."[24] Liberal education flourished when it proposed the way for a unified view of nature and man's place in it. Such an approach is slowly being forced on us once again as the entire planetary surface threatens to become more and more inhospitable to man and to all terrestrial life as a result of our pushing the discoveries of Galileo, Descartes and Bacon to the ultimate extreme.

The philosophical root of these, we remember, was Cartesian dualism: the complete separation between mind and matter, man and nature, science and culture. Today, a growing number of thinkers are rejecting this materially immensely successful, but mentally and morally stultifying doctrine, as indeed the Scottish philosophers Francis Hutcheson and Thomas Reid had done in the first half of the eighteenth century before the whole thing got out of hand. One of these is Michael Polanyi, who has said:[25] "I have tried to demonstrate that into every act of knowing there enters a tacit and passionate contribution of the person knowing what is being known, and that this coefficient is no mere imperfection, but a necessary component of all knowledge." Polanyi constantly repeats that the process of knowing starts with belief – belief in a reality as yet only dimly perceived. "This is where he breaks out of the sterile objective/subjective disjunction."[26] The process of knowing is neither "scientifically objective", an impersonal collection of data; nor is it "subjective", an ego imposing its view of the evidence. It is rather the questioning person meeting a reality which is "true out there, universal and binding." Truth is something that can be thought of only by believing in it. Knowledge for its own sake should be "knowledge for the sake of the objective reality which carries worth for the seeker." All seeking for the truth can only be done by people deeply impregnated by the traditions of their own culture because all human beings learn and grow in the "critical framework of their own culture." (This is also one of the key concepts in the thinking of Alasdair McIntyre, as we shall see in due course.) No one can set out on a discovery from a vacuum.[27] Iris Murdoch too warns against a false subjectivity in which the ego dominates: " . . .real things can be looked at and loved without being seized and used,

without being appropriated into the greedy organism of the self."[28]
She says too, like Macmurray, that our search for truth must not
be for private possession but for communication; it must be "with
universal intent", as Plato said, speaking also of the conviviality of
such sharing.

What these and other writers are saying is that we desperately need
to bring synthesis into our thinking as an antidote to the long-lasting
and very powerful bias towards abstract analysis which began with
the medieval thinkers and continued through Galileo, who said that
nature was to be grasped by measurement not sympathy; to Bacon,
for whom truth and utility were the same thing and the method
was to analyse, quantify, and organize in measurable categories; to
Locke, praised by Voltaire for applying the principles of dissection
to human psychology; and to Auguste Comte who wanted to subject social phenomena to invariable natural laws. This provoked a
counter-attack from the poets, particularly William Blake, who laid
into the scientists: "You accumulate Particulars and murder by ana-
lyzing that you may take the aggregate, and you call the aggregate
Moral Law."

> I come
> To cast off Bacon, Locke and Newton from Albion's covering . . .
> To cast off the idiot Questioner, who is always questioning
> And never capable of answering . . .
> Who publishes Doubt and calls it Knowledge; whose Science
>   is despair

The quotation is taken from Reeves who also quotes Wordsworth's
TheExcursion, lines 957–68:

> Of mighty Nature, if 'twas ever meant
> That we should pry far off, yet be unraised;
> That we should pere, and dwindle as we pere,
>   Viewing all objects unremittingly
>   In disconnection dead and spiritless;
> And still dividing; and dividing still,
> Break down all grandeur, still unsatisfied
> With the perverse attempt, while littleness
> May yet become more little; waging thus
> An impious warfare with the very life
>   Of our own Souls!

And Shelley: "The cultivation of the sciences which have enlarged
the limits of the empire of man over the external world, has, for
want of the poetical faculty, proportionately circumscribed those of
the internal world; and man, having enslaved the elements, remains
himself a slave." The conclusion he draws from this is : "The cultivation of poetry is never more to be desired than at periods when,

from the excess of selfish calculating principles, the accumulation of the materials of external life exceed the quality of the power of assimilating them to the internal laws of human nature."

If only the prescient warnings of these three great English Romantic poets could have been heeded, especially that last profound remark of Shelley. The task he implicitly sets there has still to be tackled, and the consequences, if it is not tackled soon, could be terrible. Humphrey Davy said that the purpose of man was "by his experiments to interrogate nature with power, not simply as a scholar, passive and seeking only to understand her operations, but rather as a master, active with his instruments." We can see today the damage these instruments have inflicted: on the tropical rain forests; on northern forests and lakes; on the ozone layer which protects all life; on the hunting and gathering civilizations in different parts of the world which know how to live in harmonious balance with nature; on the present starving populations of the Third World; on the human psyche in the developed nations, where gross wealth and poverty go together with a total lack of concern for the world's hungry and needy. The Romantic poets had a premonition of what would happen. Even earlier Schiller sensed the danger: "The preponderance of the analytical faculty must deprive the imagination of its energy and warmth . . . impressions can move the soul only as they remain whole."[29] The abstract, impersonal 'value-free' language that is now the fashion in certain disciplines would have horrified Schiller, Shelley, Wordsworth and Blake. We now have chairs of 'Human Resource Management'! In my opinion the connection between such language and the use of 'smart weapons' to massacre helpless peasant soldiers and civilians in the Gulf War is a close one. This is reductionism in language whose purpose is, in Humphrey Davy's words, to control "as a master, with his instruments". But now the sharp edge is turned against man as well as nature. "Knowledge", says Reeves, "has not been for sharing but for furnishing a weapon of power in the competitive struggle for the individual. Its edges are sharp and its uses self-centred."

The total effect for many students of all this analysis and abstraction is a feeling of alienation from their studies. Yet Franz Kafka said: "A book must be an ice-axe to break the sea frozen within us"; and a recent Harvard University study of businessmen's needs stated: "People need well-developed hearts. Knowledge is for the nourishment of hearts."[30] This is so because, though science is able to tell us what we can do – and it seems nearly limitless – it "cannot help us decide what we want or how much of it. (It) can only help us live by those decisions. In the search for policies, science may thus clarify and inform the discussion, but may never dominate it."[31] Kennedy speaks of another type of highly damaging isolation between the sciences and 'liberal learning'. It is the "failure to understand the powerful interpenetration of scientific and humane ideas – and the resulting loss of much of science *as* culture." The price paid for this failure has been very great in the history of thought. Yet nowhere can the case for the interpenetration between the sciences and the humanities be made more compelling than in evolutionary thought, though Kennedy points out, ironically, that it was the Darwinian revolution that probably created the 'two cultures' problem in the first place. He says that the last period of confidence in the unity of human knowledge was the Enlightenment, after which the cosmological revolution turned God into a spectator; the geological revolution of Hutton, Playfair and Lyell replaced catastrophism by uniformitarianism; and Darwin did likewise for life science. Gradualism in place of creationism was a philosophical revolution. "What Darwin had accomplished, for once and all, was the demonstration that a single way of knowing was no longer possible."

So 'human nature' was in fact phylogenetically determined. Despite the misuse of Darwinian thinking by such as Spencer and Andrew Carnegie, with their 'survival of the fittest', and their modern descendant sociobiology, the real successor to Darwin is Freud who added ontogenetic determinants to the phylogenetic ones. Human nature, in Freud's view, is dominated by evolutionary shaping and by 'early influences' on the psyche. Thus the mind is part of biology; mental illness is part of the human condition. "Indeed", says Kennedy, "in just 100 years the biological sciences have triggered a most extraordinary concept of what it means to be human and to be free. It is a view so new and so robust that it sometimes threatens to crowd out traditional choice and conventional morality. The focus on the individual is so powerful that the world shrinks as the self swells. If there is a defect in our behaviour, if we fail in what we suspect may be an obligation, there are a host of comforting explanations . . . selfish genes, oppressive early experiences, or defects in caticholamine biochemistry. Finding an ethical path within our new vision of self is one of the great tasks of contemporary humanism."

Nor is this all. Our view of reality, our perceptions, have been changed in a way that tends to internalize and therefore individualize them. It appears that our perception of the world is profoundly affected "by patterns of neural connections that have been assembled over evolutionary time . . . to extract features of the world that are of particular relevance. There is not one single, objectively verifiable world. This is to say that many of the parameters we thought belonged to the external world are in fact fixed by our biological endowment. So we may well, thinks Kennedy, be innately committed to some qualities "we thought we were choosing freely and on the basis of individual experience." The conclusion must be that *The Origin of Species* and its twentieth-century offspring have led us to an expanded view of what is within us as opposed to what is without, so that we are compelled to pay more attention to degrees of difference between individuals. This does not damage the notion of equality, says Kennedy. "Equal is not identical; different is not unequal." Society must reform social opportunity for all.

"Accelerating culture becomes the milieu in which the selection of biological capacities takes place", and the latter, in turn, speed up further cultural evolution. "So tight and so effective is this interplay that it has wrought the most rapid change in biological structure since evolution began – the growth of the human neocortex." And this has produced an almost frightening rate of change in our cultural developments. Kennedy's optimistic conclusion is that this linkage between the two kinds of evolution will in time produce "a complementary relationship between our biological endowment and our social arrangements." But for this to happen the cleavage between the humanities and science must be ended, for it "robs us of a critical understanding: that they are the products of a co-evolutionary process, just as surely as the brain and culture are. *This unity is the brightest and most exciting academic vision we could have.*" (My italics)

"Dogmas are only given up when they become inadequate not in logic but in life."[32] Kennedy's pointing up of the consequences of modern developments in biology deals a heavy blow to the dogma of the complete separation of science from philosophy, of a fundamental cleavage between man and the physical universe. So does his call for us to find "an ethical path within our new vision of self", since logical positivism had dismissed ethics as fairy tales. He is not alone in this, nor should we expect him to be, since the dangers implicit in the blind pursuit of the scientific dogma and the policies flowing from it are becoming ever more obvious. As Nash points out[33], science developed in a bourgeois society, based on a capitalist economy, and so the dogma of the scientific movement "stands in the same relation to the doctrines of orthodox economic theory as it does to the doctrines of experimental science." We have glimpsed the tracks along which the ever faster linear development of these interlinked parallel movements is leading us: in the one case ever deeper into the infinitesimally small in the pursuit of the ultimate particle; ever further out into space and back in time to get nearer and nearer to the Big Bang; and in molecular biology the unravelling of the human genome, so that, in literal fact, we shall know what makes wo/man tick – in the other case the ever faster, ever more efficient destruction and ever more wasteful consumption of the biosphere's resources, until at last man destroys species by hundreds and is near to ripping apart the whole delicately balanced ecological web of life on earth. In both cases the paradigm of linear striving towards an empty ultimate goal is the same.

Gigantic sums of money are squandered on these undertakings while a large percentage of the human race lives in sub-human conditions, with huge numbers dying of starvation. These things are being done in "the most materially blessed societies the world has ever known" and which "seem only to create an ever more mediocre culture."[34] In these societies "the contented and the self-approving" are a majority of the voters[35] and they support, so far at any rate without complaint, a New World Order, the sharp edge of which is directed against poor Third World countries whose raw materials are needed to sustain the First World's enormous wealth. It is hardly surprising that contemporary writers make statements such as "Progress culminates in the recognition that life is meaningless";[36] or "The barbarians are not waiting beyond the frontiers, they have already been governing us for quite some time. And it is our lack of consciousness of this that constitutes part of our predicament."[37] Not far short of 200 years ago Blake had damned "the idiot Questioner . . . whose Science is Despair."

So inadequate has the scientific dogma become in life that a fightback has begun, following such scouts as A. N. Whitehead early this century. One such is Patrick Nuttgens who, in a book devoted to teaching in higher education,[38] attacks the dualism which has done such grave damage to education. Paraphrasing Karl Popper, he says that there is no division between things and thoughts. It is his view that the modern world cannot be understood without some grasp of technology, yet for 150 years education has had a dislike and fear of technology.[39] The interaction of things or physical realities with thoughts and ideas or concepts is the very substance of education. An active interaction between the perceiver and the perceived is essential, he says, citing David Attenborough's *Life on Earth* as having given millions of people a new understanding of life. He also quotes Sophocles who said: "One must learn by doing the thing. You may think you know, but you have no certainty until you try it." Being an architect, he places much emphasis on design, which, he says, is "man's major activity in history."[40] He believes that, far from destroying our perceptions, technology can greatly enlarge the richness and fascination of the world. "Things contain the very essence of beauty. The beginning of aesthetic experience, of the experience of beauty, of the rightness of form, and the memorability of shape and colour and light is in the appreciation of things, either natural or man-made . . . What an astonishing world of wonder and delight is discovered by the cool observation of the mundane." Anyone who has watched a Formula One race, or an America's cup race, or an airshow must surely agree with Nuttgens.

And it relates to a training for work; it is fundamentally related to activity, rather than to inert knowledge. He maintains that there is no problem in primary education where children get to pull things apart and see how they work. But then comes a grey world of abstraction in secondary school. "My point is that by maintaining this schism between ideas and physical realities, we have placed a desert area at the heart of our learning processes in secondary school and lost an approach and incentive to living which is vitally necessary in the adult world of work and society." Or, as Robert Louis Stevenson put it, rather more pithily: "Books are good enough in their own way, but they are a mighty bloodless substitute for life." And *he* spent most of his short life writing them. Nuttgens quotes Whitehead, who seems to crop up all the time in this discussion: "The antithesis between a technical and a liberal education is fallacious. There can be no adequate technical education which is not liberal; that is no education which does not impart both technique and intellectual vision. In simpler language education should turn out the pupil with something he knows well and something he can do well." Nuttgens adds that if he can do something well, he can do so because he knows it well, and if he knows it well, he does so because he has come to grips with the experience of doing it.

Nuttgens stresses that technology is not applied science, that in fact technology, whose origins lie in the solving of practical problems, precedes science. He reminds that the Greek work for art was *techne* and quotes Robert Pirsig: "The ancient Greeks never separated art from manufacture in their minds, and so never developed separate words for them . . . This divorce of art from technology is completely unnatural. It's just that it's gone on so long that you have to be an archaeologist to find out where the two separated." He sums up this part of his argument by recalling Whitehead's affirmation that the neglect of technical education as an ingredient in the complete development of human beings has arisen from two disastrous antitheses: that between mind and body, and that between thought and action. This dualism must be overcome, and he refers to two important works by the Scottish moral philosopher John Macmurray.

9

Philosophy and Higher Education 3

From Erigena to MacIntyre
In his Reith Lectures, subsequently published as two books, *The Self as Agent* and *Persons in Relation*,[1] Macmurray discusses dualism exhaustively. Many of its aspects are unreal, he says; for example the mind/body problem is in fact "no problem but a patent absurdity". "The unity of experience as whole is not a unity of knowledge but a unity of personal activities of which knowledge is only one." Macmurray finds that unity lies in action, for action is a unity of knowledge and movement. He rejects dualism, therefore, but asserts the primacy of the practical. The practical is primary, the theoretical is secondary and derivative. He points out that in thinking the mind alone is active, but that in action both the body and the mind are active, for action is not blind. "When we turn from reflection to action we do not turn from consciousness to unconsciousness. When we act, sense, perception and judgment are in continuous activity, along with continuous movement." Thus in the nineteenth century Oxford and Cambridge were concerned with thought, reflection or knowledge for its own sake, believing that action was inferior. As we have seen, nineteenth century Oxford considered that knowledge for its own sake was the highest peak to which an education could aspire. It is not surprising that these two universities were unique in Europe in holding such a view. The tragedy is that, because of their wealth and influence, the permanent, firm backing of the English Establishment, and English snobbery, they were able to drag the whole of British education, including eventually even the Scottish universities, down the same blind alley.

For Macmurray, the starting-point of personal development is the development of the ability to act, but "the isolated, purely individual self is a fiction in philosophy". Action can only take place through interaction with others, but paradoxically it is the key to personal development. His central thesis is that all meaningful knowledge is for the sake of action, and all meaningful action for the sake of friendship. The primary critical task is the discovery of the problem. "The essential reference of theoretical to practical activities does not involve the control of theory by practice. It consists even more significantly in the control of practice by theory: in the determination through reflection of the ends of action."[2] In ancient Greece the question was 'What should we do?' Now the question is 'How can we know?' This, says Macmurray, is incomplete. The complete question is 'How can we know what we should do?' The logical empiricists, he says, have discarded the problems in order to maintain the method, whereas the existentialists have relinquished the method in wrestling with the problems. So the existentialists achieve a minimum of form, and the logical empiricists a minimum of substance. In other words, in philosophy form and matter have parted company. The existentialists see that the problem of the present lies in a crisis of the personal, whereas logical empiricists recognize it as a crisis of logical form and method. Both are correct and both are one-sided.[3] We must take the primacy of practical reason as our starting-point and eliminate dualism, "for it is the assumption of the primacy of the theoretical in our philosophical tradition which institutes a formal dualism that cannot be resolved; that the basic form of this dualism is the division of experience into theoretical and practical and that this dualism makes it impossible to think the unity of the Self and so to determine the form of a personal experience. We have therefore to begin by rejecting dualism through asserting the primacy of the practical."[4] Any philosophy which takes Descartes' 'cogito' as its starting-point creates a formal dualism of theory and practice and makes it impossible even to conceive the possibility of persons in relation, whether the relation be theoretical – as knowledge – or practical – as cooperation. If we make the 'I think' the primary postulate of philosophy, we make action logically inconceivable, because thought can never generate action. "We may formulate this dualism in different ways, as a dualism of mind and body, of mind and matter, of theory and practice, of appearance and reality, of subjective and objective, of phenomenal and noumenal worlds, but we can never abolish it."[5] When we act, our consciousness – our seeing, being, remembering, thinking does not *accompany*, but is *integrated with*, our bodily movements, and partly determines them. The body-mind problem is therefore fictitious."[6]

Macmurray was Professor of Moral Philosophy at the University of Edinburgh from 1944 to 1960, and for him philosophy is "the attempt to understand the meaning of human experience in the world". He gave radio talks in the early 1930s in which he put forward this vision of philosophy as a form of "democratic intellectualism": "Philosophy goes dry and barren and meaningless when most people are not interested in it. It really comes to life when the mass of men begin to feel the need of it, to call for it, to support the struggling intelligence of the philosopher with sympathy, with the sense that what he does matters to men." He criticises scientism and develops a 'personalist' philosophy (reminiscent of *le personnalisme* developed in a religious context round the review *Esprit* in France). He stresses the importance of self-criticism, personal responsibility, personal merit; the loss of these qualities leads to an increasing loss of the human subject. This is again reminiscent of French thinking, in particular Foucault in *Les Mots et les Choses*. "The sense of personal dignity as well as of personal unworthiness will tend to atrophy, with the decline in habits of self-examination. Success will tend to become the criterion of rightness, and there will spread through society a temper which is extraverted, pragmatic and merely objective, for which all problems are soluble by better organization."

Macmurray insists that there is no irrationalism involved in this position: "Our real nature as persons is to be reasonable and to extend our·capacity for reason." But reason cannot be "passionless reflection"; the divorce that has been created between reason and emotion is quite arbitrary and groundless, for "Reason is the capacity to behave in terms of the nature of the object". Macmurray's clinching argument is that "If our feelings are subjective because they occur in us, why not our thoughts which as surely occur to us? If our thoughts are objective because they refer to objects, then our feelings, which refer to objects in their own fashion, are objective also." Beveridge and Turnbull, in *The Eclipse of Scottish Culture*, say that, like another two Scottish moral philosophers, Baillie and Macquarrie, to whom we shall come in a moment, Macmurray is "opposed to the positivist identification of knowledge with rational scientific knowledge. He reverses the conventional notion that art is somehow less objective than science, less concerned with things as they really are, by arguing that science, which is concerned with general properties rather than individual things, yields a more superficial form of knowledge." Macmurray says: "Scientific knowledge is knowledge about things, not knowledge of them. If we have to choose, we must say that it is the person with the artist's sensibility, rather than the scientist's, who really knows the world."

Of *The Self as Agent* Beveridge and Turnbull have this to say: "This book is a deconstruction of the whole way of approaching the world and our experience of it which the successes of natural science have rendered dominant." This is at once an explanation of the little attention accorded to Macmurray by contemporary British philosophers, and of his very great importance to the revival of the democratic intellect and to rescuing the world from the high-tech barbarism which has befallen it. This was described by H. J. Paton as *The Modern Predicament* in his Gifford lectures of 1950–51, in which he said: "It is a serious matter, both for the individual and society, if men are to be told that there can be no objective moral principles – because these are not the same as scientific generalizations."

A modern Scottish school of moral philosophy has developed in the attempt to alert the world to this highly dangerous position, whose devastating concrete results we see all around us. In addition to John Anderson, whom we have dealt with, and Alasdair MacIntyre, whom we are about to discuss, Beveridge and Turnbull refer to John Baillie and John Macquarrie among others. Baillie, who was Professor of Divinity at Edinburgh from 1934 to 1956 and for whom, as he said, "reality is personal", detested the school of logical and conceptual analysis which dominated philosophy at Oxford and Cambridge. He feared that the spread of scientism, which identifies reality with the realm of natural facts, was undermining our social and moral senses – a view for which there is overwhelming contemporary evidence. "Reductive naturalism", stripping the world of ethics and interpersonal experience, has a deleterious effect on those influenced by it: "Nor do I speak here of their morals in any ordinary sense . . . but of a certain painful restriction of interest, of understanding and sympathy, which seems to leave them as very incomplete human beings . . . " Baillie was concerned about the ethical subjectivism of the positivist school, what MacIntyre calls 'emotivism'. He felt he must trust his experience – "my sense experience, my social experience and my moral experience". For him knowledge of persons was the very type and pattern of what we mean by knowledge, since "of no other existents is our knowledge so intimate and direct . . . The world of natural objects, real as it is at its own level, offers to my will a much less stubborn resistance than that offered by my encounter with my fellow men."

This challenge to the claim that scientific reason represents the primary mode of human cognition and the anxiety about its ethical consequences are shared by John Macquarrie in two works, *In Search of Humanity* and *Existentialism*. He makes a plea for a more human concept of knowledge, for "a wider concept of knowing than that of the Cartesian epistemological tradition . . ." In many subjects, and not least in the study of humanity itself, the idea of detachment is a hindrance." This does not mean that thought must become more subjective; what is needed is a broader concept of knowledge resting on a correspondingly broader apprehension of reality. "There are many rich strands in human existence that ought not to be ignored or downgraded just because they cannot be fitted into the logic of mathematics or of the empirical sciences. This is not to condemn logic or to embark on intellectual anarchy. At its best, it is an attempt to develop a logic of persons in addition to our logic of things." For Macquarrie "the goal is to become a person-in-community for no person exists in isolation". This self in situation – in his family, in his village, in his community – moving towards a goal which can be ethically evaluated, is the classical conception of the self, the conception of Aristotle.

It is this classical, Aristotelian conception of the self and of ethics that Alasdair MacIntyre intends to reassert in what Beveridge and Turnbull call his "awesome attempt to restructure the way we think about morality, the way we conceive the human self, and the way in which we live our lives". As with John Anderson, it is modernity itself which is being challenged.

Alasdair MacIntyre comes at the modern fact-value distinction through a sort of historical-philosophical analysis of what he sees as the failure of the Enlightenment project in its various avatars down to the table rase of Nietzschean nihilism. "The empiricist concept", he says[7], "was intended to discriminate the basic elements from which our knowledge is constructed and on which it is founded; beliefs and theories are to be vindicated or not, depending on the verdict of the various elements of experience. But the observations of the natural scientist are never in this sense basic. We do indeed bring hypotheses to the test of observation, but our observations in turn can always be put to the question. The belief that Jupiter has seven moons is put to the test of observation through a telescope; but the observation itself has to be vindicated by the theories of geometrical optics. Theory is required to support observation, just as much as observation theory." He finds something extraordinary in the coexistence of empiricism and natural science in the same culture, "for they represent radically different and incompatible ways of approaching the world". Yet they were part of the same world-view in the eighteenth century, which is why "that world-view is at its best radically incoherent". MacIntyre cites *Tristram Shandy* in illustration: the world as a series of jokes. Modern life is dominated by bureaucratic managerial expertise (in the universities also), and its aspiration to value neutrality (Chairs of Human Resource Management, Chairs of Management Science) and its drive to manipulative power (e.g. the bureaucratic "appraisal" of university

staffs) "derive from the history of the way in which the realm of fact
and the realm of value were distinguished by the philosophers of
the seventeenth and eighteenth centuries. Twentieth century life",
continues MacIntyre, "turns out in key part to be the concrete and
dramatic re-enactment of eighteenth century philosophy".[8]

We no longer know what the good life is. MacIntyre quotes
Bertrand Russell in *Religion and Science* : "If two men differ about
values, there is not a disagreement as to any kind of truth, but a
difference of taste." He cites also Ronald Dworkin who says more
recently that the central doctrine of modern liberalism is the thesis that questions about the good life for man and of the ends of
human life "are to be regarded from the public standpoint as systematically unsettlable".[9] MacIntyre contrasts this view with that
expounded by Aristotle: "The modern contrast between the sphere
of morality on the one hand and the sphere of human sciences on
the other is quite alien to Aristotelianism because . . . the modern
fact-value distinction is also alien to it."[10] A man in heroic society is what he does; morality and social structure are one and the
same; morality is always attached to particularity. For Aristotle the
polis is concerned with the whole of life, with man's good as such.
"Lawgivers", he says, "seem to make friendship a more important
aim than justice".[11] The virtues are embodied in practices. When,
for example, a university bears a tradition of practice or practices,
"its common life will be partly, but in a centrally important way,
constituted by a continuous argument as to what a university is
and ought to be". We have already seen that no such argument is
taking place in Britain's universities today. In modern liberalism,
which MacIntyre calls "bureaucratic individualism", all such concerns become marginal. As work is put at the service of impersonal
capital, it becomes "separated from everything but the service of biological survival and the reproduction of the labour force, on the one
hand, and that of institutionalized acquisitiveness on the other".[12]
Pleonexia, a sin for Aristotle, has become the driving-force of modern productive work, so that practices with goods, that is values,
internal to themselves, have been removed to the margins of social
and cultural life. The market economy has taken over. Jane Austen,
whose concern for her heroines' finances is a central feature of her
writing, was, says David Daiches, "a Marxist before Marx".[13]

MacIntyre's conclusion in *After Virtue* is "that on the one hand
we still, in spite of the efforts of three centuries of moral philosophy
and one of sociology, lack any coherent rationally defensible statement of a liberal individualist point of view; and that, on the other
hand, the Aristotelian tradition can be restated in a way that restores
intelligibility and rationality to our moral and social attitudes and

commitments."[14] He warns that we must preserve local forms of community that will sustain moral and intellectual life "through the new dark ages which are already upon us". One is irresistibly reminded of Walter Miller Jnr's *A Canticle for Leibowitz*.

Seven years later MacIntyre renewed his attack on dualism:

> It is a Cartesian error, fostered by a misunderstanding of Euclidean geometry, to suppose that first by an initial act of apprehension we can comprehend the full meaning of the premises of a deductive system and then only secondly proceed to enquire what follows from them. In fact it is only so far as we understand what follows from the premises that we understand the premises themselves . . . So in the construction of any demonstrative science we both argue from what we take, often rightly, to be subordinate truths to first principles, as well as from first principles to subordinate truths . . . "[15]

This view of how first principles are understood is at odds both with Cartesian accounts of the structure of philosophical and scientific theory and also with the moral theories of thinkers as various as Hobbes, Hume, Bentham and Kant. No agreed conception of the good is any longer possible. The individual is now seen as one of the most fundamental categories of human thought, and the key question for him is: why should he submit himself to the constraints of any social order?

MacIntyre now takes the case of Enlightenment Scotland to illustrate his argument. When Scotland lost its independence by the Act of Union of 1707 politics was closed to all but a few Scots. The arena moved to London, to a continuing English Parliament, and the Scots politicians who moved with it were willing to become almost totally subservient to the purposes of the English ruling elite. There was, however, what we might today call a counter-culture, an alternative mode of civil and social existence in Scotland capable of resisting, "to a large degree and for some length of time, the pressures toward the anglicization of Scottish culture and society". In this culture "the tasks of rational justification by appeal to principles with an authority independent of the social order were central". Thus, the Scottish legal, theological and educational systems had the responsibility of rationally justifying socially shared beliefs and socially approved actions and institutional arrangements. They did this by showing in detail how particular subordinate conclusions could be derived by valid deductive inference from appropriate intermediate principles that could in turn be justified by deduction from first principles.

Every individual, in making career choices and life decisions had to work them out in the light of this framework of theological, legal and moral principles. The university-educated Scot had an even more fundamental decision to make. Should he continue to live in Scotland the life laid out by these peculiar Scottish beliefs and customs or should he try to become anglicized while living in Scotland, by transferring Scottish ways into English ways, or should he emigrate? This involved fundamental choices in all areas: career, location, religion, manners, habits, and even how to talk and write. This could have comic aspects; for instance great men like David Hume and the literati of Edinburgh taking elocution lessons to learn to 'speak proper', for, as the Rev. Alex Carlyle of Inveresk said, "To every man bred in Scotland the English language was a foreign tongue." It also had supremely tragic aspects: the Gaels, mostly Catholic, had to be rejected as enemy aliens.

As trade developed, Scotland, especially the cities, became more and more anglicized; English fashions, manners, idioms and accents "were more and more invasive". Thus a variety of English stand-points appear in the Scottish internal debate of the eighteenth century, and, in the case of Hume, for example, exert a powerful influence. To bring out the great differences between Scottish and English ethical thought in the eighteenth century MacIntyre con-trasts *The Institutions of the Law of Scotland* of 1681 by Sir James Dalrymple of Stair and the *Commentaries on the Laws of England* of 1765 by Sir William Blackstone, a professor at Oxford. For Stair the primary duties of human beings are those required by obedience to God. Secondary obligations arising from human conventions and institutions serve to secure the rights that obedience to divine law would ensure. Thus the useful, the expedient and the profitable are defined in terms of what is just, equitable and right. "They in no way provide independent standards for right action." The contrast with Blackstone could not be greater; he says that God has so arranged things that "we should want no other prompter to inquire after and pursue the rule of right, but only our own self-love – that universal principle of action; God has not "perplexed the law of nature with a multitude of abstracted rules and precepts . . . but has graciously reduced the rule of obedience to this one paternal precept that man should pursue his own true and substantive happiness." This is the foundation of ethics or natural law. Further, "the doctrine of the law then is this: that precedent and rules must be followed unless flatly absurd or unjust". This is an account of the dominant English structures according to which the justification of the standards is internal to them. The standards by which established practice is to be judged are the standards already embodied in established prac-tice. The three principal differences between Stair and Blackstone are that for the former the rules of equity are among the first principles of justice; for the latter obligations depend on property, whereas Stair puts obligations before property; for Stair theology is the key, whereas for Blackstone it is redundant, since "man should pursue his own true and substantive happiness". Philosophy is at the heart of Stair's position, property at the heart of Blackstone's.

During this period moral philosophy achieved an authority in Scottish culture rarely seen at other times and places. An attempt was made in the late seventeenth century to get the universities to adopt a common philosophy curriculum, but it broke down over the well-known Scottish "philosophical itch to dispute all things". Already in 1708 the Edinburgh Town Council replaced the regents with professors of philosophy; something, as we have seen, that Andrew Melville would have liked to do in 1580. "The task of a professor of moral philosophy in eighteenth century Scotland came to be that of providing a defence of just those fundamental principles, conceived of as antecedent to both all positive law and all practical forms of social organization, which defined peculiarly Scottish institutions and attitudes." Philosophical debate began in the university class-rooms because lectures were supplemented by discussion periods where students were interrogated by the professor, and lectures were given to "tradesmen and youths from the town".[16] In addition, philosophical societies were set up in the university towns, for example, the Aberdeen Philosophical Society in 1758. The combined effect of all this was to produce a wide readership for all aspects of philosophical, sociological and scientific enquiry, and – a very rare phenomenon – a philosophically educated public "with shared standards of rational justification and a shared deference to a teaching authority, the professor of philosophy and especially of moral philosophy".

What is more, there was broad agreement between the philosophers and the professors of law, mathematics and physics as to the form of rational justification: the deduction of subordinate conclusions from evident first principles, as in Euclidean geometry. Sir William Hamilton described the chair of mathematics at Edinburgh as one "which has hitherto always owed the celebrity it has enjoyed not certainly more to the mathematical skill than to the philosophical ability and varied learning of its professors". So, says MacIntyre, moral philosophy was a system of enquiry closely related to other forms of enquiry. This resulted in an integrated scheme whose disciplinary parts involved continuous reference to each other. And this scheme was reflected in the curriculum, so that the professors who taught had to have wide general knowledge outside their own specialism, especially the professors of moral philosophy who provided the central focus of the curriculum. (We recall that one of the major reasons for the failure of the new universities, two and a half centuries later, to reintroduce breadth and interdisciplinarity into the curriculum, was precisely that the professors were so narrowly specialized, on the Oxbridge model, as to be incapable of teaching outside their specialism.) Such a scheme, with such a central thrust, necessarily conflicted with the empiricism of such as John Locke and the rationalist metaphysical constructions of Descartes, Leibniz and Spinoza. As we have seen, the conception of justice must be independent of the passions and interests, so the whole intellectual scheme was at odds with thinkers like Hobbes.

The contradiction between this cultural tradition and the demands of Scotland's growing trade and commerce was evident in the eighteenth century. Politically it was clear in the comments of Fletcher of Saltoun, the most determined and most eloquent opponent of the Act of Union in the Scottish Parliament, who said that since the Act of Union Scotland had been ruled by those who were subservient to England, with the result "that we have from that time appeared to the rest of the world more like a conquered province than a free, independent people". It was clear philosophically in the work of Francis Hutcheson, professor of moral philosophy at the University of Glasgow. His views on justice and property were remarkably like those of Stair, while his views on epistemology, strongly influenced by Shaftesbury's two great principles of altruism and egoism, aligned him with Descartes, Malebranche, Locke et al. He said: "These two powers of perception, sensation and consciousness, introduce into the mind all its materials of knowledge. All our primary or direct ideas or notions are derived from one or other of these sources." We are back to dualism, the first person point of view, in which no socially shared standards are possible. Thus following Hutcheson, as McIntyre says, David Hume, Adam Smith, Thomas Reid and Dugald Stewart were faced with a choice: either to retain Hutcheson's epistemology and reject his view of moral principles and justice, or retain his central moral and theological position and reject the epistemology. Hume and Smith chose the first alternative, Reid and Stewart the second. Thus Hume and Smith became, to use MacIntyre's phrase, anglicizing subversives, because they abandoned Scottish modes of thought on society and morality for those of England. In his *Treatise on Human Nature* Hume depicted a system in which pride in property and hierarchy was the keystone; in which property determined rank; in which law and justice exist to protect the propertied and offer no appeal against the social order.[17] Hume described this as exhibiting the characteristics of universal human nature, "whereas in fact", says MacIntyre, "it is the highly specific way of life of the eighteenth-century English landowning class". He argues in favour of anything that will lead to economic growth in an anglicized Great Britain.

Hume is a strangely ambivalent figure. He loved Scotland and infinitely preferred to London the French capital where he was called 'le bon David'. Yet he went to elocution classes in Edinburgh to improve his English. He is one of the great names in the Western philosophical tradition, at the summit of dualistic liberal orthodoxy. Yet as both Alasdair MacIntyre and, as we shall see later, Alexander Broadie, show, his philosopohical positions were inimical to Scottish traditions of thought and to Scotland's nationhood. One wonders how great his fame would have been if he had espoused the Scottish Common Sense philosophy instead of the liberal philosophy which so well suited nascent English capitalism. As Ian Bell has said: "The Scottish Enlightenment for all its intellectual glory, was simultaneously the triumph of anglicization." In any detailed history of Scottish philosophy, there will need to be a serious re-evaluation of Hume's contribution to the Scottish philosophical tradition.

The liberal order, based on self-interest and the acquisition of wealth, has as its high priests, not the philosophers but the lawyers, and its growing decadence in England is documented by the many legal decisions, often by the highest courts in the land, which have recently had to be overturned as unsafe, frequently after the accused have spent many years in prison. In such a social order power lies with the wealthy, decision-making with the educated managerial classes. It does not provide, as it claims to, a neutral tradition-independent ground. There is, says MacIntyre, only "the practical-rationality-of-this-or-that-tradition, and the justice-of-this-or-that-tradition". Yet most characteristic of the late twentieth century is a sort of rootless cosmopolitanism, a desire to be at home anywhere except in the "backward, outmoded, undeveloped cultures of tradition". A sort of cultural and social entropy is at work, evidenced most perhaps by the world-wide influence of Hollywood and the recent creation of a Euro-Disneyland in – of all countries – France!

What then is the effect of this liberal culture on the universities? The foundation of the liberal university came – and it came very late in England – with the abolition of religious tests for university teachers. The result was not, as might have been expected, that the universities became places of organized intellectual debate between contending philosophies and points of view. What happened was that, in appointing university teachers, reference was made only to a sort of generalized academic competence. To this there corresponded in the lecture room a concept of objectivity which required the lecturer to teach *as if* there were shared standards of rationality accepted by both teacher and students. Curriculum subjects too were abstracted from contending points of view. "Universities became institutions committed to upholding a fictitious objectivity." This did least harm to teaching and research in the natural sciences and most harm to the humanities in which the loss of the context of traditions of enquiry has deprived teachers of standards by which to evaluate the relative importance of texts and theories. So there is an inconclusiveness about teaching outside the natural sciences that leaves the student to his/her own preference. So the student leaves university with a set of skills, a set of preferences and little else. "There is thus", concludes MacIntyre, "a deep incompatibility between the standpoint of any rational tradition of enquiry and the dominant modes of contemporary teaching, discussion and debate, both academic and non-academic". The standpoint of a tradition presupposes debate between conflicting understandings of reality; recognition of different types of language being used; recognition of the historical situatedness both of traditions and individuals. The standpoint of the forums of modern liberal culture presupposes only the fiction of shared universal standards of rationality together with the possibility of a common language for all speakers; and the irrelevance of historical tradition. The contradiction is complete. It is such a contradiction that has been seen between Scottish and English ways of thinking about justice, natural law, community and property during the last twenty years. The Scottish traditions have not disappeared despite the efforts of David Hume's successors throughout the past two centuries, This contradiction and the growing English domination of Scotland's universities are doing terrible damage to Scotland's great traditions in higher education. It is time we reverted to our own academic traditions, and particularly to the central importance of moral philosophy, first because it is our own tradition, and secondly because the world's gigantic problems desperately need such an approach. The Scottish professional middle class, who started the rot for their own selfish minority reasons, as we have seen, must weigh their responsibilities very carefully. If they do not soon start to pay off their debt by giving strong leadership in this struggle to regain our intellectual traditions, it could be the end of the democratic intellect, *finis* to a tradition that set moral obligation higher than personal gain – the demise of "the thinking nation".

I shall deal later on with the intellectual contribution that Scotland could make towards tackling the daunting environmental and social problems that plague the world today. This, however, is the place to attempt to sum up the traditional Scottish way of thinking, in

so far as I am capable of it. The reader will recall my mentioning
Scotus Erigena at the beginning of this book, his philosophical boldness and innovativeness for which he was declared a heretic. From
whichever side of the sixteen mile wide strait between Scotland and
the northernmost tip of Ireland he came, he belonged to the same
Celtic Church[18] as Columba, and indeed as Pelagius whose heresy
was "the kindly notion that a new-born baby does not come into
the world with the name-tag 'original sinner' and that heaven could
be attained by living a life of virtue without having to be given a
ticket at the door marked 'an act of special grace'."[19] Purser adds
that centuries later Duns Scotus (from Duns in the Scottish Borders)
"echoes their faith in the power of the human will, and he too was
marginalised philosophically to such an extent that the word 'dunce'
is derived from his name" (It might not, perhaps be stretching it too
far to suggest that Macmurray and MacIntyre have similarly been
marginalised because their holistic views do not fit the contemporary
positivistic and reductionist fashion given such prominence by the
metropolitan megaphone.)

Duns Scotus in the thirteenth century necessarily had to teach and
write abroad – Oxford, Cambridge, Paris and Cologne – because
there were as yet no Scottish universities. As soon as one was created
(St Andrews, 1411) philosophy began to be taught in Scotland, and
soon the teaching was as good as anywhere in Europe. Most of these
early teachers were graduates of continental universities, above all
from Paris. It is a remarkable fact that between its foundation in
the twelfth century and the Reformation the University of Paris had
some seventeen or eighteen Scottish rectors. St Andrews was thus
run by men who had been taught and had lectured at Paris, the
great centre of excellence in philosophy at that period. St Andrews
was thus a Paris *in petto*. These philosophers included Lawrence
of Lindores, St Andrews' first rector, John Ireland, a rector of
Paris University, James Liddell, the first Scot to have a book of his
printed while still alive, Thomas Kennedy, another rector of Paris,
John Mair (or Major) from a village near Haddington, who became
Principal of the University of Glasgow in 1518, Robert Walterston,
another Haddington man, David Cranston, George Lokert of Ayr,
Robert Holket, William Manderston, Robert Galbraith, Gilbert
Crab of Aberdeen, and Hector Boece, the first Principal of the University of Aberdeen in 1491. Most of these people were associated
with John Mair at Paris. Alexander Broadie, in *The Tradition of
Scottish Philosophy*, speaks of them as "a galaxy of philosophical
talent". At the same time there were Scottish students in universities
all over Europe: Vienna, Cologne, Louvain, Bologna, Poitiers and
many others.[20]

The circle of philosophers round John Mair were mostly logicians and their major concerns were human freewill and the nature of knowledge. In their preoccupation with the freedom of the will and with virtue they are clearly linked to those early thinkers we have mentioned and, as Broadie[21] demonstrates in *The Tradition of Scottish Philosophy*, to which I am greatly indebted, there are "crucial parallels . . . between the doctrines of the medieval and the Enlightenment philosophers . . . " He demonstrates that the debate between the two central medieval doctrines of realism and nominalism – Is the 'cattiness' of cats out there in the real world or is it a mental construct? – is reflected in the positions taken up in the eighteenth century by David Hume and Thomas Reid, the greatest exponent of the Scottish Common Sense Philosophy.[22] "Hume's philosophy is in many ways a continuation, along nominalist lines, of some his pre-Reformation predecessors." Of course, he recognized that realism is the position for mankind in general: "'Tis certain that almost all mankind, and even philosophers themselves, for the greatest part of their lives, take their perceptions to be their only objects, and suppose, that the very being which is intimately present to the mind, is the real body or material existence." It was Reid who provided the philosophical justification of the realist position. Broadie not only states that a line of philosophical influence can be traced from Mair's circle to the philosophers of the Scottish Enlightenment; he argues that there are "important philosophical identities between doctrines of the earlier period and of the later". There are strong similarities between certain of Thomas Reid's most characteristic doctrines and those of the earlier philosophers. These doctrinal similarities are to be found most particularly in the eighteenth century versions of medieval nominalism and of the "theory of notions . . . found in the writings of Hume and Reid".

This is not the place nor am I the person to write a detailed analysis of the fundamental differences between Hume and Reid in these two areas. Readers may refer to Broadie's excellent book. Suffice it to say that Hume fully accepted the theory of ideas put forward by Descartes, to which we have often referred, and that he was influenced by Newtonian mechanics. Broadie says that "Hume investigated, more fully than any previous writer, the logical implications of (Descartes') theory". But he had adopted it without critical examination. Reid, on the other hand, did subject Descartes' theory of ideas to close examination and "concluded that it was incoherent".

Thomas Reid succeeded Adam Smith in 1764 as Professor of Moral Philosophy in the University of Glasgow. He published two books based on his lectures: in 1786 his *Essays on the Active Powers of the Human Mind*. They attack Hume's system and defend common sense.

"We shall see", says Broadie in a striking phrase, "that members of Mair's circle are in ghostly attendance; for a characteristic doctrine of that circle reaches out across a gap of two and a half centuries and takes its place as the central thesis of Reid's philosophy." That doctrine was the role of notions in John Mair's philosophy which, says Broadie, is the same as the role of ideas in Reid's. Mair regards notions as operations of the mind, and so does Reid regard ideas as operations of the mind. Neither Mair nor Reid see any need for an object of knowledge intermediate between an idea, considered as a mental operation, and its object. "Both Mair and Reid allowed that no notion or idea of an act of perception is possible unless we can have a notion or idea of an external object . . . Thus a perceptual notion is a mental act by which we apprehend a perceptual object. It, so to say, reaches out into the physical world, enabling us to make immediate perceptual contact with it." Mair says: 'In vain is it laid down that through the same notion we know two objects, one intuitively and the other abstractively, since everything could be maintained by saying that through that notion by itself the external object is known.' What Mair says on the matter seems common sense. And the particular common-sensical point that he makes here links him directly with the Scottish Common Sense School which flourished two and a half centuries later." Neither Mair nor Reid doubt the existence of external objects, whereas Hume sees "no rational basis for the belief that the external world has a truly independent existence".[23] In other words, both Mair and Reid reject dualism; for them "the notion is the mind in act", a phrase which forcefully reminds us of the moral philosophy of John Macmurray.

Elsewhere Broadie speaks of William Manderston's concept of will which lies at the heart of his moral philosophy. The main concept he explores is 'virtue', which he sees as being placed in the will, as being a disposition of the will. "In line with his conception of the will as the faculty of freedom, he holds that a meritorious act is immediately within the free power of a person . . . " "A person's free will can produce an act which is morally entirely good without God's special help . . . " This follows Aristotle's line that the virtues are dispositions of a rational person, that the exercise of virtue is always and necessarily an exercise of reason. Here the parallel with Alasdair MacIntyre is evident, and it also reaches back to Pelagius, John Scotus Erigena and Duns Scotus. I would not wish, being no philosopher, to push my argument too hard, but it does seem to me that one can discern a consistent thread,[24] over nearly 1200 years, in Scottish philosophy, and that its two main components are: a holistic approach to the world and to human action based on the rejection of dualism, whether nominalist, Cartesian, Lockeian or Humeian; and the conviction that virtue, right action, is a product of man's will.

We shall now examine to what extent these deeply and long held convictions, so different from the English empirical approach, are reflected in the concept of the 'democratic intellect', which has come to encapsulate the particular qualities of Scottish education, at least until the end of the nineteenth century.

10

The Democratic Intellect 1

Deduction v Induction

Henry Thomas Buckle was deeply puzzled by the Scots intellect.[1] He shared the same sort of preoccupations as J. S. Mill, Auguste Comte and Herbert Spencer, that is, he wanted to construct a science of society, a 'historical science' in the same way that Adam Ferguson had tried to create a science of morals and politics in his *Essay on the History of Civil Society* in the eighteenth century. An interesting sidelight on him is that he preferred Adam Smith to David Hume for "that invaluable quality of imagination".[2]

He set himself the task of "reducing the history of nations to the study of the logical patterns established by their characteristic modes of thought". So he was a reductionist. Scientific advance, in Buckle's view, could only stem from inductive methods of reasoning. Because of the power of the Church a country like Spain was very weak in science. Scotland, therefore, set a real problem because he saw it as being the only country in Europe where there was a continuous battle between ecclesiastical obscurantism and enlightenment, yet the former always seemed to win. "How was it that a land of great philosophers was also a land of superstition?" Why were there such differences in outlook between the Scots and the English? Why was the church history of the two countries so different? Why was the Scottish Enlightenment so different from the Enlightenment in France and England? Why was there a clerically dominated religious revival in the first half of the nineteenth century which appeared to re-establish clerical tyranny? It was utterly unintelligible to the English. For Buckle the answer to all these questions was that the Scots preferred deduction to induction.[3]

For a man who wanted to create a 'historical science' Buckle's standpoint was anything but scientific. One might have expected a sober inductive analysis from historical data, but what, to our astonishment, we get, is an attitude of profound repulsion to the evangelical Disruption of 1843. In this Buckle was at one with his English compatriots for whom 1843 was a total mystery. So also, of course, were the contemporary debates about the future of Scottish education. Buckle, like John Stuart Mill in his attack on the ideas of Sir William Hamilton in 1865, "wanted to prevent the Scots from cutting themselves off from the rest of the civilized world".[4] Incomprehension could scarcely go further, since Scotland had always been in far closer contact with the "civilized world" of Europe than England. Here we see the beginning of a trend that was to have a disastrous effect on Scottish education at all levels. When referring to Scotland, what most English writers and thinkers mean by 'international' or 'the civilized world' is England. When they refer to Scotland as being parochial, what they mean is that it is reluctant to adopt English attitudes, since it always in the past had very close and multifarious contacts with Europe. They do not realize that it is they who are being parochial and that they are forcing Scotland to share their parochialism by channelling all its international contacts through London.[5]

Buckle's book, indeed, not only reflected and strengthened contemporary English opinion, but, more importantly, it had immediate practical repercussions on university education since it was published in 1861, that is soon after the Universities (Scotland) Act of 1858. George Davie says[6] that Buckle's book "may well have been decisive in hardening British public opinion against the claims of Scots philosophical education and against the institutions designed to carry on its traditions". Hanham says that "both the English and Scottish conservatives believed that Scotland should follow the example of Oxford and Cambridge and the English public schools, and now the liberals were being urged by Buckle and then by Mill to join in condemning Scottish education".[7] There are serious weaknesses, however, in Buckle's analysis. He tends to underestimate the role of intuition and deduction in the natural sciences, "where the scientist moves from a hypothesis, arrived at by intuition and deduction from known data, to experiment and verification in order to establish both particular facts and general themes, and he placed undue weight on the merits of induction".[8] Indeed, while failing to see that Newton was as much a model for the thinkers of the Scottish Enlightenment as for himself – had indeed been taught in Scotland before he was taught in England – he exaggerated Bacon's contributions to science, and this was no doubt due to a proclivity described by David Hume: "The national spirit which prevails among the English, and which forms their great happiness, is the cause why they bestow on all their eminent writers, and Bacon among the rest, such praises and acclamations as may often appear partial and excessive."[9] A very perceptive man, David Hume, for today we could say the same about the English *Schwärmerei* for footballers, mediocre boxers, middle distance runners, a Prime Minister and the BBC! Buckle was also guilty, as already indicated, of reductionism. He was "really proposing, albeit only broadly, to begin the reduction of all human affairs to the principle of natural law".[10] Another glaring weakness, which his editor admits, is the appalling litany of inferiorisation of things Scottish to which Buckle stoops. He quite rightly says that the country was almost incessantly at war from 80 A.D. against Romans, Scots, Vikings, English, and that it lost centuries, since its richest part – the south – was almost permanently laid waste. But he then goes way over the top with cannibalism, "miserable cities", "wretched hovels", "vagabond character" of the population, "no settled habits of industry", "ferocious Highlanders who lived entirely by plunder", "freebooters from the Western Isles", no glass, no soap, no arts at all, no windows, the towns "backward, a poor village": "the fact that, until the eighteenth century, Scotland had nothing worthy of being called a city, is one of many circumstances which explain the prevalence of Scotch superstition"; "their minds must have been immersed in a darkness which we can now barely conceive"; "engrained superstition in the Scotch character"; "the Scottish people, though coarse and ignorant, still loved a certain barbarous liberty". He contrasts Protestantism in England which "has increased toleration and . . . has secured the triumph of secular interests over ecclesiastical ones" with its "entirely different result" in Scotland, seemingly unaware of the fact that as he wrote only young men who subscribed to the 39 Articles could go to Oxford and Cambridge which were totally dominated by the Church of England, whereas there was no religious test in Scotland.[11]

There is one passage in this diatribe of degradation which still rings so true that it is worth quoting in full. It provides the telling context in which the nineteenth-century commissions on the Scottish universities did their work. "In the Scotch Parliament there were 145 peers, all of whom, except 16, were, by the Act of Union, deprived of the power of making laws. These 16 were sent off to London, and took their seats in the House of Lords, of which they formed a small and miserable fraction. On every subject, however important to their own country, they were easily outvoted; their manners, their gesticulations and particularly their comical mode of pronouncing English, were openly ridiculed; and the chiefs of this old and powerful aristocracy found themselves, to their utter amazement, looked on as men of no account, and they were often

obliged to fawn and cringe at the levée of the minister, in order to
procure a place for some needy dependant . . . London became the
centre of their intrigues and hopes . . . and it was notorious that the
daily object of nearly every Scotch noble was to be made an English
peer. Directly this was apparent, the foundation of their power was
gone. From that moment, their real nationality vanished. It became
evident that their patriotism was but a selfish passion. They ceased
to love a country which could give them nothing and, as a natural
consequence, their country ceased to love them."[12]

Having got over this fine paroxysm of what we would today,
with our customary laxness in the use of language, call 'racism',
Buckle notes that, in the mid–eighteenth century, "in every branch
of knowledge this once poor and ignorant people produced original and successful thinkers",[13] having previously, in his opinion,
produced only two worth mentioning: Buchanan and Napier! He
is, of course, still mystified that "a people in many respects very
advanced and holding upon political subjects enlightened views"
should still be unable to free itself "from prejudices which make them
the laughing-stock of Europe".[14] He puts it all down, as we have
said, to the deductive method which "became supreme; it reigned
everywhere; not a voice was lifted up against it; and no on had an
idea that there was more than one path by which truth could be
reached, or that the human understanding was of any use, except
to deal deductively with premises, which were not to be inductively
examined". The poor, benighted Germans were just as bad: "In
both countries, the secular movement of the eighteenth century
was unable to become inductive, and this intellectual affinity . . .
is . . . the principal reason why the Scotch and German philosophers
have so remarkably acted and reacted upon each other; Kant and
Hamilton being the most finished specimens of their intercourse.
To them England forms a complete contrast."[15] The situation was
even worse than that, had Buckle but known it! Kant's ancestors
were the Cant family of Strachan, Kincardineshire, the same village
in which Thomas Reid, the common sense philosopher, was born
in 1710.

In speaking of Francis Hutcheson, whom he describes as the
originator of aesthetics, Buckle says that

> both parties (i.e. the proponents of deduction and induction)
> agree that we have the power of judging some actions to be
> right and others to be wrong. But as to how we get that power,
> and as to what that power is, they are at utter variance. The
> inductive philosopher says that its object is happiness, that we
> get it by association, and that it is due to action and reaction of
> social causes, which are susceptible of analysis, The deductive

philosopher says that the power of distinguishing right and wrong aims not at happiness but at truth; that it is inherent, that it cannot be analysed, that it is a primary conviction, and that we may assume it and reason from it, but never hope to explain it by reasoning to it."[16]
This excellent definition of the differences in ethical reasoning between the two strands that run through philosophy from the nominalists and realists to the logical positivists and the holists is the introduction to an interesting discussion on induction and deduction, now that Buckle has got his prejudices off his chest. He quotes Hume: "No kind of reasoning may give rise to a new idea ... but whenever we reason, we must antecedently be possessed of clear ideas, which may be the object of our reasoning."[17] He quotes Reid in a footnote; "The laws of nature are the most general facts we can discover in the operations of nature. Like other facts, they are not to be hit upon by a happy conjecture, but justly deduced from observation. Like other general facts, they are not be drawn from a few particulars, but from a copious, patient and cautious induction."[18] The difference between the schools of thought is hard to discern here; it almost seems as if Reid were a protagonist of induction, yet he says "there seems to be a great difference of opinions among philosophers about first principles. What one takes to be self-evident, another labours to prove by arguments, and a third denies altogether".[19] Yet Reid uses the deductive method exclusively in his work. "I call these *first principles* because they *appear to me* to have in themselves an intuitive evidence which I *cannot resist*."[20] This goes straight back to the doctrine of *highest evident assent* of George Lokert of Ayr in the early sixteenth century. Bacon calls this *anticipatio naturae*.

Buckle notes that Black, the great Scottish chemist who discovered latent heat, was criticised by inductive scientists who thought "that every increase of knowledge must be preceded by an increase of facts". He suggests that they have taken "a too limited view of the functions of the human mind, and of the manner in which the truth is obtained". The poet's view of nature is an emotional one, but it is no less true for all that, since "the emotions are as much a part of us as the understanding ... they are as truthful ... If the man of science despises their teaching, so much the worse for him".[21] In his view natural philosophers were imperfectly educated, they displayed "an inordinate respect for experiments, an undue love of minute detail", so that their predecessors in the seventeenth century, "by using hypotheses more boldly, "were able to do greater things than "our contemporaries with much superior resources have been able to achieve". He speaks of the "magnificent generalisations of

Newton and Harvey" which "could never have been completed in an age absorbed in one unvarying round of experiments and observations . . . our facts have outstripped our knowledge, and are now encumbering its march". We are in possession of a "huge and incoherent mass of observations" which will remain useless until they are "connected by some presiding idea". The most effective way of doing this "would be to give more scope to the imagination, and incorporate the spirit of poetry with the spirit of science".[22] He even says "our age . . . great as it is . . . has . . . a certain material, unimaginative and unheroic character, which has made several observers tremble for the future".[23] One marvels at Buckle's prescience here, at one with Carlyle's "men are grown mechanical", and true of our own time in spades!

Buckle concludes that Black had conferred a great boon "the magnitude of which it is not easy to over-rate, "before going on to show that Leslie's demonstration that heat and light were identical was a "rare stroke of sagacity," yet "the inductive mind of England refused to receive the truth, as it was not generalized from a survey of all the facts". He cites Hutton, the inventor of geology, and his book *The Theory of the Earth* 1788, and says his great prediction of the fusion of rock under heat and pressure "was conceived in opposition to all preceding experience" and that it "presupposes a combination of events which no-one had ever observed". So confident was Hutton of the validity of his theory that he left it to another, Sir James Hall, to prove his prediction by experiment, "that empirical branch of the investigation which he deemed of little moment, but which we, in England, are taught to believe is the only safe foundation of physical research". He quotes from Liebig's *Letters on Chemistry:*[24] "Cavendish and Watt both discovered the composition of water. Cavendish established the facts; Watt the idea . . . The attaching of too high a value to the mere facts is often a sign of a want of ideas." If he had his way, said Buckle, that sentence should be engraved in letters of gold over the portals of the Royal Society and of the Royal Institution. He completes his survey of the Scottish intellect with William Cullen's medical theory and John Hunter, pathologist and physiologist.

He sums up:[25]

Scotland:

> "A people who are, perhaps, the acutest reasoners in Europe, if you concede to them the principles from which they reason; but who, on the other hand, owing to their proneness to this method, are so greedy after general principles that they will accept them on almost any evidence, and are, therefore, at once very credulous and very logical."

England:
> "The most empirical nation in Europe; a nation utterly abhorring all general principles, priding itself on its common sense, boasting . . . of its practical sagacity, proclaiming aloud the superiority of facts over ideas, and despising every theory unless some direct and immediate benefit could be expected to accrue from it . . . "

He concludes by demonstrating the incompatibility of these two visions from John Hunter's experiences in London, where he arrived in 1748. The English people, says Buckle, "had become more averse than ever to inquiries which aimed at truth without regard to utility, and had accustomed themselves to value science chiefly for the sake of the direct and tangible benefit which they might hope to derive from it". When Hunter tried to mix the two methods of deduction and induction he perplexed both himself and his readers. "Only Aristotle and Newton", says Buckle, "wielded each method with equal ease". Hunter's English audiences, "prudent, sagacious but short-sighted, seeing few things at a time but seeing these things with admirable clearness, were unable to appreciate his comprehensive speculations, hence, in their opinion, he was little else than an innovater and an enthusiast. The great Scotchman, thrown among a nation whose habits of mind were uncongenial to his own, stood . . . in a position of comfortless superiority."[26]

Despite the ignorance of, and prejudice against, Scotland with which he began his study, we owe a debt of gratitude to Thomas Henry Buckle for having delineated the two national epistemological stances so clearly. He had to overcome the prejudices of his time and country to do so; after all, even Charles Darwin thought many of the peoples of what we now call the Third World were primitive savages. He seems finally to have understood the value of the two intellectual approaches, and we need to rescue the Scottish vision today before it is finally crushed out of our universities, colleges and schools. Buckle would, in the end, I think, have agreed with Voltaire: "*Vive la différence.*"

The Metaphysical Scots

During the period when Buckle was writing his book, however, the philosophical and scientific approach which he came ultimately to understand was sadly declining. David Daiches puts it well: "The Scottish Enlightenment, largely based in Edinburgh, combined paradoxically a pride in Scottish intellectual activities with an uncertainty and even a sense of inferiority about the Scots language and traditional Scottish ways . . . The late eighteenth and early nineteenth centuries was in many ways the city's golden age. But its position as the capital of a country that was itself part of a larger political unit dominated by English influences remained undefined and Victorian Edinburgh lost the cultural confidence of the Golden Age and nourished itself on nostalgia combined with a progressive anglicizing of its speech and institutions."[27] Edwin Muir, with his rather downbeat view of Scotland, has gone so far as to say that Sir Walter Scott was "a sham bard of a sham nation".

In an excellent paper on Scottish science, S. Shapin[28] says that Scottish science, like the rest of Scottish life, was, by the middle third of the nineteenth century, "being absorbed into the all-absorbing whirlpool of English culture". The Scottish identity was under threat from English forms and in this respect attitudes to Scottish science were little different from attitudes to Scottish education and the reform of Scottish political institutions. Scottish science declined "in scope, in its metaphysical framework and in general philosophical import". Science was becoming, as Carlyle had said of algebra in the 1820s, a mere mechanical knack: "little else than a cunningly constructed arithmetical mill". One simply turned the handle and ground out an answer. The distinctively Scots philosophical character of science was being eroded under the onslaught of English models. What was this metaphysical bias? It was a "pervasive concern for the foundations and uses of scientific knowledge".[29] Science wasn't simply a set of techniques, it was an "intellectual pursuit the unique certainty of which is discussed as an integral part of the exercise". For the Scots mathematics was the foundation of all scientific knowledge, and they preferred geometry to algebra. Geometrical propositions were at once statements about the real objective world and also mental abstractions from that world (again we feel the ghostly presence of John Mair's circle in the early sixteenth century). "Geometry", says Shapin, "glued together the study of the natural world and an exercise of pure reasoning". It could act, therefore, to maintain a kind of cultural solidarity.

The Scots feared educational specialization. They did not want intellectual mechanics, but liberally educated men able to reflect on the basis of knowledge. When the Scottish universities were attacked in the 1820s and 1830s for not teaching algebra, Sir William Hamilton replied that "the feeblest reasoner feels no inferiority to the strongest calculator . . . Algebra is like running a railroad through a tunnelled mountain; geometry is like crossing the mountain on foot." Geometry, epistemology and moral philosophy were seen as integrated enterprises. The Scottish Common Sense philosophy was a concerted response to Hume's scepticism and Joseph Priestley's deterministic materialism. This philosophy and Scottish views on geometry reinforced each other. "And the key to both", says Shapin, "is an overarching concern for moral and cultural solidarity". What we today would call a holistic approach. The battle between the two tendencies was fought out at the University of Edinburgh in appointing to the chair of natural philosophy on the death of Leslie. David Brewster was the 'Scots' candidate, and James David Forbes, a Cambridge man, was the 'algebra' candidate. The latter won. "The 'reform' of university education", says Shapin, "was the main agent in the erosion of a distinctively Scottish scientific tradition". Just as, today, the appointment of a large majority of English staff in all Scotland's universities has eroded Scottish traditions in all areas, but particularly philosophy. The same dichotomy was apparent in other scientific areas. William Cullen, John Gregory and others emphasised the importance of the nervous system in integrating bodily functions, thus overcoming Cartesian mind-body dualism. The antithesis here was Boerhaave's complex hydraulic machine animated by a Cartesian soul. The nerves responded to the environment and were shaped by it, so feelings were a function of how one lived. The nervous system communicated feeling between organs of the body by an act of "sympathy". So this mid–eighteenth century Scottish theory accounted for and stressed organic physiological integration; "it explained the relations between man's moral qualities and his conditions of existence". This cohesiveness and integration was the leading theme of Scottish moral and social philosophy; aspects of this physiological theory were used in their social philosophies by Hume, Adam Smith (for whom "sympathy" was a key term) and Adam Ferguson.

Why then this Scottish preoccupation with cultural and social solidarity? It would seem, according to a theory of Nicholas Phillipson and John Christie, that an answer should be sought in the historical relations between politics and culture as a result of the Treaty of Union. It was this 'national trauma' that stimulated the particular social and intellectual developments of the Scottish Enlightenment. It was a unique situation: Scottish cultural activity took on the functions elsewhere performed by political activity. Culture, including science, were "strongly loaded with political significance".[30] Interestingly, too, the membership of the Royal Society of Edinburgh, set up in 1737, was 40% scientists, 60% non-scientists; that is to say it refused to split off professional scientists from amateurs at a time when in England precisely the opposite was happening with the creation of many specialized societies by discipline.

In answer to the question why the 'anglicisers' undermined Scottish educational patterns Shapin gives an important answer: "Ultimately the answer has to be sought not in English scientific imperialism, but in changes within Scottish society itself ... The very industrializing and differentiating tendencies described by Adam Smith and deplored by the Common Sense philosophers became the agents through which the old Scottish science of solidarity was attacked and defeated." It was the Whig and radical mercantile groups of Glasgow and Edinburgh who advocated the reform of Scotland's universities "to make the curricula more responsive to the requirements of modernizing, specializing, urban economic life ... As Scottish society became more like that of England, so authentically Scottish voices were raised to bring scientific knowledge into line with the new social realities." In other words, as people like A. N. Whitehead and Nash have said, science is not independent of society but reflects it, in this case the English model of capitalism. But this begs many questions. Modern capitalism was also developing in Germany and France and the United States. Why did Scotland have to follow the English, especially as it was far from being the best? Why, above all, did Scottish universities have to follow the pattern of Oxford and Cambridge, which were the antithesis of modern and scientific? Precisely because of the powerful anglicizing pressures from the government in London, backed by what one can only call financial blackmail and by the sycophantic Scottish aristocrats who dominated all the powerful decision-making bodies. It was, of course, the Act of Union which gave them the power to do this, and they took full advantage of it. The flimsy theories of the 'no anglicization' tendency among contemporary scholars shatter against that uncompromising fact and the evidence all around us that it is taking Scotland over more rapidly than ever today.[31]

We must now ask whether in fact the traditional Scottish learning and teaching methods were inappropriate in a modern, specializing world, and whether – and this is the major question – and whether in fact they would not be better, in an up-to-date form, than the methods than were then foisted on Scotland and are so obviously failing society today. We shall continue this chapter by attempting to answer the first of these two questions.

The Open Door
Let us begin with a few quotations:

> At the same time the reform of Scottish university traditional teaching practice and curricula to bring them closer into line with the practice of Oxford and Cambridge would probably not have come about in a Scotland that had retained its independence.[32]

Scott's *Letters of Malachi Malagrowther* breathed a fiery spirit of Scottish nationalism and fierce opposition to the 'disposition to change everything in Scotland to an English model', with distinct overtones of a suggestion that if provoked too far Scotland's only course might be to secede from the Union.[33]

The characteristic excellence of the Scots colleges is the existence of an actively wrought lecture system, combined with constant and searching catechetical exercise under the highest responsible authorities of the respective classes. This, indeed, is the grand distinguishing feature which . . . has largely contributed to stamp on the national character one of its peculiar marks . . . The professor is ever in communication with his pupil, directing his energies, encouraging his exertions, resolving his doubts . . . In a word, bringing into play, in the small community of the classroom, the powers and habits which shall, in later years, be most frequently and most influentially employed in the active business of everyday life.[34]

This 'liberal' pedagogy was thought to be integral to general education, because it brought diverse ideas and diverse students into a living relationship that formed the basis of 'profession', of individuals' future character, motivation, thought and action. It thereby promoted social reproduction and adaptation and a lifelong involvement in the democracy of knowledge.[35]

Until the 1960s the Scottish universities maintained an open-door policy for virtually all applicants with minimum Highers qualifications or better. A relatively high proportion of graduate entrants to school-teaching had working-class origins . . . well represented in the inspectorate in the 1950s . . . I remember once entertaining a group of Russian educationists with a group of inspectors . . . (of) the eight I think seven were of working-class origin, which impressed the Russians so much that they thought we had chosen them deliberately. This kind of thing happens more frequently in Scotland than anywhere I know . . . [36]

We have a tradition of sound education in Scotland . . . It is our substitute for the English tradition of gentility. It is not, we feel, a thing to make a song and dance about.[37]

We have an interest in the common man, therefore we have an interest in a broad education.[38]

To go no further back than the middle of the nineteenth century
we find James Lorimer, Jun. Advocate, expressing his pride in his
country's great educational traditions. After demonstrating what an
important role Scotsmen played, both as students and professors, in
the universities of Europe in the fourteenth, fifteenth and sixteenth
centuries,[39] he goes on:

> If we can imagine a meeting between a Scotch Professor of
> Pandects of Bologna in the sixteenth century and a Scotch
> Chief Justice of New Zealand of the present day, we can have
> little hesitation, if there were to be a *Hochnasigkeit* on either
> side, in determining which would be entitled to look over his
> nose at the other. The one, in the open arena of Europe, had
> gained, by his personal qualities alone, a position of which
> few European men of that day were not ambitious; the other
> holds, by pure favour, a place which no civilized man would
> take if it were not for the pecuniary emoluments which attach
> to it. The pride of the one man was in the strength of his
> brains, that of the other in the fullness of his pockets; may we
> not add that the grounds of their respective gratulations are
> but too truly the indices of the conditions of society to which
> they respectively appertain.

This latter comment throws a strong light on Shapin's statement
that Scottish higher education and science had to change to fit the
new (and what many would now call) acquisitive society. Lorimer asks pertinently what we might not now do "with a good
and resolute will" if such man were produced "in the very dawn
of our material prosperity and our intellectual life". He complains bitterly at the discrepancy in terms of finances and chairs
between the universities of Scotland, England and Germany, at
the expense of Oxbridge and their exclusive policies. Despite this
imbalance (1190 chairs in England, 105 in Scotland) he speaks of
the intellectual character in Scotsmen "that we specially prize",
namely that "openness and freshness of mind, which is ready to
receive new truth whencesoever it may come". He cites the cases
of Newton and Kant who were both taught in Scotland before
they were taught in England.[40] He contrasts this with the attitudes of Oxbridge. "We do confess that we could not see without regret the whole youth of Scotland thus cast in the mould
of the English universities. We are persuaded that these institutions . . . exercise on second-rate minds an influence unfavourable
to originality and freedom of thought. Such . . . is peculiarly the
case with Oxford. Here pupils are struck, as it were, with one
mental die, and on every subject which is presented to them, the
opinions to which they give utterance, in place of being the

results of their own individual thinking, are too frequently nothing more than an expression of Oxford views."[41]

The contrast with Scotland is very great, according to Lorimer. He lists Scotland's great contributions to contemporary civilization: the mechanical inventions of the early nineteenth century, the medical and legal reforms "now running riot among our English neighbours", the great debt systematic, scientific agriculture owes "to the free experimental research of Scotland during the present century".[42] Yet he says that more is done to help Oxford than all the Scots universities together. There had been 130 new posts in the English universities in the previous 50 years, and 70 in Ireland. There were about 35–40 learned posts in the Arts Faculties of Scotland. This was a staggering deficiency as compared with England and Ireland. Often in a single college at Oxford the Fellowships greatly exceeded the learned positions in Scotland. "The claim of Scotland", he says, "surely is not weaker than that of Ireland . . . a grant similar to that recently given to the Queen's Colleges in Ireland would fully satisfy all the reasonable longings even of those whose views, regarding the universities of Scotland, are most advanced."[43] He points out that while large public grants had of late years been made both in England and Ireland for the establishment of new universities and colleges, "the interests of Scotland in this respect have received no such attention and . . . even the recommendation of the small additional Endowments In the Report of the Commission on the Scottish universities in 1830 have not yet been carried out." When it is considered that this discriminatory neglect was taking place at the same time as the series of commissions to bring the Scottish universities' "teaching practice and curricula closer into line with the practice of Oxford and Cambridge", there is a very strong case indeed for the accusation made by at least one scholar[44] that there was and is an English conspiracy against Scottish education. At any rate it demonstrates the insubstantiality of the claim of those who say there was no such thing as anglicizing pressures.

The comparison with Oxford and Cambridge was a constant in mid-nineteenth century writings about the universities, showing in itself what the writers knew to be the central thrust of the commissions on the Scottish universities, whose work went on throughout the middle two-thirds of the century. It was claimed that the Scottish 'catechetical' system was superior to the Oxbridge tutorial which produced 'dungeons of knowledge' rather than 'enlightened and enlightening' members of society. This was because the real teaching of the colleges was carried on in the rooms of the 'coaches' or 'grinders'; it was a 'forcing-house' system (as the English public and

grammar school sixth form still is today). The Scottish system produced graduates who, while having 'varied and extensive reading',
and not having been forced to learn a vast mass of facts, yet "excel
the mass of English graduates in the knowledge of first principles
and in the fundamental laws of language and of science".[45] The
North British Review echoes the claim of Francis Jeffrey and Lord
Broughton referred to in an earlier chapter: "On the adaptation
of our colleges to the genius of the people we need not enlarge.
Their great mission has been to leaven the masses, and this characteristic has been scrupulously preserved. Our students are drawn
even from the lowest classes . . . But the gulf between the Oxonian
and the mechanic is a wide, nay, almost impassable one . . . "[46]
The anonymous author admits that there are weaknesses in the
Scottish universities: the students are too young, there is a lack
of regular examinations at the beginning and end of each session;
there should be more prizes for merit. There is not enough money,
not enough staff, not enough books. He insists nonetheless on the
value of the traditional Scottish system whereby a student should
graduate in Arts before going on to professional training, this being
"the foundation of all professional training". He says that "many
of our reforms are led astray by the contagion of the English
example and stay not to inquire whether the cases of Oxford and
Edinburgh be similar . . . the desire for English models has led us
into many misconceptions . . . "[47] He warns – and the warning is
even more valid now than then – that "the direct result of a mere
professional training is to produce empirics, and not ornaments of
science and society . . . We consider the compulsory graduation of
professional students a matter of so vital moment that we place
it at the foundation of our scheme."[48] The great objection to an
entrance examination which the reformers were calling for – and
the author is one of them – is that it will "exclude from our seats
of learning many of the poor, hard-working, *seri-studiorum* men,
who are the very bone and marrow of our country; and admit only
the youths whose means allow deliberate and minute preparation
for the competition."[49] In other words, the introduction of the Jude
the Obscure syndrome into Scotland. We must, above all, he says
"scrupulously guard against the possibility of modern utilitarianism converting our mental training apparatus into a mere 'useful
knowledge' grubber".[50] Again the warning which has now in our
day become a chorus from the most far-seeing of today's university scholars in Europe and North America. I have come across
no text which encapsulates so succinctly the various aspects of the
democratic intellect, which, some contemporary scribblers assure
us, is a myth.

The same points are taken up by Professor John Nichol, a Balliol graduate and long (twenty-six years) the Professor of English Language and Literature at the University of Glasgow, in a pamphlet of 1888 in which he describes the recent university bill as likely to lead to the "disintegration" if not the "effacement" of universities long nurses of the higher thought. He makes no bones about saying that the bill adds to its predecessor of 1858 "new provisions till now upheld only by those avowedly hostile to a system *whose very success has excited their hostility* . . . "[51] (Our italics). It would give a baleful stimulus to "the vicious modern subordination of teaching to examination", Nichol says, quoting T. H. Huxley: "The educational abomination of the present day is the stimulation of young people to work at high pressure by incessant examination."[52] The demand to exclude professors from examining their own subjects "would soon degrade them into crammers". The Bill is "essentially hostile to the higher education of Scotland" and is in principle "opposed to the best interests of higher education everywhere". He complains that the introduction of an entrance examination at Glasgow was "a self-denying ordinance", since it led to a decrease in Arts students.[53] He is entertaining on the subject of utilitarianism and specialization versus general education, quoting Cobden – "who found more wisdom in a number of the *Times* than in all Thucydides" – and Bright – who saw culture as "a smattering of two dead languages"; and citing on the other hand Matthew Arnold – "the university of Mr. Ezra Cornell is calculated to produce miners and or engineers, not sweetness or light" – and Goethe – "Take care of the beautiful, the useful will take care of itself". His own conclusion is that "'Over-specialization' is now more frequent than 'diluted omniscience', and if it came to pass that the majority of undergraduates follow, in parallel and consequently never intersecting lines, 'mechanics, law and physiology', they will fail, from want of any common base, to 'enlarge each other's horizon'."[54]

Nichol argues that the ancient Scottish universities are "seminaries for the nation; comparatively poor, they are institutions for the comparatively poor . . . open in practice as well as theory to the more thrifty, intelligent or aspiring of the lower (classes), they are in effect great public schools for the bulk of the middle classes of the country."[55] This is something the English universities could not do. The Scottish universities had been unfairly criticized "because the conditions of their existence make it equally impossible for them to discharge the functions of the English".[56] The latter stood accused of being mere "training-schools of literary rhetoric for the upper classes" and of teaching their able students "how to sneer". He concludes that, with all its defects of detail, "our university system supplies the most enlightened and useful general training anywhere open, among us, to a mass of young men of comparatively limited means". He adds that "too much honour cannot be paid to some of the men, to whom the bar of poverty is not unconquerable, who, under pressure of almost incredible toil, stint themselves of rest, of sleep, even of food, inspired by a zeal for a more intellectual life, often vindicated by a distinguished career". The basic reason for this is "the thirst for knowledge that animates the mass of the people".[57] The persistence of certain contemporary authors in decrying the Scottish concept of the democratic intellect as a myth, usually on the flimsiest and most hypothetical evidence, should be put to the question. After all, Professor Nichol was a graduate of Balliol and twenty-six years a professor at Glasgow when he wrote these words, and may therefore be taken as an intelligent judge not prone to myth-making. A. D. Lindsay was not the first Balliol-trained Scottish Professor to reject the Oxbridge system and the damage it was doing to Scottish university ideals and practice.

11

The Democratic Intellect 2

Arduous and generous emulation
Moving forward some 30 years we find twentieth-century confirmation of the Scottish way of thinking about education: "Experience has shown that brains, capacity, talent are not the prerogative of any one class, but are diffused in an irregular and uncertain fashion through all classes, though unfortunately arrested, stunted, perverted through lack of training. All this store of potential capacity must be conserved for the nation . . . Every child of every grade must have his chance . . . The possibilities of extended education for the mass of boys and girls is not less important and urgent than the training of the specialist . . . The close bearing of the Representation of the People Act upon the Education Act is here revealed . . . the latter renders the extended franchise a measure of benefit rather than of danger – which is the prime requisite and condition of sound democracy."[1] These words are taken from a book published just after the First World War, the intention of which was obviously to get in quickly and influence further educational developments. It contains essays by various educationists, and two of these, by Herbert Grierson, Professor of English at Edinburgh, and John Burnet, Professor of Greek at St. Andrews, are of particular interest to us.

Herbert Grierson begins by making a point that needs making. He say that Scotland's universities are "modest matrons" beside those of Leyden or Berlin, but their value can be seen in their having trained "a people whose service to the world in character and intellect has been altogether out of proportion to its wealth and numbers.[2] They had no fellowships like those of Oxford and Cambridge and were thus unable to build up postgraduate research in the pursuit of higher scholarship, but as teachers they set in motion through the country "waves of intellectual activity to which the intensified spiritual life of the Scottish people is in no small measure to be traced".[3] Grierson points to the difficulties the universities had since the Act of 1889, with the introduction of a school leaving certificate and a university preliminary examination, both of which were initially set at far too high a standard. The greatest blow was the breaking in pieces of the uniform course of study for the MA "which included all the chief factors in a liberal education", upon which J. S. Mill had commented so favourably. With it disappeared the single class, the great factor in the intellectual life of the universities, in which the students were all united.

The Scottish professorship, too, lost its financial and otheradvantages which had retained in Scotland men like Lord Kelvin, Clerk Maxwell and many other famous names. All this led to uncertainty, so that the universities in Scotland no longer knew what their exact function was. "They no longer put the coping-stone upon the general liberal education of the best youth of the country . . . and completing the cycle by introducing them to the study of philosophical methods and speculation."[4] What can we do, Grierson asks, "to recover what may be recovered of the loss entailed when the universities ceased to provide the last stage in a good general education?" He makes it quite clear that nothing is to be gained by taking Oxford and Cambridge as models, since their history is so distinct and different from that of Scotland's universities. He states categorically that the work of the Commission of 1889 "suffered from nothing so much as from the fact that the dominating influence on it was that of men who were not deeply imbued with the spirit of the Scottish universities, and had no adequate faith in their capacity for development on the lines of the past".[5] So strongly does Grierson feel about this that he wants to explain his own experience as student and teacher before 1892.

In response to the criticisms of the Scottish lecture system as being unnecessary with the increase in the number of books and tutorial exercises, Grierson says he found something "wonderfully awakening" in following a well-constructed course of lectures by someone who is a master of his subject. What was wrong with the Scottish system was that the examinations followed the lectures too closely, "partly from the inability of most of the students to obtain an adequate supply of books. Many were too poor to buy, and shrank even from the deposit required for the use of the library."[6] (How say you now, proponents of the mythical nature of the democratic intellect?) But what left the greatest impact on him – greater than that of any teacher – was the class itself. "There is nothing anywhere – not even perhaps in America, where the system of options as now in Scotland prevails and where there is no honours degree – quite like

a Scottish university class as it then was. It was a heterogeneous but
united body from first to last . . . (including) students of all degrees
of excellence and variety of capacity.." The honours students took
all the subjects required for the pass degree and he took them in
the same class as the rest of his year, so that the class contained the
strongest and the weakest in classics, mathematics, philosophy and
science.

> In none of the subjects were the attainments probably yet high
> but the capacity was there; and a professor who passed from
> Aberdeen to Cambridge has confessed to me that there was
> nothing he missed so much as the opportunity of addressing an
> audience which included such a range of ability and interest . . .
> The effect for the students was an enormous volume of eager
> and generous emulation . . . The atmosphere was one of work
> and competition. No one who remembers it in tranquillity but
> must feel he owes a deep debt to the spirit of arduous and
> generous emulation which breathed from these lads carving
> out their own careers on the rudely cut and hacked benches
> of King's College.[7]

There, from the pen of one of Scotland's finest professors of English
literature and language, and in the twentieth century, breathes the
very spirit of the 'non-existent' democratic intellect.

No doubt Grierson, like all who love teaching, looks back on his
early career with slightly rose-tinted spectacles. His analysis of the
destruction wrought by the 1889 Act is nonetheless spot on. Here
is not the place to go into great detail, but Grierson demonstrates
the disintegration of the curriculum brought about by the introduction of specialization with honours degrees, and the downgrading
of the Ordinary degree by making it an *alternative* to the honours
degree. The degree came to represent the study for a single year –
sometimes not even that – of seven disconnected subjects. A superficial knowledge of seven subjects took the place of a good general
knowledge of classics, mathematics and physics, and philosophy,
with an introduction to English literature and natural science. The
result was "a steady fall in its value as an introduction to, and preparation for, vocational and professional study", so that there was
"a steady diminution of interest in it on the part of both students
and professors". "The interest of the professor", says Grierson, "has
centred more and more in the group of honours students who work
with him throughout their course".[8] And of course these honours
students missed out on their general education in such subjects as
philosophy and history, not studied at school. Thus was created
"one of the worst results of the present arrangement, the imperfectly
educated honours graduate . . . who has left incomplete his general

education in order to specialise without distinction".[9]

The honours degree was an Oxford invention and so was the very narrow specialization in classics, on which Grierson expresses grave doubts: "It is because the mere disciplinary study of Latin and Greek was continued so long, with no introduction to their unique literary and historical interest, that it remained so barren of humanist value."[10] He quotes Matthew Arnold on the great classical public schools: "Here are our young barbarians all at play." Grierson says the First World War demonstrated the need for a liberal education for technical specialists and the vital importance of a greater width of humanist culture, literary, historical and philosophical. He then launches on a credo which needs to be quoted in full, since it is as valid today as it was seventy years ago.

> Men and women are not only, and less and less will they be, expert (or inexpert) lawyers, doctors, merchants, manufacturers, bankers, clerks and artisans; they are also citizens of the world and the state. Regarded in its simplest and most practical way, they are voters on whose understanding and temper the security of society and its callings and institutions depends. It is the immediate and insistent interest of every profession and industry that the education of its members and servants should include elements of a liberal education *which do not belong to the school stage* (our italics) – philosophy, history, economics, literature, art – and that, so far as practicable, they should be encouraged to pursue such studies even after they have begun their professional training . . . and it is the duty of the state and the universities to provide the necessary means . . . The university will have to enter in a more generous spirit than in the past into the humanist education . . . of all classes and conditions of the community.

This is a fine modern restatement of yet another aspect of the democratic intellect, very necessary today in the age of the tabloid and competition on the ratings, but of course our universities have been heading faster and faster in the opposite direction under pressure from philistine governments. The fatal step was taken by the Commission of 1889 which, says Grierson, lacked any sort of guiding principle in legislating for the honours degree and its relation to a general liberal education. It should either have excluded all extraneous subjects or selected them on some rational principle. In fact, the one clear desire of the Commission was to "weight the balance in favour of classics and mathematics",[11] in the Oxbridge manner, by making conditions on extraneous subjects much easier for an honours classics degree than for any other subject, English, say, or modern languages. The result was that in Scotland, as in

England, the honours work was so narrow that the student could spend all his time in one department, and that a Third Class honours graduate, who had included a couple of irrelevant soft options in his degree course, was less well educated than a graduate with a good ordinary degree. One more very large and very obvious nail in the coffin of the 'no-such-thing-as-anglicization' myth!

The really sad feature in all this was that honours work did not differ in essence from ordinary work. It consisted in preparing for an examination: dogmatic instruction supplemented by reading and tutorial instruction in what was already known, but not investigation. "A business", says Grierson, "of training pupils in examination gymnastics". He asks whether one can justify encouraging young men and women to continue till the age of 23 or 24 (as the situation then was) an education whose main aim is to enable students to make a brilliant showing in papers that have to be written in three hours. Such students should have entered a purposeful vocational training by the age of 21. In other words he advocated earlier entry, at 17 instead of 18 or 19. Grierson also preferred to the training for three-hour essay writing "the tradition of eloquent exposition on which France and Scotland have laid stress".[12]

Grierson makes salutary reading today because we see how little we have advanced since his day in the things that really matter in higher education. The 1889 Commission left lecturers without any voice in the management of the university outside their own classes, something which, in Grierson's opinion, "is self-confessedly absurd".[13] The Senatus is a conservative body, so conservative that no reconstruction of the curriculum had ever been carried out by the universities themselves. The reason for this "is that it consists of a congeries of experts, each primarily interested in his own subject and department and jealous of interference from without". We may well ask ourselves what has changed for the better since Grierson's day. He himself was quite clear that there was no other body "so well fitted to carry on the general educational policy of the university as the general body of teachers".[14] For the same broadly democratic reasons Grierson was against the adoption of the English collegiate system: "The freer, more responsible life of the Scottish student is an element in his moral and intellectual training."

Grierson's peroration reflects this deep Scottish sense of popular democracy so well that it is worth quoting at length: "To enhance their efficiency, to maintain and strengthen their democratic character, must be the sole aim of a reformer of the Scottish universities, for their prosperity must depend upon the degree to which the Scottish people feels them to be its own peculiar care . . . A democratic people like ours wants not only an intelligent and educated ruling and

directing bureaucracy, recruited from every class, but an intelligent
and educated people to criticize, direct and control its bureaucratic
administrators. It matters less who administers if an intelligent people knows what it wants and is determined to get it. The Scottish
universities have drawn into their classes at all times the young
intelligences of every order. To widen, on no account to contract,
their clientele – by going out to it if it cannot come in to them –
while raising ever higher the level of the culture they afford, must
be the earnest and sleepless endeavour of the native universities, as
of all who have served and serve the great Scottish people."[15] No
doubt the denigrators of the democratic intellect consider Grierson
to be an innocent dupe.

   This is perhaps an appropriate point at which to discuss the 'democratic intellect' concept and its critics. The fact is that they have never
understood it. So much is evident from an article by R. D. Anderson
on George Elder Davie entitled *Democracy and Intellect*.[16] In it he
asks whether Scotland would become more democratic "if Davie's
programme were adopted and all university students were trained
in metaphysics?" His answer is that, "It is difficult to see why, and
clear in any case that the 'democratic intellect' does not mean the
democratization of education as this is usually understood socially
or politically". He describes Davie's programme as "a philosophical
training for the elite" which is "so little concerned with broadening
the popular base of education". Of Anderson's book, *Education
and Opportunity in Victorian Scotland*, a *TESS* review[17] says that
"it is a theme of his excellent book that the 'egalitarian myth' surrounding Scottish educational history blurs the fact that the much
vaunted 'democratic' tradition meant in fact equality only of opportunity and the selection of talented individuals for social promotion
through secondary and higher education". "True egalitarianism",
it tells the reader, "came only much later, with the introduction of
comprehensive secondary schools". And, of course, the "myth of the
'democratic tradition' is powerful" because supported by Davie's
The Democratic Intellect, "a book whose main thesis Anderson specifically seems to demolish". Similarly, R. Houston, in his book on
Scottish literacy – a work of inferiorisation if ever there was one –
claims the democratic intellect is a myth because all it involved was
equality of opportunity.

   The use of terms like 'selection' and 'social promotion' in a
deprecating sense of an educational system which was offering
places to as many children (of both sexes) as it could take in the
seventeenth and eighteenth centuries is, quite simply, ludicrous. As
the quote with which we opened this chapter says: "Every child
of every grade must have his chance" because brains are not the

prerogative of any one class. R. E. Bell, who at one time shared many of Anderson's views, says[18] that the contest ideal (keeping as many children as possible as long as possible in education) favoured in Scotland has suffered its worst erosions – high prestige accorded to specialist courses, ever more rigorous entrance standards demanded of those with a deprived background, the emphasis on research at the expense of teaching – because of Scottish university principals abandoning Scottish traditions and becoming directly dependent on London. The *TESS* reviewer's "true egalitarianism" with the intro- duction of comprehensives is somewhat wide of the mark, at least in England. Bell points out that there is no separation of sheep and goats in Scottish comprehensives, whereas in England CSE and GCE pupils are separated. This has led to increased academic achievement in Scottish schools "when many English teachers *were scorning scholarly achievement in the name of equality and anti-elitism*" (our italics). The result, says Bell, is that there is a higher number of working-class children at university in Scotland than elsewhere in the UK.

The danger italicised above (the subject of discussion on the TV news programme *Scotland Today* as I write) is also referred to by Davie:[19] "We have done a lot these past ten years to redress the balance, providing goals in education for the less able which are both attainable and satisfying. We sometimes have the impression that what the Scots are aiming at is *democracy without intellect*. It is almost as if, in a dramatic reversal of the original position, the Scots were leaving the lads and lassies of parts to their own devices and concentrating their whole educational energy on developing the lads and lassies whose potential is not academic or intellectual." (our italics). Nevertheless, he goes on, "what is happening in the schools shows that the new system is by no means forgetting the old intellectual values". The democratic intellect found a place in the comprehensive system, as Bell showed. Left to itself, the Scottish system "seems to have considerable potential for a regeneration of the education system which would do justice both to the values of common humanity and common intellectuality". Davie looked forward to a time when, with the repatriation of the universities, it would be possible to recreate a system in which, as in the nineteenth century, egalitarianism did not exclude intellectual distinction.

Davie shares with John Anderson a distrust of progressivist, mod- ernist optimism and theories of education. Anderson argued that progressives overlook "qualitative distinctions and oppositions, neglect the incompatibility of different values and traditions, differ- ent moralities and forms of life, and collapse ethics to questions of distribution". To those who argued that his was an elitist position

Anderson replied: "It is argued that I exaggerate the intellectual element in education, that not all children are fitted for an intellectual
training. My answer is that the only alternative to the development
of understanding is the development of submissiveness." If education is simply vocational training, "thought is at a discount and the
social consequences will be gullibility and acquiescence". The truth
of this statement is borne out by the contemporary political and
social situation in Britain.

Beveridge and Turnbull[20] maintain that discussion of the 'democratic intellect' clouds the issue by debating how open Scotland's
education system was to all social classes and thus diverting attention from cultural to sociological issues. Davie's book, they say, "is
essentially a description of the long nineteenth-century *Kulturkampf*
in Scotland, which pitted those who wished to see education evolve
in the spirit of local traditions against those who favoured the adoption in Scotland of the specialising and untheoretical approaches
to education favoured in England". There was a long tradition of
Scottish commitment to theoretical reasoning, "to applying first or
philosophical principles to literary, historical, linguistic and economic subjects. The emphasis was on 'enlarged investigation', 'the
philosophic itch to dispute all things.' "The 'common sense' of
subjects was put before questions of detail. It is in this sense that
Davie uses the idea of 'democratic intellectualism' to characterise
the Scottish mind."

We have all stood in Scottish pubs where the discussion ranged
from first things to last things. Perhaps the most sensible conclusion
to this discussion is L. P. Hartley's comment in the prologue to *The
Go-Between* : "The conclusion of both historians and moralists is
that it makes no sense, intellectual or moral, to describe the past in
the present's categories. To attempt to do so is worthless, because
it makes it impossible to explain the past, and arrogant because it
assumes that the past has been merely a preparation for the present."

An activity of the soul
Several times in his paper Grierson refers to the work of John Burnet,
professor of Greek at St. Andrews. Burnet has a paper[21] in the same
book which is very important because in it he tells how he favoured
the reforms of 1889, indeed made them the subject of his inaugural
address at St. Andrews in 1892 ... and then admits how wrong
he was: "The measures then adopted only made things worse than
they were before."[22] The university entrance examination was "a
failure from the first". The papers set in Latin and Greek both in the
entrance examination and the leaving certificate examination were

"impossible except for the best pupils in the best schools" (meaning those that most resembled English public schools). This was because the conditions under which the Scottish schools worked – "and we certainly did not foresee that the conditions would become ever more unfavourable as time went on" – made it impossible for even the best of the state schools in Scotland to produce the same results in classics as in other countries. He stresses that it is not the fault of the schools: in Germany students on entering university had nine years of Latin and six of Greek, whereas in Scotland the corresponding figures were five and two. "That is inevitable", says Burnet, "and no entrance examination can make the slightest difference to it. Schools don't have the staff". Then comes the leitmotif we have heard in all Scottish discussion of higher education and which so displeases our democratic intellect myth makers. "In the second place we are bound by all our best traditions to keep the door wide open as long as possible in order that a higher education may be within the reach of every class in the community."

The important point to note here is that this utter fiasco was the result of sixty-three years (1826–89) of Commissions and reports on the Scottish universities whose sole aim was "to bring them closer into line with the practice of Oxford and Cambridge". It must have cost a great deal of money which would have been better spent on an educational system which was so poor and yet had achieved so much. It also, and more seriously, knocked that system clean out of kilter and prevented it from developing along its own lines. Our universities have never been able to recover from that blow; indeed some of them have been turned into second-rate copies of English universities. Only when planning as well as financial control is returned to Scotland will they be able to try and pick up again where they were forced to leave off a century ago. It will be very hard, but not impossible – the vision is still alive.

In another book[23] Burnet makes a very useful comparison of Scottish higher education with that existing in Prussia. He shows that all German boys destined for positions of authority and responsibility must have a general education which was mainly humanistic in character and lasted till age 20. No specialisation at all was allowed till then. Burnet, who is much concerned with the formation of an elite, says that this emphasises the strong conviction of the Germans that higher work can only be done on the basis of a thorough and prolonged general education.[24] He quotes a German educator who says that *Bildung* i.e. education, "is the sum of all we have forgotten." He makes a statement which is important in the light of today's preoccupation with "transferable skills". The further a general education is carried, "the more does the possibility of transference from one department to another increase, and it is probably at its highest at the close of a well ordered course of such training".[25] He goes on to say that those subjects are of highest educative value which have potentially the largest number of common factors with as many other subjects as possible. "Whether, in a particular case, actual transference of trained ability from one department to another takes place depends entirely on the subject's sense of the importance of the other department and the interest he consequently takes in it."[26] The work of a Greek scholar, he points out, is just as much a specialism as that of an engine-driver. The more thorough the humanistic training which has gone before, the higher will be the level of the specialized work. "That is just because there is a greater number of identical factors which connect the specialism with human life as a whole."[27] So the teaching of the Greek scholar should aim not at producing Greek scholars, but at producing men and citizens. What he is often tempted to regard as his higher work, i.e. his research, "is really of far less importance". Aristotle had said it would be strange if carpenters and cobblers had a specific function and a corresponding excellence, and man as such had none. Was there such a thing as a good man? The Greeks answered the question very much in the affirmative, and its rediscovery at the Renaissance led to the modern world. At this point in the argument we feel the spirit of John Mair's circle hovering somewhere about, and we cast a glance forward to the ideas of John Macmurray and Alasdair MacIntyre.

In an essay entitled 'Ignorance'[28] Burnet says that knowledge – living, first-hand knowledge – is "an activity of the soul", whereas ignorance is passive and inert, and he discusses the growth of ignorance in this sense. He speaks of the danger of a new Dark Age despite nineteenth-century optimism in the progress of knowledge, and we recall that fifty years later MacIntyre says, in *After Virtue*, that the new Dark Age is already upon us. "We are told that specialism is the remedy", he says, and quotes an example to illustrate the danger he foresees. At an archaeology conference on the subject of palaeontology people walked out when someone spoke about the Bronze Age. "There must be something wrong here", he says, "for the suggestion, if pushed to its logical conclusion, would land us in a society where no-one knew anything that anyone else knew. The mass of men would take refuge in scepticism and the dark age would be upon us at once."[29] This sort of approach to knowledge – and it was the Scottish moral philosopher Professor James Frederick Ferrier of St. Andrews University who invented the term epistemology, or theory of knowledge – had led to a situation where standards of teaching and examination had to be progressively lowered

in all departments over the thirty years since 1892. The only exceptions, significantly, were the physical and natural sciences. "I am
certain", he concludes, "that the young men of today are absolutely
and relatively more ignorant than those of 40 years ago and, what
is worse, they have less curiosity and intellectual independence".[30]
What would Burnet say if he could see our situation today, with
the decimation of departments of philosophy, fine art, music, and
so on in our universities?

He also has some interesting things to say about research and
teaching.[31] If you listen to those who talk most about research, says
Burnet, you learn that it is research to study the manuscripts of
an author's text, but it is not research to interpret his meaning to
students. This is quite new, says Burnet, because the great scholars
of the past never talked about research though they did a great deal
of it. The worked for the sheer enjoyment of learning and teaching.
A perfect example of this springs to mind. One of the greatest ever
works on linguistics, a book which revolutionized the subject, was
only given to the world because two of the great man's students
met for a reunion dinner and reminisced over the wonderful lectures
he had given. They soon realized that they had kept careful notes,
so they got together and produced the book which was to become
a bible for all linguists. It is de Saussure's *Cours de Linguistique
Générale* and the students were Charles Bally and Albert Sechehaye.
Nowadays, the most important criterion of a university's success
is the amount of research moneys won, and there is much talk of
the "endowment of research", "research scholarships", etc. "True
research", says Burnet, "can never be fostered in that way. I don't
suppose any of the great discoveries have been paid for at all, and I
am sure that they have all been made by men who had no thought
of being paid for them."[32]

On the Snow-line, that is the relationship between science and
arts, Burnet goes back to the Greeks: "The great lesson that Greece
has to teach us at the present day is the folly of any estrangement
between Science and Humanism."[33] His view is that science depends
upon humanism, since it is only the humanist point of view "that
can furnish an adequate motive for its pursuit or even a justification
for its existence".[34] This was precisely the characteristic feature of
German higher education as created by Wilhelm von Humboldt at
the University of Berlin. For "men of science who are tempted to
rest their claims on merely utilitarian grounds are really betraying
their own cause".[35] He points out that the German universities did
not yoke themselves to the chariot-wheels of industry and commerce; it was just the other way around. German manufacturers and
industrial leaders were better educated than ours. All the German

higher schools taught both literary and scientific subjects, but only
a comparatively small number of hours were devoted to science. No
boy intended for the professions, even for such a position as mining engineer, was allowed to make science his chief subject until at
least his nineteenth year, and usually older. The great weakness of
the German system, however, was that it kept the boys too long at
school, till age 20 – and this had a bad effect on German student life.
This was the fault of the German universities during the nineteenth
century, which had allowed their faculties of arts to disappear,
and the Philosophical Faculty that took its place to become over-
specialised. But since they insisted on a long and thorough general
education before specialization for the service of the Prussian State,
it could be done only by keeping the young men at school till they
were 20. "Higher education falls properly into three periods and not
into two, and if we ignore that fact we get into trouble at once. There
is the period up to about 17, in which the pupil is chiefly employed
in entering on the inheritance of humanity; the period from about
18 to 21, when he makes this his own and forms a personal view
of the world, and the period from 21 onwards when he is ripe for
some special study in the department he has chosen for his life's
work. The intermediate period is really the most important, but it is
the one we are most apt to go wrong about."[36] In Germany it had
been tacked on to the school course with unfortunate results, while
in Britain "some people, who imagine they are 'practical', would
have us omit it altogether and start special training at 17 or 18".

The French had the same sort of problems. Up till 1870 their
Faculté de Lettres gave the same sort of broad general education
as the Scottish Arts Faculty did. They then concentrated more on
research in the German manner, and this led to *la crise du français* –
the students could no longer write French and they had no "idées
générales". So then a classe de rhétorique (as in the Middle Ages)
and a première supérieure were added to the school course, and
finally an année propédeutique in the Faculté de Lettres devoted to
philosophy and literature. A Professor Coste of Bordeaux praised
the American liberal arts college for giving young people heading for
very different professions "the opportunity of preparing themselves
for the life of a man and a citizen. In my view it is a grave defect of
our university system that it offers the majority of young Frenchmen
the Baccalauréat as the termination of their moral and intellectual
training, when they leave the lycée, where they have been subjected
to the discipline of children. Our young men would gain much in
strength of character if they attended university for a year or two
after the lycée, and if, free from professional preoccupations and
open to generous enthusiasms, were initiated by associations of a

scientific, literary or social character . . . into responsibility, decision and tolerance. That is the lesson the French might learn from the American college."[37]

In Germany, too, there were educationists who considered the American liberal arts college – which in Burnet's view is the exact equivalent of the traditional Scottish arts faculty – as the solution to giving a broad and thorough general education to students before starting on their specialist professional studies at the age of 21. Scotland had certain advantages, not least the fact that her system drew talent from every section of the community – a problem not solved in England or Germany – and that her universities had retained their arts faculties, whereas the German universities had lost theirs. "Everything depends on that, just as everything depends on the College of Liberal Arts in America."[38]

At this point Burnet reverts to the matter with which we began, namely the total failure of the Universities Act of 1889. The reforms had never done the least good, hope had been swept away; they had not raised the standard of work in university classes; they had kept back students who were perfectly ready to go on, they had let through students who should have been kept back. The universities should not be relieved of the duty of providing preliminary instruction in subjects not compulsory at school, so that the Junior Classes which the reforms had abolished should be reintroduced, and, above all, obstacles should not be put in the way of young people wishing to come to university, as they had been by the preliminary examination and by the Carnegie Trust, despite its original aims. The benefits of the Carnegie Trust were more and more confined to the middle classes in the towns, who didn't need them. (This is the same phenomenon as that noted by Sheldon Rothblatt when scholarship competitions for Oxford and Cambridge were made open in the nineteenth century.) He quotes President Nicholas Murray Butler of Columbia University: "It is far better educational policy to let ten unfit boys into college there to prove their unfitness and drop out, than to keep one thoroughly fit and ambitious boy out of college, perhaps to the discouragement and detriment of his whole life."[39] This is the Jude the Obscure syndrome again. The important conclusion Burnet draws from all this is that his examination of Prussian higher education has shown "that it is impracticable for us to throw the whole burden of a complete liberal education on to the secondary schools, and that it would be most undesirable even if it were practicable".[40] All experience had shown that if the general education of young people stopped at 17, one could not expect to get the best out of them. If we wanted to do as well as the Germans had done then we needed to continue general education until the age of

at least 20. This, of course, was precisely the role of the old Scottish
arts degree, and its truth was recognized in Germany, France and
America – precisely the countries which are outstripping Britain in
higher education today in the late twentieth century.[41]

The central element in such a broad, general education should
be philosophy, in Burnet's view. "It seems clear to me that in one
form or another Philosophy ought to hold the central place in the
stage of education we are now considering. This is in accordance
with Scottish tradition, and I am convinced that it was just this
that enabled Scotland to do as well as it did in the past . . . It is the
study of philosophy alone that can help a young man to approach
all other studies aright, and can save him from the narrowing influence of special study."[42] Despite the excellence of the teachers in
the French classe de philosophie and the French for *idées générales*,
philosophy at school must tend to be more dogmatic than it should
be. "It is only in the free atmosphere of the university that philosophy can flourish, and this is one of the strongest arguments for the
retention and strengthening of the Faculty of Arts . . . The school
is unable to give just that finishing touch to a general education
which is necessary if it is to become a proper foundation for a more
specialised training."[43] This would not mean that the universities
were doing school work; it would mean simply that it was thought
better to teach young people from 18–21 in the universities and not
in the schools. It would be much better to say that the French and
German schools were trying to do college work. "University work
proper should normally begin only after the Arts degree has been
taken."[44]

Nothing is missing in this remarkable seventy-five-year-old
prefiguration and proposed solution of the problems which beset
our universities today even more than in Burnet's time – not even
interdisciplinarity and the two cultures. "I have indicated already
that both the students of the Humanities and those of Science will
naturally find their work running up into the study of philosophy,
but there is a further principle which seems to me of great importance . . . It is extremely desirable that the students of the Humanities should know something of Science, and the students of Science
should know something of the Humanities . . . I think we ought to
insist on some science in every arts course."[45] Burnet says that the
American distinction between the liberal arts college and the university is a great help to clear thinking on this subject. It was not,
in his opinion, the High School or the Graduate School which was
the key feature of the American system, but the liberal arts college.
He also says that we need superior faculties of science and letters
like the American schools of graduate study. Readers will recall that

this had been proposed in the mid–nineteenth century but that the money was not forthcoming from London. "The expert training which crowns the whole system couldbe completed by the 25th or 26th year, and one has no right to expect it to take less time than that."[46] The Scottish faculties of arts should become the pivot of our system of higher education, like the colleges in America. "The alternative is to keep our boys at school till they are close on 20."[47]

What Burnet was seeking to do was to reinstate the traditional Scottish university system, updated to meet the situation in the twentieth century, following the dismal attempt to Oxbridgise it which had stalled the whole system. I think he was right, not because of what the "no anglicisation" people called the "nationalist" attitudes of a George Elder Davie, but because that system, appropriately adapted, would be far better than the bureaucratic-utilitarian, finance-led system we now have. Nor is it only Scotland that needs it -the world needs it.

Knowledge as an activity

Burnet's dreadful discovery and honourable retraction begs a very big question, of course. Why did Westminster and its aristocratic Scottish allies spend more than 60 years and a great deal of money on destroying a university system and curriculum which, in the opinion of such able men as Grierson and Burnet -having seen the effects of the reforms -was far better than what had replaced it? Presumably because they had a different agenda and were in a position to impose it. Yet there has never been any real certainty that they were right, as can be seen from the influence of the Scottish general approach in England, both before and after the reforms of the nineteenth century.

For example, when dissatisfaction with the narrowness and exclusiveness of Oxford and Cambridge led to the creation of University College, London, in 1826 (the year when the first Commission of the Scottish Universities met), the project was launched by Thomas Campbell, who had studied at Glasgow and Edinburgh universities. The first Education Committee, as it was called, had 10 members of whom 6, including its chairman, Henry Brougham, were graduates of Edinburgh. Similarly, graduates of Scottish universities were prominent among the professors appointed. Three out five appointees with established reputations were graduates of Edinburgh, as was also the secretary to the Council of the university and the warden appointed to manage its day-to-day affairs. The Medical School was modelled on Edinburgh "and manned almost entirely by Scotsmen." "The extended range of the subjects of the university, the lecture system, the non-residence of the students, the admission to single courses, the absence of religious tests, the dependence of the professors on fees, and the democratic character of the institution were all deliberate imitations of Scottish practice." Similarly, at Owen's College in Manchester, founded in 1851, the curriculum was divided into two main sections, Mental Philosophy and Physical Philosophy, a typically Scottish emphasis.[48] We have also seen in an earlier chapter the same Scottish influences at work at Keele and Sussex universities.

The contradiction between the two approaches – generalism and specialism – is still very evident in the recent period in official reports on higher education. The Crowther Report of 1959, for instance, says that specialization is inevitable, that it is "a product of the nineteenth century and a consequence of the tremendous advances in knowledge which from that time on began to mark all branches of study . . . The argument is not whether specialisation is desirable or unavoidable; it is about when it should begin." It says that "able boys and girls are ready and eager by the time they are 16 to get down to serious study of some one aspect of human knowledge." The Dainton Committee Report of 1968, on the other hand, says that "there should be a broad span of studies in the sixth forms of schools", and that "irreversible decisions for or against science, engineering and technology (should) be postponed as late as possible". It further states that "the swing from science is evidence of a reaction against a narrow concentration on studies in a particular field and a desire to bridge the extremes of specialization that have developed in school . . . It may be evidence that the gulf between the two cultures is a consequence, not a cause, of the curricular problems we have discussed." The Swann Report says: "it is evident that the great preponderance of present and future jobs for scientists and technologists, in industry and in school-teaching, are generalist in nature and do not require, or utilize in any direct way, specialist knowledge and skill, certainly not to the degree that it is developed in undergraduate courses in this country". Finally, the ten-volume Robbins Report of 1963 repeatedly makes a plea for broader first degree courses. It was not listened to, any more than Dainton or Swann.

It is clear from all the above that the specializing system imposed on the Scottish universities in 1889 was never seen as quite obviously educationally superior by some of the top people in higher education in Britain. Why, then, was it imposed? "Why", asks Professor Andrew McPherson, "should there be selection within the Scottish universities and how has the horizontal distinction between two intellectual styles, the generalist and specialist, been turned into a single vertical distinction between students who have been judged more or less able?"[49] After all, the Scottish Arts course in the nineteenth century had, as we have seen, a coherent educational philosophy and a clear economic function. It provided a broad general education such as could not be supplied by the schools, with their severe financial and staff limitations, before the student then went on to specialize in the law, medicine or theology. The main reason put forward by the "anglicizing reformers" was, as we have seen, the poor performance of Scottish candidates in the Indian Civil Service examinations, though this affected only a tiny minority of middle-class students, and was in any case to be expected since the examinations were set by Oxbridge men and therefore favoured students who had been through the intensely narrow classics and mathematics courses at these two universities. McPherson makes the key point that the relevance of this narrow training to the needs of the ICS were never questioned. He points out that it was only after the First World War that the numbers taking Honours degrees increased. Why? Was it economic and social factors that were responsible? Were the anglicizing university staffs building up the Honours courses to boost their CVs with the ultimate aim of applying for chairs in England? Did the Honours degree improve the job prospects of those moving to England in search of work, since this has been an essential career move for large numbers of young Scots throughout this century?[50] During the past hundred years 50% of Scottish graduates worked outside Scotland in the British Empire and in England where the general degree was not understood.

This is one very obvious reason for the gradual contraction of the Ordinary degree. "There are now 14,000 fewer graduates working in Scotland than in 1983, and during the period 1983–87 only Scotland's share of graduates fell, from 9.4% to 7%, with London having 45%, and this at a time when the graduate population of Britain rose by 230,000."[51] These figures show that the English labour market has always exerted a powerful influence on the Scottish university curriculum and teaching style. The English did not understand an open system where anybody who could pay the low fees could get to university, where they could follow any courses they wanted and so had a variety of qualifications, where they did not need to sit a degree examination but could show class tickets as proof of attainment. Furthermore, the education was a general one and based on a common philosophical core. What the English job market wanted was a "standardized specialist graduate product".[52] From this followed the need to formalize the whole higher education process from matriculation through to graduation by formal written examinations and formalized instruction.

Some of those who reject the anglicization thesis see this type of sociological analysis as supporting their position, whereas in fact it utterly undermines it. It was English political domination and economic power which destroyed the Scottish university system, so beloved of men like Grierson and Burnet; and this would probably not have come about in a Scotland that had retained its independence, as David Daiches has said. We can never know for certain, of course, but men like the above, and all the others whom we have had occasion to mention, would have wielded very much more power in an independent Scotland; whereas the Oxbridge-educated aristocracy, who did so much of the damage, would have had very much less. Also, the influence of the Continent, of France and Holland and Germany and Norway and Sweden, would have been very much stronger.

This, however, is speculation. What we do know is that the English purse-holders required the Scottish universities to demonstrate their 'efficiency' before they would release any money. The traditional Scottish ends were undermined by the equally traditional lack of means. They needed money for new chairs, but did not wish to raise students' fees and thereby exclude poor students. Graduation was taken as the sign of the efficiency of teaching and learning, and everything else then fell into place. "Matriculation defined potential candidates and ensured efficient spending on those 'most able to benefit'.[53] Since graduation conferred privileged status a century ago, there was need for a greater uniformity of teaching and learning, of syllabus and assessment; hence the written syllabus and curriculum and the written examination. The free-wheeling, democratic, exciting Scottish system was bureaucratized out of existence. The parallel with what has been done to Britain's universities as a whole in the 1960s is quite striking. Interestingly, too, much of the critique of what is being done today echoes the vigorous opposition of the Scottish academics of the nineteenth century who first experienced this modern liberal capitalist model of the university. Such a bureaucratic model of higher education necessarily influenced the student's attitude to knowledge, both then and today, as a number of contemporary writers have noted.[54]

The emphasis in Scotland was on "knowledge as an activity". The traditional teaching method was 'Socratic' and 'catechetical'. Lectures were followed by companion classes called 'examinations, in which the professors argued with the students, using a question-and-answer approach. They were considered to be very important for training the mind; and the reader will have noted that they were a direct descendant of the 'disputations' that were such an important part of the learning process in Scottish universities in earlier centuries. As McPherson points out, no distinction was made between the pedagogic and evaluative functions – between teaching and assessing – in these discussion hours, and of course the student was free to argue and disagree with the professor, a freedom impossible in the schools. This is why Burnet and others insist that general education must continue at the university, since it cannot be properly done in the schools. The value of these 'examinations' was not simply that they gave the professor an opportunity to gauge how much his students had understood and correct any misunderstandings. "It also assisted the essential function of education which was seen as the acquisition by an individual of a capacity to relate his specific and local vocabulary and modes of thought to more general and universal categories. The emphasis was on the student's making this relationship and respecting the authority that was implicit in knowledge as distinct from that in the person of the lecturer. The ideal product of the system had acquired skills and habits of thought which might be applied 'generally' – in other subject areas and, more importantly, outside the university in the business of life."[55] The vast gulf between this active method of learning – some elements of which have been rediscovered by contemporary authors – and the valuation of knowledge for qualification rather than for its own sake, is very obvious. The final justification of the bureaucratic system, with its written examinations, is, says McPherson, political and economic; it leads to passivity and boredom on the part of the student, and hence – since s/he is going through the hoops to get a job ticket – to the fragmentation and irrelevance of much of the knowledge gained. This necessarily destroyed 'general' or 'liberal' education, because the written examination, not life in the world, was the be-all and end-all of the student's life.

The result was a complete transformation of the way the university taught and the student learned. Teaching and assessment were separated and so were subjects. Separate subject departments developed. Previously, professors had relied for their income on students' fees which were handed directly to them. This is nicely illustrated in a delightful story from J. M. Barrie: "It was the opening of the session, when fees were paid, and the whisper ran round the quadrangle that Masson had set off home with 300 £1 notes stuffed into his trousers pockets . . . his pockets . . . were unmistakably bulging out. I resolved to go in for literature."[56]

In other words an element of supply and demand operated. Under the new system there was a common salary structure, so that the professor was no longer dependent on his popularity with the students and was in a monopoly position in his separate department.

The appointment of teaching assistants to help the professors led to a career hierarchy, especially for those educated in the specialist tradition of Oxford and Cambridge. They could move between Scotland and England, they became 'researchers', 'specialists', and the boundaries between departments, arising from the peculiarly English style of specialist education, became set in concrete. As late as the Robbins Committee in the early 1960s there were still depositions condemning this trend. McPherson gives some student opinions on the situation from the late 1960s. "The unstimulating nature of the lecture system made the subjects boring. Moreover the (essay) exams require no real knowledge of the subject, but merely the regurgitation of notes, understood or not. Courses are too narrow in outlook – too much specialization." "I thought university would teach me to think – but I was only required to memorize on the whole." "I have found that one can develop a technique for passing exams without doing nearly as much as first appears necessary. Furthermore, the necessity of passing exams makes them the only consideration in academic life." Economic criteria are now more important than knowledge criteria; graduation is, as it were, the termination of a contract. The student's place in the professional market is decided by the quality of his degree. Thus in view of the degree's importance for an individual's life chances it had a backward effect on the schools, making for earlier specialization. This is at its most intense and most narrow in the schools that set Oxford and Cambridge as the goal of endeavour.

Another major question raised by the liberal capitalist model of the university is: who decides the content of the curricula? Clearly the people who have power and influence within the educational system. The political nature of these curricular decisions has never been clearer than during the 1980s when the supposed university-friendly attitude of the University Grants Committee was swept aside, and the universities were told in no uncertain manner that they would do the government's bidding or they would not get money; and the ultimate power in money matters lies with the Treasury and the Cabinet. Starting with Sir Keith Joseph, supposedly a brilliant, Oxbridge-trained intellectual, curricular and all other decisions relating to the universities were taken on the basis of a crude interpretation of the needs of the British economy. The speed with which any real autonomy has been stripped from the universities and they have been reduced to executants of government policy through such a comically incompetent body as the Universities Funding Council, which replaced the UGC, is truly alarming.

Is there any way back for the Scottish universities? That is a question we shall look at in detail in the final chapters of this book.

There are certain elements, however, which make for a cautious optimism. The generalism versus specialism problem simply will not go away, as we have seen from the various solutions to it propounded in the Crowther, Dainton, Swann and Robbins reports. It is also being debated in other countries such as the USA, Canada, Australia and New Zealand. It appears to be a fundamental and permanent dilemma of higher education. The British Government thinks that higher vocational training is what universities are about, but more and more British leaders in technology tend to believe that what is needed is a generally-educated student who can think for her/himself, ask questions, who knows something about the problems of the world today, and can express him/herself articulately, logically and convincingly. That was precisely the aim of the traditional general Scottish university education. The problem is well stated for our day by the University of Edinburgh in its submission to Robbins: "The polymath and the educated man are becoming increasingly difficult to equate."

McPherson gives a clear definition of the problem: "The ideal of a liberal education originally meant that an accepted body of knowledge should form the cultural inheritance of all educated men and should be transmitted in its entirety to the next generation. When that became too large a task, one decision which might have been taken would have been to define an essential core of knowledge which every student must master before branching out into other fields or taking further the study of one aspect of the core. That decision was not taken."

If the fact that the problem refuses to go away is an element encouraging optimism, then its intractability puts some propounded solutions out of court. The Robbins and Swann committees both called for raising the status of the general degree. The latter even called for the removal of the terms Honours and Ordinary and for making the degree courses the same length. We have seen how little attention has been paid to them. In any case, as McPherson says, these proposals would not be enough. It would be necessary to make radical changes in the methods of instruction and assessment and in departmental structure, though we have seen how far Tom Cottrell got with his teaching innovations at Stirling. McPherson does not mention Stirling but says that there is no longer a coherent philosophy of general education in Scotland, which is why the Scottish representatives (if they were indeed Scottish) could give no coherent educational justification for the Ordinary degree to the Robbins Committee. Hardly surprising, one is inclined to say, when there is a large majority of English academics at Scottish universities who have no idea of general education, as the Stirling failure showed.

His own suggestion that perhaps Scotland could learn from the innovations of some of the new English universities fares no better since the phenomenon known as "academic drift" soon pulled these universities back into line.

The one true element of hope is that there continues to be much discussion of the problem around the world, and there still exists real understanding and appreciation of the traditional Scottish approach to higher education. What is more, there is a rapidly growing realization that our present, fragmented and over-specialized training is not fitting the present generation of students to understand and face up to the great and growing problems confronting us, and a strong sense that a more holistic approach is needed. Therein lies the hope for the democratic intellect. We shall have to look squarely at the situation in Scotland's universities today before we can give voice to that hope, but first we must make a broader examination, in the light of contemporary comment, of the perennial problem of generalism versus specialism.

12

Generalism v Specialism
"Atomism packed tight"

Aristotle, demonstrating that there is nothing new under the sun, asked: "Should the useful in life, or should virtue, or should the higher knowledge, be the main aim of our training?" More than 2000 years later Herbert Spencer asked: "What knowledge is of most worth?" The answers to these questions have been clearest when times were settled, for example in the Middle Ages, when the trivium (grammar, rhetoric and dialectic) and the quadrivium (arithmetic, music, geometry and astronomy) reigned supreme. The Scottish Ordinary degree, providing a broad general education in the arts, science and philosophy, gave a confident answer in later days. But today uncertainty prevails over the issue of general versus specialized degrees.[1] Dissatisfaction too.[2] At the Annual Conference of Adult Education in 1966 Professor Ronald Fletcher of York University gave vent to his: "I personally am becoming deeply dissatisfied with what is going on in the universities. They seem the last place where you can be educated; they are BA factories whose professors are like works managers, mere admin men."[3] One wonders what Professor Fletcher might think of the present situation where the bureaucrats and accountants have taken over totally and department heads are now line managers, and where everybody has to have a 'mission statement'. Indeed the *Times Higher Education Supplement*[4] speaks of the Jarratt Report's "offensively managerial language" and cites the recommendation to the Committee of Vice-Chancellors and Principals from its national co-ordinator of academic staff training that academic staff in universities should receive training in management techniques, entrepreneurship, marketing methods and media presentation, in addition to improving their more traditional teaching skills. This is so ludicrous as to be almost unbelievable.

Ex-Provost Alastair Thompson of Callander gives us the *vox populi Scotiae* on the subject; "The aspirations of the Scottish system were as important as the achievements. The ideals were that all children should have a basic education as cheaply as possible, and that as many as possible should have a secondary education. What is the purpose of education?[5] Is it to train the mind in a narrow channel for a particular job, or should it consist of a general training which would fit the person to acquire the skills of any job? The latter has been the case in Scotland. Should we continue with this policy or do we have to consider what is happening to our young people? They may have to leave Scotland to find a job and their qualifications may not be recognized as they are different from those in England."[6] So different that an article describing the English system in *TESS*[7] can be titled 'More and more about less and less' and can ask "What is the difference between a specialization that narrows and a specialization that liberates?"

Professor Tom Cottrell, Stirling University's Principal, was quoted in the editorial of the same number of *TESS* as saying that the capacity of Scottish higher education to innovate and to rethink itself would be judged to some extent on the performance of Stirling University where they were reaffirming the importance of a general and flexible education as compared with a specialist and rigid one. At Stirling they believed in the virtue of variety within a system. Variety, like the innovation which often creates it, leads to a constant rethinking and should therefore be welcomed. Speaking, in a later issue of *TESS*,[8] as a former professor of chemistry, he said that he would not want his students to be taught more chemistry at school. If people wanted to get intellectual maturity by working on their own at school, they could very usefully spend a year on history or English or maths and come and be taught chemistry by the professor of chemistry. This was backed up by Professor John Lamb, of the chair of engineering at Glasgow, who said he preferred students coming to his department to have as broad an education as possible without being taught engineering at school. "We would like them to have a good grounding in maths, physics and chemistry in particular, with knowledge of the foreign languages and competence in English. This is the prime requirement."[9] And Professor Raymond Smart, Vice-Principal of Heriot-Watt University, gave it as his view that "over-specialization in university education can produce graduates who lack the basic knowledge to widen the scope of their work". Professor Reichman of City University makes this more explicit. "It can be fruitful to start from some basic problems and bring together the disciplines which have a bearing on them, for no subject is self-contained, confined to its own corner of reality."[10]

We recall the views of John Burnet who said: "The most important side of any department of knowledge is the side in which it comes into touch with every other department. To insist on this is the true function of humanism." On this issue, clearly, the two cultures are not as far apart as they might seem.

The very antithesis of this attitude was expressed in the media hype surrounding the award of a First in mathematics to Ruth Lawrence, a 13-year-old Oxford student. An editorial in the *THES*[11] had this to say:

> The democratic quality of excellence needs to be insisted upon (because) there are too many who are more happy to set excellence on some unscaleable pedestal, rather than base it firmly on accountable merit. Such a view justifies their commitment to an inflexibly hierarchical society ... The second message (of this award) is that education is a narrowly focussed business, that it is about economics or biochemistry or, in Ruth's case, maths and not much else. This concentration on carefully restricted disciplinary territory is particularly strong in higher education, despite a century or more of rhetoric in favour of a broader and more liberal university curriculum. Such concentration is probably not even profitable in its own narrow academic terms; certainly it disables many of the best intentions of a higher education. Education, even higher education, is not just about intellectual excellence in the narrow sense ... It is about the acquiring of wisdom, a much broader circle drawn round this narrower excellence that also embraces maturity, experience, judgment and, yes, humanity as well."

How ludicrously at variance with such a commonsense judgment the specialization craze can be is shown by the story of Ganesh Sittampalam, a 13-year-old mathematics genius who took a First in mathematics at Surrey University, "beating the previous record-holder, Ruth Lawrence, by seven months", gloats the newspaper report.[12] But Ganesh is obviously a very level-headed boy. His comment was: "I jumped up and down and yelled 'Yippee' when I found I had a First", but he is thinking of giving up maths to concentrate on his GCEs at school. One wonders if they will insist on putting him into the Guinness Book of Records, and whether this will become a regular event in the sporting calendar like Wimbledon or the Open Golf Championship. "What is worse", says another report, [13] "such specialization has invaded the schools. I wonder in what other civilized country children, at the tender age of O-levels, are asked whether they prefer to be natural scientists, humanists, or even social scientists".[14] Seventeen years after his famous report on the universities Lord Robbins had to admit that his key proposal for the provision of broad, non-specialized undergraduate courses had not been fulfilled. Instead, he said, the English (though not the Scottish) universities had created more and more sophisticated undergraduate courses and thereby undermined their ability to turn out generally well-educated young men and women. In their turn, the universities, through their entrance requirements, had imposed on schools a habit of specialization that forced children to choose ludicrously early between arts and sciences. In his book *Higher Education Revisited*[15] he described this as "little short of a national disgrace". In conversation he grew even more vehement, thumping his desk at the London School of Economics and deprecating those professors who, in a scrabble for self-aggrandizement, had promoted narrow honours degrees and neglected broad degrees more suited to the majority of students destined never to become dons or high experts. Such is the power and mystique of the Oxbridge-created honours degree that even so prestigious a figure in higher education as Lord Robbins was completely defeated on what he considered to be the most important aspect of his report. It has to be said, however, that even he gets it wrong – and in a way that helps his opponents – as to the original purpose and role of the Ordinary degree. It was not for the non-high-flyers, as he says. It was for all students before they specialized; its role was to civilize them.

The predictable result of this seemingly ineradicable fix on specialization was noted in the higher education press: "Britain is one of the best educated nations, and yet among her politicians and academics she has perilously few people with the broad view, capable of thinking – and thinking ahead – in economic, political and multi-scientific terms."[16] Britain's bumpy ride through the 1980s and into the 90s was precisely the product of such limited thinking. In December 1973 the Association of University Teachers had come out against specialization in the Sixth Form.[17] In 1990 it was still at it. As a result of the Higginson Report on A-levels its Council called for "broader but leaner" A-levels along the lines of the *baccalauréat* or the Scottish system. This would greatly improve access to the university, said the Council, and would possibly result in a four-year degree.[18] Yet not much more than a year later the Howie Report was proposing the abolition of the Highers in Scotland and their replacement by a six-year baccalaureate which, whatever its stated intentions, would be likely, because of the almost certain refusal of adequate funding, to end up imitating the English paradigm of the six-year A-level course plus three-year university degree course. Certainly Sir Christopher Ball and Dr John Ashworth, Director of LSE, were loudly calling for a reduction of the Scottish four-year degree to three years. Confusion and uncertainty could scarcely go further, with cost-effectiveness being the only immovable criterion. The dangers, however, were growing greater all the time. In an article entitled *Science Approaches Point of no Return*, Dr John Mulvey, of the Save British Science committee, said: "Measures need to be taken to tackle what amounts to a national emergency in our education system, which is preventing more people with better standards of qualifications entering higher education science and technology courses."[19] The strongest message from both students and teachers (on the basis of an enquiry by Oxford University Department of Educational Studies) was that the present A-level system gave too little choice and caused premature specialization.

At this point Dr Graham Hills, the maverick English Principal of Strathclyde University, enters the lists. He speaks of the practical advantages of delaying specialization in his column in the THES, since it allows time for a better fit between the students' aspirations and talents and the opportunities open to them. "Common sense therefore suggests that students should initially read for a general first degree as [was] . . . *de rigueur* in Scotland . . . The unnecessary imposition at the age of 17 or less of a premature commitment to a small number of specialized subjects should be pruned and discarded together with the A-level examinations which thrive on it. Schools could then return to their civilizing task of encouraging the young to enjoy learning and to leave school with an appetite for more (in contrast to the feeling of surfeit after sixth form scholarship swotting we noted in Chapter 3) . . . A liberal education is desirable for all and we should not let the premature pursuit of nuts and bolts obscure that."[20] This, says Professor A. J. Beattie, of the chair of Greek at Edinburgh, would enable them to come to university "in a sober and relatively emancipated frame of mind", especially if they didn't have too many exams to sit at either school or university.[21] Even the Universities (Scotland) Bill of 1965, which was a compromise between conflicting views, said: "We believe that there are good educational reasons for combining subjects in such a way as may cut across the conventional divisions such as arts, science and social science."

Principal Tom Cottrell, speaking to the sponsoring committee of Stirling University before the university existed, said it would be very important to secure academic staff of high quality who were like-minded in their concern for teaching and following knowledge, regardless of the formal, and often largely out-dated, divisions between subjects. Clearly he did not succeed in this since his innovative attempt at a broad, integrated first year university course – *Approaches and Methods* – met with resistance from staff and students and had to be abandoned.[22] Professor Jack Johnston, of the Chair of Economics at Manchester, chips in that one of the diffi-

culties of recruitment lay in the arts/science dichotomy that existed
certainly in English grammar schools. With early specialization,
the intellectually gifted boy or girl tended quite naturally to think
of a science or an arts faculty as his/her natural university development.[23] Too much specialization too early and the lack of the
opportunity to change disciplines between school and the first year
at university are post-Dainton and post-Swann themes dealt with
in the McCarthy Report.[24] It points out that American high school
and first-year college curricula encourage more general study. The
first-year engineer in America is taught law and sociology, and the
system tends to produce the 'science-based generalist', the type of
scientific all-rounder who can switch from one specialism to another
in a fluid labour market.[25] In Great Britain, per contra, there is,
according to McCarthy, a lack of versatility among its scientists due
to the narrowness of English and Welsh sixth form and first-year
university courses.

At this point we come across a confusion typical of many in
educational debate in Britain because of a failure to think problems through. Professor Norman C. Hunt, of the Department of
the Organization of Industry and Commerce at the University of
Edinburgh says he agrees with Robert Presthuis of Cornell on what
he calls the British 'generalist myth' – "the assumption fostered
mainly by the public schools and Oxbridge that a liberal education augmented by certain personal qualities of 'character', 'poise'
and 'leadership' provides the best basis for dealing with complex
problems of modern government and industry". If future managers
are not given a training in subjects which are relevant to a career
in the highly complex technological world of modern industry,
"British industry will continue to be starved of the able managers
trained in the natural and social sciences who are so significant a
component in the most successful Continental and American industries".[26] The confusion here is brought out well in Sanderson and
was foreshadowed earlier in our demonstration that the Scottish
universities followed the medieval tradition of a *broad* arts course
before specialization, whereas Oxford and Cambridge provided
only a *deliberately narrow and specialized* arts course ("exactness
within a narrow range", said Sir John Seeley) for training gentlemen.
Sanderson points out that there was mutual suspicion and contempt
between the Scottish universities and Oxbridge, and that the Scots-
inspired University College in London "betokened both the sharp
differences between the two national systems of liberal education
and their mutual incomprehension".

As we have seen Oxbridge won that battle because of their political power and influence and through their sycophantic aristocratic

Scottish alumni. As Sanderson delicately puts it, the "later nineteenth century systems grew closer together as the Scottish universities were anglicized to some extent by accepting a narrower degree of specialization". He quotes the General Report of 1900 of the Commissioners under the Universities (Scotland) Act of 1889 to show where the fatal damage was done: "We found ... that the existing course of study in Arts was too rigid; it admitted of no adaptation for individual taste or bent of mind, nor did it offer any encouragement to the higher and more specialized study of any subject. Under the new scheme the Honours student is exempted from some of the Pass subjects, and is able from the outset to lay out his whole course with reference to the Honours Group in which he proposes to graduate." Thus was the excessive specialization that is being so widely complained about today imposed on the universities of Scotland. Sanderson is in no doubt what the purpose was: "The first major change was the revolution which anglicized the Scottish universities." There is something far wrong with the scholarship of people who today loudly affirm that there was no anglicization of the Scottish universities.

The answer to Professor Hunt's problem is that the influence of Oxbridge is all-pervasive in our universities and must be greatly reduced. More importantly, we must find a way of re-introducing the Scottish ordinary degree course, containing elements of arts, science and philosophy *for all students before they specialize*, because, as Professor Hunt says, specialization is indeed necessary. John Grierson speaks of "the specialization which is the distinctive aim and end of university education, but not to be begun till the right time"; yet Grierson was a great enthusiast for a good general knowledge of "every essential department of general culture". General knowledge and professional specialization were complementary at the Scottish universities, whereas at Oxbridge the arts course was narrowly specialized and exclusive, wanting nothing to do with science and technology.

Dr W. H. F. Burns, Vice-Chancellor of the University of Liverpool, takes the opposite position to that of Professor Hunt.[27] Speaking to the pupils of Morrison's Academy, he says that it was very common now to hear criticism of the educational system as not preparing people for real things such as management and decision-making, and that he believed this whole approach to be a misconception. "I believe", he said, "that the most important function of education is to give the mind a general training which will serve its owner in good stead no matter what profession or occupation he chooses to pursue and no matter what demands life makes on him." This was the goal sought by Tom Cottrell when he said[28] that the formal part of modern university education tended to concentrate a student's powers in a relatively specialised field, and that the informal part – general discussion among contemporaries – tended to encourage thinking at large without much check on its accuracy. The careful study of general intellectual methods at a fairly elementary level was not usually part of the curriculum, yet many who worked with recent university graduates found them lacking in just the ability to think carefully and simply about new problems. The Academic Planning Board of the University of Stirling was aware of this deficiency and sought to remedy it by recommending a course for all students on general intellectual methods. The idea of such a course is not new; in the medieval university there was a generally accepted basis for the master's degree, consisting of seven liberal arts: grammar, logic rhetoric, music, arithmetic, geometry and astronomy. Three of these arts appear in the Stirling course, not because they were accepted in the Middle Ages but because they are still important. Such a sentiment would have been welcomed by Principal Steven Watson of the University of St Andrews, who said at a graduation ceremony that universities were now the organized interest which has to "take the leading part in the battle for lasting truth against temporary convenience".[29] That the memory of these historical traditions is still very much alive is confirmed by the remarks of Dr John McIntyre, Professor of Divinity at Edinburgh, at a conference organised by *TESS* in 1975. He said it would be wrong to be silent about the continual emphasis on broad requirements, the reluctance to narrow down a pupil's options in later life by a premature option for a science-type or an arts-type course, "as well as the primacy of place given to philosophy . . . and the requirement of an arts degree for entry to all of the professions up until living memory."[30]

A significant number of reports, including Leverhulme, which we have not yet mentioned, have favoured broad-based courses. In response to a questionnaire from the chief executive of the UGC, Sir Peter Swinnerton-Dyer, in 1983, not one university supported the Leverhulme concept of two-year, broad-based degree courses. Many considered that an opening-out of sixth form studies could only be achieved by extending degree courses to four years, a view supported by the Committee of Vice-chancellors and Principals but unlikely to receive funding. This rare but welcome example of English readiness to learn from Scottish experience was followed by the Higginson Report's call in 1989 for broader A-levels. This was supported by the AUT, which said that "students should be encouraged to think for themselves and gain a real understanding of their subject rather than stuffing themselves full of half-digested facts. There could well be a demand for a much less specialized first year or indeed degree programme with pressure for broader ranges of modes of study." Such a volume of complaint might seem irresistible, yet nothing is done. Sir Graham Hills again puts his finger on the obstacle in the way: "The jackpot prize for stubborn durability must go to A-levels and the conspiracy of interests supporting them. Despaired of by most as a sad English anachronism, the A-level examination system sails serenely on regardless of its critics. On its way it continues to debilitate higher education by delivering to it students narrowly and miserably prepared for the wide spectrum of subject opportunities in front of them ..."[31] Roger Young, the headmaster of George Watson's College in Edinburgh, called in to report on Stirling University's difficulties after the Queen's visit in 1972, called in vain for the resuscitation of the *Approaches and Methods* course we have spoken of. He said that the weakest part of most sixth-formers' educational equipment was methodology and the approach to learning, and that the lack of a real understanding of approaches and methods in their studies exacerbated many Stirling students' academic difficulties.[32]

Michael Swann, then Principal of the University of Edinburgh, speaking of the growing numbers of students and of the fact that inevitably there would be more who would not reach the highest grades, said this did not matter. "Indeed, one good result might be a greater concentration on broad general degrees ... The Scottish educational system has got this much more nearly right than anyone else in the UK." There was much to commend the ordinary degree. It had great flexibility and considerable width, and it provided the pattern of the sort of thing the universities ought to be doing. Many students who were not future specialists were taking biology as part of an ordinary degree. Biology was the science that linked the humanities with the physical sciences. It should be taught to more students and perhaps taught in a more enlightened way.[33]

What is more, such an approach seems to pay off. Michael Gavin points out in an article that Scottish graduates seem to succeed in getting jobs and suggests that "the nature of the traditional Scottish university course is indeed such that its breadth and relative lack of specialization make its graduates easier to employ". He cites what he calls the "quite extraordinary fact that 145 out of 6,153 1970 first degree graduates of Scottish universities were still seeking employment at the end of 1970 compared with some 2,500 in the UK universities as a whole, and including 715 from the University of London alone where 8.1% of students were in this plight". The editorial in the same journal says "it may well be that by coming to

Scotland the English student improves his or her chances of eventual employment", though it points that Scotland can ill afford to lose 400 graduates a year who are finding work elsewhere.[34] (This has been Scotland's fate for centuries). The unfortunate result has been that more and more English students have flooded into Scotland, so that four of our universities (Edinburgh, St Andrews, Stirling and Dundee) now have a majority of English students. This helps create enforced uniformity of the Scottish system with the English one, as Dr John McIntyre, of Edinburgh University, was already pointing out in 1975.[35]

An article entitled 'The Passing of the Polymath'[36] goes so far as to say that within the established educational framework there is little or no chance of anybody having a sufficiently wide education for him to be well educated. "This increasing academic specialization", the author continues, "is having unfortunate results in that it is becoming ever more difficult for people to take a broad view of even one subject and interpret and synthesise the latest findings and theories to see how they fit in together, to put them in their time perspective, and thus point the way for further research". There are few academics who dare to be generalists even in their own field "for fear of being 'knocked'."

This lack of perspective can be seen in industry and government as well as education. The government seeks to appear more professional by having all sorts of specialist advisers and committees. "This", says the writer, "is most unfortunate as all specialists must, almost by definition, advocate the use of their specialty." He concludes that the universities should be producing generalists who understand both scientists and artists, and put both in their proper perspective. Wilson[37] says that almost any area of knowledge may be of direct professional use to a lawyer in untangling the legal ramifications of a case: building practices, appropriate pedagogy for deaf children, or the classification of renaissance art. "A manager who is to get the best results from his team could have use for almost realm of discourse in order to interpret a target or to get an agreement properly understood." But Robinson gets it wrong when he says that "people wanting vocational training should not go to the university but to some vocational, further education centre". It is perfectly possible to do both in the same institution by the simple expedient of a general, broad first degree followed by specialist training.

Furthermore, "many students of science and technology are glad to include some study of the humanities in their courses", says David Raphael, Professor of Philosophy at Imperial College, London.[38] "They are interested in debating questions of value, of critical appraisal, of the foundations of belief (scientific, ethical, political, religious), of the explanation of human actions – individual and social." He says that this is well recognized in the USA, "where the basic form of higher education for most students is a BA course in the liberal arts and sciences", after which many go on to graduate school to specialize in science, law, medicine, etc. But at the level of the BA the Americans still believe in the value of the liberal arts and sciences "for giving young people an all-round appreciation of human knowledge and human values". He then remarks, in a way that should sadden Scottish readers, "it is also recognized in Scotland to some extent, though to a lesser extent than a generation ago". He goes on to explain what they did a generation ago. They got "a sound general education preliminary to a more vocational training". It included "as core requirements" a course in philosophy, a foreign language, and one in mathematics or a natural science, and not less than five subjects had to be studied. He adds that when specialization was introduced at Glasgow University after the Second World War the bridge between the humanities and the natural sciences simply disappeared. This was followed by pressure to remove the foreign language, and then to remove philosophy. He calls for the revival of the Ordinary degree, which should include mathematics and science because of their importance in the modern world; philosophy for its fostering of a critical attitude; some form of history, language and literature. "All the central humanities should do more than cater for the specialist." He concludes with a very important perception: "The English universities are falling down on their job when they insist on squeezing all their undergraduates, whether square pegs or round, into the one kind of hole called an honours course. They deceive themselves into thinking that they have raised the standards of higher education for the average undergraduate by getting rid of the ordinary or general degree." To sum it up, members of the university teaching profession "are increasingly oriented to research rather than teaching . . . experts embedded in ever more narrowly defined knowledge traditions. Their organizing principle is speciali-zation, itself a product of the reductionism inherent in the scientific method . . . "[39]

There are problems in Australia too. According to a Senate inquiry into higher education Australia's universities are producing a race of 'barbarian' graduates with poor analytical, creative, communication and social skills. The Senate committee found that courses were too specialised, lacked a social context and did not prepare graduates for their working lives. "Hyper-specialism runs throughout academic life", said a delegate at an LSE Contemporary Research Group Seminar. "We divide into our little groups and spend our academic careers organising conferences for the same group of specialists."[40]

The American, Allan Bloom, says that a highly-trained computer specialist need not have had any more learning about morals, politics
or religion than the most ignorant of persons, because his narrow
education can cut him off from the "liberal learning that simpler
folk used to absorb from a variety of traditional sources . . . When
a youngster like Lincoln sought to educate himself, the immediately
available things for him to learn were the Bible, Shakespeare and
Euclid." Was he really worse off than youngsters today, asks Bloom.

Perhaps all is not gloom and Bloom. In an article in the *Scottish
Educational Review*[41] J. P. B. Lovell speaks of a course at Edinburgh
which was stimulated by *Natural Sciences 10, Aspects of the Natural
Environment*, created at Harvard, which was taught with excep-
tional care, all for the benefit of students who would never take
another science course. "*Natural Sciences 10* was just one part of a
general education programme, the scope and quality of which would
grace any university, no matter how specialized or unspecialized the
academic backgrounds of its students." It contained a great range of
thought, experiment and exposition which was put over by a young
team encouraged to take a professional pride in teaching, including
teaching designed to produce breadth in university curricula. Its
value was, among other things, that it gave students a chance to *do*
some work in science – which reminds us of Whitehead's dictum
that pupils should be given the opportunity both to know and to do
and of Macmurray's philosophic emphasis on action. Again, we are
disagreeably reminded that Scotland exported to America what was
choked off at home. As an editorial in the *THES* said,[42] "American
undergraduate courses aspire to a breadth that is never attempted,
or only feebly so, in Scotland." The point had been rubbed in in
the previous issue in which it was stated that the State University of
California was raising the stakes for entry. From 1994, in addition
to four years of college-preparatory English, three years of mathematics, two of a foreign language, one of laboratory science and
one of US history, students must take a single one-year-long world
history class or one semester in world history and another in world
geography and culture. They will also have to take an additional
year of biology, chemistry, physics or earth sciences. Professor Helen
Henry says that this is "an attempt to address what many faculty
see as a deficient global perspective. Students increasingly need to
look at their world as the entirety of human experience, not just the
Eurocentric perspective." The astonishing thing is that apparently
this will do little to check the enrollment boom, because 90% of
the 165,000 students alreadymeet the strengthened criteria. It is, of
course, true, that in education as in most other things, California
is ahead of the rest of the United States, but even so the picture of

mass access to higher education is splendid to behold. It proves that mass access and excellence are not incompatible. It is hardly surprising that in BBC 2's scientific and environmental blockbusters the researchers consulted are nearly always relaxed youngish Americans in jeans.

Here and there one finds beginnings of a new approach. For example, at the University of Bielefeld, the professor of education was setting up, in 1970, a new type of college, the *Oberstufencolleg* for students from 17–21 years of age, which dispensed entirely with the Abitur, the German equivalent of Highers or A-levels. Students were to spend two fifths of their time on two subjects, while the rest of the time would be given over to communal projects covering all subjects, and complementary studies covering five basic ways of approaching knowledge.[43] In 1985 the Swedish Minister of Education, Lennart Bodström, said that Sweden's emphasis on expanding its pool of qualified technologists must not be accompanied by neglect of the humanities. Technicians themselves tended to benefit from a broad humanistic tradition. In 1980, the Saudi Arabian Minister of Industry, on a visit to Sweden, did not want to talk about experts and technology, but to discuss poetry and meet Swedish poets. The Swedish minister receiving him was understandably astonished, and Lund University was encouraged to set up crash courses in Arab culture for Swedish companies, and 2,500 businessmen had attended 50 courses in the last five years (one remembers that we owe our knowledge of ancient Greek and Roman literature to the Arabs). At the seminar Mr Bodström was attending, speakers said that "industry needs humanists" because they understand the importance of developing themselves and listening to others and "they have a talent for an overall view, not limiting their analytical powers to any one sector". But a few swallows do not make a summer, especially when they are abroad, and it remains true that, as F. R. Leavis said in 1943, "the idea of liberal culture has been defeated and dissipated by advancing specialization, and the production of specialists . . . tends to be regarded as the supreme end of the university, its *raison d'être*". This is true even of the universities of Scotland, which more than any others in the past set the general education of all students as their goal, and only renounced it when compelled to by *force majeure*.

In reflections on the universities of Cambridge and London,[44] George B. Jeffery says that the universities are turning out men and women who are narrow specialists in the sense that they have great technical knowledge in some small field, "but have little or no conception of knowledge as a whole or of the part which is played by their particular specialty within the greater structure". This again is the exact opposite of the traditional Scottish system which trained students to see the systematic interconnections of things and their relationship to a wider context. Jeffery does not think "that anything is likely to be done until a university is prepared to stand up to its own specialists".[45] He shows that the specialist university teacher insists on putting more and more of his specialty into the courses of his students. The next stage is the brilliant undergraduate who undertakes research and realises that if he is to make his mark he must concentrate on a tiny section at the boundary of knowledge, so that he becomes even more specialized than he was as an undergraduate. "Later he attains to seniority within the university and by this time he is all too often a cobbler fully convinced that there is nothing like leather and prepared wholeheartedly to legislate for the propagation of his species." The trouble with the specialist is not that he knows a lot about his subject; "it is that he knows nothing about anything else and that he therefore in any ultimate sense knows very little that is significant about his own subject".[46] For Jeffery the answer to this problem is that anyone working in a special field should, from time to time, pause and ask what is the nature of enquiry in this field, what questions does it give rise to, what kind of answer does it give to these questions? "In brief he should have some grasp of the philosophical nature of the work . . . and he should try to appreciate the place which his work takes in the general body of knowledge."[47] He regrets that philosophers have allowed their subject "to become a specialty among other specialties", because as soon as we begin to ask what is the true significance of our work in relation to the whole body of knowledge "we find ourselves asking in our amateur way the questions which have been asked in differing form throughout the whole history of philosophy"[48] – the point made earlier by I. F. Stone. Jeffery would like to see the philosophers offering lectures and opportunities for discussion to students in other subjects, for it is the philosophers who have "the best opportunity to make an effort to bring back our lost sense of unity". Philosophy in this sense was the keystone of the old Scottish ordinary degree. There could hardly be a better plea for its reinstatement.

Ortega y Gasset is a scholar who has much that is interesting to say about this problem.[49] In the introduction to his book Harvey Lee Nostrand says:

> If we could solve the problem of general education, we could confidently strike any third world war off the calendar. General education means the whole development of an individual, apart from his occupational training. It includes the civilizing of his life purposes, the refining of his emotional reactions and

the maturing of his understanding about the nature of things according to the best knowledge of our time. *In this sense general education is the fundamental problem of modern society.* (Our italics)

Ortega y Gasset waxes very ironical about the sop that is thrown to 'general culture' in our universities. "The absurdity of the term, its Philistinism, betrays its insincerity." It betrays an underlying notion that the student ought to be given some ornamental knowledge which will somehow educate his moral character or his intellect. For such a vague purpose, he says, any old non-technical discipline will do. In the Middle Ages, on the other hand, "all was general culture", because general culture then meant "the system of ideas concerning the world and humanity which the man of that time possessed . . . the effective guide of his existence . . . clear, firm ideas concerning the universe, positive convictions about the nature of things. That is true culture – the opposite of external ornament . . . Culture is what saves human life from being a mere disaster."[50] We cannot live without ideas. Living is nothing more nor less than doing one thing instead of another. "Culture is the vital system of ideas of a period." Life and planning are inseparable, and man's or woman's plan has to be based on an 'idea' of the world and the things in it. This concept of the world and man has to be 'wired in', as it were, because life is always urgent, it is "fired at us point blank". Culture, which is but its interpretation, cannot wait any more than life can. Science, research, is not something we live by. "The internal conduct of science is not a *vital* concern; that of culture is."

Compared with the medieval university, y Gasset says, the contemporary university has abandoned almost entirely the teaching or transmission of culture. (We must remember that he was speaking 50 years ago. What would he think of today's universities?) "It is evident that the change has been pernicious. Europe today is taking its sinister consequences." This is because the average European is uncultured, that is, ignorant of the essential system of ideas concerning the world and man which belongs to our time. This average person is the new barbarian (we are reminded of MacIntyre); he lags behind the contemporary civilization, archaic and primitive, in contrast with his problems, which are grimly, relentlessly, modern. "This new barbarian is above all the professional man, more learned than ever before, but at the same time more uncultured – the engineer, the physician, the lawyer, the scientist." He quotes Chuang-Tsu: "How shall I talk of life with the sage, if he is the prisoner of his doctrine."

If any professional man – what Edwards would call the decision-makers – is ignorant of the physical cosmos, does not have a coherent

picture of the great movements of history, of the key contemporary
ideas of philosophy and biology, then he is not an educated man, "he
is a perfect barbarian". There is no other way: "to move with assurance in the tangle of life one must be cultivated. Civilization has had
to await the beginning of the twentieth century to see the astounding
spectacle of how brutal, how stupid and yet how aggressive is the
man learned in one thing and fundamentally ignorant of all else. *Professionalism and specialism, through insufficient counterbalancing,
have smashed the European man in pieces.*" (Our italics)

Another great failing of the contemporary university is that it lives
a lie, it lacks authenticity. It caters for Ashby's "thin, clear stream of
excellence", not for the ordinary student; and "failure is taken for
granted". Institutions exist because the ordinary man exists; they
are made for the person of ordinary endowment and s/he must be
their unit of measurement. Leonardo da Vinci said; "Chi non puo
quel que vuol, quel que puo vogli" This, in Gasset's opinion, must
be the guide to any real reform of the university, if it is to regain
authenticity. "Instead of teaching what *ought* to be taught, according to some Utopian desire, we must teach only what *can* be taught,
that is, *what can be learned.*" Rousseau was right, says Gasset, to
shift the centre of gravity to the learner. If we then take the ordinary student as our starting-point, the university should provide the
education that will make him/her a cultured person, "at the height
of the times". This education will then consist of:

1 The physical scheme of the world (physics);
2 The fundamental themes of organic life (biology);
3 The historic process of the human species (history);
4 The structure and functioning of social life (sociology);
5 The plan of the universe (philosophy).

There is no cogent reason why the ordinary man or woman should or
ought to be a scientist or researcher, so we must get rid of delusions
of grandeur. In a phrase which reminds us strongly of Macmurray
and Whitehead, y Gasset says that "the virtue of the grown man is
to will, to do and achieve".

The trend towards a university dominated by 'inquiry' has been
disastrous, for it has led to the elimination of the prime concern,
which is culture. The result has been 'scientism' with its "pedantry
and lack of reflection. Anyone who makes a tiny discovery or goes
to American or German laboratories for six months is a *nouveau
riche* of science". But he can't teach his own courses because he
has no grasp of the discipline as a whole, and he hasn't a clue
about the mission of the university. "One of the evils attending the
confusion of the university with science has been the awarding of
professorships, in keeping with the mania of the times, to research

workers who are nearly always very poor teachers, and regard their teaching as time stolen away from their work in the laboratory or the archives."

We are passing through an age of terrific *un-culture*, says Gasset, so it is of historic importance to restore to the university its "cardinal function of 'enlightenment'". For this we need "sound syntheses and systematizations of knowledge" because "from all quarters the need presses upon us for a new integration of knowledge". The labour of this undertaking is enormous and requires teachers with a genius for integration. "*Of necessity this means specialization, as all creative effort inevitably does; but this time the man will be specializing in the construction of a whole.* " (Our italics). The pulverization of research must be compensated for by a centripetal force to constrain centrifugal science.

The reader will have noticed that Gasset's views approximate very closely to the purposes of the old Scottish general degree for all students. Understandably so, since it is a direct descendant of the trivium and quadrivium taught in the classical and medieval universities of which Gasset approves. It can be seen, too, that his scheme of instruction could, with minimal modifications, be the basis of a revived three-year general degree for all students, to be followed, if desired, by two Honours years and then graduate school.

It is interesting, too, and indicative of the chronic nature of the problem, that much of what Ortega y Gasset says is today echoed by Sir Keith Thomas, President of Corpus Christi College, Oxford.[51] The traditional role of teachers of the humanities was to train their students, not to become scholars, "but to be useful citizens and inhabitants of a larger world". But we live in a vastly different world now, says Thomas, with enormously increased access to the universities, so that the original justification for the humanities as being the appropriate education for an elite is now no longer valid. The humanities have always been criticised: in the seventeenth century the cry was for more attention to mathematics, science and modern languages; now it is for business studies, law, accountancy, economics and computational skills, and the future of the humanities is seriously endangered by their lack of obvious practical utility.

Nowadays in the arts the fashion is for research, but this distracts from training the young and leads to the relative downgrading of the humanities because they are 'unrigorous'. Scientists dismiss them as 'soft' (I remember a professor of engineering at a meeting asking what was the point of teaching archaeology!). In any case what is arts research? The texts are there already, so this 'research' cannot be measured by 'output' or 'productivity'. "The time would be far better spent teaching", says Thomas. But the triumph of the research ethic means that many teachers are rather contemptuous of such activities. They write primarily for each other and they are more concerned to produce future scholars than to educate a wider public. "Is it too much to say", asks Thomas, "that we are now members of a self-perpetuating interest group of scholars who have half forgotten their original social function and whose professional status is based on a misleading analogy between their activities and those of the physical sciences?"

The humanities no longer claim to teach people how to live. "We educate for feeling and understanding, *but not for action.* [Macmurray again] Moral philosophers no longer teach morals. Historians do not draw lessons from the past." There has been a growth of historical relativism, so that we are all pluralists now. [MacIntyre again] Today the notion that the study of the humanities somehow makes people morally better is found embarrassing by most teachers, says Thomas, citing as example George Steiner's reference to concentration camp guards reading Goethe. Now academics do not have an accepted set of values to transmit to the next generations; their god is rationality, that is "the capacity to make problematic what had hitherto been treated as given". Thomas's conclusion is that the real case for the humanities is the intrinsic value of the subject matter for throwing light on human beings, human society and the human imagination. They provide an enlargement of experience, enhance self-consciousness, and widen our sense of what is humanly possible. Most importantly, they enable us to step outside the assumptions of our own day, "escape the tyranny of present-mindedness", and achieve a sense of detachment. Thomas ends with a question: "Should we give more attention to values and standards, even the implicit morality, our teaching inculcates?" We know the reply Gasset, MacIntyre and Macmurray – to name but three – would give to that question.

In this rapid review of what scholars have recently had to say about this seemingly intractable problem I should now like to bring in a Scottish professor of education, Nigel Grant, who has thought long and hard about these questions and has given his ideas powerful expression in a pamphlet, *The Crisis of Scottish Education*, published in 1982. He says:

> One can argue that specialization limits the potential of the individual, closes his options, and is an ill preparation for future learning, since the developments that will have to be coped with are quite as likely to be in the cracks and overlaps *between* subject areas as within them. At bottom, one can argue that there is a difference in philosophy: general education . . . seeks to help the individual to maximise his or her potential,

and can even serve the development of learning by producing people more likely to see the connections between things. It is worth noting in this connection that works such as Darwin's *Origin of Species* – and, we might add, Adam Smith's *Wealth of Nations* – were triumphs of generalism, not of specialization. Specialization is more likely to train functionaries, to produce highly capable personnel to work in pre-determined slots in a pre-determined structure of knowledge and ideas. The constant chorus of calls to relate education to the needs of working life is essentially the specialist philosophy carried to its logical conclusion in defining people and their needs by one of their functions. The generalist philosophy, while not denying the validity of this function, insists that there are others, and that education must serve the whole person and the whole community, not just the employee and the industrial complex.

We shall end this chapter with a lengthy exegesis of the views of an American scholar who has thought even more about it, and who writes imaginatively and satirically in an area which could do with a bit of savage humour. It is not unusual, he says, for a history scholar to specialise in the first half of a century of American, European or Asian history, and then select only one aspect of the field. "The assumption here is that the university, as producer of knowledge, must be composed exclusively of productive scholars, which means specialists who specialize."[52] The new member of staff toils in the library or laboratory "under the mantle of his discipline, meaning not the medieval hairshirt but the silk-lined cloak of professionalism". He and his peers constitute the chief asset of the university, "the prevailing belief being that research is the great justification of the whole enterprise". The analogy here is with science and industry; only R&D keep the nation thriving. "New is the keynote. New products, ideas, ways of doing the same thing, on the chance that they will be better, newer."[53]

This approach of course downgrades teaching, which was the most important part of university work until the nineteenth century. Again Barzun is witty about a very sore point: "Even on his own campus the 'great teacher' can be explained away as a lovable man of average competence – 'not enough for a great university'. His counterpart, the average man of research, lovable or unlovable, is still felt to be worth more."[54] Barzun quotes Leslie Stephen to show where this sort of attitude can lead: "What a blessed place this would be if there were no undergraduates ... no waste of good brains in cramming bad ones." It also leads to the decay of the art of the formal lecture, so prized by John Grierson, David Daiches and others. The order and connection among the different parts of the formal lecture is being lost, and there is too much chat as a result of the free and easy tutorial. "The student sees and resents the fact that teaching is no longer the central concern of the university or its members."[55] 'Publish or perish' is the slogan of the profession, so the scholar is interested in his field, not his class.

Barzun pulls no punches. He speaks of "the higher bankruptcy", the impersonality, the loss of organic cohesion because of the concentration on an ever-growing number of specialisms – "atomism packed tight". "The association of older and younger in the enterprise of learning is that idea, that routine which is now despised because the disinterestedness of its effort has evaporated. The feeling of making, building, resisting, overcoming is gone. The young are sullen and indignant. They feel exploited, because they are surrounded by the perfunctory, not making by making believe – casual teaching, mechanical scholarship, assembly-line research."[56] Barzun's approach to the subject may seem too aggressive and high voltage to us in Britain, but at least in America they do question the purposes of higher education, something absent in discussion on the subject in Britain. He outlines the various stances on the purposes of higher education: research, vocational, social. These are rejected by another group which says college is for education. "Specifically, it is for injecting the necessary dose of the liberal arts into the undergraduate before s/he enters economic and social life. At this shaming reminder, everybody begins to praise the liberal arts. They are indispensable – to what, is not clear: some say, the good use of the burdensome leisure that is coming; others, to inculcate 'values' – we need citizens, democrats, humanitarians; still others, the making of strong critical minds for all uses; and yet others, the development of native gifts: we need artists and such people – creativity."[57] The true purpose of education is given in a quote from a college dean: "America's education system is in danger of becoming a vast factory committed to the production of specialists, technicians, and fact collectors . . . making it increasingly difficult for the college student to achieve a mature understanding of himself and his proper relation to society – to achieve, in short, a liberal education." Again we see that the central function of a liberal education is to provide the means to enable the student – *all students* – to ask the half-dozen basic questions that have endured since the beginnings of philosophy, and to see things in their interconnections and relationships. As Barzun points out in a footnote: "Soldiers in camp, workmen along the road, strangers in a stalled bus will, given the chance, wonder about matter and God, discuss the nature of love, or grow vehement about justice and the criteria of truth."[58]

This true, central purpose of education is drowned in a flood of what Barzun calls "preposterism". We say to the intending university teacher: "You shall write a book and it shall be a contribution to knowledge." This is now endemic in the system. Everybody shall produce written research if s/he wants to eat, and "it shall be decreed a knowledge explosion". It may be an explosion of print and paper, but the knowledge is very tenuous. According to Barzun an enormous amount of research output is: "Repetition in swollen fragments of what was known more compactly and elegantly before; repetition, conscious or not, of new knowledge found by others; repetition of oneself in diverse forms; original worthlessness."[59] The best liberal arts colleges in the USA "have insisted that the brilliant PhD be able to keep the class awake and moving through the syllabus".[60]

We now see the ubiquity of specialization. Even the American higher education system, which has held on so long to the broad approach followed in Scotland, is succumbing to it. Barzun explains the mechanism. The compulsion to produce research is strongest among young lecturers, since promotion – in the USA as in Britain – depends on it. They are thus deflected from devoting their energies to time-consuming teaching. In teaching "an experienced, well-stocked mind can take a single book, author or small period and make the scholarly virtues of thoroughness, accuracy and precision accompany the discovery of ideas, facts and suggestive relationships". But it is much easier to teach technique which bores students who do not yet know the subject, or teach listlessly what is not linked to the lecturer's research interest'. The important thing is to be 'scientific', 'professional', to pass on the approved techniques to the next generation. Barzun calls this a 'mandarin system'. So the aim becomes to get the general educational requirement of the lower years out of the way. Able students can go straight into second year, and specialise in the upper years. Thus, since the high schools have pre-empted freshman courses, "college work is squeezed flat". It becomes a "thin partition" between the improved high school and the professional, specialized university. This partition is a nuisance, to be got rid of by the apprentice specialist, who serves as assistant to a scholar, verifies footnotes, does his/her PhD, then post-doctoral work, then on to become "a sure-fire grant collector". This cycle, says Barzun, "seems designed to prevent an excess of well-educated persons in the university faculties, in college teaching and in the nation at large". He quotes Ortega y Gasset: "The contemporary university has developed the mere seed of professional instruction into an enormous activity; it has added the function of research; and it has abandoned almost entirely the teaching or transmission of culture." As a result, for most students, the shift has been from studying to qualifying. This whole invidious system, which makes everybody, young and old, miserable, has developed as a result of "the menage à trois that united business, government and the university. The young mandarins accordingly pawn their intellects at the institution for a number of years and expect, on retrieving them, a passport to the available affluencies."[61] The humanists are accused of slavishly imitating the sciences and ignoring meaning in favour of technique. The scientists are called 'campus mercenaries' because they can be easily led by the nose in their pursuit of funding.

What keeps this great imposture going? asks Barzun. The answer is money. Federal support grants to "create new centres of excellence"; it becomes a self-perpetuating system. It needs big names with contracts, "suitably sterilized from teaching". Also prestige, a post-war invention which is not the same as reputation, or greatness, or glory. "Prestige is acquired first, instead of arriving last." Barzun's description of prestige is so humourously and wickedly accurate that it merits quoting in full: "choosing faculty appointees who will look stunning in press release; getting the man or line of goods that has just come into prominence; picking up top people in mid-career so nobody can fail to see their beauty, instead of far-sightedly judging and picking the future stars when young; image-coddling for maximum visibility; good ratings in surveys and polls of excellence; avoiding trouble, so as to appear in the press frequently and favourably. Prestige, in a word, is commercial advertising."[62] Barzun's comment on this is that "self-praise rots judgment, false standards usurp the mind – it is the drug experience". He quotes university president Gideonse: "Are we in positions of educational responsibility really engaged – as we say – in the 'promotion of learning' or are we involved in the competitive merchandising of social status?" He refers to the need for "toughness in the exposure of moral or social illiteracy in high places".

There is no need to underline the relevance of Barzun's views to much that has been said in this book and to the situation in British higher education today. Barzun's conclusion is that of H. L. Mencken: "Let us not burn the universities – yet." Not, at least, until I have had an opportunity to look at the current position of Scotland's universities.

13

Scotland's Universities Today 1
Academic Entropy

Describing the nineteenth-century reforms prescribed by government for the universities in England and Scotland, R. E. Bell, having dealt with the attempted modernization of Oxford and Cambridge, goes on to say: "The Scottish universities, in a less rewarding economy, had lowlier aims – to provide high-standard courses for entry to the professions (especially medicine and teaching) and within these limits to follow the fashionable English to the greatest extent possible. Those Scots seeking political leadership had, clearly, to go south – if necessary as postgraduate undergrads."[1] This "Scottish desire to emulate the English" meant that they recruited English academic "beginners" (from Oxford or Cambridge of course) as professors, "thus drawing the Scottish universities into the more prestigious English career structure." In addition, academic selection committees showed great respect for the distinction of Oxbridge candidates for posts, even, in the case of Edinburgh and St Andrews, playing up their 'medieval picturesqueness' as a suitable setting for Oxford-style academic activity. What we today call the 'Scottish cringe' or 'inferiorism' of the growing Scottish professional middle class was already well in evidence. This "English tendency", as Bell calls it, was reflected even more in the universities' attempts to cater for "the cheaper middle-class schools (George Watson's, Heriot's, etc.)" which had mushroomed in the major cities after 1870, so that "the old 'open' tradition" of going straight from the parish school to the university became less and less possible. This new elitism was, however, slower off the ground in Scotland, partly because of the 'open' tradition and because the universities were poor and needed every reasonable student they could lay their hands on.

Robert Anderson, in an interesting article[2] on student life at Aberdeen, paints a similar picture. 'Student life' and student mags were invented at Aberdeen in the 1880s to meet the complaint that there was no "corporate life". Anderson gives two reasons for its creation at that time. The age of admission rose from 15 or 16 in 1860 to 18 in 1900, as a result of the 1889 Bill. Also, "In the late Victorian age the structure of bourgeois careers took on a new stability which crystallized around the organized professions, university qualifications and competitive examinations. The tone was set by the reformed English public schools." It is not clear what Anderson means by 'reformed', but we recall that Sheldon Rothblatt showed that there was a great growth in the number of public schools in England at this time because of the new money seeking status, and that Oxford and Cambridge became more exclusive than they had ever been because of the opening of scholarship examinations to general competition. Anderson explains that Aberdeen exported half its graduates outside Scotland, so that Scottish education had to adapt to put the Scottish students on equal terms with the English ones, and "this was reflected in the far-reaching reforms of secondary schools and of the university curriculum, completed by the 1890s." There are many major questions begged in this explanation, not least why the half of Aberdeen's graduates who went south needed a university education based on the Oxbridge model, since they could not all be going into the church or the civil service or government or public school teaching, which was what Oxbridge prepared its students for. It was, after all, precisely because Oxbridge was failing to meet England's need for trained scientists, technologists and industrialists that University College, London, had been set up on the Scottish model as early as 1826, to be followed by Owen's College and other university colleges in the north of England. Surely Aberdeen's student emigrants would have been less, rather than more, likely to get good jobs in an England undergoing Victorian industrial expansion with an Oxbridge-style education. It was because the Scottish university curriculum was *different from, and broader than,* that of Oxford and Cambridge that Scottish engineers and technologists had played such a disproportionate role in the industrial revolution.

One of the immediate effects was not pretty and it came in a speech of the Principal of the University of Aberdeen in 1876: "There would be some opportunity for the rustic class of students learning to use their knife and fork; in fact, for their learning the usages of society, by which a number of young men from the country destined in after life to move in the sphere of gentlemen would be greatly benefited." Worse still, the Aberdeen University Gazette, a student mag, claimed that from the development of *esprit de corps* "a higher type of morality and manners would result, and outsiders

would look on our graduates as, in the highest sense, gentlemen."
Anderson's comment on this – which I quote without comment –
is: "It was a gentlemanly social polish which Scottish students were
thought to need and did in fact successfully acquire, in order to
compete with the products of English schools and universities and
to assimilate with the British elite and its values. To this extent there
was a process of anglicization at work."

It is hard to believe that Aberdonians, as eager to prick pretension as
other Scots, could have spoken or penned such words as these. I hope
readers are squirming, because this process of cringing inferiorism,
and the pompous pretension that is its *doppelgänger*, have never
stopped from that day to this and it is high time they were stamped
on. Here are three contemporary examples, two of them from a seminar run by Mrs Thatcher's Centre for Policy Studies. Lord Annan,
one of the great panjandrums of English higher education, making
a transparent piece of special pleading for Oxbridge: "The great
institutions should be treated differently to the other universities . . .
It is wrong that all universities should be treated alike . . . Most
institutions should be teaching something much more vocational."[3]
Next Lord Todd (of Trumpington, if I mistake not): "There are
too many so-called universities, most are akin to polytechnics . . .
training people for useful things . . . traditional university was never
designed for so many people." "Such is the fantastic arrogance of
the London-Oxbridge golden triangle", concludes the author.[4] The
awful irony is that these are precisely the policies that are being
implemented now with 'selectivity' and the division of the universities into research sheep and teaching goats. The third is taken from a
review of Sir Charles Carter's book *Higher Education for the Future*
in SER, Vol 6, No 2, 1981. The author, Tyrell Burgess, quotes Sir
Charles: "At one extreme, no-one would consider a twelve-session
course in lampshade-making for bored suburban housewives to be
higher education . . . " and says: "On the evidence of this book the
insulting assumptions of this sentence are not in the least justified."

Meanwhile, as the Oxbridge norms for civil service entry were
being foisted on Scotland's universities, they were being criticized in
the United States where, in 1867, in the House of Representatives,
Frederick Woodbridge, speaking on a bill for administrative reform,
said: "There are other objections to the bill. One is that it is anti-
democratic . . . it is undoubtedly true that Belgium and Prussia and
France and England have a similar system of appointing officers to
the civil service. But where is the analogy between England and this
country? That, sir, is a country of aristocracy, a country of classes,
where as a rule a man cannot rise unless he is born to position. In
England the coal-heaver of today is a coal-heaver on the day of his

death. Here the avenues to position, to power, to wealth, are open
to all, and they ought not be any legislation of ours to be closed . . .
The race is to all men. The avenues are all open; and I think it would
be dangerous for us to close the avenues to the many and provide
a royal road for a fortunate or favoured few." There were to be no
'obscure Judes' in the USA.

There are, of course, none so blind as will not see. Both Bell and
Anderson, having clearly demonstrated the anglicization of Scottish
higher education in their writings, nonetheless deny that it existed
and still exists. Bell, for example, writes[5]: "Many of Davie's statements were of course strong ones and he soon became a rallying
figure for those who regretted the passing of what they took to be
a Scottish educational tradition free of social class barriers, generalist, based on the study of philosophy and linked to the more open
world of the Continental universities – a tradition that had been
betrayed in favour of an English model based on class distinction,
pedantic specialization, and the inward-looking petty preoccupations of Oxford and Cambridge." Bell and Anderson see all this as a
groundless myth. They refute the myth of widespread anglicisation,
they reject the notion that it needed an English hand for example
to encourage such city schools as Fettes and Edinburgh Academy
to strive for greater and greater social exclusiveness. The trick here
is transparent. Describe correctly, but with a faintly mocking tone,
the features of the Scottish educational tradition, but then throw in
such tendentious terms as 'rallying-figure', 'what they took to be',
'betrayal', and above all erect an Aunt Sally, i.e. that it was not
Englishmen who created such schools as Edinburgh Academy or
Fettes. No-one has ever claimed that it was. We have shown clearly
in Chapter 4 that a prime role in the anglicization of Scottish education was played by Scottish aristocrats educated at Oxbridge and the
upwardly mobile Scottish professional middle classes (David Hume
was an angliciser!). The regrets of the Edinburgh professional man
confirm it.[6]

The example, however, was English, whatever Anderson may
say about the need for change in nineteenth-century Scotland,
since English public schools and Oxbridge were unique in Europe.
Furthermore, the power to impose these reforms came from the overwhelmingly English government at Westminster. Do Bell, Anderson
and others deny the evidence of the universities (Scotland) commissions of the nineteenth century? The claim that "Much of the
change, far from being an English imposition on Scotland, was happening throughout the industrialized world", will simply not hold
water. Great changes were of course taking place throughout the
industrialized world both in Europe and America, but they were

assuredly not based on the example of the English public schools and Oxbridge. Indeed, it was to combat German industrial and technological supremacy that university colleges were set up in the northern towns. In the USA university curricula were in fact based on the Scottish model, and they created the graduate schools proposed by Scottish academics in the mid–nineteenth century but deliberately refused funding by the Westminster government.[7] Had they come into being they would assuredly have done far more to equip Scotland for the changes that were happening throughout the industrialized world than imitation of Oxbridge. Anglicization of Scotland's universities, in other words, was a very negative phenomenon. They were prevented from carrying through, a century and a half ago, an innovation that would have put them indisputably in the lead and which, today, is the great success story of the American university system.

Another scholar who questions the anglicization theory is Walter M. Humes.[8] He states the problem correctly by saying that "the culture of Scotland is seen to be constantly under threat from England, which, by virtue of its economic and political dominance, tends to penetrate all aspects of Scottish life." He then qualifies this statement by saying that the understandable desire to defend the principle of Scottish autonomy and distinctiveness in education leads to a limited and perhaps questionable interpretation of historical developments, particularly during the modern period. He claims that the existence of a separate institutional apparatus in the form of the SED, the SCEEB, the CCC etc. "tends to disguise the extent to which educational thinking has been shaped by a climate of ideas which is by no means peculiarly Scottish." What he does not do is give any evidence of these influences, particularly of any that are non-English.[9] He quotes James G. Kellas[10] on the degree to which Scottish education has been "subject to the assimilation process in British society", and Kellas's affirmation "that the grounds for maintaining it as a distinct form seem less clear." That looks to me like a euphemism for an English takeover of Scottish education. Humes quotes a whole number of instances which would seem to support such a conclusion. He shows how, despite successive claims for a separate national system of state-supported education by Sir James Moncrieff and others, legislation for Scotland was delayed until a full two years after the 1870 Education Act for England and Wales. Worse, it failed to provide properly for secondary education in Scotland and thus "could be seen as assuming an essentially English pattern of extensive private involvement in post-elementary education."[11] (They are still at it with 'opt-outs' in 1992.) He shows how the first separate Scottish Education Department was set up in

London, not Edinburgh, in 1885, and quotes the Duke of Richmond who described it disparagingly as "simply a room in Whitehall with the word 'Scotland' painted on the door." He even refers to the four university royal commissions of 1826, 1858, 1876 and 1889 and quotes George Elder Davie to the effect that the members were Scottish neither in feeling nor in education, being aristocrats with Anglican sympathies and being connected with Oxbridge rather than the Scottish universities.

Having made these historically accurate points, Humes then goes on to say that such explanations are attractive but dangerous. He admits that there has always been a body of Anglicisers in Scotland, but there is a danger that all changes will be seen as an English conspiracy. By whom, he does not say. Is he perhaps imputing such an attitude to Davie, the scholar who first opened up this field? If so, he greatly weakens his own case. No-one would dispute his affirmation that sources of social and intellectual change are not reducible to single chains of cause and effect. His claim that "to look only for cases of 'English' influence debases the character of Scottish culture and suggests a very restricted range of appropriate research strategies", would be exaggerated even if accurate. But since no-one is looking "only" for cases of English influence, and he does not indicate what the "appropriate research strategies" might be, his claim is rather supererogatory. As are his further recriminations that "the conceptual categories here are decidedly crude" and that they "exaggerate differences and ignore similarities". Weakest of all is his accusation that, "because of their preoccupation with questions of nationalism",[12] they "fail to take account of over-arching concepts and ideas which go beyond nationality and help shape the perceptions of men and women in many different cultures". Again the Aunt Sally: these are questions of the history of ideas, not nationalism. This is even more strongly the case in his statement that "Conventional accounts of Scottish history centred on institutions such as education and relying heavily on notions of England as predator need to be supplemented and counterbalanced by an awareness of the part played by international keywords such as science." Is he asking us to ignore the facts of Scottish educational history, as accurately presented by himself among many others? Does he imagine that Scottish thinkers – the heirs to the Enlightenment, to the enlightened views on science of an evangelical like James McCosh or a great scientist like James Clerk Maxwell – are likely to overlook the international influence of science? Is he denying that England was a predator in all areas of Scottish life for centuries, and that the Scots have reason to be suspicious? Humes' thesis, I regret to say, is a modern, up-to-date version of inferiorism.

For anyone who reads, without preconceptions, the voluminous literature on Scottish higher education in monographs, articles in educational journals, and contributions to the academic press, there can surely be little doubt that for more than a century-and-a-half there has been a determined, prolonged and cumulative effort to bring the Scottish universities into conformity with those of England. For example, the following comes from a letter to the press: "No-one but the most obscurantist philistine would deny the inestimable contribution of the ancient Scottish universities to our life and culture. That a small nation should support for hundreds of years four major centres of learning and teaching is a unique aspect of our heritage. It is therefore a matter of considerable historical importance why the presence of these institutions in Scotland did not prevent the decline of morale and national consciousness during this century. One answer must be that they have become somewhat remote from the realities of Scottish life. Indeed, only one of the four original universities, Glasgow, truly reflects in its location and the catchment area from which it draws the bulk of its students the social environment in which most of the Scottish people live."[13]

Principal J. Steven Watson of St Andrews University, arguing against university devolution, says parochialism would be the result, and "the end of such a process might be an all-embracing regional education authority."[14] Inferiorism again, and of a peculiarly blinkered variety. One of his lecturers clearly does not agree: "The case for any Scottish executive taking responsibility for Scotland's universities is simple and urgent. The degree of alienation between the key opinion-forming departments of Scottish universities and the Scottish nation is already extraordinary. Furthermore, it is likely to grow worse. Academic jobs are already scarce. In the coming economic blizzard they will be even scarcer. Products of the over-inflated graduate schools of Oxford and Cambridge are likely to compete for what is available in Scotland in large numbers and, given current appointment criteria, they are bound to reinforce the already excessive grip of the English universities on the whole structure of Scottish life."[15] A third letter[16] deals with the university curricula: "Parochialism does not enter into the argument, as Scotland is unique, as far as I know, in putting more emphasis on an alien culture than on its own within its establishments of higher education. As a radical nationalist I would be very disappointed indeed if the first independent Scottish government did not legislate for the long-awaited change of history and literature syllabi." I am afraid Mr Lawson may have to wait rather a long time. Meanwhile, the indications are all in the opposite direction. It was reported in that same year[17] that Stirling University's M. Litt in Scottish Studies was doomed. The first course, in which the philosophy, history and English departments were to have participated, was to have been *Scottish Culture 1740–1840*. The Academic Board was unwilling to finance the course. Proposals for courses in Gaelic fared no better. I note that at Stirling, as at all our universities, there was, and is, a large majority of English staff.

These quotations are picked almost at random; the pages of TESS and THES have contained a large number over the years. For example, in April 1966 TESS refers to the appointment of English Principals to Scottish universities and to the argument put up in such cases, namely the number of Scots holding high offices in England. Its counter-argument is that "England does not feel defensively about Scotland; it can scarcely suspect a takeover. There would, however, be some worry in England if a series of American Principals were appointed there. It is surely unreasonable to suggest that if all Scotland's Principals were English then there would be no cause for Scottish concern." Some 15 years later the same journal[18] thus described Sir Fraser Noble, the Principal of Aberdeen University: "Among the serving Principals of the four ancient Scottish universities only Aberdeen's Sir Fraser Noble is a Scot. Presumably Bell, Anderson, Humes, Houston *et al.* would say that this is an inevitable development in an interdependent world; that it is the Scottish universities which are doing the appointing; and that it therefore cannot be put down to Anglicization.

Still, they have their allies. Professor S. C. Frazer, of that same Aberdeen University, speaking to the students, [19] had this to say: "I urge you, as graduates of a Scottish university, to look to the motives of those who would turn us into a tartan university. Theends which they seek are their own, not those of the Scottish community, still less those of the Scottish universities." Had he spoken in a similarly militant vein on the other side of the argument he would have been accused of an outrageous attempt at indoctrination. He was not, however, shall we say, the most fervent opponent of the repatriation of the Scottish universities. At a World Education Fellowship Conference at Stirling University a Mr. James Scotland (Can it be the same man who wrote an excellent history of Scottish education?) warned his audience that devolution would afford an opportunity for the lunatic fringe to boost Scottish studies and elevate Burns and Henryson to the status of Shakespeare and Chaucer simply because the record on behalf of Gaelic and Scottish studies had been so poor in the past.[20] With such allies, who needs enemies?

On the other side we find a distinguished leader of the E. I. S., John Pollock, who said:[21] "All the present government pressures are towards making the Scottish system conform with a pattern of educational provision which is not designed for Scottish circumstances" – a rather more objective statement of the facts by a kenspeckle member of the Scottish community. Even R. E. Bell saw the anomaly in running the Scottish universities from London, in an article entitled *Subservient Universities*.[22] "Certainly nobody's interests will be served in the long run by leaving such a large chunk of the Scottish education system under an often uncomprehending DES, turned into a part-time colonial office to oversee the institutions which, as Vice-Principal Walsh (of Edinburgh University) never fails to remind us, the Scots cannot be trusted to run by themselves."

It is hardly surprising that N. U. S. /Scotland should have said that Principal-led scaremongering had superseded principled discussion as the basis for government decisions on university devolution. The Government did not trust a Scottish administration to govern the Scottish universities competently.[23] One wonders that the students had the nerve to say anything at all in view of what Professor T. C. Smout of St Andrews University had declared at the beginning of the year when speaking on the theme *Scotland and the Future* at Edinburgh University's School of the Man-made Future:[24] "Scotland's unenviable education record had produced falanges of schoolchildren who arrive at university with pens poised to catch the truth as it drips from their teacher's lips. Scotland's miserable education system . . . The Scottish traits are suspicion, conservativeness and inflexibility . . . Education in Scotland has consisted of smashing facts into children and teaching them to compete with each other." This is the man of whom St Andrews' Principal, Struther Arnott, had said, when a celebrated television programme on the *Englishing of Scotland* pointed out that only 12 of St Andrews' 50 professors were Scots, that he would rather have one Englishman like Smout than any number of Scots. One can only describe Smout's views as the macho or tough-it-out school of inferiorism.

His opinions are not shared by Frederic Lindsay in an article entitled 'A Fundamentally Non-autonomous System'[25] in which he says: "Scottish education is best understood as an example of a partial system, that is one which, while possessing some overtly independent administrative machinery, is fundamentally non-autonomous . . . (it) may be likened to a branch factory which is allowed quietly to deteriorate until it would seem irrational to argue against closing it down . . . Symptomatic of the imminence of our intellectual redundancy has been the influx of English people into higher education appointments. Presumably most of them would hope to obtain a similar post in England. It is difficult to see how any system can do other than decline which makes a habit of importing self-confessed

failures . . . No interested foreigner could fail to find it instructive
that a people can be educated into a version of their past in which
a poverty-stricken nation is rescued by Union from semi-barbarism
and elevated into a region soberly proud of its careful businessmen and reliable infantry. The latest blueprint has been provided
by Dr Smout. Rather as though the late, unlamented Dr Goebbels
had embarked upon a scholarly and assiduously compiled history
of France."

An equally strong statement of Scotland's educationally dependent
position had been made a year earlier by Brian Dockrell, Director
of the Scottish Centre for Research in Education.[26] "There are, too,
fears of cultural and educational assimilation . . . there is a growing awareness that the educational tradition is slowly being worn
away and replaced piecemeal by procedures, practices and materials
imported from the South. Two aspects of this 'cultural imperialism'
are the large proportion of university professors, particularly in the
social sciences, from south of the border, and the acquisition of local
publishers by concerns whose primary concern, it is thought, will
be to sell textbooks and materials produced for the larger market."
Dockrell points out that the fundamental concerns are the same for
Canada as for Scotland. Can a country maintain its standards if
its economic policy is made elsewhere in the interests of its bigger
neighbour? "Can a country preserve its identity if its culture and
education are largely imported from that same neighbour?"

Bruce Millan, Secretary of State for Scotland, answered that question[27] with the bland statement that there was no anglicization in
the schools, but excluded the universities where he said he knew
the charge was most strongly made. Since he had been Under-
Secretary of State for Education one might have expected some
evidence for the first statement and a rather more open and honest
statement about the position in the universities. His explanation
for his failure to offer anything more on the universities would no
doubt have been that they were not his responsibility but that of the
DES in London. Having for the first time cited a politician, I must
give the opposition view. This was put forward in an article entitled 'More Money and More Freedom'[28] by James Halliday, SNP
vice-president: "The danger (anglicization) is particularly obvious
at university level. The integration of Scotland's universities with
Scotland's educational system cannot be indefinitely postponed. It is
absurd to have universities staffed by sad exiles, lagered-up in their
campus compounds, wistfully hoping for that posting to Sussex. As
for students, the argument is simply about proportions. Ten percent
of English students in a Scottish university might be regarded as a
defensible leaven in the lump. At 50 percent they have taken the

lump over, and detached it from the community around it." Now in the 1990s, of course, the exiles could hardly be described as sad. The flood of English immigration into Scotland is at an all-time high, because of the declining quality of life in the South of England.

That same issue of TESS contained a very long letter from R. E. Bell replying to Bruce Millan, in which, *inter* many *alia*, he wrote: "Of the desirability of all this (English pressure on the Highers, marked intolerance of Scottish forms, etc.) I as an Englishman, born eight miles from the Border, retain an open mind; but if I were a Scot and I valued what is supposed to be the real kernel of Scottish educational tradition, its non-elitist, generalist curriculum, pursued in 'democratic' institutions, then I would be very worried indeed, and the survival of Highers, the GTC, the tawse, the SED . . . would give me no comfort at all." Nationalism may be outdated, and even a sentiment to despise. But writers on Scottish education cannot have it both ways. Either a small nation nurtures and cultivates its distinctive institutions and protects them from encroachment, or it frankly leaves them open to international influences, and once their distinctiveness is dead it frankly admits they are dead. The former requires an immense act of dedication on the part of the nation itself, or some outside pressure which helps to create a national determination. Such miracles happened in Israel and Finland, where moribund languages were brought alive again . . .

"I do not believe there has been either the will on the part of Scots or the pressure of external events (he was writing before the advent of Mrs Thatcher) to cause a strengthening of Scottish educational forms and institutions. The miracle having failed to appear, perhaps it is after all best to sit back and accept that international (perforce largely English) influences have triumphed and to accept the benefits they have brought to Scotland's changing institutions." This is a very clever call to the Scots to disarm. He issues a challenge which has still not been taken up, though the situation is now in the 1990s even worse than it was then. One would cavil at his use of the words 'international' (he is himself slightly embarrassed by this word, for in matters of higher education 'English' and 'international' are at opposite ends of the spectrum), 'benefits' (there have been none) and 'changing' (Scotland's educational institutions were not, and are not, changing of their own volition but under English pressure, as he himself admits, contrary to all his previous denials of anglicization).

Bell also says that, as far as the universities are concerned, he is not quite so sure that there isn't "a sinister English plot to take over." He accuses Millan of ignoring the key issue by excluding the universities from his comments, for "the university, through its high status and its function as the trainer of educational and intellectual leaders, sets the whole tone of the country's corporate culture." This failure of an able Under-Secretary for Education at the Scottish Office to take an interest in "such key institutions is both no surprise and one of the major problems. The Scottish educational system, administratively, has had its head cut off, and that has happened, we are constantly assured, at the request of the universities themselves, a fact significant in itself from a national point of view." What Bell does not say, though we have seen it referred to by many contributors to the educational press, is that there is a large majority of English staff at all Scotland's universities, and that sometimes there is a majority of English Principals as well. So it is equally no surprise that the Scottish universities consistently rejected repatriation both in the 70s and at the time of STEAC in 1985.

What is surprising, and justifies Bell's low estimate of Scottish determination and self-respect, is that neither the Scottish middle class as a whole, the professions, nor any of the political parties have so far put up any sort of a battle to defend Scotland's educational and cultural soul, in other words her national identity. History will deal particularly harshly with the Labour Party which, despite large majorities of seats, and despite having able people like Bruce Millan, has not lifted a finger to protect the Scottish universities. Nor can the Scottish National Party escape criticism. It has made the odd general statement, treating education like a PR matter much less important than oil or steel – whereas in fact it is much more important if Scotland is to continue to exist as a nation – but has never waged a sustained campaign based on a real understanding of the issues and their now quite desperate urgency.

Just three months before the publication of this important letter an article entitled *Scots can't go it alone* appeared in TESS of 30 November 1973. It was largely a rehash of an editorial in *Scottish Educational Studies* written by the same R. E. Bell who has been very active in Scottish educational publications and thereby gained a strategic position. It is full of determination-sapping doom and gloom: "The editor of such a journal as *Scottish Educational Studies* is all too well aware of how deeply integrated English and Scottish educational thinking now is and of how weak a thing is really independent Scottish educational opinion. Compared with the educational worlds of England and Ireland, each with its own climate of opinion and zest for policy-making, that of Scotland seems more and more dependent as each day goes by." This is a much more subtle and effective form of inferiorism than that of Professor Smout, skillfully sounding the authentic note of Scottish inferiority complex and dependency. The author points out that many of the contributions to SES are the work of English academics temporarily working in Scotland but seeing themselves as belonging to a career structure that is now world-wide. Also much interesting work by Scottish academics on Scottish matters bypasses SES completely because the authors wish to display their wares in the international arena where they feel their future academic activities will undoubtedly lie. The result, says Bell, is that Scottish educational thought is now totally international.

Huge questions are begged. American universities contribute more than any others to the "larger scientific world" in the international arena, but that does not mean that their university system becomes indistinguishable from that of other countries, especially that of England – which is the fate the author has in view for the Scottish universities. He makes this quite clear by writing : "With the gradual spread of English-style examinations and the CNAA and Open University degree systems, with the abolition of the Ordinary Arts MA at Edinburgh, with the introduction of English-style BEds, and with the appointment of more and more inspectors, advisers and college and university lecturers from outwith the Scottish system, it is doubtful whether the distinctive Scottish forms can or should survive. How many people any longer believe in them, except in competing political slogans? The death throes, which George Davie saw beginning with the university legislation of the late nineteenth century, are now almost complete."[29]

The most frightening symptom of all of the decline and decay of Scottish higher education is that an Englishman with the views of R. E. Bell, despite his undoubted ability, should ever have been appointed editor of *Scottish Educational Studies*. Was no Scottish voice raised to show the devastating effects of all this, to demonstrate just how wrong Bell was when he spoke of the "benefits" for Scottish education of the anglicization whose existence he elsewhere denies. Yes, one – but a singularly powerful one: the voice of Nigel Grant, now Professor of Education at the University of Glasgow.[30] As J. Derrick McClure puts it,[31] "This fact-filled, closely reasoned and powerfully argued booklet has the force of a bombshell . . . there could be no more depressing symptom of a servile, defeatist national mentality than Scottish education as it is described here. Emphasis is placed throughout on the random, unthinking, accidental nature of changes in the system: the direct result of the fact that insofar as there is a single body responsible for education in Scotland as a whole it is the Westminster Parliament, to which (and not to the Scottish people) the SED is responsible." The booklet deals mainly with the schools but much of its message is relevant to higher education. The nature of the crisis is triple: there is a crisis of direction, a crisis of resource, and a crisis of identity. Despite

the changes brought about at the end of the nineteenth century
the Scottish universities are still relatively open as compared with
those of England, and there is much less of a pecking order than
in England where the Oxbridge, Civic, Redbrick league table has
stultified English education, where academic considerations have
long been confounded by social elitism. They are still slightly less
specialized than their English counterparts, but all these characteristics were being rapidly eroded at the beginning of the 1980s.[32]
Similarly, there are still some hopeful features in the secondary
system: there is no systematic creaming-off of talent as in England;
independent schools don't dominate the system; specialization is a
little less premature; all teachers have been professionally trained
graduates for more than half-a-century. But again these features are
dwindling fast. One of the continuing problems of Scottish education has been the devaluation of Scotland's cultures, both Gaelic
and Lowland, the provincialisation of the country and the uncritical
acceptance of norms imported from elsewhere. "Concern for local
cultures . . . usually bring accusations of 'parochialism' from the
more metropolitan-minded, little suspecting how narrow *their* view
is from an international standpoint. What Scottish education has
failed to do has been to give adequate weight *either* to the immediate
culture *or* to the wider complex of cultures of which it is a part
and in which we all live. Neglecting both to concentrate largely on
English norms is to do ill service to the future citizens of a pluralist
world."[33]

Grant points out that Scotland is unique in teaching its young
people more about someone else's history than their own, the only
parallel being the colonial territories during the heyday of the British,
French and Portuguese empires. "The World view thus presented is
not only parochial – it is not even their own parish."[34] An Edinburgh
pupil once asked: "Has anything happened in Scotland between
Skara Brae and the '45?" The arts, both Scottish and other, are
largely ignored in Scottish schools. Grant does not say so, but the
S(0)ED bears a heavy responsibility in all these areas.

The structure, curricula and functioning of the Scottish education
system is also being diluted. "There used to be a fairly coherent curricular policy in Scottish schools and higher education institutions,
based on a broad and balanced range of subjects, deriving from
the Renaissance ideal of the well-rounded, harmoniously developed
and broadly cultured and capable individual, and from the Knoxian
idea that it was in the interests of the community to produce such
citizens."[35] Thus specialism was avoided at school and university,
since even the Honours degree keeps some breadth in the first two
years. This 'generalist' policy was however severely eroded in the

1960s and 70s, so that the top end of secondary school is now almost as narrow as the English VIth form. There is a danger of ignoring Highers for A-levels even in the public sector. We shall see how prophetic this last warning was to be ten years later. The same thing was happening at the universities. Both the 'ordinary' degree and the honours degree were becoming less and less broad: at Edinburgh, for example, selection for specialized courses was done right from the start.

The great danger in accepting A-levels and Highers on an equal footing for entry to university resulted in differential failure rates in first year at university, because English academics at Scottish universities (in a large majority) design courses for A-level students, so that Scottish students, with more breadth but less depth, are at a disadvantage. Yet the case for specialization or for accepting special- ised A-levels on the same footing as students with Highers was never put or discussed. "It has been happening at random, uncritically – partly through the collapse of previous controlling mechanisms (like the university entrance requirements), partly through an infatuation with English models, and it has been happening at potentially influ- ential points of the system, without much consideration of what these imply for policy. Scottish education has been going specialist in a fit of absence of mind." [36] It is highly ironic, of course, as Grant points out, that this has been happening while doubts are being more and more openly expressed in England about the wisdom of early specialization (see, for example, the Higginson Committee's call for five subjects at A-level, "broader, leaner A-levels" as opposed to the so-called 'gold standard' of Oxbridge and the public schools and their numerous powerful allies in high places). These doubts are expressed because English educationists and businessmen are now realising that their overseas competitors produce more flexible, more capable and more broadly educated people in management, administration and politics. "It would be truly ironic", says Grant, "if the Scottish system were to go specialist just in time to see that policy discredited in its country of origin."

This copying of English educational methods is "piecemeal, uncriti- cal, often unconscious and frequently dysfunctional", but there is a much greater danger in borrowing so much from one system and so little from others. It is here that one sees the disingenuousness of using the word 'international' in reference to external influences on Scottish education. "Usually outside influence means English influence, so Scotland depends to an unreasonable degree on one of the world's more eccentric education systems." This makes it more difficult for Scotland to learn from the USA, Germany, Denmark or any other country. Indeed, "it makes it more difficult for Scotland to learn that it *has* anything to learn from other countries." The odd-man-out English system looms so large and has such powerful political control over Scotland that the Scottish system is in great danger of being completely absorbed by it. What is more, it makes it very difficult to think hard and carefully about our real educational needs "if we insist on constantly defining ourselves with reference to someone else."

The most glaring defect of all is that we have no effective control over our own educational system. It is administratively devolved, but. there is no political control *in Scotland* over what even specifically Scottish government departments do. Even educational legislation that applies to Scotland *only* is made by the whole Westminster parliament, and this has always been the case. To rub this in, as it were, the SED (Scottish Education Department) has recently been changed to SOED (Scottish Office Education Department), thus making it quite clear that it is under the control of a branch of the Westminster government. The situation is politically no different from what it was more than a hundred years ago when, as we have seen, the office was in Whitehall. The power of control over the universities is just as great: "All government needs to do is to control the supply of funding and make it conditional on certain things being done." The UGC, supposedly a university-friendly body acting as a buffer between the universities and government, in fact 'recommended' departments for closure. Even this was insufficient in the light of the government's free market polities, so it was replaced by the UFC (Universities Funding Council) with its system of 'bids' by universities on the 'customer-contractor' principle – which collapsed in ignominy after a year, having produced a million pieces of paper and little else. Its Chairman, Lord Chilver, believed in higher education as charity, using means-testing to direct help towards the poor. The irony of imposing such a system on Scotland's universities, which a century and a half before had practiced an 'open door' policy, does not need underlining. "Through the crisis and chaos of the last few years (Grant is writing in 1982, since when things have got much worse) the Scottish universities have managed to retain some of their own characteristics, some remnants of a distinctive educational tradition, like the *relatively* generalist approach to the curriculum . . . But they do so on sufferance; if central government decided to impose a uniform UK pattern on the universities, it is hard to see how it could be prevented. In a random sort of way, that is what is happening already."[37] And has happened much more forcefully and directly in the decade since, under the enormous centralising pressures the Westminster government has exerted. It remains to be seen whether the return of financial control of our universities to

Scotland in 1993 will be able in any fundamental way to change this situation.

The changes in university entrance requirements have the effect of increasing specialization in the secondary schools. "As long as they included English, a science or mathematics, some minimal breadth was maintained." But these requirements have been dropped by most of Scotland's universities, so that the universities' slide into specialization has been accompanied by a similar drift in the schools. Thus the Scottish system is being sucked into the English specialist pattern without any discussion of the educational merits and demerits of specialisation as such; worse, it is well on the way to becoming a provincialised version of the English system. There is not, even, an effective forum for discussion of the system as a whole, anywhere." The Scottish educational system is unique: control, policy-making, even administration, are fragmented and lie outside Scotland in certain vital areas, and political control is exerted by London government. "It is small wonder, in this semi-detached system, that there is little evidence of any general policy, let alone anything as ambitious as vision, and that the various crises, some receiving piecemeal attention and some utterly neglected, continue to fester."[38] One feels a desolating sense of shame that our teachers at all levels, from primary to university; our professional people in all fields; our politicians of every shade from right to left and from unionist to nationalist; our religious leaders of whatever denomination; the leaders of professional associations and trade unions – that all these, so many of whom have received a good Scottish secondary and university education, do not seem to realize, as Nigel Grant so passionately does, that the great educational tradition from which they benefited is in imminent danger of disappearing for ever; or, if they do, it does not seem to worry them since they have made no effective protest.

Grant nonetheless believes that a co-ordinated system of higher and further education could provide a national service to take care of all the various needs, such as part-time courses for professional development, transfers from one institution to another, advanced study, distance learning etc., and "make a quite fundamental contribution to the learning requirements of a much larger section of the Scottish adult population, without doing violence to variety and institutional autonomy – indeed it could make them substantially more real than they are at present".[39] He stresses the need to build up international links to maintain Scottish educational integrity, because assimilationist pressures will always be strong because of the mass media, publishing etc. which all necessarily work in favour of the larger system, i.e. England's. We should seek good ideas from everywhere, not just from England, in our efforts to develop our system. "We have a better chance of being ourselves in an international context rather than being in the shadow of one system only . . . We must not be inhibited by the one-sided 'special relationship'." To this end, Grant concludes, we need a Scottish Parliament with a Ministry of Education which has an international relations department.

This is the definitive answer to Bell's thesis that Scotland's educational system should simply relax and let itself be absorbed. But what chances are there of a vigorous reaction to his justified challenge that if we want to preserve our system we must be ready to fight hard for it? What, I repeat, is the matter with our thinking classes that they seem incapable of acting against what McClure, in his review, calls the "the anti-Scottish conspiracy in Scottish education – there is not the slightest doubt of the appropriateness of that phrase – (which) has not only deprived generations of Scottish children of their cultural heritage and come near to extinguishing the two indigenous languages, but has instilled as the norm an Anglocentric attitude which is as parochial as anything could be."

14

Scotland's Universities Today 2
The Wasteland

Certainly the omens were not good. Scotland's university principals had rejected university repatriation and only began to think again when the UGC's notorious cuts letter hit the universities in 1981. Pressure of circumstances forced the eight Scottish Principals to act together to a novel extent, said a leader in *TESS*.[1] If, however, the cooperation were to be formalised and if there were to be a single body speaking for the university sector, the staffs of the universities would no doubt argue that it should not comprise only the eight Principals.[2] "The 'Octet' sounds like a relic of the Venetian Republic, with all the drawbacks of such an oligarchy." In fact, the staffs had very little to say. The students seemed to be more aware of the implications for democracy of the way the universities were being run. Tony Martin, the Honorary President of the Heriot-Watt Students' Association, had said already in the 1970s that the "artificial separation of interests between students and lecturers is a separation that the administration of the university are always keen to promote ... Members of the Court have to rely too much on officials of the university for the provision of detailed information, reducing the staff members to little more than rubber stamps." And that was long before the real managerial blizzard hit the universities in the 1980s under the Thatcher-Joseph-Baker dispensation.

There was one very serious symptom of the 'takeover' Grant had prophesied: "The path of Scottish education seems set on the slippery slope to eventual total integration with the English system."[3] This was the way in which A-levels, since the 1960s, had more and more been accepted as on a par with Highers for entry to Scottish universities. They are, of course, very different animals. A-levels are highly specialized in two or at most three subjects taken over two or even three years; whereas Highers are much broader – four, five or even six subjects taken over one or two years. A-level students had the added advantage of generally being a year older. Already in 1967 a *TESS* editorial[4] was saying that "some of the Scottish universities are rightly worried about the large unleavening lump of entrants from the South". Then in 1968 the Thistle Group, a Scottish radical Tory pressure group, published a pamphlet on education, compiled by three law students. They said that the UCCA system was a threat to Scottish education since it had led the Scottish universities to prefer A-levels to Highers and consequently to threaten the breadth of sixth year curricula in Scotland. They pressed for a guaranteed number of places in Scottish universities for Scottish students to prevent sixth year work becoming a glorified university entrance course as it had become south of the border.[5] This problem has kept on cropping up, getting more and more serious as the years passed; it is bigger than ever in 1992, as we shall see. It has consequences which have regularly hit the headlines over the years – we shall give one example. In 1975 a student report[6] said that Scottish failure rates were "staggeringly high at St Andrews University". In 1973–74, even after resits, there was a failure rate of 35% of first year geography student with Scottish Highers, whereas there were no failures among those with English qualifications. The corresponding failure rates for English were 23% for Scots and 3% for those with A-levels. The university blamed the declining standards in Scottish schools, but the students refuted this thoroughly disingenuous and dishonest idea. They said that the university's courses were orientated towards the GCE early specialization approach rather than towards the broader based SCE approach. The students proposed that foundation year courses could help to resolve the dilemma, but this idea, said *Student Opinions*, had been rejected by the university. The *THES* commented: "The obvious trend for SCE students to fare worse than their GCE counterparts leads one to the unwelcome conclusion that there is a failure on the university's part to respond to the needs of Scottish students." Unwelcome perhaps but hardly surprising in view of the large majority of English staff at the university. That is the central problem and it will have to be faced up to some day.

Even more unwelcome is the conclusion that that failure has gone on until today, yet the evidence shows that this is so. It would be tiresomely repetitive to report all the occasions on which this problem has surfaced and the to-and-fro arguments that have frequently been indulged in, so we will cite the most recent one. In a press report[7] it is stated unequivocally that in practice, at the University of Edinburgh, a direct comparison is made between Highers and A-levels when deciding who to admit. We have seen that this cruelly penalises Scottish applicants. To make sure that they cannot escape this mechanism an UCCA spokesman said that it should make no difference where a student lives, in other words that there should be a standard procedure throughout the British Isles (which is what the St Andrews students were complaining about nearly 20 years ago). The English applicants for university places being so much more numerous than the Scots, the result is obvious. So is the resulting attitude of Scottish applicants who shun Edinburgh and flock to Glasgow, which has remained more loyal to Scottish traditions. We have seen that Dr Graham Hills despaired of the A-level system as "a sad English anachronism". In the same column[8] he said: "But behind Hadrian's wall it is quite different. The well-educated Scots have remained uninfected .. (they) have the great good fortune of not having to specialize before they enter higher education." Much good it has done them since, as a report *School to Higher Education – Bridging the Gap*[9] notes in its conclusions: "Scottish students are disadvantaged at Scottish universities compared to A-level entrants from south of the Border." The report says it is clear that A-level students are the majority group in some courses (this is a gross underestimate), and it adds there must be serious concern that this is creating "a learning environment inimical to students with Highers alone". The same report says that there is a 5% to 6% difference between average drop-out rates in England and Scotland. It is remarkably small in the circumstances and would probably disappear if one were comparing like with like. Many Scottish students at university would not have got there at all because of the elitist A-level system. The savage irony is that young Scots are being penalised, their life's goal destroyed in some cases (the writer knows a university Senior Lecturer whose son, with four Highers, could not get to university) by the preference given to A-level entrants at a time when the A-level system, fiercely criticized by Dr Hills and many English educationists, is clearly on the way out.

Even worse is the fact that slavish adherence to the UCCA system has turned at least four of our universities into English universities. All our universities have long had a majority of English staff. Now at least four of them have a majority of English students too. Throughout most of the 1970s and all of the 80s I never taught an Honours class at Stirling University that had more than a small minority of Scots in it, and this was also true of other years. When I was put up by students as a candidate for the post of Honorary President of the Students' Union, I found that the student hustings were overwhelmingly English and that the student radio station was almost entirely run by English students. Interviewed by a lad from the South of England I felt quite out of place pushing a Scottish programme. This takeover must have grave consequences for the self-confidence and self-respect of the Scottish students. To have allowed this unplanned colonisation of Scotland's universities by English students is a complete betrayal of generations of young Scots; it also reveals the poverty of thought among the people who are put in charge of our universities. Some day young Scots will demand an explanation.[10]

What makes this treatment of Scotland's young people even harder to take is what one learns from an article entitled *The Oxford Experiment*.[11] The author explains that when Scottish students go to English universities, especially Oxford and Cambridge, "the deal is": In the one or two school subjects they put forward as 'specialisms' in this context, the Scottish student who has studied five or six Highers subjects cannot hope to profess a quota of 'ground covered' comparable with that of the GCE Student who has concentrated on two or three A-levels for two (or three) years. "The philosophy implicit in the 'deal' is that he hopes to compensate for a less massive attainment in two 'specialist' subjects by having continued a far wider spectrum of academic subjects to a further level than his competitor." That, in turn, explains the author, John Marshall, is linked with the question: "How well, if at all, do the Scottish entrants catch up on what must plainly be a handicap of attainment? To this question an Oxbridge don answers: "In degree subjects for which previous school attainment bulks large the Highers qualified candidate does start under quite a handicap. But all the evidence of the trial year indicates that he catches up by the end of the first term or the start of the second. And an encouraging number not only 'catch up' but even start to 'overtake'." One's immediate reaction is to be irritated by the laboriousness of the explanation of the obvious and the patronising tone, but a moment's reflection makes one ask "So how massive is massive?" To exchange breadth for so little depth is surely not a sensible proceeding. The 'handicap' is clearly not so great as to make it either reasonable or fair to give preference to A-level students at Scottish universities. Yet that is what has been done on an increasing scale for nearly three decades. It is inconceivable that this could have happened – at least one hopes so – if our universities had not previously been inundated with English members of staff and even Principals, for whom this must have seemed a quite natural thing to do – though that does not say much for their professional competence and understanding of the different Scottish educational situation and the needs of Scottish students. It says even less for the Scottish members of staff.

One of the most thorough examinations of the problem is an article by James Robertson entitled *A Question of Identity in the Scottish*

Universities.[12] He says that Scottish students at some of our universities might be forgiven for wondering if 'cultural reorientation' was now a part of their higher education experience. There was a growing resentment among them at the increasing numbers of students from down south which reflected a justifiable concern for the integrity of the upper echelons of the Scottish education system.[13] "Why are these universities catering more and more for people from outwith that system who have no interest (in the sense of 'stake' rather than 'quaint curiosity') in it or the country and culture which it represents, while Scottish students are squeezed out of university places?" At St Andrews Scottish students were only one third of the total student population; at Dundee and Stirling they were barely half; while at Edinburgh 11% fewer of the students were Scots than was the case in 1981. In 1985 there were 1200, i.e. 13%, less Scottish undergraduate entrants to Scottish universities than in 1980–81, as well as a slight decrease in numbers going to study outside Scotland. These estimates were borne out early in 1989 in a detailed argument between three Edinburgh researchers and Michael Forsyth, who was responsible for education at the Scottish Office.[14] They showed that the cuts in funding to the Scottish universities had a knock-on effect on opportunities for entry. To take just two examples: In 1976 an estimated 70% of qualified school leavers went straight on to some form of higher education. The comparable estimate for 1986 was only 59%. In 1980 37% of school leavers with four Higher passes went to university. By 1986 the proportion had fallen to 12%, that is by an enormous two-thirds, at a time when 'access' was one of the government's favourite academic buzzwords. As the researchers said: "The greatest single contribution government can make to wider access is to raise the opportunities for higher education at least to the level at which they stood in the second half of the 1970s."

At the same time the Edinburgh MP Nigel Griffiths was strongly complaining, in a letter to the Secretary of State for Scotland, Malcolm Rifkind, against the discrimination by English universities against Scottish applicants with Highers, the examples he quoted being Leeds, York and Newcastle. With the decimation of departments in Scottish universities at that time as a result of government policy, it could mean that Scottish students could have nowhere to go. This was more than a possibility because at that very time Strathclyde University was rejecting the UGC's request that it discontinue teaching and research on mining and petroleum engineering on the grounds that, if it pulled out of the field, there would be no undergraduate teaching in it in Scotland, in spite of a demand for courses and ample job opportunities. Yet at the very time all this was happening places were being filled by English students "for whom", says Robertson, "three or four years at university is often little more than an extended exercise in leisure", and who fail to appreciate "that in Scotland a separate set of values and historical traditions exist which do not defer to Anglocentric metropolitanism".

One of the most forceful statements of the need to preserve the integrity of Scottish university education with its four-year Honours and its three-year Ordinary degrees is to be found in the STEAC (Scottish Tertiary Education Advisory Council) report presented in December 1985 and entitled *Future Strategy for Higher Education in Scotland* : "It is in our view essential that Scotland's broadly-based educational tradition should be protected so that when priorities change higher education is able to respond and adapt. As full a range of academic subjects as possible should be provided and new subjects should also be accommodated." It speaks of Scotland's "valuable tradition in both vocational and non-vocational subjects", and stresses that "key subjects must not be lost to Scottish higher education as a result of nationalization of provision on a UK or GB basis". All well and good but, on the other hand, STEAC also said that "Nothing should be done . . which would prevent Scottish universities from recruiting a substantial part of their student population from the rest of the United Kingdom and from overseas."

The trouble with this is that it undermines the defence of the Scottish system quoted above. Now it is a good thing that there should be substantial numbers of young people from different cultures and ethnic backgrounds at our universities; indeed there always have been. The problem is that the proportion of the nationals of one country, England, has been allowed to rise until they are well in the majority in at least four of our universities. There has also been an increase in the numbers from North America, from European countries as a result of EC legislation, and from richer parts of Asia like Hong Kong and Singapore, while the numbers from Third World or poorer countries have fallen. "In other words", says Robertson, "there appears to have been a general shift in the constituency of the student population as a whole (and at certain universities in particular) during the 1980s, away from the disadvantaged and towards those, whether from home or abroad, with more wealth." For example, in 1985 Eton supplied more entrants to Edinburgh than any other school.

Add to this the fact that there are large majorities of English staff at our universities and you arrive at a position where Scottish studies, Scottish history, literature and politics "are ghettoized, becoming the concerns of a dedicated minority instead of major sections of general teaching. It is in fact quite usual for history students to graduate from Edinburgh without having taken a single course in Scottish history". At the time Robertson was writing Edinburgh University was trying to obtain money from private sources to fund a Chair of Scottish Politics, without success at the time. In 1986 those with Highers formed only 52% of admissions to Social Sciences, while in Arts Scots were less than 50% of the student intake. In Modern Languages studies were so geared to A-levels that Scottish applicants were strongly advised to wait a year and try to travel to raise their standardsof. There was not one permanent Chair of Scottish Literature in the whole of Scotland, "while what in most self-respecting countries would be a centrally-funded and much-treasured repository of national culture – the School of Scottish Studies – in fact exists as a semi-official department of Edinburgh University, housed discreetly in a corner and heavily dependent . . on charity". Again it baffles the mind to try and understand why the writers, artists, musicians and intellectuals of a country so rich in contemporary art and culture, and so lively withal, do not raise loud, sustained protest against this inferiorisation of Scottish culture.

In his Annual Report to the General Council of the University of Edinburgh, on 27 June 1992, the Principal, Sir David Smith, tackled two questions which had aroused media comment: the proportion of the student body which is Scots domiciled, and the freezing of the Chair of Scottish History. He shows that there is a net inflow from south of the border of 2000 students per year and that this inflow is of great value to the Scottish economy, worth at the very least 40 million per year and providing more than 3000 jobs. The pattern of applications from south of the border is unevenly distributed, "with particular preference being shown for Edinburgh and two or three other Scottish universities, some of whom have significantly lower proportions of Scots-domiciled students than Edinburgh". He also says that the largest expansion in intake in the university's history, more than 3000 or 15%, took place in October 1991, and that the continuation of the national drive towards mass higher education will present the university with a challenge.

But surely, since the economy of the UK is an integrated economy, 2000 extra Scottish students would bring in just as much money as the 2000 English students, with due allowance made for the higher standards of living of a considerable number of the English students. And surely, with a 15% expansion in first year entrants that year and the continuing drive towards mass higher education, the English majority of students will become ever greater unless measures to restrict it are taken. Indeed, the education correspondent of *Scotland on Sunday*, on 30 August 1992 expressed great fears for the future of Scottish applicants to Scottish universities, saying that "Scotland's renown as a highly-educated nation is under threat". Nowhere does the Principal mention the equivalence between A-levels and Highers through UCCA and university admissions boards as the mechanism which has made such an invasion possible. Indeed, in almost the same breath he speaks of "the pressure of competition for entry" and of "a drive to increase the numbers applying from local schools which traditionally send few students to university". This must be self-contradictory, since we have already seen the press reporting abandonment of the University of Edinburgh for the University of Glasgow by Scottish applicants because they know they have no chance against A-level applicants at Edinburgh.

The Principal deals in similar vein with the freezing of the Chair of Scottish History, accusing the press of giving the impression that the University was "generally not giving a damn for Scottish traditions and culture". He claims that, "At present the University of Edinburgh makes greater provision for the study of Scottish issues and Scotland's culture than any other university in the world", i.e. nineteen departments spread across five faculties offering courses on specifically Scottish issues. He says it is "ludicrously malicious" to suggest that they had ever intended abandoning the Chair of Scottish History. The Principal protests too much. No-one ever suggested that; protesters were angered at the freezing of a chair in an absolutely central subject for any country: its history. A subject, moreover, which has been neglected for far too long in Scotland's schools and universities. Would Sir David freeze the chair of English history in a university in his own country, England? One has only to ask the question to see the double standards which are operating here. One does not underestimate the financial problems facing university principals in these philistine times, but the Principal's statement that it was, after all, "only one of the seven vacant chairs in the Faculty of Arts which the Faculty has publicly committed itself to filling as soon as its resources permit, shows that he did not see it as of absolutely central importance. If he had, it would have been quite easy to find the necessary money by cutting back on the teaching of English history and literature, which dwarf Scottish studies at Edinburgh. (They also dwarf French and German historical and literary studies, which are very important to Scotland.) That, sadly, would never occur to him nor to the Arts Faculty, since he, and they in their large majority, are English.

He also protests a great deal about the University's commitment to Scottish culture, with the establishment of a Chair of Scottish Ethnology and an attempt to establish a Chair in Scottish Literature, "a subject very popular with students". (Why then have they had to wait until now for it?) Unfortunately the fund-raising campaign to establish an endowment for the Chair failed: "Hardly a single one of the many wealthy Scottish bodies which were approached offered any support for this key aspect of Scottish culture." So they are to blame, not the university! He says it is a 'key aspect of Scottish culture', yet he and the Arts Faculty had done nothing about it. Had it been a 'key aspect' of English culture it would have been a very different story. Again, as with the Chair of Scottish History and the Chair of Scottish Politics, the answer to the problem is obvious, but would never have occurred to him. The weakest and, I have to say, the most distasteful part of the Principal's case came when he said: "Our Trade Unions are apprehensive and angry when they perceive that some of the outside attacks and pressure on the University to immediately fill the specific post of the Chair of Scottish History are simply riding on the tide of the increasing desire for devolution or independence." This looks uncommonly like smear tactics, and that in a matter of great importance to nearly all Scottish academics and teachers. It casts doubt on the honesty of the Principal's case.

Edinburgh is not the only example of this English takeover. Robertson quotes the journalist Joyce McMillan:[15] "At St Andrews University I ran full tilt into what is possibly the most anglicised of all Scottish institutions and found myself in classes and coffee-rooms where mine was the only Scottish voice. The Honours English examination demanded *one* paper out of *nine* on Scottish literature, and that was regarded as something of an imposition by the two-thirds of arts undergraduates who were in fact English." The position at Stirling at the end of the 1980s was similar, as pointed out earlier. English students were in a considerable majority, and to this must be added the staff composition. The Scots and those who had taken their first degree in Scotland only got anywhere near 50% in two of Stirling's schools (in Arts, arguably the most important school, it was 28%); less than 20% of the professors were Scots; and almost the entire top academic and administrative echelon who ran the place were English. The only thing Scottish about half of our universities is their geographical location.

In 1991 the Stirling Principal revealed a hitherto unsuspected vein of black humour when he said in a press statement: "It is important that we retain the character of a Scottish university because that is one of the reasons that attracts students from elsewhere." He did not seem to realise that this statement is self-contradictory. At least half of our universities have in fact acquired colonial status. A letter to the press[16] points out that our languages, literature, history and culture generally are largely displaced by those of the metropolitan power, which claims and asserts superiority: "These are the distinguishing characteristics of colonial status." He cites the American sociologist Michael Hechter who, in his book *Internal Colonialism*, said that the purpose of the denigration of the culture of a colonised people is to undermine their will to resist the colonial regime. This can obviously take many forms, suited to different circumstances, different audiences, and different immediate purposes. "Colonialism is at its most complete when many of the colonized no longer recognize the reality of their status." This seems to be the case with nearly all our leaders and opinion-formers in view of their failure to speak out against what is the now fairly imminent destruction of Scotland's higher educational soul.

This is no empty accusation (if I may digress for a moment), since most of the top posts in the Scottish arts and culture generally are cheerfully given to Englishmen, who have brought with them in some cases the empty pretensions of the metropolitan art world. It is surely extraordinary that, for example, the Director of the National Galleries of Scotland and the Director of Glasgow's galleries and museums should both be English.[17] Other small countries like Sweden, Norway, Denmark, Austria, Belgium see no need to import cultural leaders *en masse* from outside, and it cannot be that they all produce more home-grown talent than Scotland. Can it conceivably be that there is a deliberate, unspoken and perhaps only half-conscious intention to destroy Scottish cultural identity and therefore her national self-awareness?

To return to our theme ... Robertson's suggestion of a positive remedy to counter what he calls the "Yah factor" in our universities is the adoption of an official, high-profile approach to Scottish schools liaison with the conscious aim of increasing Scottish representation among the student bodies of the most affected universities. In 1987 Edinburgh's history department suddenly realized that more than half the students were now non-Scots (clearly one of the motives for not hesitating to freeze the Chair of Scottish History); and this prompted a campaign to attract new applicants from Scottish state schools. He says there are some other examples in other departments but they are unfortunately not concerted, "are often made in spite of a lack of official approval, and arise largely out of a realization that the situation in a department or faculty has already got out of hand".

To an informed English observer like Stanley Adams, rector of St Andrews, it seemed logical "that Scots should be the chief beneficiaries of their own universities". A policy to ensure that they were could form part of an overall strategy for Scottish education such as that proposed by STEAC in 1985. "Positive discrimination of this kind would be entirely appropriate to the attitudes which inform the general perception of the problem: that the universities of Scotland should perform their proper function as the upper-level institutions of a national education system, catering for Scots and for the international community, not operating as branch organizations of another country's educational apparatus." Robertson expresses the hope that it should become national policy that at least 70% of students at *each of the universities* should come from Scotland, and that overseas students should also be recruited in higher numbers and their fees paid by a Scottish-funded system. There is certainly no reason why English students should be more than 10% of the student body at any of our universities in view of the very large number of higher education institutions in England with university status. At that level, however, they would be very welcome, as they were in the eighteenth century when the only way English non-conformists could get a university education was by coming to Scotland, in view of the religious test for entry to Oxford and Cambridge. It would obviously take very much longer to reduce the proportion of English academics at our universities to a level at which they would no longer dominate the system. Concern to avoid any individual hardship would dictate a long-term recruitment policy which over a generation or so would return our universities to their Scottish roots. Our universities, like the Scottish people as a whole, are deeply internationalist in sentiment, but that must not be allowed to mean the total anglicization of our universities. As Jean Jaurès said, to be a good internationalist one must first of all be a good nationalist, in the sense of loving one's country.

One might have thought that, after rejecting the repatriation of our universities in the late 1970s and then having their fingers burnt in the cuts onslaught in 1981, our university Principals, even the English ones, would have welcomed STEAC's call for the academic devolution of the Scottish universities and the establishment of a body "with responsibility for academic planning across the university and non-university sectors of higher education in Scotland and for allocation of resources within a system of funding unified under the Secretary of State for Scotland". It seemed that at last we were going to able to take a comprehensive look at the totality of Scottish education and perhaps, with luck, do again for it in the late twentieth century what the *First Book of Discipline* had attempted to do for it more than four centuries ago. But no, once again the Scottish universities opposed the proposal. The *Times Higher Education Supplement*[18] commented: "It is now clear that Mr Rifkind's (then Secretary of State for Scotland) was a finely balanced decision. Despite the difficulties, the Secretary of State had been prepared to jump the other way if he had been assured of greater support in the Scottish universities". Worse still, the AUT (Scotland) opposed it as well, opting instead for a Scottish sub-committee of the Universities Funding Council, set up in 1989 and quickly found to be unsatisfactory. Of this sub-committee the THES said: "Some will regard this body as a deliberately feeble institution designed simply to defuse devolutionary feeling . . . The fact that the committee will not become involved directly in detailed negotiations between the Scottish universities and the parent UFC in London may seem to support this view." This prophecy turned out to be spot on, and the AUT (Scotland) quickly reversed its policy on 29 April 1989 and moved towards accepting, in principle, a single funding and planning body for Scottish higher education, and backing "the principle of an elected Scottish Assembly which would have, inter alia, responsibility for higher education in Scotland".

The informed onlooker, of whom there were and are all too few – might well look on in bewilderment at such behaviour by the leaders of Scotland's universities. In editorial after editorial[19] the *Times Higher Education Supplement* (a London publication) argued the commonsense advantages of the repatriation of Scotland's universities, above all ending the anomalous situation whereby Scotland's universities were under the UGC/UFC, that is, an English body accountable to the English Department of Education and Science and the British (to all intents and purposes the English) Secretary of State for Education, while all the rest of Scottish education – the schools, further education and all non-university higher education – remained under the responsibility of the Secretary of State for Scotland. In October 1988 the THES was saying: "The attention of the Scottish committee of the UFC should be directed at least as much to the future role of the Scottish universities within Scottish higher education as a whole as to their present place within the British university system . . . The focus must be on Scottish higher education, not British universities." It saw a danger that, following the rejection of the STEAC proposal in 1985, the evolution of Scottish higher education would be over-influenced by the apparently more dynamic example of England, in other words that "creeping anglicization which Scots educators already discern in the Scottish Education Department's policies on school boards, curriculum and testing, and the accreditation of skills . . . a process of one-sided convergence which has been under way in the Scottish universities for a century or more".

The THES sees the importance of preserving the Scottish tradition in Scottish higher education. "It is as much in the interests of England as of Scotland to maintain models of diversity. Uniform arrangements are generally bad arrangements." It even says that Scottish higher education is an inspiring example, being "more populist, offering broader degrees (still) and enrolling more young people. It is more relevant and there are fewer barriers to access". On January 29 of that same year, in an editorial entitled *Ane Old Song*, it showed a remarkable understanding of the situation in Scotland, and followed this with a clarion call for intellectual diversity. No-one, in or out of Scotland, has written better on the subject, so the peroration is worth quoting in full:

> University devolution is above all a political and cultural question – better still, a national question. The present constitution of Britain is unlikely to be maintained for much longer. The arrogance of South Britain would be enough to overturn it even without proud memories of Scotland's nationhood. It is no longer a question of if but when a Parliament sits again in Edinburgh. Those who seek to limit the march of a nation, in Parnell's famous threat, risk being trodden on or, worse still, forgotten – even if they are among that nation's most ancient institutions.
> But there is an even more powerful reason for favouring university devolution. In the face of the frightening integration of the world's economy, intellectual as well as material, the uniformity of mass attitudes, the conformity of our values, there is an urgent need to reassert the claims of cultural pluralism. For on cultural pluralism is built the capacity to imagine otherwise that is the root of freedom and science. Scotland is a better place than most to start.

Would that our pragmatic, money-grubbing Principals had such vision! The THES also made the commonsense points that the shape of access is quite different in Scotland and cannot be reduced to an appendix to English policy; that the pattern of industry and employment is different. "Above all Scotland's culture, which embraces the nation's expectations of education, is unique. Yet serious discussion of these fundamental questions remains difficult as long as the universities, the larger part of Scotland's higher education are managed on London's terms."

Despite all this good advice Scotland's universities resisted repatriation to the end. Can any reader doubt that the English majority on all university bodies, and even in AUT (Scotland), is the principal reason for this quite extraordinary position? Had there been a majority of Scots it is all but certain that repatriation would have been preferred. It is a huge historical irony that repatriation was "almost accidental", as the THES put it on 4 October 1991 – the product of the amalgamation of the UFC and the PFC in England. It is, though, a shade premature in its surmise that the inner intellectual life of the Scottish universities may be transformed, that this may lead to a cultural resurgence (well under way already, without benefit of the universities) and that "old philosophical ghosts" may emerge from the shadows of Scotland's history. It is certainly true that Scotland's 'social ethics' are different from those of England, as underlined by Mrs. Thatcher's "There is no such thing as society". It should not, however, be forgotten that, though the universities will be responsible to a funding body set up by the SOED (itself a loyal transmitter of Westminster government decisions), they will in reality still be dependent on funding decisions involving the DES and other funding councils in London. The AUT, through its regional officer in Scotland,[20] warned about "the nightmarish complexity" that will result from this situation, and about the dangers of the purely administrative devolution of higher education.[21] "We are convinced", he said, "that academic devolution can only be complete when there is democratic accountability to a Scottish Parliament."

The AUT had clearly thought the position through. Not so the Principals, whose fear of, and resistance to, real repatriation continues. For example, Glasgow's Principal, Sir William Fraser, warned the Scottish Office, whose top civil servant he once was, that its paternalistic approach in funding Scotland's central institutions should not extend to the universities when they came under a Scottish funding council from April 1993.[22] The Scottish universities have always distrusted the SED (now SOED), which is seen as high-handed in its administrative style and anti-university in its attitudes. "It is essential", says Sir William, with an insider's knowledge, "that the Scottish Office realises that what is happening is not the gathering of a few wandering sheep of different ages and sizes into its existing flock, with the appointment of a new shepherd in the shape of the funding council, operating on the same basis as the old shepherd with the old sheep." It seems strange that this noble resistance to petty tyranny was not given more powerful expression, or any expression at all, at the exactions and authoritarian policies of the UGC/UFC as the 'hit man' of the Westminster government, and that there was hardly a squeak of protest at what the THES called the "ruthless anglicization" of Aberdeen by the UGC under Sir Peter Swinnerton-Dyer.

Sir Kenneth Alexander, Chancellor of Aberdeen University, took a more balanced stand,[23] expressing the hope that academic institutions would reap the benefit of the changes in university funding. He told graduates at Marischal College: "For the first time education in Scotland from primary to university and beyond will be under Scottish administration: a seamless garment, as yet not of an altogether pleasing design. However, if we are wise enough, this garment can be cut to fit our social, cultural and economic needs more

effectively than ever before." Professor Maxwell Irvine, Principal of
Aberdeen University, on the other hand, pinpointed another great
threat coming from the UFC: "We now face the threat of a creeping
bureaucracy which could stifle higher education in Scotland to an
extent that we have managed to avoid for over 500 years – all this
in the name of quality control." Quality control could not be measured on a simple numerical scale. "Quality – academic quality –
is the essence of a university. The ability to deliver that quality is
threatened by government's desire to expand higher education and
its determination not to pay for it."[24]

In fact, the wolves that threaten to come down on Sir William
Fraser's sheep-fold are external ones, as witness the extraordinary
lucubrations of Dr John Ashworth, Director of the London School
of Economics and former science adviser to Mrs. Thatcher.[25] He
was one of two dozen academics who wrote to Tam Dalyell MP,
a member of the House of Commons examining the Further and
Higher Education (Scotland) Bill, to express doubts about government plans to set up a Scottish Higher Education Funding
Council. Mr Dalyell believes that a separate funding council will
lead to Scottish universities becoming isolated and could stem the
flow of 3,500 English students who study in Scotland each year.
Mr Dalyell's renowned abilities in research evidently do not extend
to the universities, since the four ancient universities did rather better in isolation for 500 years than they are doing now being run
from London. At any rate, Dr Ashworth gave it as his personal
view that it was "a mistake for there to be a separate council for
Scotland". He then, like Sir Christopher Ball in a lengthy article in
The Scotsman,[26] makes a scarcely veiled attack on Scotland's four-
year degree pattern,[27] backing it up with the scare story that "the
English universities are already restive" and brandishing the bogey
of "internecine warfare". He says the Scottish universities would
become "inward-looking", which is rich, coming from the adviser to
the greatest 'little Englander' of them all. With sublime arrogance he
says that "quality assurance" (one of the many fashionable jargon
terms borrowed unthinkingly from business school lingo by our
supposedly top drawer academics) would suffer under a separate
funding council – probably ignorant of the fact that throughout the
eighteenth and most of the nineteenth centuries Scotland's universities were much superior to those of England. They only dropped
back when forced into the English mould and measured by English
criteria in the late nineteenth century.

These are the people Sir William Fraser should be directing his fire
at. Sir Graham Hills is in no doubt where the threat comes from.
He said[28] that much rested on the UFC Scottish sub-committee's

determination to stick up for itself. It would have to deal with those who still believed they could manage Scotland's universities as if they were merely a small part of the British set-up. "The new body is an unknown quantity, but it is likely to be constrained by the requirements of Britain as a whole." He didn't think the committee was a token gesture because "anything that ameliorates centralized decision-making is a good thing". We now know, sadly, that the Scottish sub-committee of the UFC did not stand up for itself and has been a failure, as the THES predicted. The important thing, now that Scottish higher education is to have its own funding council, is precisely that it should stick up for itself against control from the 'golden triangle' in the south-east and not contract the Scottish disease of petty, internecine squabbling.

The creeping bureaucracy, of which Professor Maxwell Irvine warns, means that Scottish higher education, having so little in the way of powerful, determined advocates at Westminster, always comes off worse. Even the UGC shut down 30 university departments in Scotland between 1979 and its demise in 1989, and cut finance by 12.6 million between 1985 and 1989.[29] The axed departments included Heriot-Watt's Department of Pharmacy and the Edinburgh Dental College, and would have included Glasgow's Veterinary College as well had there not been such a public outcry. Examples of this devastation of Scotland's higher education are so numerous as to defy selection. At the beginning of 1989 there were some 14,000 fewer graduates working in Scotland than in 1983. That is a very large number for a small country, especially at a time when there were more graduates than ever working in Great Britain. More than 45% of all Britain's graduates were working in London and the Southeast. A quarter of all Britain's working female graduates were in London. During the period 1983–87 the only part of Britain where the number of working graduates fell was Scotland, from 9.4% to 7.0%. This in a country which has always produced more graduates per head of population than England.

The sociologist Isobel Lindsay has shown that one third of Strathclyde University's 1987 graduates – the vast majority of them Scots, unlike St Andrews or Edinburgh – got their first job outside Scotland.[30] It is a safe bet that a large majority of Scottish families with graduates see them go out of Scotland to find suitable work. During the graduation season of 1992 the prospect of unemployment had never loomed so large. At Stirling's Arts graduation no-one had a job lined up. One had applied to work behind a Post Office counter until something better came along. Of Edinburgh's 1991 crop of graduates only 43% had found jobs in the UK. The story was the same at Napier College (now Napier University) where in one of its vocational – and therefore supposedly job-rich – courses: the two-year diploma in journalism, only 5 out of 33 had found full-time jobs in the media.[31]

An even worse symptom of the academic wasteland Scotland's universities have become is the increasing difficulty students are having in finding books in their libraries. "In the past decade student numbers at Scotland's universities have increased by 33% – from 44,500 to 60,000 – while the number of books purchased has dropped by 17%, from 70,000 to 60,000." The result is that many students now find it impossible to get hold of the texts they need for their courses – as in earlier centuries. The dangerous consequence of this is that some "lecturers have responded by reducing the breadth of reading they recommend to students". This affects staff as well as students. At a time when they are being compelled to do more 'research' as well as teaching 33% more students, more than 30% said they were losing touch with developments in their fields because they could not get access to new publications. The inevitable result of this squeeze on books and periodicals is that the quality of teaching and research must suffer. This is precisely the opposite of the goal the Government thinks it is pursuing with its 'performance indicators', 'productivity-related pay structures', 'efficiency gains' and all the other business-school jargon it has introduced into the universities. When to all that are added the salary constraints inflicted on university teachers as on no other section of professional workers, the effect on morale has been quite devastating. Edinburgh's Principal said that in all key indicators – such as numbers of students, volume of research and higher external income – university performance had increased by 50% over 10 years but pay had fallen by 25%, and this at a time when top people in industry were awarding themselves huge pay increases and even MPs were giving themselves a 38% increase in expenses.[32]

Nor with the change of Prime Minister in 1991 was there any sign of a let-up of the pressure on universities as a result of government policy on the reduction of public expenditure. Sir Ron Dearing, the successor to the incompetent and reactionary Lord Chilver[33] as chairman of the Universities Funding Council, said[34] the universities faced a radical shake-up (yet again!) to find room for the growing numbers of students. The traditional academic year must be sacrificed and buildings used more efficiently to cram in extra students. Opening up lecture halls on Saturday mornings and Wednesday afternoons alone could allow a 20% increase in the use of facilities. Stirling University's Principal, over the opposition of the students, was already calling for lectures to continue till 21.00 hrs. No-one appeared to realize that students need time to study, to do part-time jobs if they can find any, to relax and take part in leisure and sporting activities, or simply to socialize and grow up. Extra private sector money and better management of university buildings – though Glasgow's Principal had declared that £50 million was needed just to repair and maintain its buildings, yet its annual budget for this was just £4 million – were essential for expansion. The great delusion continued: that it was possible to treat universities like a production line, with heads of department turned into line managers, and to manage them along the lines of British industry, whose managenent was one of the weakest in Europe.[35] As early as 1968 Principal Stevens of St Andrews was attacking the "conveyer-belt" concept of the university: "At a time when we are discussing what has gone wrong with the relation of students and staff, when we are lamenting the failure of the generations to communicate, deploying technical enrichment with spiritual impoverishment, could anyone dream up a more ridiculous proposal (a 50-week university year, i.e. four or five 10-week terms) than to break the social bond of a university and to turn the young into packages on a conveyer-belt and to give the staff the job of stamping the packages as they pass."[36]

Sir Graham Hills was still plugging the Chilvers charity-cum-workhouse approach to university education by advocating means-tested charges for it.[37] These should be set at about 20% of the real cost. "Then", said Dr Hills, "the universities could afford all the books and facilities they need". Well yes, provided they had any students, especially in Scotland where, it was estimated, 50% of young people were below the poverty line. No exaggeration, as the heart-rending sight of young people begging in Edinburgh and Glasgow confirms. Dr Hills and others seemed not to see the glaring inconsistency between calling for mass higher education and driving young people away from the universities because they cannot afford it. (Yet, for reasons best known to themselves, this was the man the authorities in Inverness asked to investigate the possibility of a university in the Highlands!) This delusion stemmed in part from the visit of Mr Baker to America when he was Secretary of State for Education. There he had a brainstorm: American higher education = private funding, European higher education = public funding. So let us privatize British higher education on the American model! The only problem here is that American higher education is just as heavily subsidized from public funds as British higher education. Nor is "working your way through college" possible in Britain – above all not in Scotland with its long-lasting recession and heavy unemployment. Nor has private industry ever shown itself ready to finance higher education on the scale necessary. Nor is it possible for British universities, with the possible exception of Oxford and Cambridge, to raise sufficient funding from their alumni by well-organized fund-raising, as the major American universities do.

Certainly the squeeze was being inflicted on all Britain's universities but it affected the Scottish universities more, as the financial crises at Aberdeen and Edinburgh showed. Symbolic of this situation in Scotland were the freezing of the Chair of Scottish History at Edinburgh at the beginning of 1992, which we have dealt with, and the proposal in June 1992, also at Edinburgh, to end the historic role of the Rector – elected by both staff and students – as chairman of Court, the university's ruling body. Initially this proposal was not made by the university authorities themselves but by the firm of management consultants advising them on the running of the university;[38] but the university's leaders were determined to implement a proposal made by people who have no understanding of the ethos of a university. They see the university as a large business and want a bureaucrat chairing its leading committee, as in commerce and industry generally. A university, however, is not a large business and can never be properly or successfully run like one. This does not mean that a university cannot be run efficiently, only that turning it into a carbon copy of Britain's poorly run industries is not the way to go about it.

A shining example of how to improve at secondary and higher levels has been set by the French Government during these last years. In 1989 spending on education was 18% of all government expenditure and was to rise by 3% in real terms.[39] The Government had just put forward an educational programme the aims of which were "staggeringly ambitious: to ensure that no child leaves school without reaching a recognized standard of education"; to bring 80% of pupils up to baccalaureate level (by comparison the 1992 Howie Report in Scotland gave a figure of 25%); to guarantee that everyone with a 'bac' pass gets a university place if s/he so wishes. In other words more than 50% of the age group would get to university by the year 2000. There are already 1.3 million students in higher education in France – twice as many as in Britain. The French Government expects that number to rise to nearly 2 million by the year 2000. An enormous programme of refurbishment, building (four new universities) and staff recruitment is under way. Something like 1500 new university teachers were being appointed. The French Government apparently does not suffer from the current Westminster mania for cutting public expenditure. It clearly realizes that no national possession is more precious than the trained minds of its young people. There has been regional consultation, talks with interest groups, and an upbeat public presentation of the plans at every stage.

When compared with this, and remembering Scotland's great 'open door' policy for university education in the nineteenth century, one blushes for shame at the present position in Scotland as described by Edinburgh's Principal:[40] "The plan was to build up our major source of income, which meant student numbers, and to reduce our major expenditure, which is the wages and salaries bill. The problem is that we didn't have a sufficient number of students to justify the staff, so we had to bring these back into balance." This Children's Hour type explanation omits to mention that the result of this double ploy would be a huge increase in staff-student ratios, and therefore increased pressure on staff, who had already had a large increase in their workload over the past 10 years. Sir David Smith accepted that the rapid increase in student numbers meant "some measure of decline in quality". This is not surprising when one reads that the university had been saved by its students "packing ever more tightly into lecture halls, laboratories and libraries and bringing plentiful fees with them" (and clearly getting less for them)[41]. In the last three years the undergraduate intake had shot up by 40% to more than 3000 per year. As a result of this "success" the plan to shed (more value-free language) more than 200 academic jobs had been revised down to 160 – for which relief much thanks! "We have an ethos", says Sir David, "which is now spreading, that the majority of academic decisions are inseparable from resource decisions". What he means is that university teaching, learning and research is now *finance-led* or *market-led* and that Edinburgh university is now in the hands of the accountants. When one sees what they have done to British industry as a whole, the prognosis for Scotland's universities is a bleak one.

The reason for obeying the management consultants in the matter of removing the Rector as Chairman of Court is now quite clear. The role of the Rector is the one element remaining of the consensual method of running universities that began at Bologna more than 800 years ago. It is one of the rare truly Scottish traditions left in our universities. It offers some slight democratic resistance to the bureaucrats and accountants who now run our universities. Muriel Gray, a former Rector of the University of Edinburgh, explained just why the Rector's role is so important[42]: " . . . by chairing the Court the rector has enormous influence . . (it) is essential to enable the rector to carry out his or her full function in the university. To the chair of Court nothing in the university is secret, and so investigations of complaints brought to the Rector's office can be fully pursued without obstacle. This unlimited access is just one of the useful powers bestowed on the Chair of Court, but the other more rigidly constitutional ones, such as the right to set the Court agenda and monitor the minutes appear to terrify those who live in fear of any Rector who doesn't take tea with Michael Forsyth." (At that time in charge of education at the Scottish Office). It is essential, she adds, that an independent outsider should retain this power because it is a great and ancient democratic Scottish tradition: "a vocal, active, independent Rector in a position of strength". Clearly such a person could get in the way of the streamlined academic production-line Sir David Smith has been talking about. Much better to have 'one of us', so that proposals to turn Edinburgh University into 'Knowledge plc', as Glasgow's Rector put it, can go through on the nod. As Muriel Gray points out, "The retired captains of industry currently sitting . . on our Courts mostly obtained their previously-elevated positions in management through privilege, not skill."

For this position to be reached there has been an enormous *trahison des clercs* on the part of our senior academics, because Mrs Thatcher's governments were only able to inflict such great damage on our universities, and with such speed, because there was so little resistance. Academic staff are urged, by a CVCP committee no less, to receive training in entrepreneurship, marketing methods and media presentation; the language is offensively managerial. At least a third of all teaching and research staff are now on short-term contracts, thus casualising a profession it takes a lifetime to master. One wonders how a David Hume, an Adam Smith, or even a James Clerk Maxwell would have fared in such a situation.[43] The *Scotsman* interview with Edinburgh's Principal speaks of "the present climate of fierce competition between Britain's universities", and Sir David Smith even wanted them to be competitive with Europe. Such a concept has nothing in common with good teaching and research and should be resisted rather than compliantly accepted. Knowledge is co-operative, not competitive.

Sir William Fraser, then newly appointed as Principal of Glasgow University, had already nailed this nonsense in 1989.[44] He said that, on being "parachuted into this field" he had been struck by the ruthlessly competitive atmosphere between universities. "The Government seems to regard competition as the well-spring of all worthwhile human endeavour. But the degree to which universities are in competition with each other, not simply for students but in particular for resources from outside, seems to me to create a danger of distorting the purpose for which the universities are there – the provision of high-quality teaching and facilities for research." It had been condemned long before by Patrick Geddes in his unique series of vacation courses at Edinburgh from 1887 to 1899. The *Scottish Review* of 1888 quotes him: "And a yet more important side of the teacher's own education is in progress – the moral one – he learns that study can be well done for love, and without competition; his every day's work goes towards righting the vicious modern subordination of teaching to examining."

In this quite unwonted academic climate there must be grave doubts about the government's call for mass higher education. It is right to make such a call but it must also be compelled to put up the necessary funding, following the French example, so that standards do not fall, as Sir David Smith and other Principals fear. I repeat: nothing is more valuable than trained brains, and therefore also their education and training, yet, somewhere between 20 and 30 billion pounds is thrown away on nuclear weapons that will never be needed, far less used. Finance for higher education is a political matter, as Sir David says, and is not to be obtained by packing students in, reducing them to the breadline, or dunning them when they have graduated. If the management consultants and Sir David Smith have their way, the Rectors of Scottish universities will no longer be in a position to resist the management consultants and the business-school whizz kids who will deprive Scotland's universities of what little Scottish character they still have left.

Yet Sir David Smith admits that the increased financial pressures on students are damaging their ability to learn. The first concern of every university teacher must be the welfare of his/her students, so why does Sir David and his senior colleagues in Scotland not do something more effective to protect them than accepting the advice of management consultants? There are plenty of forums for them. Their failure to do so is a betrayal of Scotland's young people. Indeed, at a graduation ceremony on 16 July 1992, Sir David himself spoke in a manner which can only be interpreted as in opposition to the very policies he seems to be tamely implementing: "Education which aims too narrowly at preparing people for jobs in a market-oriented, highly-competitive world carries the serious risk of minimising the qualities of altruism and unselfishness." That could not be better said. "Mass education", he goes on, "will be of little value if it simply increases the number of people who are pursuing their own selfish ends. Remember, it is within the lifespan of today's new graduates that major changes have to happen." That is excellent. It harks back to the great moral philosophical traditions of Scotland's universities and forward to the devastating problems that today's students will have to tackle.

It is not the commercialised universities of today that can fit them for this task, for they are sent out into the world with a specialism but little cultural background or understanding of society's problems. More, the students themselves show they are aware of these needs by flocking to the arts and sociological subjects. They need a broad, philosophy-based education, as well as a specialism, and that was precisely the traditional approach of Scotland's universities. We need to get back to that tradition, in a suitable contemporary form: a tradition which produced students who could think analytically and for themselves, who could ask questions and see the systematic interconnections of things. The memory of that great tradition is still with us. What Sir David Smith said in that graduation speech about environmental problems, on the need for North-South dialogue, showed just how badly we need to revive it.

But can we do it?

15

The Revival of the Democratic Intellect 1
The Blocked Society

In attempting to answer that question we must not forget how difficult the task will be. We must keep always in mind R. E. Bell's challenge: either make a tremendous national effort or, and preferably in his view, sit back and allow our universities to be totally anglicized. If the only thing at stake here were Scottish pride and self-respect, even then the great effort would be worth making. Scotland over the past three centuries has been a frustrated girning nation and will remain so until she wins through to a full and free outpouring of her cultural uniqueness in all areas of life; intellectual, artistic, social, both at work and at play and at all levels of society. As David Daiches has said: "It is the picture of Scotland as we should like to see it that lies in the imagination of those who live here that alone can be decisive in shaping the country's future. In the last resort a country's destiny depends on the imagination of those who live in it."[1]

Important though Scottish pride and respect are, there is something even more important at stake. Throughout the industrialized 'West' there has been during the last twenty or thirty years a growing volume of anxiety and criticism about the goals of 'Western' culture and hence about the role of the universities. A voluminous literature has grown up. Has Scotland a contribution to make to this debate? If Scotland's holistic tradition of higher education could be revived, would it not be the answer to what one author sees as the central problem. "The problem is the dualism in Western thought", says Patrick Nuttgens[2] – who had a thrilling time at Edinburgh as a student – thus bringing the non-dualistic Scottish Common Sense philosophy and its modern descendants such as John Macmurray and Alasdair McIntyre back to centre stage. The revival of the democratic intellect is not some Scottish nationalistic parlour game, as

Bell, Anderson, Houston et al would have us believe. On the contrary, it may well be the leading edge in the battle to renew 'Western' higher education as a whole. If so, we must do our utmost to bring it about, not just for Scotland, but for the world.

That may seem a vainglorious claim, but it is no stranger than the creation of the American and Russian navies, and of the Indian National Congress, by Scotsmen. A Scotsman, too, as we have seen, played a part in drafting, and was a signatory to, the American Declaration of Independence. It is as if the Scots performed at their best on a world stage. "All nations can point to their geniuses in many realms of human endeavour: but, for a country of its size, Scotland's contribution is almost disturbing in its scale."[3] So let us measure the full extent of the problem we face and see whether there are any grounds for such a proposition.

Let us begin with Alfred North Whitehead who devoted a great deal of thought to these problems.[4] In his chapter on the universities and their functions he says that though universities are schools of education and of research, this is not their reason for existence. After all, he says, books have existed since the fifteenth century, so that if passing on knowledge and information is all that is required, there has been no need for universities since that time. "The justification for a university is that it preserves the connection between knowledge and the zest of life, by uniting the young and the old in the imaginative consideration of learning . . . A university which fails in this respect has no reason for existence (a rigorous judgment which would eliminate many of today's universities). This atmosphere of excitement, arising from imaginative consideration, transforms knowledge. A fact is no longer a bare fact: it is invested with all its possibilities."

The imagination is not to be divorced from the facts: it is a way of illuminating the facts. "It works by eliciting the general principles which apply to the facts, as they exist, and then by an intellectual survey of alternative possibilities which are consistent with these principles." The resemblance between this epistemological schema and the traditional generalising approach in the Scottish universities is quite striking. This use of the imagination "enables men to construct an intellectual vision of a new world and it preserves the zest of life by the suggestion of satisfying purposes". The task of a university is to weld together imagination and experience, to prepare the young for business and the professions by "promoting the imaginative consideration of the various general principles underlying that career". The students then pass into their "technical apprenticeship" with their imagination "already practised in connecting details with general principles". Thus the proper function of a university is the imaginative acquisition of knowledge. "A university", says Whitehead, "is imaginative or it is nothing – at least nothing useful".

The symbol for learning has always been a lighted torch, and the cliche has it that "the imagination is set alight". Whitehead concludes simply but devastatingly for our universities as they are today: "If this problem is mishandled, then the vast extension of universities (and he was writing in the 1920s!) will fail to produce proper results." His solution of the teaching/research problem was equally direct. If you want imaginative teachers, then get them to do research. If you want imaginative researchers, get them to teach, to explain themselves to minds that are active and plastic, and with the world before them. "Knowledge does not keep any better than fish. You may be dealing with some old truth; but somehow or other it must come to the students, as it were, just drawn out of the sea and with the freshness of its immediate importance."

Practically everything Whitehead has to say on this subject runs exactly counter to what is being done in the vastly larger higher education industry (for that is what it has turned into) of today. He points out that some of the more brilliant teachers are not among those who publish. Their originality requires direct contact with the students and such people are immensely valuable. "It would be the greatest mistake to estimate the value of each member of a faculty by the printed work signed with his name", says Whitehead, adding that "there is at the present day some tendency to fall into this error". He calls for an emphatic protest against this attitude on the part of the authorities which is "damaging to efficiency and unjust to unselfish zeal". What is important is not the number of words but the weight of thought. One can only wonder what Whitehead would say today confronted by our bulging universities, high staff-student ratios, greatly increased teaching loads and more importance than ever attached to 'research' for promotion purposes. The damage to efficiency must be enormous, yet efficiency is precisely what is sought with 'performance indicators' and all the rest of the managerial paraphernalia.

Flexibility and originality have been lost too, and innovation has been driven to the fringes of the system. "No-one today would undertake those ambitious attempts to redraw the map of knowledge that were so popular in the very early days of the new universities."[5] The movement towards interdisciplinarity, as the epistemological approach most likely to encourage the flowering of new ideas, since it reflects the fact that new ideas mostly occur in the interstices or on the borders between disciplines, has also been stalled.[6] So has the democratization of the universities, so necessary to foster the flow of ideas from the bottom up. as urged by T. H. Huxley

and Sir Eric Ashby. The attempt to impose change from above
has entirely ignored the central issue of the values and purposes of
higher education. The nuclear department has remained the holy
of holies, so that whatever the apparent diversity of the system (a
vast array of universities, polytechnics, central institutions, further
education colleges, etc.), the phenomenon of 'academic drift' shows
the underlying homogeneity based on an unhealthy desire for status.
"Correct form is clearly a deep-rooted English characteristic", says
the educationist Eric Robinson.

In the late 1960s the American writer David Riesman said: "The
very centralization of academic life in Britain, the insistence on a standard examinable curricular coinage, enforces limits on innovation."
This bureaucratization and hyper-specialization of knowledge, adds
Peter Scott, have given rise to a conflict between "professional and
highly specific values and the older values of a general education",
and this conflict is felt in the competing demands of teaching and
research – the point made by Whitehead 50 years earlier. What
should be complementary activities are seen as competitive, and this
has led to what is known as "selectivity", as Scott foresaw: "There
may even be more insistent demands for the more effective separation of teaching and research . . . perhaps by creating a hierarchy
of institutions with 'research universities' at the top and teaching
institutions underneath." Thus the retreat from general education
has crumbled the cement that held the university together. "Without
common values the case for maintaining the university as an institution becomes essentially a bureaucratic one concerned with efficiency
and economies of scale." It has become a part of Galbraith's 'techno-
structure', upholding the "centrality and codification of theoretical
knowledge".

The dilemma of higher education in the late twentieth century is
clear. There is a very urgent need to establish values and priorities
within the whole system: institutions, departments and disciplines.
But it has never been more difficult to do so because the developments
we have mentioned have made it impossible to establish a consensus
on the basis for establishing priorities. The norms of a bureaucratic
university are also a threat to the traditions of academic freedom
and of pedagogical freedom (*Lernfreiheit and Lehrfreiheit*). The
enthusiasm for the new utilitarianism is such that it is undermining
the conditions of free enquiry. As the customer-contractor principle
spreads from research into teaching, and with the introduction of a
rigid, bureaucratic form of staff appraisal into the universities following the Jarrett Report and Mr. Baker's Education Bill of 1987, it
has become very difficult to insist upon a proper level of autonomy
for the individual teacher or department. The abolition of tenure

for all new staff and for those changing posts, and the possibility of redundancy for purely managerial reasons of cost-efficiency have dealt a severe blow to the traditional liberal values of higher education.

The universities have become almost entirely instrumental institutions which are seen as being able to make a direct and powerful contribution to the acceleration of economic growth, not simply by the production of students and by discovery, but in quite immediate and specific ways. (For example, one of our universities in Scotland has become a business school with trimmings.) So research is looked upon as the production of marketable knowledge rather than innovative thinking. Such knowledge and those who produce it are markedly more subservient to political power, if for no other reason than obtaining grants to carry on the work. Since fully a third of all university teachers and researchers are on short-term contracts, boat-rocking becomes a very unpopular activity. The upshot of all this is that the distinction between the political authority of the state and the intellectual authority of the universities, strictly observed in the Middle Ages, is now greatly weakened.[7]

Any plan to renew higher education, to reintroduce humanist, general education, has to contend with this fact: that the modern university is seen as mobilising the intellectual resources of society to manufacture progress. The size of the British higher education system more than quadrupled between 1945 and 1980 and is still growing more rapidly than ever with acceptance of the goal of mass higher education. As A. N. Whitehead said in 1916: "In conditions of modern life, the rule is absolute: the race that does not value trained intelligence is doomed." Clark Kerr foresaw this development in 1966:[8] "This evolution has brought departments into universities, and still more departments; institutes and ever more institutes; created vast research libraries; turned the philosopher on his log into a researcher in his lab; taken medicine out of the hands of the profession and put it into the hands of the scientists; and much more. Instead of the individual student, there are the needs of society; instead of Newman's 'truths of the natural order' there was the discovery of the new; instead of the generalist, there was the specialist." The university is no longer an academic community; it has become a bureaucracy. The decisions are now taken by academic politicians with their bureaucratic language: talk is all of 'cost centres', 'performance indicators', 'mission statements'; classes are now 'delivered' etc. This meta-language of bureaucratic command used by the knowledge bureaucrats has filled the vacuum caused by the disappearance of a common intellectual language, says Peter Scott. "In a strange and disturbing inversion of the natural order of the liberal university, essentially administrative values would then become superior to intellectual values."[9]

The process started in America so it is to another American that we turn for a definition: "In mass higher education, the institutions are still preparing elites, but a much broader range of elites that includes the leading strata of all the technical and economic organizations of the society. And the emphasis shifts from the shaping of character to the transmission of skills for more specific technical elite roles."[10]

But there is a problem. "The intrinsically dynamic force of the specialized sciences did not compel those exposed to these sciences to think anew about the fundamentals – continuously. The dynamic force of the specialized disciplines was turned outward . . . Society was influenced, even changed, by the application of new knowledge "persons were not".[11] There is a widespread feeling of regret, even of unease, that modern universities have adopted an attitude of ethical neutrality, even amorality[12], which they justify by an appeal to their positivist ideology.[13] It is here that such an unwontedly popular philosopher as Ayer has played such a destructive role. "The true has become the pharisaic enemy of the good and the beautiful." Robbins' claim that education administers to ultimate ends, to the good society, and Matthew Arnold's statement about man's need to relate knowledge to his sense of conduct and his sense of beauty are now simply swept aside. So the university seems to many to be a prisoner of amoral, technocratic or cognitive values[14]; but the intellectual adequacy of such a position, from an ethical and logical point of view, is more and more being called into question, especially by the young in the general green and environmental movement. The rationality of allowing millions to starve in the Third World while the industrialized world enjoys great prosperity, of destroying the world's rain forests and many species of animals – of great value to science and medicine apart from anything else – is being strongly challenged. The intellectual limitations of a rationality which provides such an incomplete description of the world are being exposed.

Again, however, we must stress just how difficult it will be to reverse this trend. Universities have split into a mosaic of non-communicating departments not solely because of the country's economic and technological needs, but also because of the internal momentum of the development of knowledge. This makes a change of direction difficult because it involves a major reorientation of mind and values in our society. "Remoralisation and reindustrialisation are parts of the same process of rebuilding modern society . . . the role of the educational system as a source of engaging values is as important as its capacity to act as an instrument of socio-economic change."[15] But how is such a momentous change to be brought about? The major source of the crisis is intellectual and one of the keys to a change "must be a new respect for intuitively based knowledge". The problem then becomes one of restoring the capability of men and women to find meaning at first hand. Does not the answer perhaps lie in tradition, as Alasdair McIntyre believes, in the process, not just the product, of knowledge?

Scott shows that the philosophical differences between culturally based knowledge and scientifically determined knowledge are slight. Historians, sociologists and physicists work through hypotheses based on intuition informed by empirical information and theoretical tradition. All disciplines contain both 'cultural knowledge' and 'scientific knowledge'. Darwin used imagination and intuition informed by practical observation: his theory was indeed a grand holistic theory. Historians and philosophers, in other words, do not operate by different intellectual rules from physicists and biologists. Both accumulate knowledge in a piecemeal way that is entirely consistent with the empirical traditions of science. With knowledge-as-process the emphasis is on education: people-through-knowledge, whereas with knowledge-as-product the emphasis is on technology: knowledge-through-people. So good teaching and good scholarship go together.

The reviewer then points out that Professor Roy Niblett refers in a paper to Alasdair McIntyre's *After Virtue* as being the most outstanding recent contribution to the remoralisation of society. Niblett, being an educationalist, realises just how profound are the remedies needed. How in practice, he asks, can "spiritual nourishment" be given to the vast numbers of students whose preoccupation will be with acquiring saleable technical skills? We know that McIntyre says, with Aristotle, that values are rooted in tradition. We also know – it bears repeating – that Scottish higher education, up till a century ago, was that all students went through a broad general Arts course, including elements of science and giving a central place to philosophy, especially moral philosophy. That tradition was centuries old and somehow deeply rooted in the "perfervidum ingenium Scottorum" with its distinctive "scholastick itch of disputing all things". This would seem to provide a possible answer to Niblett's question. Students will always, and rightly, seek to acquire saleable skills, especially in a mass higher education system; but it would be possible to give them Niblett's "spiritual nourishment" by restoring the old general arts degree for *all* students, and not, as the Act of 1889 had done, making it an *alternative* to the Honours degree for supposedly weaker students.

If it could be done, it would certainly be a consummation devoutly to be wished. Scott points out that the tension between academicism

– the concentration on purely cognitive values – and instrumentalism – the State's determination to get a saleable bill of goods
from the universities – is a source of pessimism for the future. "A
generation ago, the scholar and the senior administrator still had a
great many common values, intellectual as much as social. Today
the professional academic working away in the factory of his discipline and the practitioner in one of the technological professions
are likely to be at best ignorant and at worst actively hostile to
each other's values[16]. "All professionals, he says, need a generalist
or integrative element, because the cultivation of rationality in a
specific cultural context is just as important as the codification of
theoretical knowledge. His hope, though it seems a faint one, is that
the epistemological topography of the university will be changed by
the undoubted fact, mentioned above, that in a number of disciplines
the exciting areas are to found on the periphery, in the borderland
between disciplines. We remember how John Burnet said in 1929
that the most important part of any subject was the one where it
came into contact with others. Scott's hope is sustained by Thomas
Kuhn's thesis that revolutionary, new scientific paradigms occur in
the border areas where the weight of orthodoxy is less oppressive.
"If this is ever true", says Scott, "the modern university's com-
manding assumption that knowledge is best advanced through a
process of concentration rather than generalisation appears much
more doubtful".

However that may be, there is certainly a growing unease about
the purposes of modern science and technology, about the moral
inadequacy of technocratic values. This is taking two forms. On the
one had there is the general environmental movement – mainly supported by the young – which wants technology subjected to humane
purposes and whose central theme is the all-round protection of the
biosphere and all its inhabitants.[17] On the other hand, there is a mood
of pessimism, a loss of faith in science and technology, a distrust
of learning and a contempt for reflection. "The moral mechanism
of Progress has broken down", says Scott, describing England as a
"blocked society" whose "public conscience has become degenerate". He speaks of the "frightening prospect . . . of the unravelling
of modern society, not so much of its material structure, but of its
political, intellectual and possibly even moral, fabric"[18]. He stresses
the great importance of higher education in the remoralisation of
society because it forms "the cognitive and cultural mirror in which
we remember our past, experience our present, and anticipate our
future. If the mirror is cloudy because higher education regards
knowledge as a product rather than a process, then "we misremem-
ber our past, misrepresent our present, and shrink from the future".

Thus the task of remoralisation is very urgent. If most people engaged in higher education are prepared to accept that reason now has an instrumental rather than a critical character, "that it should be used to improve the means, not question the ends",[19] then reason may as a result lose its ability to create value and meaning and become instead an instrument of direction and even oppression.

This is what has now happened in our universities. If there is worry and anxiety about the situation, it does not find expression because of the precarious situation teachers and researchers find themselves in. It has of course led to a great loss of morale and zest which must in the end, lead to a loss of quality. The more expert individual disciplines become, the more isolated from each other they are and the less they seem able to contribute "to a sensible redefinition of our common culture, which is the means by which the ultimate ends of society and of knowledge can be submitted to constant and critical examination". The result is a drift towards an increasingly philistine culture. One main avenue of hope in this bleak situation is "to attempt to place the modern project within a context not simply of continuing intellectual vitality but of a particular national experience, of a particular place and time".[20] Once again we come back to MacIntyre and the fact that values belong to particular cultures: we are brought back to the inescapable conclusion that if Scotland's universities are to flourish again as they did in the eighteenth and nineteenth centuries, they will only do so by a return to our own traditions and values. Scott's analysis seems also to show that England has a lot to learn from this tradition and that the century-long trend of academic influence from South to North needs to be reversed.

For the modern university, in the generic sense, must try to restore a better balance between knowledge in the sense of positivist data and utilitarian techniques, and culture in the sense of cumulative human experience. "Even in a post-industrial age, in an information society, the university must remain a thoughtful, a reflective, even a philosophical institution. In a busy world it must be calm. In a noisy one, still."[21] Any solution to the central problem, though, must take into account the exact historical perspective of university development if it is to have any chance of success. Four out of five universities in Europe were founded in the 20th century, most of them, certainly in Britain as a whole, after 1945. "They belong to a future-oriented present, not a tradition-encrusted past. The long centuries before, from Abelard's Paris to Humboldt's Berlin, were simply the university's prehistory." Fortunately, Scott recovers from what might have seemed an unwisely dismissive attitude by saying that prehistory is still worth examining in any discussion of the links between knowledge, culture and the university. One of the lessons of that history is that, unless backed by powerful cultural and socio-economic forces, intellectual change is not enough in itself to transform the university. For example, "The physics of Isaac Newton, the philosophy of David Hume and the political economy of Adam Smith were only fully realized when social and industrial change towards the end of the eighteenth century created a new cultural environment, a new way of imagining the world." The great moments in the history of the university: in the Middle Ages with Bologna and Paris; at the time of the Renaissance; in eighteenth and nineteenth century Scotland, were all times when it was a formidable cultural vehicle as well as a great scientific institution. If we are to restore the widespread cultural influence of the universities in Scotland, it must be, it can only be, in the context of the present social-political-economic topography of the world: the dominance of information theory and of high technology theory and practice; the growing importance of the Third World; the rapid development of the environmental movement; the domination of the world economy by multi-national companies.

It is in this world that the "university must be philosophical not because it is against the world but because it is of the world. It is only by being a thoughtful institution that it can produce knowledge of genuine value, the logos that makes sense of the bewilderingly exploding data of the modern age".[22] It must meet the demands for expertise and for wisdom of a high-technology economy with its enormous demands for ever-increasing expertise, but at the same time for ever greater flexibility. In the contemporary situation it is not enough for the universities to help individual students to create a better future for themselves. It is not enough to shatter the social limitations of the old higher education – still embodied in Oxford and Cambridge – with its preoccupation with elites and experts. It is not enough to transform the world's societies and economies through the application of science and technology. Unless the university can remake the moral as well as the material world, these projects will falter.

"Individual students will be discouraged by the gap between things that are and the better things they glimpsed. Mass access will be frustrated by arguments that society and the economy need fixed numbers of relevantly trained graduates, not undetermined numbers of critically educated citizens . . . Only a university that is free and philosophical can fulfil its modern mission."[23] And of course at the present time it is neither. With the new enterprise system under the Universities Funding Council the academics have been evicted, the universities are being run by academic managers who lack both culture and imagination.[24] Together with the ceaseless subdivision of knowledge and the triumph of positivism, this has resulted in a strange paradox; the contradiction between the institutional coherence of universities and their intellectual incoherence.

It is a situation in which the ordinary university teacher feels quite powerless. The Westminster government has taken to itself the power, through the UFC, to interfere completely in the life of the universities, and staff are muzzled: many because they are on short-term contracts, many more through the abolition of tenure, and the rest by the staff appraisal scheme, which applies to teachers alone among professionals. Not to mention the oligarchical structure of universities today which delivers them into the hands of the administrators. The university is now one of the least democratic institutions in the British polity. It might seem a barren terrain for propounding solutions; but only if the gigantic problems that are piling up untackled are ignored. The university's age-old moral duty to speak truth to power is very pressing today in late twentieth century Britain "where there is widespread moral confusion, little cultural consensus and a marked decline in traditional cultural values, yet many of the most pressing problems facing society are ones which have to be addressed in moral and ethical terms. Questions such as pollution of the environment, genetic engineering and nuclear power have a serious moral element; they cannot adequately be resolved by technological and financial criteria alone."[25] The authors of these words speak of the radical re-evaluation of the function of universities carried out by the Government. The universities are to be seen in cost-benefit terms, "but is the apparent funding crisis being used to increase governmental control over the universities to their great detriment . . . the crisis before us is philosophical rather than financial". One of the major doctrines produced by this re-evaluation is that higher education is not a matter of knowledge or learning, but of picking up skills. Of this Kenneth Minogue says: "Like the ideal of criticism, this once said something important. It is now the vehicle of a dreadfully unreflective philistinism which is destroying the culture of the West."[26]

The threat, the challenge, then, are great. Man, however, has only ever solved major problems when they threatened to overwhelm him; and now the problems are global. The universities must clearly now start educating the young, who must face these problems, in a way that prepares them adequately for the task. What, in this context, is adequate? For Bernard Crick the answer is clear: "We must turn out each student both trained and useful and also critically minded, and with a passion to pursue argument for the sake of truth alone."[27] Further, society is composed of diverse elements, so an education for diversity along with critical method is necessary in a pluralistic, free society: "An education to understand and empathise with diverse truths must include not merely different ways of looking at the disputes of one discipline, but some knowledge of the different forms of knowledge. In Europe we have a lot to learn from the best North American curricular practice." The debate about whether universities should be cultural, scientific or vocational is meaningless: "We need all these, as does any possible form of human society." Indeed, these three have gone together since the beginning of the human story, as a look at the superb hunting technology as well as the splendid art of Cro-Magnon man 30,000 years ago and of the San people of southern Africa 15,000 years ago makes plain. Thus school pupils must be exposed to all three, and those involved in the government of universities – "the self-government, I hope", says Crick – must have some understanding of, and respect for, all three. But there is a priority: "The vocational, the professional and the technological must be infused by the cultural and the scientific, and this does not occur simply by geographical closeness. It must either be built into the curriculum, certainly in the first years, or be deeply embedded in the culture of the professors. Which is the more realistic practical assumption?" Professor Crick is an English academic, but his long and distinguished years at Edinburgh have clearly brought him to a position where what he is in fact – and perhaps unconsciously – proposing is a return to the traditional general degree for all students. He quotes Bertrand de Jouvenel who once said that education had a dual purpose, "to make man's labour more productive and his leisure more fruitful". Crick adds, "the greater the gain in one direction, the more necessary is progress in the other".

The unity of the cultural, scientific and vocational goals of higher education had already been stressed by Whitehead when he said that "First-hand knowledge is the ultimate basis of intellectual life", and "There is no substitute for the direct perception of the concrete achievement of a thing in its actuality".[28] Yet, as Nuttgens (a student at Edinburgh in what he describes as "one of the most stimulating periods of my life") points out, the irony is that over the last century we have developed an education system that rewarded and elevated precisely those people who can least contribute to society. "Imprisoned in their disciplines, narrowed into their specialisms, we train them with the utmost rigour to be unable to cope with the real, immediate world ... as soon as advanced knowledge is applied to the real world, the boundaries of the disciplines become a barrier to progress." Students must be trained to know and to do in real life, which can never be as neat as the scholar's summary in his book. A scholar of a previous generation[29] had stressed the vital importance of 'relevant knowledge', that is knowledge which recognises its connections with all the forms of knowledge and which is purposively related to human ends. For Robertson the danger did not lie in a philistine ignorance or contempt of science, "but in mistaking advance in the material mechanism of life for progress, and when advance in knowledge is demonstrably outstripping the advance in moral power". There was, he thought, a real need for the universities to be the starting-point of a new renaissance to raise moral power: "If it does not start with them it will probably not start at all." Similar views are expressed by a contemporary scholar in the jargon of today. Specialist honours courses, he says, "neither provide for a truly liberal approach to undergraduate education, nor do they facilitate the development of the general and transferable skills the achievement of which is the mark of intellectual excellence . . . such general intellectual skills are developed most readily in an interdisciplinary context – one given focus and coherence by the identification of themes and problems which have both theoretical and practical significance."[30] These specialist courses reflect a closed and exclusive set of values elaborated by Newman at Oxford (called by Robertson "an imperial university") which has had an enormous influence on the whole British education system, on British society generally and its attitude to practical affairs, including the creation and distribution of wealth. This disinclination – typical of dualism – to relate theory to practice, has resulted in an immensely serious blockage of technological transfer between the scientists and the technological process.

Nuttgens[31] adumbrates a modern alternative: "If we use the culture of doing and making as a guide to the development of our education, it must be the case that it leads to a system of learning very different from the traditional one . . . It must be characterized by the fact that things happen, that new things are made, that new cognitions of nature are achieved, that things work or do not work. It must be an education based on doing something, not passively receiving it, but, as *homo faber*, worrying one's way through to the goal. It involves intuition as well as rationalization, and the development of an acute perception in the active understanding of things. If its starting-point is activity, its great moment is discovery and its reward is freedom – the freedom to do and know and change and invent." The image recurs of James Watt in his workshop at Glasgow University surrounded by the thinkers of his day for whom there was no division between knowing and doing. Or of Jolly Jack Phosphorus, John Anderson, spending his salary on creating the instruments and the library to teach chemistry to hundreds of working men, and thereby creating the first 'mechanic's institute' in Britain – which was to become the University of Strathclyde.

The Robbins Report had said that, "the essential aim of first degree courses should be to teach the student how to think". Yet through its failure to think through the changes that would be needed in teaching, research and structure, nothing was done. The White Paper of 1972 put it even better, concluding: "The wider the span of student motivation the greater the need to match it with a wide and flexible choice of courses." Yet nothing was done. The Leverhulme inquiry of 1982 said: "We are convinced that a more operational style of thinking is not incompatible with the cultivation of individual sensibility, delight and moral awareness, or with the engagement at the higher level with theory." Which did not stop the Westminster government shutting departments of philosophy, music and fine art. In 1985 the response of the UGC and NAB (the corresponding body for the polytechnics at that time) to the Government's Green Paper, entitled *The Development of Higher Education into the 1990s*, had the following to say: "The abilities most valued in industrial, commercial and professional life, as well as in public and social administration, are the transferable personal and intellectual skills. These include the ability to analyse complex issues, to synthesise and integrate disparate elements, to clarify values, to make effective use of numerical and other information, to work cooperatively and constructively with others and, above all perhaps, to communicate clearly both orally and in writing. A higher education which provides its students with these skills is serving society well." Yes, indeed, if you create it. But nothing effective was done. One has to suspect a hidden hand. It was, of course, the power of the so-called 'Golden Triangle', the Oxford-Cambridge-London axis with its mythic 'Gold Standard', the A-level system with its defenders in all the important positions of State and its bland but powerful mouthpieces, such as Lord Annan.

"A broader definition of the academic ethic is needed", says E. Shils, an American scholar. "It is important to remove ... the tendency within the basic academic ethic to separate theory from action. This is a deep-seated problem within the high culture of Britain and finds expression in the over-evaluation of abstract argument as against practical concerns." He also says that "the Humboldtian idea of the unity of teaching and research remains a valid one."[32] There is too much emphasis on passive learning; undue academicism 'turns off' young people who are stimulated by the interplay between theory and action. As so often in this book, we find that Whitehead has the most succinct formula: "Education is the acquisition of the art of the utilization of knowledge."[33] And it has to be utilized in the world of today. "The purpose of higher education", says another American scholar, J. O'Toole, "should be to prepare people to work in the emerging systemic problems that beset society. At all levels of public and private institutions there is a growing need for people capable of divergent and holistic thinking about alternative solutions to problems of the future . . . Traditional vocational and liberal approaches to higher education are inappropriate to the challenge because they are based on outmoded assumptions about the tasks that need to be done in the world . . . the discipline-based pedantic system closes minds to the new and untried, while focussing attention solely on the safe solutions of the past. "[34] One of the most powerful impediments to progress in teaching has been the widespread conservatism of academics in regard to innovation in teaching; their tendency, as a result of the academicism we have discussed, to prefer a didactic to an interactive method, which is more demanding; and the priority that must be given to research if they want professional advancement.

We may sum up this run-down of the problems facing the modern university by citing Clark Kerr, one of the most eloquent writers on the subject. Quoting James Bryant Conant, a celebrated American university leader, he says that the Western world has had for a thousand years a continuing problem of "keeping a balance between the advancement of knowledge, professional education, general education and the demands of student life". He goes on: "Knowledge is now central to society. It is wanted, even demanded, by more people and more institutions than ever before. The university as producer, wholesaler and retailer of knowledge cannot escape service. Knowledge, today, is for everybody's sake."[35] He explains that over the previous thirty years nearly half of American national growth can be explained by the greater education of the American people and by better technology, which is also largely a product of the education system. "The university has become a prime instrument of national purpose. This is the essence of the transformation engulfing our universities."[36] Basic to this transformation is the growth of the 'knowledge industry' which is equivalent to 29% of GNP. As a result the two worlds of the university and business are merging physically and psychologically. In this situation the university should create an environment that gives its members a sense of stability; a sense of security; a sense of continuity; and a sense of equity. Britain's universities have entirely failed to create that atmosphere. This is certainly because of what Kerr calls "a loss of unity – intellectual and communal unity", which "can be attributed to what Robert Oppenheimer calls 'a thinning of common knowledge'. Knowledge is now in so many bits and pieces and administration so distant that faculty members are increasingly figures in a 'lonely crowd', intellectually and institutionally."[37]

As a result of this situation there are many important problems to be faced. "One is the improvement of undergraduate instruction in the university. It will require the solution to many sub-problems: how to give adequate recognition to the teaching skill as well as to the research program of the faculty[38]; how to create a curriculum that serves the needs of the student as well as the research interests of the teacher; how to prepare the generalist as well as the specialist in an age of specialization looking for generalizations . . . Another major task is to create a more unified intellectual world; to open channels of intelligent conversation across the disciplines and divisions, to close the gap between C. P. Snow's Luddites and scientists; to answer fragmentation with general themes and sensitivities. Even philosophy, which was once the hub of the intellectual universe, is now itself fragmented into such diverse areas as mathematics and semantics."

Karl Jaspers' "sense of the unity of all knowledge" seems still to be a very long way off.

16

The Revival of the Democratic Intellect 2
The Famed Learning of the Nation

We are still seeking an answer to the question whether, faced with these truly enormous difficulties but at the same time with the inescapable intellectual and practical needs of our society, we can restore our tradition of the democratic intellect and thereby make what I believe could be a key contribution to the development of higher education at an absolutely crucial moment in human history. What then have we to offer?

"People who attend schools are too often approached as merely fodder to meet our society's needs. Education begins in acknowledging what a libel on their natures this is. Teaching should be an attempt to meet the needs of the taught, not of the teachers. Illich's distinction between 'hope' and 'expectation' is relevant here. We should never, through a desire to equip them with the means for having expectations, forget that what they have a right to is hope. A career is a poor substitute for a life." Thus the writer and former teacher William McIlvanney gives the modern vision of Scotland's perennial preoccupation with teaching the young.[1] A few years earlier Aberdeenshire's Education Committee said there should be explicit teaching of morality in school for one or two periods per week. It considered that the general principles of clear and logical thought could and should be taught in secondary school. The subjects or topics should be: consideration for others, truthfulness, honesty, self-control, kindness to animals, love of beauty, self-esteem, forethought, responsibility to the community, goodwill towards other peoples, courage and obedience.[2] There we have the modern version of Scotland's perennial preoccupation with moral philosophy and logic. The profound influence of these two permanent elements of the Scottish psyche and society have given Scotland a 'social ethic', as George Elder Davie called it, very different from that of England.

In a profile of Davie[3] the author says that the basis of this distinctive social ethic was the Scottish educational tradition, formed as it was on a thoroughly democratic principle of access and a generalist approach to the curriculum. His colleague T. C. Smout, showing an extraordinary lack of historical perspective, argued that it was "only a bourgeois democracy", yet for Morton it remained true that the Scottish universities, with an entrance threshold as low as 14, 15, 16 (the age at which Adam Smith, David Hume, Sir William Hamilton, James McCosh and many other Scottish thinkers went to university)[4], the 'catch-up' junior class (which McCosh attended) to counteract the worst insufficiencies of the schools, and no entrance examination to exert downward pressure on admissions, embodied a philosophy of 'access' that is still in advance of current policy.

It was philosophy, pre-eminently, that dominated the Scottish universities, says Morton. Just as Oxford stood for classics and Cambridge for mathematics, Edinburgh, Glasgow, Aberdeen and St. Andrews stood for a very distinctive blend of logic and moral philosophy which imbued every other discipline. Mathematics, medicine, the classics, were taught with a heavy philosophical bias; emphasis lay not in algebraic or philological detail but in a general approach that held the whole to be more important than the parts. This is the exact opposite of the modern reductionist tendency which sees the parts as more important than the whole. Stephen Rose, in an article entitled *A Vision out of Focus* in the THES, refers to the reductionist mode of thinking which has characterised science, discussed in a previous chapter: "It believes not merely that to understand the world requires disassembling it into its component parts, but that these parts are in some way more fundamental than the wholes which they compose."

The pressure that brought about the final destruction of the system was "the improving spirit of the nineteenth century Anglophile reformers who sought to bring the Scottish universities into line with England". This, argued Davie, was the fatal error since English higher education, as we have seen, was demonstrably out of line with European and American norms. The English scholar Harold Perkin, in the THES, even speaks of "the Victorian Scots who sold out to an unprincipled and class-based, anglicized educational immobilism". In his Dow lecture on the *Social Significance of the Scottish Philosophy of Common Sense* [5] Davie uses the very same language that we have seen repeatedly used by contemporary English and American writers. He warns against the "intensive specialization (that produces) the dangerous consequences of an intellectual atomization of society", to which he preferred the traditional approach of "an all-round spiritual participation by means of educational democracy". That could well be a definition of what these contemporary authors are calling for. He is also in the direct line of Francis Jeffery's declaration to the 1826 Royal Commission.[6]

That declaration is echoed by many contemporary writers. William McIlvanney again[7]: "The most striking feature of Scottish literature is the democratic principle. This tradition of awareness of the people went back before Barbour's *Brus*. It had its first flowering in the makars and its ultimate expression in the ballads. Burns never lost touch with the people, nor Scott, though he showed signs of the deterioration of the tradition with his fixed backward look." Those who criticise Davie's concept of intellectual democracy can only do so because they are not themselves, any more than Smout, in touch with that tradition. Donald Withrington, a Scottish Studies specialist who has no patience with romantic notions, says, in a very interesting description of eighteenth century school education in Scotland[8]: "By the later decades of the seventeenth century, in the Lowlands at least, almost every parish had a school, and the vast majority were Latin grammar schools. Most parochial schools taught reading and writing, some arithmetic, sometimes church music, frequently 'good manners' as well as Latin."[9] In the large towns, the burgh schools, supported by separate English and Scots schools in the districts, concentrated on Latin, with Greek on occasion and mathematics more frequently. With such widespread availability of schools and with the universities open to all likely to profit from them. all seemed well. But Scottish hardheadedness wanted more 'modern', practical subjects than Latin, so such subjects as algebra, plane and spherical geometry, trigonometry, mensuration and land surveying, accounting and bookkeeping, astronomy and navigation, perspective and drawing, natural history, commercial history and geography, French, Italian and Spanish were introduced. This was done at the demand of parents, children and others, and is a further example of what Davie means by the words 'democratic intellect'. As Withrington says, these developments were quite different from the movement in England which left endowed grammar schools untouched "with a bleakly narrow language training". The Scottish universities followed suit, their view being expressed by the Principal of King's College, Aberdeen, in 1760: "Now that education is put on a more natural and useful footing, there are many students who know nothing of Latin and Greek. Their plans and schemes for life do not depend on the knowledge of these languages, and yet by attending the other classes they may learn a great deal of useful knowledge ...

it is highly inexpedient, as well as unreasonable, to think of fixing down one uniform and determined scheme of education so as to oblige every individual student to learn the same things." (It took us a further two centuries, as a result of the anglicizing pressures that demanded that Latin and Greek be taught more intensively in Scottish schools and universities, to return to that commonsense view. It has now been generally adopted throughout Britain.)

I am sure that Alfred North Whitehead and Patrick Nuttgens, to name but two, would thoroughly approve of these sentiments. Withrington concludes: "The continuing thread in the historical development of the curriculum in Scotland is not in an academic tradition but in the vocational emphasis (with the academic included) that has been made since the Reformation. What was studied was always seen as a preparation for further studies (and then for further vocational needs) and for employment 'in the world'." Hence the emphasis on "the genius and capacity of the student, his situation and connections in life and the desires and inclinations of his parents" that has often been made. Hence the interest in maintaining a broad basis to our school and university training.[10]

Withrington's detailed historian's approach is quite different from the epistemological approach of Davie, the historian of ideas, but their conclusions are very compatible. Withrington says that this new "mixed teaching" did not replace classical by modern studies. This is a further aspect of the democratic intellect, which is in fact a many-sided, holistic concept. This 'cafeteria' system of the mid–eighteenth century – reminding one of the system of 'electives' at Harvard very much later – was destroyed at the end of the eighteenth century by the 'Thatcherites' of that day. Teachers' salaries were too low, Benthamite utilitarian views of public accountability led to official inspection of schools and standardization to get value for money. These inspectors "introduced plans for courses and laid down expected standards of attainment decided by government agencies of one kind or another and not by students or their teachers". (*Plus ça change . . .*) These pre-ordained curricula were finally enforced in the universities too, in 1892, as we have seen.

In an interesting article[11] Colin Radford, Reader in Philosophy at Kent University, demonstrates the contemporary relevance of eighteenth century Scottish educational philosophy, what was called the 'open door' approach. "I believe that all courses at universities should be open in this sense: anyone should be allowed to attend lectures and seminars . . . Some might even claim that the presence of large numbers of 'visitors' would be disruptive. Why? They are not in the USA or Australia where large numbers 'sit in' on courses, i.e. do not take them for 'credit'." All classes should be advertised in the local press, libraries, schools etc., transport laid on, lectures arranged in the evening for those at work. "But could we cope?", asks Dr Radford. "Of course", he says, "though that and how we coped would require political decisions. But having to cope is exactly what is required. We are a philistine, under-educated, unproductive, class-ridden society, divided into officers and other ranks. Improving attitudes to knowledge and making university education genuinely available are necessary to change this". Dr Radford's plea had in fact been preceded by a similar call in the Report of the Second European Conference on Higher Education, held in Edinburgh. "The achievement of a system of higher education with complete freedom of entry for all with the ability to benefit from it should be a fundamental aim in every country."[12] Scotland, a very poor country, got nearer to this ideal in the eighteenth and nineteenth centuries than any other country until very recently.

Withrington, in a paper presented at a conference on *The Scottish Gift*,[13] said that one of the most remarkable aspects of the development of the Scottish education system had been the way in which the whole community came together to support the school, clubbing together to ensure a headmaster of the highest quality. The openness of the schools to all backgrounds was paralleled by the low entry qualifications for the universities. The major characteristic of Scotland's education system was the close links established between even the smallest parish school and the universities, whereby the bright boy, no matter how poor, could 'get on'. This urge to make sure the bright boy or girl, whatever their social circumstances, get the fullest possible education, is still very strong in Scotland. And it helps all children, as shown by a report in the educational press. Dr Dickson of the SED told West Lothian teachers that progress towards comprehensive education in Scotland had been smoother than in England. It was difficult to be confident about the reasons for this. There was something about the Scottish tradition – an element which we had cause to be proud of – that children from poorer homes were able to go to university. The contemporary critics of the concept of the democratic intellect, showing a total disregard for historical perspective, call this 'bourgeois' or 'meritocratic'. They deliberately – so it seems – ignore the fact that it was very advanced for its time: the case was the very opposite in England, which stopped the 'lad o' pairts' from 'getting on' – *vide* Jude the Obscure. The parochial school as the main avenue of advance was the major distinguishing principle of Scottish education from the seventeenth century onwards, and another was universal schooling, at least in the essential elements. It should be said, too, that the State supported the schools earlier in Scotland.

The intellectual quest that began in the parochial school was anything but 'parochial' in the invidious sense so often used by those
who defend the present set-up in Scottish education and do not wish
it to run its own affairs. Reporting on a Channel Four television
series on *How to be Celtic*,[14] a *TESS* article says: "In the best Scottish
tradition the issues raised through the deceptively 'Celtic' prism are
of a profoundly universal nature and are presented in a way which
vividly illustrates just how many of the issues that we face on the
'periphery' of Europe go the heart of the problems of twentieth
century industrial society." It speaks of "the recurring way in which
the big issues touched surface again and again in different settings –
issues of culture, politics, personal and collective identity, the environment and the economy, all interlocked in a questing examination of the dominant political culture of Europe." And Asa Briggs,
speaking at Edinburgh University's Quatercentenary Conference of
the common "universe of thought" of the medieval universities,
the development within them of "a kind of intellectual state", their
common curriculum and way of life of their students, says they raise
issues which are not yet dead. "There may well be features of 'post-
industrial society', to use another fashionable and question-begging
term, that may have more in common with pre-industrial society
than with the societies of the nineteenth and twentieth centuries."
Tantalisingly, he does not elaborate, but it is a visionary gleam which
we shall attempt to follow up later.
    This feeling for universality in space and time seems to be a
uniquely 'Celtic' characteristic and is found in all sorts of contexts.
There is a tendency to turn outwards, to embrace the wider world,
to build a sense of nationality on a wider appreciation of the human
condition . . . "[15] It is to be found in a particularly concentrated
form in the work of Hugh McDiarmid, of course, and also in that of
Kenneth White, who has been a leading light in French intellectual
life for years and is a professor at the Sorbonne, as so many Scots
were four centuries ago. William Cobbett did not like this side of
the Scots. He accused them of the absurd belief that the best way
to improve the condition of the working man was not to give him
bacon with a small 'b' but Bacon with a big 'B'. He was notoriously
prejudiced against the Scots and especially their "feelosofers".[16]
An 'imaginary debate' between him and John Maclean would be
very interesting. "The Scots, at their best, were philosophers; the
English, at their worst, philistines." So says the THES, adding that
this difference has been powerfully reflected in their universities. It
quotes a mid-nineteenth century Edinburgh professor. "No, his (the
Scotsman's) walk as a thinker is not by meadows and wheatfields
and the green lanes and the ivy-clad parish churches where all is

gentle and antique and fertile, but by the bleak seashore which parts
the certain from the limitless, where there is doubt in the sea-mew's
shriek, and where it is well if, in the advancing tide, he can find
a footing on a rock."[17] The same powerfully exhilarating theme is
expressed *passim* in the work of Hugh McDiarmid:

>Let there be licht, said God, and there was
>A little . . .."

and

>To hell wi' happiness,
>I sing the terrifying discipline
>O' the free mind that gars a man
>Mak' his joys kill his joys,
>The weakest by the strongest,
>The temporal by the fundamental
>(Or hope o' the fundamental).

These quotations are taken from an article on George Elder Davie[18]
in which the author speaks of how the Scottish intellectual tradition has always been drawn to the 'fundamental' as opposed to the
'temporal', with philosophy as a 'privileged' subject "whose critical
function is to keep asking what knowledge is and what man's chief
end might be". In other words to keep putting the same half-dozen
questions which were broached in Greece and are endlessly brought
up again and again, as I. F. Stone has said. The Scottish mind seems
always to have been preoccupied with first and last things. The
writer has some fascinating things to say about the relation between
this kind of thinking and "the ethos of Celtic elaboration": for
example the strap-work of Pictish carving and jewellery, the beautiful elaboration in the *Book of Kells* and, as we saw in Chapter 10,
the "preference of Scottish mathematics for the conceptual purity
of geometry over the applications of algebra".

  Susan Manning, an American scholar, writing about the Enlightenment[19], describes it as a "quite extraordinary flowering of intellectual achievement in areas as diverse as philosophy and palaeontology, ethics and economics, anatomy and agriculture, rhetoric and
religion", and the eighteenth century's "most systematic enquiry
into the relationship between Man and Nature across all fields of
endeavour then open to investigation". It astonishes her that it could
have taken place in a small, economically backward country which
had recently lost its national independence and from which there
was "a steady drain of Scottish talent and ambition southwards to
London, of Scottish enterprise and adventurousness westwards to
the American colonies, and of Scottish missionary fervour and mer-
cenary acquisitiveness eastwards to India". A massive brain drain
that has continued ever since.

The other side of this philosophical tradition is moral philosophy, the sense of obligation to society: for example, "Adam Smith's 'common sense' reliance on mutual social observation and interaction as a reply to Hume's total scepticism about what we can possibly know about ourselves and the world around us;"[20] or, today, Alasdair MacIntyre's view that "philosophical ideas are influential in social, moral and political life", expressed in an essay on Marcuse.

Jo Grimond expressed penetrating views on this aspect of Scottish thought a number of times over the years. When he was installed as Rector of Aberdeen University in 1970 he said: "The Scottish universities were founded not only to encourage learning and to teach, but to serve the community by turning out democrats fit to sustain, inform, criticize and change society. The task of social obligation is more important than it has ever been since the Middle Ages. The Scottish universities were committed to humanism, dedicated to human values, to positive assent in the possibilities of human beings, *and to the paramount importance of value judgments.*"[21] Five years later he was showing just how much damage had been done to that tradition:

> Scotland is on the road away from the democratic intellect, let alone the Greek ideal of the economical use of resources, and the pursuit of beauty and excellence by personal endeavour. When we come to education over the age of 14, will the Scottish tradition be developed along the lines *of teaching moral philosophy applied to the modern world* ? Our society suffers desperately from the lack of any overall moral belief."[22]

Another two years later he expresses his realization that the weakness is the excessive concentration on specialized vocational skills. "The measure of skill, quite unjustifiably, is being narrowed to skills needed in industrial production. But a skilled nation should be skilled in all walks of life . . . The greatest of these (skills) is skilful judgment. That is the ability to see beyond the immediate. It is the ability to look wider than oneself and longer than the next year. It is the essential ability in a democracy. Alongside the development of the individual capacities of the pupil, the most important skill which a pupil must learn is to be a good citizen in a free society . . . Britain has become unskilled. Its unskillfulness starts at the top. We used to be skilful in government. Now we are not."[23] (Our italics) Contrast with the bleak picture Jo Grimond paints, and the very much bleaker situation that has developed in Scottish higher education over the fifteen years since then, the following item of news.[24] Laurance S. Rockefeller, who majored in philosophy and graduated from Princeton in 1932, has given his *alma mater* $21 million to establish a centre for the study and teaching of human values. The new centre, says a statement from the university, will focus on "moral, political, social and spiritual aims and aspirations and their influence on human character, conduct and communal life". In fact, as long ago as 1978 Professor Alvin Goldman of the University of Michigan was saying that "political philosophy has come back in great strength in the last 10 years. Normative ethics, which had lain dormant for the previous 50 years, have had a clear resurgence." Vietnam and Watergate were cited as reasons for this renewal of interest.[25] The former Education minister, Mr Baker, was too busy on his American trip, trying to find out how to create mass higher education on the cheap, to have time for such philosophical trifles.[26]

A Scottish academic emigrant to the United States, Professor Ninian Smart, Professor of Religious Studies at the University of California at Santa Barbara, has different ideas. He would like to see a Scottish Institute of Advanced Study (similar to that of Princeton University) set up in the Stirling area.[27] This is a great historical irony because, as we remember, the Scots universities wanted to set up graduate schools in the mid-nineteenth century but were refused funding. The Americans did set up graduate schools, so it is left to a Scot in America, 150 years later, to propose the development of advanced study in Scotland. Professor Smart believes that such an institute would enhance higher education and research in Scotland. The Scottish universities enjoy easy mutual accessibility and, says Professor Smart, there has been a long tradition of pioneering work in the sciences and arts in Scotland, with the country playing a leading role in "international intellectual and practical development, especially during the Enlightenment and the industrial revolution". He also believes that finance could be raised from the prosperous Scottish diaspora all over the world, "both because of their emotional attachment to their homeland and because of the high regard for education among all Scots".

He thinks that such a centre could perhaps begin with five main areas of study. First of all there would be Scottish studies, including the history and analysis of Scottish philosophy, economic thought, literature, science, the arts, music and religion, together with technology and social evolution, and Scottish history in its broadest sweep. He considers that Scotland's great achievements, ranging from the thought of such as David Hume and Adam Smith to the poetry of Robert Burns and Hugh McDiarmid, and from the inventiveness of James Watt and Robert Adam to the remarkable contributions of the Scots in their world-wide diaspora – such as those of Andrew Carnegie and John Muir, one of the earliest environmentalists and the creator of America's national parks – "provide a very rich scenario for cultural and social history". Indeed, the history of the diaspora itself could constitute one vital area of research.

Another valuable area of research would be a high-powered approach to the Celtic languages and civilization, "examining the whole great Celtic heritage stretching deep into the heartlands of European civilization". "I think", says Professor Smart, "it is a fine and worthy vision to help put Scotland back near the centre, or at the centre, as it was during the eighteenth century and the early nineteenth century. Once you have produced Adam Smith and invented the steam engine, you have launched the modern world." It is sad indeed that such a vision can only be produced by an expatriate Scot; that it would occur to no-one here to expect the SOED – busy executing Westminster educational policies – or our university leaders to put forward such a plan.

It is, however, not surprising, since any kind of vision is utterly lacking in government policy. Writing about the Swinnerton-Dyer/Keith Joseph papers, David Holbrook, Fellow of Downing College, Cambridge, asks "Where is the idea of a university in these exchanges? Do we want a civilized country or not?" The questions to be asked are about hopes, knowledge, values and beliefs. Also questions of truth, of ideas, and the vision and imagination with which ideas and the truth are pursued. The sciences and the arts are united in this. The difference between a Japanese motorcycle and a British one is a difference of imagination and, with imagination, more complex dynamics such as hope, morale and spirit. "A mean-spirited educational system, manipulated by mean-spirited administrators, will never stir up a nation to lead the world in anything or even to solve its own problems." The collapse of the British motorcycle industry is a symbol of what has happened over the last thirty or forty years. "As a nation we have become dispirited, materialistic, unimaginative, hedonistic, inflexible and lacking in foresight. These problems are the marks of our half-education, our mis-education."[28]

Holbrook says these papers contain no sense of the dread and anxiety of our time, or any hint that *"ours is an era in which there is a philosophical crisis in which science seems to have stripped the world of meaning"*. We have seriously lost our way in educational matters and especially those areas with which the humanities deal. "Surely this is an age in which we desperately need more intelligent and trained men and women who can confront chaos and assert, against the brutalities and miseries of our world, some confidence in humanness and creativity, in the powers of mind and sensibility, in the capacity of human beings to create meaning and values, and to take their fate upon themselves." And isn't the university precisely the place where young men and women "are trained in this kind of confrontation with life – as teachers, doctors, engineers, lawyers, readers, writers, biologists, journalists, politicians and members of an educated public to whom issues are serious and values significant?" Holbrook concludes that technology provides the tools society needs but that they may well be unable to save us "unless we have a more adequate, visionary and hopeful sense of the uses to which they can be applied. That is a question that belongs to the humanities."

There can be no doubting the great anxiety Holbrook feels. The tragedy is that the institution in which he teaches, Cambridge, has done, and is still doing, so much to perpetuate an educational system which makes the production of what he calls "these dreadful documents" inevitable: a system which after all produced the authors of the documents in question (Keith Joseph was even revered as a great intellectual!); a system based on the A-level "gold standard", on elitism, ultra-specialization and a scarcely veiled contempt for technology and industry. It is a system based on philosophical dualism: mind and matter, theory and practice, thought and action, abstract and concrete, gentlemen and players. As the THES of 20 October 1987 points out in an editorial dealing with Allan Bloom's book *The Closing of the American Mind*, "the difficulties faced by higher education, not just in the United States but throughout the West, are philosophical rather than educational. They arise from a confusion about ends, more than an inadequacy of means".

There is, however, evidence that philosophy, in the sense of the search for ethical values, is fighting back. More than a decade ago Lancaster University launched a new degree in Philosophy and the Arts because, it was said, students find themselves faced, in studying the arts, with conceptual puzzles and presuppositions as they attempt to evaluate works of literature, music and the other arts. They lack suitable training and adequate acquaintance with philosophical aesthetics and relevant philosophical work on perception, emotions, imagination, language and problems of value. Hence the use of the term "applied philosophy" in describing the course.[29] In 1984 Alan Wilson was saying that "philosophy should be a significant part of multi-disciplinary teaching and indeed should be available as one of the foundations for students in most disciplines ... A new dimension becomes available to research and scholarship in many disciplines."[30] Indeed, by 1990 applications for philosophy places were rocketing. By the 26th May of that year there were 4,446 applications in Britain, which was a 23% increase on 1989 and a doubling since 1987.

In Scotland there appeared to be a fairly constant demand for the introduction of philosophy into the 6th year in schools. For example, in 1966 Mr D. R. Gordon of Strathclyde University was teaching philosophy in the English Department and his subject was "the possibility of introducing philosophy as a study for Sixth year pupils in Scottish schools." [31] Students could best be encouraged to philosophize through the discussion of problems. A letter in the same journal asks "headmasters and all those concerned with curriculum to consider the possibility of introducing philosophy into school education.. because of its potential contribution to intellectual development and because of its potential interest for young people".[32] Three years later an article in the same journal describes how a teacher had a group of pupils in Sixth Year Studies "who wanted to read some serious philosophy". This forced him to work out a list of his top ten books which were "all within the understanding of a good 6th year pupil".[33] The operative word here, of course, is *good*. What about those who are not so good; and what about those who have gone off to university after 5th year? They all need some form of philosophical study, and there is certainly no room for it in the crowded and rushed 5th year curriculum. With mass access now almost a reality, there can be little doubt that the best place for such study would be the university, and the best form would be a general arts degree for all students with *philosophy linked to contemporary problems* at its heart.

Two excellent articles by Roger Young[34], then headmaster of George Watson's College in Edinburgh, demonstrate a possible philosophy curriculum for the first year of such a general arts degree for all students: "For each one of us, be we teachers or sixth formers, (first year students) there is the common problem at the centre of our lives: 'Who am I, and what is to be my response to the world in which I find myself? The question 'What is man?' has challenged man's mind since history began. Can we not use our curiosity about the men and women we are, or are to become, and about the world we are growing up into, to provide the fundamental *raison d'etre* of the sixth form year (first year at university)? So if we ask 'What's all this sixth form (first year) education about and for?', the answer is that it's about us and it's for life. Nothing less."

In the second article Young describes the work of tutorial groups and the questions they would analyse under a number of headings: Who am I? What sort of world do we live in? Do our lives mean anything? Who is my neighbour? And how are we to live together? What do we value in life? And why?

He then lists the possible results of such a study:

1 Discovery of ideas;
2 Development of creative and critical thinking;

3 Acquisition of the capacity for independent study;
4 The dialectic of discussion, the pressure of facts, the challenge of evidence, wrestling with words are all necessary, hence the need for the writing of essays and the oral articulation of thought. Without all these neither creative nor critical thought amounts to anything.

Finally, in 1980, in an article entitled *The Process of Judging Art – the case for teaching philosophy in a comprehensive school,* William Scott says the purpose of teaching philosophy in school is so that pupils may learn the relationship between the different forms of knowledge and to what extent they are true. "It seems desirable at the end of school life to try to draw together all the separate strands of knowledge and to examine them for a view of knowledge as a whole and the process whereby it may be acquired. Pupils should not leave school without considering the process by which art is judged: whether, for example, their response or their teacher's response is enough", for this too lies within the province of philosophy. He lists questions similar to those posed by Roger Young:

1 What ought I to do with my life? How ought I to live my life? Why should I live in this or that way?
2 Is there a God?
3 Who am I? How did the world come to be? What ought I to do in it?

The aims of the course would be *practical,* i.e. it would examine the answers great philosophers have given to fundamental questions. These answers would then be critically examined in discussion. They would also be *technical,* i.e. the procedures of philosophy would be analysed. What is philosophical argument like? How does one conduct it? The need for definitions, the precise use of language and striving for clarity would be emphasised. The only thing wrong with this is that it is vastly over-ambitious for school study, but would fit very well into the sort of three year general arts degree we are advocating. And all these requests for philosophic study for young people constitute an eager return to the traditional purposes of philosophy by demand from the grass roots. They have looked up for too long – and have not been fed – to the barren aridities of logical positivism.

At any rate, all the things Holbrook calls for existed in the traditional Scottish system which Oxford and Cambridge, through their Scottish aristocratic alumni and a government and civil service largely staffed also by their alumni, contrived to suppress and subvert after a sixty-year-long war of intellectual attrition in the nineteenth century. Holbrook graphically documents the failure of the Oxbridge system which, like an academic cancer, has colonized every higher educational institution in Britain. It is time for Scotland to return to its traditional system[35] in an up-to-date form.

Have we any indications as to how that might be done? John Macmurray says[36] that a university is not just a collection of young people waiting to be educated. "The education provided must be unified. Behind it must stand a philosophical theory of education which can determine the place of different departments of study in moulding a full human maturity." The danger that universities faced was the great expansion (and this was before 'mass access') which might make them come apart at the seams and concentrate on producing technical specialists – which is precisely what has happened. Macmurray says we must answer the question "What constitutes the unity of the university?" His own answer is that, "The business of a university is to be the cultural authority of the region that it serves. In virtue of this it can and should hold together every aspect of human culture, in its widest sense, in a unity."[37] The university is an institution of higher *education*, so research is secondary. "The first duty of the working university is to carry the cultural heritage through the succession of the generations faithfully and effectively." During a lifetime in universities he had often been disappointed and angered to find members of academic staff who professed to have no interest in education and who "seemed ashamed to be thought of as teachers. Surely this can only express either a pitiable blindness or a despicable snobbery. Surely the profession of teacher is one of the most honourable and exalted to which any man can aspire. If academic staff are primarily teachers it would seem to follow that the most important people in a university are its students." A university was best judged by its ability "to inspire its students with respect, gratitude and loyalty".[38]

What, then, must be done? Science should be seen in proper perspective: it deals with facts, not values. It can tell us what is possible, but it is culturally neutral. Its results can be used for good or evil. We need to develop philosophy whose traditional task has been to maintain and to further the integrity of culture. We need to take up again the quest, not for knowledge merely, but for wisdom. Philosophy had tended to abandon this quest, "in large part through a misplaced belief in the universal beneficence of scientific method". For Macmurray, therefore, the heart of a university's function lay in the faculty of arts, and philosophy needs to be given back its central role of cultural leadership. "Finally, and this is the cutting edge of the whole strategy, we need (we must) set at the head of the philosophy departments a philosophy of education, to convince us that we are indeed teachers, and to make us proud of it." Many of Macmurray's ideas are similar to the thinking of that extraordinarily innovative polymath, Patrick Geddes. As G. R. Tudhope, President of the Association of University Teachers, said in 1954: "A university in his (Geddes's) view should be the spiritual, the intellectual and the artistic centre of its region." His daughter Norah said of his work for the University Extension Movement: "Its aims were to bring to the smaller provincial centres the best the universities had to offer." Another facet of the democratic intellect, which is clearly more attractive to the Scots than Brideshead Revisited, if I may plagiarise a *THES* editorial. At his celebrated vacation courses he held constantly before the teacher and students the single goal of reuniting the separate studies of art, literature and science into a related cultural whole which should serve as an example to the universities, mainly engaged in breaking knowledge up into particles unconnected with each other or with life.[39]

Socrates and Peter Abelard would have approved of Macmurray's emphasis on teaching and philosophy. So would Derek Bok, President of Harvard University, who says[40] that in the nineteenth century American universities devoted great efforts to the moral development of the students and considered this an integral part of their mission. To emphasise the importance of this task many college presidents took it upon themselves to present a compulsory series of lectures on moral philosophy to the entire senior class. According to one scholar this course "was regarded as the capstone of the curriculum. It aimed to pull together, to integrate and to give meaning and purpose to the students' entire college experience and course of study. In so doing it even more importantly sought to equip the graduating seniors with the ethical sensitivity and insight needed if they were to put their newly acquired knowledge to use in ways that would benefit not only themselves and their own personal advancement, but the larger society as well."

This emphasis on moral philosophy, as in Scotland, was muted at the end of the nineteenth century by scholars "who emphasised the scientific value of their work and its freedom from romantic judgments". Presidential lectures on moral issues disappeared, without any visible replacement, "a casualty of the search for value-free learning and the reluctance to engage in any form of teaching that could be criticized as doctrinaire". Interestingly, however, there has been a new development of applied ethics courses since Watergate. "Such courses", says Bok, "have important contributions to make. There is value to be gained from any form of instruction that acquaints students with a rich literature in moral philosophy and forces them to think carefully and rigorously about enduring human problems ... It warrants a determined effort ... also because the goal is so important to the quality of the society in which we live."

Interestingly, there have been a number of broadcasts on BBC television tending in the same direction. One on nuclear power on 16 July 1992, part of a series dealing with science entitled *Pandora's Box*, said that science and technology don't decide; man does. Science offers a range of possibilities, but the choice to be made is a moral choice. The conclusion for higher education is clear. Students need to be trained to be able to make those choices in the difficult, chaotic world of today and tomorrow. This is reinforced by the conclusions reached by Dr Robert Foley in a programme on evolution in a series called *Antenna* on 20 July 1992. Our mistake, he said, is that we think we are the crown of creation, and that our latest technological invention is evolution's highest point to date. In fact, the only appropriate comment at each new evolutionary stage is "So far, so good".

Our intelligence is simply the result of a long line of ancestors having to solve their problems. But in evolution the margin between success and failure is a very narrow one. Every evolutionary advance creates as many problems as it solves. Dr Foley concludes that the brain will probably be our downfall; meaning presumably that, like so many species before us, we have become too rigidly specialized (in our case culturally) to adapt to new conditions. Certainly the contemporary myth that 'economic development' and 'progress' will in linear fashion lead us to a paradise on earth seems instead to be leading us inexorably by positive feedback to the ever-growing destruction of the biosphere, which includes man.

A good succinct summary of the position is given by Dr Grover Foley:[41] "In the modern age we have seen the return of the power machine. To control Nature, modern science disassembled it (Bacon's *dissecare naturam*), denied Nature value, purpose or meaning. Galileo reduced Nature to matter and motion, while Hobbes made a machine even of the mind. Society lost any intrinsic value and became a mere constellation of forces. Science reduced man to cosmic dust, the plaything of chance and necessity. For what then does man live? Having driven out all other goals, power science itself becomes the only goal. Losing all other values, such as the Good, the True, and the Beautiful, man becomes, as with Hobbes, a creature of pure self-interest. Even the True is reduced to the Useful."

Yet, despite the warnings of such as Macmurray, MacIntyre and Bok, and the voluminous publications of the ecology and Green movement – from Frank Fraser Darling, Barry Commoner, Peter Scott, Rene Dubos, Paul Ehrlich and many, many others to the well-researched work of Friends of the Earth and Greenpeace – the universities have not been listening. On the contrary, they are driving, or being driven, ever faster down the road of scientific and technological specialization, with the humanities getting an ever smaller piece of the cake and playing an ever smaller role. Our universities are no longer the critics of society, training their students to understand, and play an effective role in, that society. They have become the prisoners of the system; in the case of the Scottish universities, the prisoners of a system which runs counter to all their centuries-long traditions of a general education before specializing, embodying an analytical understanding of the relatedness of all knowledge, the need to express ideas clearly, logically and articulately, and a sense of mutual responsibility and desire for social justice.

This sad scenario can be clearly seen in the triumphalist advertising of the new 'universities': Napier, Paisley, Robert Gordon's in Aberdeen and Glasgow's third university.[42] The talk is all of manufacturing, engineering, electronics, computing, business studies, information technology, business management, science and technology. These are what the publicity blurb calls "the major study components of a rapidly evolving and increasingly comprehensive campus scenario". (We are not immune to Jacques Barzun's prestige bug.) "Our areas of interest", says Professor John Woodward of Paisley, "involve people who are readily employable and vocationally oriented. As long as people need food, shelter, clothing, transport, and all the basic facilities, our graduates are the sort who provide the services and there will be a growing demand for such people". But for how long? – one would like to ask Professor Woodward. And are these the only skills they will provide? What about Jo Grimond's "skilful judgment"? What about his "teaching moral philosophy applied to the modern world"?

There is no mention of culture or the arts here. Indeed Dr Turmeau, the first Principal of Napier University, "insists that Napier University has no intention of either changing its mission – the provision of courses which lead to a wide range of careers –or of aping the older universities". Indeed, he believes that it "is much better positioned to cater for the additional 16% of school leavers entering higher education during the next ten years". Presumably because of the vocational nature of the courses offered and because so many Scottish students are being excluded from Edinburgh (now listed as third in the *Times* league table of British universities and busily selling off its art treasures), St Andrews, Stirling, Dundee and other Scottish universities by the invidious preference given to A-levels over Highers.

It is because of their failure to mention the arts that I put quotation marks round the word 'university' as applied to these institutions, not because I share the Oxbridge contempt for technology. It is also no doubt the reason why such a trustworthy authority as

Professor Nigel Grant was recently quoted in the press as saying that employers will no longer simply ask job-seekers if they have a university degree, but will want to know in what subject and at what university they obtained it. Scotland's universities, as we have seen, have had a strong vocational tendency ever since the Middle Ages, but specialist training was always preceded by a three or four year all-round training in the 'Arts', including philosophy and basic science. This was so much a part of the Scottish tradition that it took more than sixty years to destroy it. The new institutions give no sign of losing any sleep over it; their advertising shows they mean to continue sending young people out into the world with a specialism of some kind and little else. They are thus not universities in any Scottish sense of the word. The title 'university' gives them status, that is all. As Dr Turmeau says: "People's perception of us has changed and we have had companies coming to us simply because we are now a university – and we have gathered in contracts we would not have got before . . . university status is the seal of approval for us." *Status*, the English disease, which has nothing in common with the traditions of Scottish higher education.

17

The Revival of the
Democratic Intellect 3
An Ecology of the Mind

The whole approach to higher education we discussed at the end of the last chapter is not a cure for any problems – it is a major part of the problem. And the problem is not going to go away: it is the problem of planetary and human ecology. It may come as a surprise to the reader that this is not a recent issue stirred up by the Greens or by the militants of the counter-culture. As early as 450 BC Artaxerxes I attempted to restrict the cutting of the cedars of Lebanon. Since the mid–eighteenth century the conservation of the environment has been an important strand in science begun by the French, including the writer Bernardin de St. Pierre, in Mauritius, where they were working on the relation between deforestation and local climate change. This was then taken up by the British in the Caribbean, and by von Humboldt who "promulgated a new ecological concept of the relation between people and the natural world: that of the fundamental interrelation of humankind and other forces in the cosmos. His ideas, which drew extensively from *the holistic thinking of Hindu philosophers* (our italics), presented a scientifically reasoned interpretation of the threat posed by unrestrained human activities".[1]

Several Scottish scientists, including Alexander Gibson, Edward Balfour and Hugh F. C. Cleghorn (who worked for the British East India Company) became enthusiastic conservationists. "They advocated establishing a forest system in India that was unequalled in scale. In an 1852 report they warned that a failure to set up an extensive forest system would result in ecological and social disaster."[2] Disasters duly occurred in India and South Africa, and their warnings and the work of Charles Darwin compelled legislation to protect the environment in India and Africa. J. Spotswood Wilson

even presented a paper to the British Association for the Advancement of Science in 1858 in which he raised "the spectre of human
extinction as a consequence of climatic change". We cannot say we
have not been warned! The writer concludes: "Our contemporary
understanding of the threat to the global environment is thus a
reassertion of ideas that reached maturity over a century ago. It is
to be regretted that it has taken so long for the warnings of early
scientists to be taken seriously."

The point, however, is that they are still not being taken seriously enough. The rain forests are disappearing at a great rate with
incalculable consequences, the industrial nations are destroying the
ozone layer, heating up the earth, poisoning the rivers and oceans
(the latest victim of organochlorine pollution is the polar bear),
causing species to become extinct and cetaceans and fish stocks to
dwindle alarmingly; a hugely costly war is conducted against a poor
Middle Eastern nation to ensure oil supplies for the grossly wasteful
transport systems of the developed countries, while millions starve
in Africa; there are droughts, floods, famines, epidemics and pan-
demics – all the things we were warned about a century-and-a-half
ago, plus the decay of cities and the evil menace of drugs.[3]

We have, fact become cognitively disoriented in relation to our
environment, and the universities must bear a major share of the
blame for this, since they have insisted that their role is a cognitive
one.[4] Their pursuit of positivistic, reductionist, objective, value-
free knowledge is shown not only to have major weaknesses, but
indeed to contain a positive threat to our continued existence. As
C. H. Waddington has said: "A scientist's metaphysical beliefs have
a definite and ascertainable influence on the work he produces." Karl
Popper also realized that "scientific discovery is impossible without
faith in ideas which are of a speculative kind, and sometimes even
quite hazy; a faith which is completely unwarranted from the point
of view of science and which, to that extent, is metaphysical".[5]
Science and technology can never be value-free.

It is, therefore, a welcome sign that Sir David Smith, then still
Principal of the University of Edinburgh, should call for that city to
host top-level meetings to tackle the world's environmental problems and the North-South divide as a follow-up to the 1992 Rio de
Janeiro Earth Summit.[6] He stated that the conditions necessary to
sustain civilization in its present form are at risk, and that, though
we need industry, it needs to modify the way it behaves. The most
heartening thing of all was that in 1991 he had begun a programme at
the university aimed at introducing environmental elements into all
its courses, research and administration. Such issues raise problems
of challenging complexity, whose analysis would be particularly

good for training the mind, and would also be excellent vehicles for interdisciplinary teaching, showing how important social, moral and ethical questions are inextricably linked to science. *The university could also implement a programme to improve a sense of environmental responsibility*. (Our italics)[7] He said too that education had a role to ensure that people acted for the good of all.[8] This is the beginning of a return to the traditional holistic Scottish approach in higher education. It is to be hoped that it is the swallow that heralds the summer, for we are clearly at a turning-point, a moment of mutation, in man's relationship with the planet, brought about by the exponential development of industrial civilization, which is now all but out of control.[9]

Why not then pick up on Sir David's innovation by restoring, *for all students*, the traditional Scottish Ordinary degree covering the arts and sciences and with the central emphasis on an *earth ethic*, after which those wishing to specialize at Honours level would do a further two years. This idea is in the wind. A report in 1990[10] says that the Scottish universities are now highlighting the general degree to attract students and achieve wider access. In the early 1960s up to 50% of students took ordinary or general degrees. This had fallen to 33% in 1990, with some universities as low as 15%. According to the report the universities were stressing the deliberate emphasis of the general degree on breadth of study rather than specialization, saying it was of particular interest to those wishing *a general higher education before pursuing vocational studies*. Readers will recognize the traditional Scottish approach. Dundee's Principal Michael Hamlin has urged the Scottish universities to revive the status of the broad three-year Ordinary degree to aid student recruitment.[11] So has Dr Turmeau, Napier's Principal[12], adding the interesting comment: "The goal of an institution like Napier University is not just being effective and efficient in producing high-quality teaching and research. Our major goal is to ensure that as many of our young people as possible are provided with an educational process which will enable them to develop their knowledge and freedom of thought and which will encourage them to ask the question 'Why?'" Turmeau is here reflecting the unease about the present imbalance in the universities, so often referred to in the contemporary literature, and which is mentioned in a THES editorial on the two cultures.[13] "Within it (higher education) there remains an attachment to the former view of its responsibilities. Its goal is not simply to enable but to enlighten. The third version of the two cultures debate is present in all the detailed issues that excite policy-makers – the relationship between teaching and research, academic quality, the reform of honours degrees, even the funding of higher education institutions. These are not simply technical; they are permeated by fundamental value judgments."

In the same speech at a graduation ceremony, Dr Turmeau, no doubt – and understandably – buoyed up by the euphoria of the occasion, said that Scotland could become the envy of the world by returning to its one-time role as leader in the field of higher education. Vainglorious though this may appear, it is an inchoate sentiment that keeps cropping up. Writing on Hugh McDiarmid,[14] Neal Ascherson refers to his "Scottish Messianism, " his claim that Scotland had given to the world in the fourteenth century the earliest version of modern political freedom" in the Treaty of Arbroath, and had "offered the human race the chance of permanent escape from the tyranny of economic necessity" through the Industrial Revolution. "Now", writes Ascherson, "there approached the time when Scotland would break the third seal, and lead humanity into a new universalism which understood the oneness of all 'living' and 'inanimate' creation", and, in the words of McDiarmid, "commence to express the unity of life". This had also been the message of Patrick Geddes and is today the message of the modern ecological movement; it is also the message, however cautiously and diplomatically advanced, of Sir David Smith. It is another deeply rooted desire of the *perfervidum ingenium Scotorum*, another reflection of the democratic intellect, reaching out literally to the whole of creation. For it was also the message, more than 200 years ago, of Robert Burns when he wrote in *To a Mouse*:

> I'm truly sorry man's dominion
> Has broken Nature's social union
> And justifies that ill opinion
>> Which makes thee startle
> At me, thy poor, Earth-born companion!
>> And fellow mortal.

And also when he wrote in *On the destruction of the woods near Drumlanrig* :

> "Man! cruel Man!" the genius sighed,
> As through the cliffs he sank him down –
> "The worm that gnawed my bonny trees,
>> That reptile wears a ducal crown."

And every Scot knows his clarion call that "Man to man the world o'er/Shall brothers be, for a' that."

The central importance of biology as a unifying discipline is forcefully stressed in a thoroughly scientific context by Dr Ron Roberts, Professor of Biology and Director of the Institute of Accquaculture at the University of Stirling.[15] He says that the Scottish school and higher education system has a tradition of breadth and that this tradition has a noble pedigree. He adds that, given the rapidly changing work environment, the complete disappearance of many traditional occupations and their replacement by completely new ones, "the breadth of the Ordinary Degree has a positive virtue. In its integrated, basic natural science form, biology has become "a central subject in school and university curricula – the new classics, a subject which has intellectual rigour, academic acceptability and significance to all aspects of modern life". He points that few used the classics as linguists; they were usually colonial or civil servants. So with biology: "It is important to have a biologically-educated electorate capable of being rational decision-makers and opinion leaders in whatever capacity they reach."

Professor Roberts criticizes the UGC for "striking particularly viciously at those universities which have a strong adherence to the broad educational value of higher education", and expresses his amazement that Sir Edward Parkes, Chairman of the UGC, should have declared to the parliamentary Education, Science and Arts Committee that "the nature of biology is changing. Some of the developments have great potential and economic significance. On the other hand there is an area of biology which has really been more in the nature of a sort of general education discipline not aimed at a particular career, a good deal of the ecological end of the subject, so now we have shifted resources from one to the other." Professor Roberts finds threatening to both university and school biology, "indeed in its logic a threat to education as a whole, the suggestion that since some aspects of biology as a subject do not aim at a particular career but are in the nature of a 'sort of general educational discipline', they have to have resources shifted from them. This to me appears to be folly of the first order. The core university and school subjects are taught as the basis of an education for living." Again we see the fundamental contradiction between the educational result of English logical positivism and utilitarianism and the Scottish tradition of a general education to set up young people for life.

Olga Wojtas, in an article entitled *Greening Higher Education*,[16] explains how Edinburgh University is currently exploring how far environmental education can become part of all undergraduate teaching, as proposed by Sir David Smith, and not simply be restricted to such obviously relevant subjects as scientific monitoring of the environment for global warming and other threats, or developing technologies for controlling pollution and acid rain. The intention is that it should cover ethical, aesthetic, legal, economic and consumer considerations. The Edinburgh Centre for Human Ecology reports that many students are concerned about how their careers will relate to the world. Ms Wojtas, striking a rather jarring and, in present economic conditions, unrealistic note, suggests that environmental concern could well give universities a competitive edge in attracting students, and that employers could find it hard to attract good students if they do not show this concern. But, she says, Edinburgh recognizes that broadcasting ecological education beyond the subject-specific area to cover human behaviour and culture is a challenge to conventional university teaching, since it would have to deal with ways of life. It is unclear, she concludes, how willingly academics will rise to this challenge. Certainly the failure of similar earlier attempts to change direction at Keele, Stirling, Sussex and other new universities of that period does not augur well. It is, however, true that to those educated in the Scottish tradition it poses much less of a problem than to those educated in the narrower English tradition.

Admittedly, there is now a School of Environmental Studies at East Anglia and an Environmental Institute at Imperial College, but these are not at all the same sort of animal as Edinburgh is proposing. Wojtas points out that one of the concepts of human ecology, namely that the ecological behaviour in which changes need to be made is strongly determined by culture, is likely to be seen as irrelevant in many subject areas. She fears many lecturers will feel innovation requires increased resources, and that there will also be problem of curriculum overload, "with departments unwilling to jettison existing elements of courses for something they see as peripheral". Edinburgh's Centre for Human Ecology recommends an evolutionary approach, strengthening and co-ordinating existing environmental interests and promoting stronger links between departments on these, helping to rouse environmental consciousness among academics. Developments in this area will quite obviously be cross-disciplinary

Welcome as they are, these suggestions seem to me to be too little too late, too complex and insufficiently concentrated, and above all flying – on a wing and a prayer – in the face of the endemic tendency to academic fissiparousness and departmental isolation which has so far defeated all attempts at greater breadth and interdisciplinarity. The only way to make the fundamental change of direction that is essential, while satisfying all the disparate needs and demands, is to bring back the Ordinary or General Degree *for all students before specialization*. I can certainly agree with Wojtas, however, when she says that this problem is not going to go away.

Indeed, that is very much of an understatement. According to Auslan Cramb[17], "the world's deepening environmental crisis is causing the deaths of 35,000 children under five every day". A stark report from the United Nations Environment Programme covering

the past two decades, reveals that ecological destruction has esca-
lated, malnutrition has increased and the gap between rich and poor
has widened since 1972. The report identifies children as the main
victims. Population rates are the highest in history. Destruction
has reached planetary dimensions with man-made depletion of the
ozone layer, global warming, mass extinctions and the increase in
toxic wastes. Transboundary and freshwater pollution, deforestation, expansion of deserts and the loss of agricultural soils are all
increasing. 900 million people in cities are exposed to unhealthy
levels of sulphur dioxide; one in four Europeans drinks water with
pollution levels higher than EC minimum health standards; one
quarter of the world's plants and animals are in danger of extinction
in the next 20 to 30 years because of human activity

The number of chronically hungry people in the world increased
from 460 million in 1970 to 550 million in 1990. As I write these
words we watch on television, stunned and horrified, the terrible
humanitarian tragedy of mass starvation and death in Somalia.
Yet, at the Earth Summit in Rio de Janeiro, the United States, the
world's biggest producer of carbon dioxide and by far the largest
consumer of the world's raw materials, refused to agree targets for
the reduction of carbon dioxide emissions or to sign a document
to protect rare species. It is hardly surprising that the reviewer of a
book by Robert N. Procter, *Value-free Science? Purity and Power
in Modern Science*, says[18]: "In our current situation it is especially
important that scientific research and the knowledge it produces are
evaluated from a position of strong moral commitment." Thus the
Scottish Environmental Forum, not long before the Earth Summit,
called[19] for the radical reshaping of the world economy and society,
with a reversal of the 'south to north' flow of resources. It went on:
"History will judge the Earth Summit, not by its words and intentions, nor by minor successes in tackling immediate problems, but
by whether it grasps the urgency of the crisis and the opportunity
for entering a new era of human society. It is a chance to rethink
and reshape our relationships with one another, in a global society,
and our relationships with the Earth, in a global economy. It is a
chance to create a new world order which is just, participative and
sustainable."

Alas for that noble, idealistic dream – the Earth Summit was by
common consent, a failure; it did not even begin to tackle that
agenda. It was flatly condemned as a debacle by one commentator:
"For the major players, the Summit was a phenomenal success.
The World Bank emerged in control of an expanded Global Environmental Facility, a prize that it had worked for two years to
achieve. The US got the biodiversity convention it sought simply by

not signing the convention on offer. The corporate sector, which throughout the UNCED process enjoyed special access to the secretariat, was confirmed as the key actor in the 'battle to save the planet'. Free-market environmentalism – the philosophy that transnational corporations brought to Rio through the Business Council on Sustainable Development – has become the order of the day."[20]

Whatever one's particular stance on these momentous questions, it seems clear that Edinburgh University's innovative plans to develop environmental teaching are too tentative and will be too complex in operation to make the impact and give the lead to other higher education institutions that is needed by the end of the millennium. One of the major reasons for the failure of the Earth Summit, alongside the basic economic one, is that most of the key actors there approach the problems from the scientific, technological, philosophically positivistic and reductionist standpoint which the universities have done so much to spread, and which is the disease, not the cure. Time is not on the environment's side. The world-wide network of computers, rapidly growing ever faster and more powerful, together with the instantaneous communication of masses of information by fax machine and other high tech methods, are almost literally creating Teilhard de Chardin's *noosphere*, but in a sense very different from that which he envisaged. Man's power to damage the biosphere is thereby enormously increased.

Ad hoc methods, however enthusiastic, are inadequate in dealing with such a vast and all-embracing subject. Max Nicholson explains[21] that what so sharply differentiates environmentalism from preceding movements is that it is scientifically based but, as Darwin showed, it contrasts with other scientific approaches in involving direct confrontation with beliefs about the origin and nature of man. In presenting the human species as one among the rest, ecology not only implies obligations on man for harmony with nature, but indirectly challenges such deep-seated traditions as men's status in relation to women. It also advances the thesis, strongly resisted by religious leaders among others, of "the human applicability of the concept of limits of carrying capacity for a given species in a given environment". Nicholson shows that ecology is unique among sciences in that its focus is mainly on interrelationships not only between plants and animals, but between both and features of the environment which fall within the physical, and even, to some extent, the human sciences. "The philosophical and ethical implications tend to split ecologists between those frightened to stray beyond the limits of laboratory research and those, like A. G. Tansley, ecology's European father, who readily pursue wider issues."

One of the fundamental ethical problems is that most human leadership for the past few thousand years "has assumed the validity of a hierarchy dedicated to the build-up of power over nature and over men's hearts and minds in order to achieve visible material progress". This has resulted in a strongly man-centred culture, oblivious of the need for the sustainable use of resources and of any ethical claims to the survival of the biosphere, "even if God created it". How does it come about then, asks Nicholson, that the ecological movement has an effective world-wide organizational structure with a rich diversity of activist bodies? Why such strong motivation and such instinctive support from so many people? Nicholson's view is that the prolonged exposure of a species to the experiences man must have had between his emergence from the forest and the development of modern civilized living during recent millennia "must have involved intense natural selection in favour of lifestyles in harmony with the environment". Primitive man had a very long time in which to hone his skills in identifying plants for food and medicine and in "using them for survival with a success modern science can hardly surpass".[22] The hunting group was a most successful prototype for modern management and military operations.[23] The remarkable expansion of the human neo-cortex long antedated civilization.

Nicholson thinks the environmental movement has tapped a deep well, including ethical influences. "A new order", he says, "implies new values and ethics". The environmental militants do not wear their ethics on their sleeves and think that it is what they do that is the most important thing. "They openly challenge claims to human mastery of nature, and the exploitation, aggression and sheer greed which accompany these. Insistence on the sacredness of biological diversity, and on the criminality of causing extinctions of species represent another strong bond between the movement's scientific and ethical bases." Ethical issues, however, become more difficult and complex the further the attention is shifted from stopping damage to nature in the wild and concentrated on tackling attitudes and habits which indirectly conflict with its welfare and sustainability. "Far-reaching changes in life-styles, demanded by recent discoveries, are not easily carried through, even by green enthusiasts, and present frequent difficulties when they have been adopted by organizations with opposite habits and attitudes." And this despite the fact that measures to reduce air pollution, for example, largely coincide with savings in energy through readily attainable improvements in efficiency and consequent savings in family expenditure. Nicholson concludes that, paradoxically, it has taken the movement for the conservation of nature to bring true human needs back to the forefront, after decades in which they have been brushed aside for the convenience of technology, mass marketing, and arrogant politicians of all colours. 'Sacrifices' imposed by the need to avoid ecological catastrophe are actually measures of liberation. Simplicity and frugality are good for you. The economic use of resources is a good thing, as the Greeks thought, and as Jo Grimond reminded us in the last chapter.

The most pertinent and the most hopeful feature of all this for the universities is that it is the young people who are the most active in the environmental movement. Until, that is, they are subjected to the sort of courses the new, and not so new, universities are touting to prepare them for the rat race. It looks as if we need a new ethic for a new earth[24] and that we have a ready-made audience for the courses that will impart it. *A New Ethic for a New Earth* – that is the title of a book by an American author, Glenn C. Stone, quoted by John Passmore, an Australian philosopher who was a student of John Anderson (referred to in Chapter 5) in his book *Man's Responsibility for Nature*.[25] This new ethic, says Passmore, must incorporate a careful, scientific approach to the building of a new ecological earth. Both are the job of what he calls "the new university training" which, if Edinburgh's activities are any guide, could well begin in Scotland, thus fulfilling Dr Turmeau's vow. Passmore says: "The task we have now to undertake in attempting to estimate the long-term effects of our actions, both on the biosphere and on human societies, is so immense that in relation to it our ignorance is almost total. To correct this situation may well require . . . a minor revolution within science (20 years later this seems a gross understatement). The scientist will be forced, in the unenthusiastic words of one of my scientist colleagues, 'to slosh about in the primordial ooze of interdisciplinary studies'."[26] He will need to work with scientists who do not work in laboratories; with the natural historian and the field naturalist who have traditionally been at the bottom of the scientific pecking order, for "interdisciplinary investigations are in this area not a luxury but a necessity". "Only if men see themselves for what they are, quite alone, with no-one to help them except their fellow-man, will they face their ecological problems in their full implications."[27] It is towards this "sombre realization" that they must move.

Passmore then lays down a philosophical underpinning which could well be the philosophical core of a new integrated three-year Ordinary degree for all students, in the traditional Scottish style but constituting that "new university training" which Passmore considers essential. It is so important that it merits quotation at length:

> What about the metaphysical outlook characteristic of the West? That . . . is exceptionally complex and diversified, by

no means to be summed up in the view that nature is wax in man's hands. Nor is the West ... irrevocably committed to the Aristotelian-type metaphysics for which nature consists of substances with distinct properties, each of which can be separately modified without altering anything else. One of the most important alternative suggestions, dating back in essence to Heraclitus, is that the world consists of complex systems of interacting processes varying in their stability. Each such system – of which a human being is one – can survive, like a flame, only so long as it can interact with surrounding systems in certain particular ways, drawing upon and giving out to the systems around it. It can die by choking in its own wastes or because it has exhausted its resources. That way of looking at the world, which ecological investigations help to substantiate, makes it perfectly plain that you can't do one thing at a time; it destroys, too, the belief that human beings are somehow different, outside the eco-system, whether as villainous intruders or as heroic manipulators. But it does so in a manner not the least mystical, not the least anti-scientific in spirit, not in the least implying that there is something wrong with any attempt to make the world a better place.

Scientists too are beginning to think along similar lines. In his book *La Logique du Vivant* the biologist François Jacob, the Nobel Prize winner, says that it was not only the purely experimental aspects of science that interested him. The influence of the French educational system in stimulating an interest in philosophy was not far behind. It led him to an interest in why various concepts about heredity and the nature of evolution had emerged at particular points in history, and how they related to other ideas going round at the time. "I began to read what the scientists themselves had written in the past, and was struck by the fact that at a particular point in history they were all talking about the same thing ... I also found that the history of science has to be linked with everything, with technology, with politics, with other social activities." So he decided to write a book and tried to show that scientific ideas evolve, not in a linear way, but in a way that involves a complete rearrangement of the way that we look at time and space and objects. "The type of arrangements we look for in one field is the result of a tremendously integrative process which takes things from a wide variety, not only of scientific domains, but also social actions and interaction with the environment."[28]

This has never been truer than of the present time and the sense of it keeps cropping up all over the place. For instance, a *THES* editorial, reporting on a Swedish conference which discussed 'knowledge policy' and knowledge traditions, asks whether higher education has become dominated by an over-narrow scientific tradition, a tradition that is mechanistic, amoral and dismissive of values that cannot be reduced to reason. This tradition aspires to provide a complete intellectual description of the natural world and of man's place in it, "but it can only succeed by the sustained inhibition of our moral imaginations". But there is a difference between the technocratic approach and the tradition of scientific inquiry. Science is by its very nature modest and tentative. Its most important principle is "I know that I do not know". "So science is not the enemy of intuition or imagination. Indeed, it positively encourages both." Knowledge can certainly be based on reasoning and experiment; but it can also be based on faith or tradition, ethical values, practical experience and aesthetic sensibility. But "a technocratic society is not ennobling", in the words of Daniel Bell.[29] Material goods provide only transient satisfaction or an invidious superiority over those with less. "Yet one of the deepest human impulses is to *sanctifying* their institutions and beliefs in order to find a meaningful purpose in their lives and to deny the meaninglessness of death. A post-industrial society cannot provide a transcendent ethic . . . The lack of a rooted belief system is the cultural contradiction of society and the deepest challenge to its survival."

Statements similar in purport come also from the side of the environmentalists. "Atomism or holism on its own, either one without the other, is not only incomplete, it is incoherent. We can understand neither the tree without the leaf, not the leaf without the tree . . . Neither can we morally understand things in isolation. The wellbeing needs of an individual are a matter of its nature, and the nature and needs of a being cannot be understood except in context. We are what we are as individuals, but we are also what we are with respect to our social group, our species and the biosphere, and this affects moral issues. Morally and ontologically, then, we must recognize different aspects of reality."[30]

We learn, in an only apparently lighter vein, that Japanese companies are seeking "creative dropouts" rather than conformist achievers.[31] In other words they want lateral thinkers rather than logical positivists. Nigel Calder, editor of the *New Scientist*, giving a lecture on his father Ritchie Calder at the University of Edinburgh, said that the world needs "gangs of intellectual lager louts to deal with the scientific challenges of global change". Gatecrashing into academic research by non-experts had played a key role in scientific evolution: examples were Watson and Crick, who were physicists, discovering the structure of DNA, and the advancement of astronomy by radar experts during the Second World War.

"You can't do one thing at a time." That is the opposite of what Galileo, Bacon and Descartes told us, and of what the logical positivists in their supposedly objective, value-free, linear drive to a material paradise on earth are still telling us. "The task we have now to undertake is so immense . . . that in relation to it our ignorance is almost total." For such a task – involving a fundamental rethink of the philosophy, science, ethics, aesthetics, politics and economics of the past nearly 400 years – a boldly and determinedly radical approach is needed. Civilization, as Sir David Smith told us, is at risk.[32] At this point we pick up again Asa Briggs' throwaway insight that "there may well be features of post-industrial society . . . that have more in common with pre-industrial society than with the society of the nineteenth and twentieth centuries". He was referring to the universities and their "universe of thought". If there was one feature that was more responsible than any other for the success of the Scottish universities it was the three or four year general arts degree preceding professional specialization, based on the classical trivium and quadrivium, and covering the arts and sciences, with philosophy holding a central position. Even a figure like Lord Todd of Trumpington was declaring over twenty years ago[33]: "There is much talk of a new system for British universities in which there would be a three-year general degree followed by a two-year specialized degree for a selected group, and finally a very restricted two-year doctorate group."

The harping on selection and restriction should not blind us to the value of this proposal in that context and at that time. Lord Todd's proposal was of course not taken up, but there is nothing to stop the general degree for all students being revived in Scotland, except lack of imagination brought on by our cognitive disorientation. One can imagine the outcry – where will the money come from at a time when such as Sir Christopher Ball and Dr John Ashworth are calling for the shortening of the Scottish four year honours degree, when students are being forced by debt created by student loans to go for the present debased pick'n'mix form of the ordinary degree rather than the four-year honours degree.[34] Therein lies our cognitive disorientation. We ignore the real, fundamental threats to human civilization and starve of money the bodies most able to tackle them, while we spend many billions on unnecessary nuclear weapons and vastly expensive and murderous armed forays for ephemeral political and economic advantage. Because of an unthinking and totally anachronistic dogma about reducing public expenditure we handicap ourselves in the real battle for survival by skimping on higher education – packing students in, reducing them to the breadline or proposing to dun them when they have graduated – while France in 1989 was spending 18% of its national budget on education.

The fact is that the English three-year Honours course is ludicrously short in this day and age; nowhere else in the developed world are university courses so short. Even the Scottish, American, Canadian, Australasian and European four-year courses are too short now. It is noteworthy that the country with the longest university courses in Europe, Germany – where students can still also follow the medieval practice of attending courses consecutively at several universities – is also the country with the most powerful economy and the richest cultural provision. Well over a century ago Professor John Stuart Blackie, Professor of Greek at the University of Edinburgh, was speaking of the

> professions which cannot dispense with a long preparatory training, and in which an early start is in the long run often more prejudicial than advantageous. These are the proper subjects for university as distinguished from school training; and taking our measure from the existing state of the more intellectual professions in the best educated countries of Europe, we may lay down for them an academical curriculum of six years – three years for those studies in science and literature that belong to a man of solid information and large thinking in this nineteenth century, and three years for strictly professional study. The young man who shall have finished his course of study according to this gradation will be 24 years of age, – soon enough for any prudent person to meddle seriously with the thorny perplexities of the law or the obscure experimentations of the medical art." [35]

This is even more true in our day than it was in the 1860s in view of the enormous growth and flowering of knowledge in all areas of human experience. There are indeed five-year degree courses (not compulsory but taken by most Honours students) in Scotland – Stirling's modern language departments have them. Geoffrey Squires declares categorically [36] that the English university norm of three years is quite simply too little time in which to acquire the necessary amount of knowledge in its depth, relativity and reflexivity. He refers to the four-year patterns in North America and other parts of Europe and says that "there is a certain nostalgia in higher education for unifying ideas or models such as the medieval trivium or quadrivium, or the original notions of a liberal or polytechnical education. The nostalgia is more interesting than the ideas, because it points to a sense of loss of institutional and communal coherence." The famous Harvard University report of 1945 on general education says that "students, whatever their specialization, should become familiar, through formal, examined courses, with a body of knowledge, ideas and values which constitutes the heritage of western civilization". When reviewed twenty years later, it was found to have failed. Not surprisingly, in view of the climate in the universities. Now – if it is not already too late – a re-examination of the heritage of western civilization is imperative, if that civilization is to continue.

The argument that a three-year integrated general course for all students, plus a further two years for those going to Honours, would be too expensive, is, in the light of European experience, quite simply disingenuous. Dutch universities, with which Scottish universities had such close contact and from which they learned so much in the eighteenth century, have no such difficulty. Like the Scottish universities in the eighteenth and nineteenth centuries, they have no form of entrance examination. Students are funded for *six years* and they have a free public transport card. In Germany, too, as we have seen, students spend at least six years in higher education. It is noteworthy that Dutch and German people in politics, industry and other professional fields (including footballers!) are much more skilful in the use of foreign languages than the British – again largely because they spend much longer at it.

The introduction of a three-year integrated general degree – a modern equivalent of the trivium and quadrivium, covering the arts and sciences and with a planetary or earth ethic as its core – would, I am convinced, be a roaring success, and would quickly bring Scottish higher education levels up to those of California in terms of the proportion of the age group entering higher education. As evidence I would advance the fact that the thirst for knowledge in Scotland, always great, has never been greater than it is now. The demand for Open University places in Scotland is at an all-time high, yet here again spending cuts threaten a vital part of many courses.[37] "More than 100,000 students have gained Open University degrees, a disproportionate number of them Scots. Applicants for next year's 2,900 Scottish places have reached record levels, breaking the 10,000 barrier. This year 773 Scots graduated, more than in any other of the university's thirteen regions. Yet the Open University courses are no soft option and it takes a six-year slog to get a degree. "Our students are really fired up", says a lecturer. It was always thus in Scotland.

To this inspiring picture one has to add the extraordinary blossoming of the arts in Scotland, whether it be poetry or painting, the novel or the theatre, music both traditional and classical, or even the desperately under-funded film industry. Nowhere in the world, even in the richest parts of it, is there such a concentration of arts festivals as in the Edinburgh-Glasgow area, including the biggest in the world, the Edinburgh Festival. Scotland is an incredibly fertile field for all intellectual and artistic undertakings, despite the fact that, every year, the country's brightest and best are forced to emigrate to find suitable work. Dr Turmeau's dream that Scotland might again lead the world in higher education could come true, but it will need a mighty effort of imagination and determination.

For there are many difficulties to surmount. Our university finances may have returned into Scottish hands but finance will still be controlled by the Treasury in London through the SOED. The Scottish Universities Funding Council will need to draw inspiration and courage from Scotland's great higher educational traditions in order to show a more combative attitude; to oppose with resolution Government meanness towards higher education; and to stop in its tracks, and then reduce, the utterly inappropriate anglicization of Scotland's universities and colleges. The Government's attitude to a proposal to lengthen courses to five years, with a three-year general element and two-year specialization element, can be foreseen, though in fact a well-integrated three-year course giving students an understanding of the modern world and its problems, teaching them to ask questions, to debate and express themselves articulately, could well considerably reduce the numbers going on to Honours, since they would in many cases – feeling that they had a good education – want to go on for training in industry and business.

Such a scheme would, in fact meet everyone's needs: the industrialists and businessmen complaining about the excessive specialization of university courses and the need for recruits with commonsense, the ability to handle people and to think on their feet; the educationalists – particularly in England – who constantly complain about the narrowness of the A-level curriculum and created a committee – the Higginson Committee – to do something about it. (As we have seen, that committee's proposals to broaden A-levels along the lines of the Highers were not listened to.) It would be a wise response to the warnings of the humanists – the teachers of the arts and philosophy – that it is madness to deprive young people of a knowledge of their country's cultural past. Countries like France and Germany, so successful in the economic field, lay great stress on culture and philosophy in their higher education institutions, while young Scots have for generations been taught to think of Shakespeare and Chaucer, Dickens and Thackeray, Keats, Wordsworth and Shelley, as their literature, and a great scientist like James Clerk Maxwell as being of little importance alongside Newton or Darwin. The establishment of an earth ethic at the heart of such a general course would begin to meet the warnings of the environmentalists and train our young people to tackle the vast problems the world is facing. It would above all – half a lifetime as a university teacher convinces me of it – meet the needs of the young people, who throw themselves with such generosity of spirit into saving whales and baby seals and feeding the starving children of Africa.

It has to be said that they often show more imagination and courage than the academics who teach them; for another difficulty, which has caused the failure of all previous attempts – listed in Chapter 6 – at a general, all-round education at first degree level, is the resistance of many academics who are strongly thirled to specialization. Here, however, the views expressed by Sir David Smith of Edinburgh University and Dr Turmeau at Napier University would seem to indicate that there is a new spirit abroad at the highest level in our universities. Their conviction, no doubt shared by others, of the need for change may bring about more determined leadership in the direction so clearly seen by so many to be necessary.

Last of all, we should not forget the imagination, determination and resilience of our students and the combined power of staff and students working together, as in the noble case of Peter Abelard. Dr William Gaillard, the Director of the UN International Drug Control Programme, whom we have already quoted, had some inspiring things to say on this, and I cannot do better than end with his words: "Cultural change is next on the agenda, the young generation is the key to the solution of the problem but also the group which is worldwide most at risk ... The young generation itself, however, is giving all of us some hopeful signals. Young people have been the first to react against a world that values so highly the individual, the material, the chemical, the fake, the polluted. It is the young who developed what has become our ecological conscience. We need to strengthen this impulse by redefining a new set of values for the twenty-first century which will take into account the new needs that have emerged so clearly over the last decade. We desperately need an ecology of the mind."

Envoi

Benjamin Franklin, that gifted, creative polymath and *uomo universale*, liked nothing so much as to be in Scotland; and when he was in London he spent all his time with his Scottish friends there. One may take from that what one wishes, but I like to think that a man so talented in both theoretical and practical matters found himself at home among Scots, who had precisely the same balanced attitude towards reality.

When, some years ago, the Queen visited the People's Republic of China, she went to a large gathering in a Shanghai theatre. As she came on to the stage, a little Chinese girl, dressed in tartan, walked on stage from the other side and sang Auld Lang Syne to the Queen . . . in Mandarin! How does it come about that a simple song about friendship and nostalgia, from a small country, has become the world's anthem, as it were? The genius of Robert Burns, certainly – but it should be noted that he is one of the most popular poets of all time, in both senses of the word 'popular'. The Scottish people repaid the compliment by making the exhibition of the *Emperor's Warriors* in Edinburgh the third largest exhibition ever held in Britain, with ordinary Scots queueing for hours in the street in their tens of thousands in cold weather. National pride must have had a lot to do with it, for the exhibition was not put on anywhere else in Britain.

A *TESS* editorial tells the following story: "The old Scottish universities have their proud legends. It is said that one lad o' pairts, a scholar from Elgin Academy, arrived in Aberdeen in the 1840s, having walked all the way from Glass on the far west side of the county. Round his legs, the story goes, were tied bands of straw to keep out the drifting snow, and on his back was the sack of oatmeal which was to be his main sustenance till he could walk home at

Christmas for more. Some 40 years later this youth was to become Principal at Aberdeen."[1] This anecdote too strikes a popular note.

Further enlightenment is to be found in an article entitled *Beyond the Kailyard to Virginia Beach*,[2] in which Dr Noble of Strathclyde University says that Scotland is seen by American historians, especially in the eighteenth century, not only as an extremely interesting laboratory for the analysis of social change but as a "vital source of the political, cultural and economic evolution of the USA". It is no accident, he says, that the *Wealth of Nations* and the creation of America were almost simultaneous events. "Much of the secular, rational, technological world was invented in eighteenth century Scotland; we therefore had a profound religious, theoretical and personal influence on that state of modern material and political progress which is America." Speaking of the Scottish colonies in Virginia and especially the Carolinas, he says: "It is easy to mock the florid plaid carpets, the tartan wallpaper as backdrop to crossed claymores and iconic monarchs of the glen. Such things are, however, testimony to the unassuaged pain of exile. Such jumbled, crass symbolism is also no more than an extension of our post-union native confusions of identity."[3] Noble refers to David Daiches' demonstration of the impact Hugh Blair's rules of rhetoric in the eighteenth century had on the drafting of the US constitution. He then asks in conclusion: "Having created so much of modern society it is long past time we Scots became intellectually responsible for what our hands and minds so astonishingly wrought. Can we have commerce and virtue? What does technology do to human nature? Do we have a definable national identity, and what are the political consequences of this? Were we but to tell ourselves our true story, it might be the beginning of resolving many of our intractable difficulties."

As to our national identity, Dr. Noble may set his mind at rest. Precisely the same cultural characteristics, the same drive to spread the word across vast geographical spaces, were true of Columba and the Gaels. The north of Ireland and western Scotland were the most civilized places in Europe during the Dark Ages, and Columba's monks took their educational mission across Europe. Their traces are there to this day: L'Eglise Saint Thomas (or Thomaskirche) in Strasbourg has a notice outside which says: "The first church on this site was built by Scottish monks in the 6th century." Then there is Sanct Gallen (he was an Irish Scot) in Switzerland, with a beautiful copy of the Book of Kells in the Stiftung; the Schottentor in Munich; and the Schottenring and the Schottengasse in Vienna. The cultural patrimony goes further back even than Columba: everywhere there are Scots you will find jewellery and other artifacts that bear the mark of the beautiful art of the Picts.

His point about a sense of intellectual and political responsibility is, however, a very valid one; and his sense that Scotland still has a great deal to give the world if she can but find her feet is echoed by Tom Nairn.[4] "The deep underlying strength of the nationalism of Scotland is a simple one. It is simply not possible for anyone from within the culture to resist at least part of its appeal. Nobody with any imagination can fail to be moved by the stubborn dream of true existence which has survived this desperate history without truth, this long sterility where all dreams were in vain. Misplaced, sentimental, archaic, it is nonetheless a dream of wholeness – a wholeness which will express life instead of hiding it, which will free the national tongue and will from their secular inhibitions, a realness to startle itself and the watching world. It is a dream of release and affirmation, shared by many; and, as such, more important than most of what passes for reality."[5]

I agree with both these authors that the greatest frustration for Scotland is not to be able to give to the world as generously today as she did in the past.[6] There is a large book yet to be written on the quite extraordinary contribution this small country has made to modern civilization and the people who fashioned it all over the world. And a large question to be answered as to what made such a thing possible. I personally believe a large part of it is due to the Celtic inheritance, because we share many of these characteristics with the Irish people. The urge for release and affirmation of which Tom Nairn speaks is certainly a very powerful one. John Buchan, who was a Conservative MP as well as a popular writer, felt it. In a speech in the House of Commons he said: "We do not want to be like the Greeks, powerful and prosperous wherever we settle, but with a dead Greece behind us. We do not want to be like the Jews of the Diaspora – a potent force everywhere on the globe but with no Jerusalem."[7]

Nor was he the only Conservative to feel it. So did the late and much lamented Alick Buchanan-Smith, who refused Cabinet office because of government attitudes to Scotland and its universities. So does Michael Fry, the journalist, in an intelligent article entitled *University Challenge of Home Rule*."[8] Many rejoiced, he says, at the Government's decision to repatriate the funding of the Scottish universities on the grounds that for the first time it would bring all Scottish education under the Scottish Office. This was wrong, he says, because earlier in the century it was the Scottish Office's views on the universities that were sought and deferred to in London. "These views were clear", he goes on. "However glorious the Scottish academic tradition, it merited no leading place in the modern world. In Britain, that belonged properly to Oxford and Cambridge alone. The Scottish universities' job was efficient production of school-teachers. Their little provincial lives might sometimes be lit by sending a brilliant pupil on into a higher sphere. But the essential task and tenour of the system was to be, in Davie's chilling word, subaltern." Later in the article he says: "Scotland, alone in the world, was left with a system of higher education guided by the assumptions and priorities of another country .. Scotland sacrificed the independent academic tradition which had once been her pride."[9]

A very serious consequence of this was that the confirmed subaltern status of the Scottish universities in this all-British bureaucracy "has opened a divide from the nation at large. Once, the universities were Scottish culture, high culture anyway. Today, with the honourable exception of half-a-dozen scattered departments, they make no contribution to Scottish culture." Angus Calder bears this out.[10] He writes of the recent rediscovery and reassessment of Scotland's past by historians who show that pre-Union Scotland was a stable and harmonious country by European standards, with a strong intellectual culture. "As against this", he continues, "the drive from London seems to be towards a situation where elderly English academics in decimated departments teach an Anglocentric view of culture and history to English public school boys amid the ruins of the broad Scottish curriculum."[11]

This desire for release and affirmation – to give the world of Scotland's best – has been constantly expressed for nearly three centuries now. As John Buchan put it in 1932: "We are in danger very soon of reaching the point where Scotland will have nothing distinctive to show the world." And, a century earlier, Sir Walter Scott: "There has been in England a gradual and progressive system assuming the management of affairs entirely and exclusively proper to Scotland, as if we were totally unworthy of having the management of our own concerns."[12] Today this latter threat is greater than it has ever been, as Tom Nairn shows: "In today's Scotland there is – in certain cultural trades and types of management – a visibly growing predominance of individuals from metropolitan England." The latter qualification is vital, he says. We are not talking about the 'English' as such or about a geographical entity. We are talking about "the dominance of the UK heartland – of the specific imperium denoted by phrases like 'the Home Counties'. This power-node is at once imprecisely territorial, socio-cultural and institutional: *the bastions of Oxbridge university are its most prominent landmark*" (our italics). Higher education is the "outstanding example" of this dominance, to which Scottish culture is clearly succumbing, "But an analogous trend is visible in other public-sector professions and in the arts: there, too, the 'best man' (or woman) is increasingly often from Oxbridge England and, once installed, will recruit others from a like background."[13]

If Scotland is ever to throw off this "London-centralist hegemony" of which Sir Walter Scott and so many others have complained, the recovery of Scottish identity is much more important than a mere change in political behaviour, says Professor Christopher Harvie of the University of Tübingen.[14] He outlines that identity in four points:

1 The importance of the 'concept of society' in Scottish social thought;

2 The Scottish notion of the division of political power, namely that power lies with the people, not with the king or absolute parliamentary sovereignty, which, said Lord Cooper in 1953, was "a distinctively English principle which had no counterpart in Scottish constitutional law;"

3 The ideological-religious basis of Scottish social institutions which reflect principles of morality and social justice; and

4 The multiform nature of Scottish cultural identity.

Harvie stresses the difference between Scottish and English social thought. Since the Reformation the Scots had tended to "derive the principles of social organization by deduction from general theories of man and society rather than rationalize them via induction from particular instances."[15] This difference is reflected in the contrast between Roman Law and English Common Law. "The essential unity of men and society is, in the thought of Andrew Fletcher or Adam Ferguson, as important a legacy of the Scottish Enlightenment as the economic atomism of Adam Smith." Perhaps the most important fact of all about the Scottish philosophical tradition is that it stressed "that facts acquired significance through their relationship to one another and to historical change," and thus "the whole society and its culture became the frame of reference of Scottish philosophy". This philosophy was, as we know, the central core of the general degree for all students until it was dethroned at the end of the nineteenth century. There is a clear resemblance between it and the metaphysical stance put forward in Chapter 17 by John Passmore, as being in tune with the environmental needs of the contemporary world. Passmore was a student of the Scottish philosopher John Anderson, who is described as a Heraclitean. The central core of Scottish philosophy, as described by Harvie, bears more than a passing resemblance to Heraclitus' "Everything flows". Little wonder then that there should be such a fundamental conflict between Scottish and English epistemology and methodology in higher education, since logical positivism is at the opposite philosophical pole to that great fundamental intuition of Heraclitus. This Scottish philosophy also affirmed that social institutions should not be passive in the face of industrialization and the division of labour, but should intervene to humanise it. There is to this day a basic 'solidarism' in Scotland, says Harvie, "an acceptance that we are all members one of another". Or, in the popular Scots saying, "We're a' Jock Tamson's bairns."[16]

The difference between this philosophy and these social attitudes and those that prevail in England needs no underlining. The effect of the anglicization of Scotland's universities has consequently been quite devastating.[17] These ill effects led John Buchan, a Tory MP and Establishment figure, to make the following statement in that famous parliamentary speech of 1932: "I believe that every Scotsman should be a Scottish nationalist. If it could be proved that a separate Scottish Parliament were desirable, that is to say that the merits were greater than the disadvantages, Scotsmen should support it. I would go further. Even if it were not proved desirable, if it could be proved to be desired by any substantial majority of the Scottish people, then Scotland should be allowed to make the experiment." Politics is not my subject in this book, but it must by now be fairly evident that the merits far outweigh the disadvantages in a country whose industry (Steel, coalmining, car manufacturing, shipbuilding) has been decimated by Government and at least half of whose universities are now English academic colonies. As to the wishes of the Scottish people, 75% of them voted for parties supporting a Scottish Parliament at the 1992 General Election, and the governing party has just 11 of the 72 Scottish parliamentary seats. It is time, therefore, that the opposition parties, and especially the 61 opposition MPs in Scotland, heeded John Buchan's call. Campaigning for a Scottish Parliament before a General Election and then dropping the idea like a hot cake when, for the fourth time, they have lost, is no help to our beleaguered universities. These parties do not seem to realize – at least one hopes that it is a matter of belated realization on their part – that putting up a fight at General Elections and then acquiescing in the status quo controlled by a small minority party for the next four or five years is destroying Scotland's identity, with frightening speed, in all areas of the national life, and especially in higher education.[18] They do not engage in any vigorous way with the great problems Scottish students are having to face, nor with the terrifying fact, if looked at squarely, that, with the now near total undermining of Scottish higher education, the very soul of Scotland is at stake. I repeat: when a country loses control of its universities and its culture, it is about to lose its soul. Cultural and political power are indivisible. Is there any other country in Europe indeed in the non-colonial world which allows its universities to be run by academics from a bigger and more powerful neighbour, and their policies to be largely decided by that neighbour's government – for that is the truth of the situation? The English would never allow Oxford or Cambridge to be run by non-Englishmen, nor would the French allow the Sorbonne, nor the Germans Heidelberg or Berlin, nor the Italians Bologna, nor the Americans Harvard or Yale, to be run by people from another country, especially if their basic social and philosophical assumptions were as different as are those of Scotland and England. Our higher education institutions cannot go on waiting much longer. It is good that funding is now back in Scotland, but London still holds the pursestrings and the SOED does Westminster's bidding. We need a Scottish Parliament soon, and a Minister of Education and a Higher Education Council[19] with both academic planning and financial responsibility and control in Scotland, and a long-term appointments policy which, over time, reduces the large English staff majority in all our universities to more sensible proportions, so that eventually there is a solid majority of Scots men and women teachers and researchers. Nor need anyone fear that over the long term there will be any shortage of good Scottish applicants. The Scottish diaspora is one of the largest, best educated and most effective in the world,[20] and when they see Scotland once again led by a recalled Scottish Parliament ready to wipe away the effects of centuries of neglect, distortion, destruction and waste, they will be queueing up to come back. We don't sing only *Auld Lang Syne* ; we also sing *Will ye no' come back again.*

What a great day it will be when the Scottish universities are at long last free to undertake their own programmes. The AUT and the EIS agree that we need a programme which respects the integral links between higher education and the schools, which reflects the role of universities and colleges in their local economies and in Scottish culture, and recognises the need for proper planning and co-ordination of all the institutions of higher education. What an enormous and exciting programme, too, lies ahead of our universities to help rejuvenate the arts, literature and music, both Gaelic and Lowland; to literally recreate Scottish history and Scottish traditions in philosophy and science and have them taught in all our educational institutions; to tackle the problems of the Scottish economy and agriculture, particularly the revival of the Highlands and Islands.

Finally, we need to open the universities and colleges to all who can benefit from studies that are broadly based and flexibly organized, in the European tradition. We must also create a genuine democracy of the intellect in our universities and colleges, so that all members of staff may participate, instead of the oligarchical leadership by bureaucrats and accountants which we have at present. Having had the honour to chair a committee which prepared such a scheme at the University of Stirling in the early 1970s, saw it adopted unanimously at a large meeting of the university's General Assembly and then shelved, I know it can be done and I know it is wanted. (See Annexe.)

Throughout the writing of this book in the hope of helping to rescue and rehabilitate Scotland's splendid higher education traditions, I have been encouraged and driven along by two unforgettable images.

The first is the warning given to Samoan chiefs by that political troubleshooter and diplomat extraordinary in Samoa, Robert Louis Stevenson.[21] Because of his friendship and kindness to them when they were political prisoners, a group of chiefs – some of them old and unwell – decided to do him the unheard-of honour of building a road for him. This they did – he called it the *Road of Gratitude* – and a celebration was held at which he made a noble speech to them in Samoan. He warned them "to occupy and use your country. If you do not, others will .. And I repeat to you that thing which is sure: if you do not occupy and use your country, others will. It will not continue to be yours or your children's if you occupy it for nothing .. I who speak to you have seen these things .. I have seen them with my eyes .. I have seen them in Ireland, and I have seen them in the mountains of my own country, Scotland – and my heart was sad. These were a fine people in the past – brave, gay, faithful, and very much like Samoans, except in one particular, that they were much wiser and better at that business of fighting of which you think so much. But the time came to them as it now comes to you, and it did not find them ready. The messenger came into their villages and they did not know him; they were told, as you are told, to use and occupy their country, and they would not hear. And now you may go through great tracts of the land and scarce meet a man or a smoking house, and see nothing but sheep feeding. The other people that I tell you of have come upon them like a foe in the night, and these are the other people's sheep who browse upon the foundation of their houses."

The second is the image of the philosopher Peter Abelard – physically diminished, his life shattered, denounced as a heretic for his independence of opinion and banished from Paris to the forests of Champagne, followed by several thousand students from all over Europe who insisted that he teach them. "Erecting their tents and mud huts covered with thatch, they prosecuted their studies in the wilds, contenting themselves with the simplest rustic fare."[22] They rebuilt for him in stone the oratorio he had only been able to construct with reeds and thatch. It was truly a *monumentum aere perennius*: that simplicity, that frugality, that courage proved more powerful than all the forces arrayed against Abelard, for he it was who founded the reputation of the University of Paris.

Annexe

UNIVERSITY OF STIRLING: ACADEMIC ASSEMBLY
REPORT OF THE WORKING PARTY   21.3.73

INTRODUCTION

1.1 The University of Stirling needs to get its second wind. This, if one had to put it in a nutshell, is the message that comes across from the thirty or so members of the University who presented their views, either orally or in writing, to the Academic Assembly's Working Party.

1.2 In its early days there was an intimate, informal, almost family atmosphere on the campus, and because numbers were small people were fairly well informed about what was going on. Thus there was little felt need for the formal trappings of democracy, and corners could be cut in decision making without any apparent ill effects. On the contrary, the most beautiful and most speedily constructed building on the campus was designed by two people during a train journey from London to Edinburgh. It must have been an idyllic time.

1.3 However, as numbers grew, it should have become apparent that such methods possible in a small community where everyone knows everyone else were no longer adequate. The proportion of people who did not belong to the magic circle of those who came in with the breeze-block and "compo" grew to become a large majority. At the same time university qovernment relied heavily on a small number of people who, because of the principle of overlapping membership of Court, Academic Board and Academic Council and the manner of appointing committees of Court and Council, seemed to wear an altogether dis-proportionate number of hats. Such a steeply hierarchical arrangement can become too cosy. There is insufficient feedback. Experierce, expertise become the watchwords; critical judgement is not brought sufficiently to bear. The views of the vast majority of teachers and researchers who, with the students, are the soul of any university, are not seen as indispensable to healthy decision making. The Academic Assembly is looked on as a "safety valve" or even as a pointless nuisance. As Nobert Wiener says : "Men of ambition for power are not entirely unknown in scientific and educational institutions. Such people prefer an organisation in which all orders come from above, and none return." He calls this an inhuman use of human beings because "any use of a human being in which less is demanded of him and less is attributed to him, than his full status is a degradation and a waste." With such a structure and in such an atmosphere mistakes are all too easily made.

1.4 The Working Party has therefore sought, in a constructive way, to introduce more feedback loops from teaching staff to governing bodies at all levels and has been guided in this by the following criteria.

1.5 Firstly that, where practicable, election is preferable to appointment since it empowers individuals who are held by the majority to be best qualified for the nature of the task. Also, the collective-responsibility for the actions of elected bodies is more widely based and should help to get rid of the us-them mentality. Thus, under the arrangements we propose, all members of Academic Council and academic members of Court are elected at one level or another.

1.6 Secondly, and arising from the last point, the only distinction that should be recognised between professor and non-professor is the academic one: professors are (or should be) the best teachers and scholars and the professorship is therefore the best paid and most prestigious university teaching post. All full-time teaching staff should be eligible for election and appointment to the various university bodies. The present arrangement based on tradition rather than currently acceptable reason – which gives professors privileged access to the major decision-making bodies, should be changed.

1.7 Thirdly, all executive bodies and committees should be made responsible to one or other of the major representative and deliberati bodies, i.e. Court and Council. The power of delegation should be curtailed and in many cases replaced by the devolution of decision making with obligatory ratification by the parent body. This would simplify, streamline and rationalise decision making.

1.8   Fourthly, while we feel that properly accountable executive bodies should not become too large, we take Perkin's point when he says, "Efficiency is not necessarily confined to the rapid despatch of business: the consultation and acquiescence of interested parties may be just as important". For this reason we feel that a body like the Academic Assembly, where all staff can be present, is of vital importance in university government. The case is argued in detail in the body of the report.

1.9   Fifthly, we have made brief reference to weighted student representation on Court, though it lies outside our remit, again because we believe it to be vitally important for a number of reasons: representation of student views on the top governing body, freshness of approach to problems, the learning by students of the disciplines of responsible decision making, and so on.

1.10 The structure of university government proposed in this report is essentially democratic, but the type of democratic representation we suggest has a dual aspect. On the one hand there is representation of subject areas which is achieved through the sequence Department–Board of Studies–Academic Council–Court; with each lower body providing elected members for the higher body. Thus, elected Chairmen of Departments and Boards of Studies are automatically members of Academic Council. On the other hand there is representation of the University-wide body of opinion which is achieved through the members of Court and Academic Council who are elected directly from the Academic Assembly. Though it is expected that the former will not simply see themselves as representatives of subjects and subject areas, the presence of the latter is an important component of the proposed structure since it provides a counterweight to the increased importance given to sectional academic opinion as represented by Departments and Boards of Studies.

1.11 We realise, of course, that our major proposals involve changes in the Charter and that the process might take years. However, as will be seen, we also make a number of proposals which could be implemented immediately.

1.12 We would like to make the further general point that the proposals contained in the report are not made for idealistic reasons. It is not a matter of democracy for democracy's sake or representation for the sake of representation. What is wanted is democracy to facilitate the taking of correct decisions, representation in the cause of greater efficiency. Our recommendations are not seen as any kind of panacea or instant solution of all our problems. It is hoped, quite simply that they draw some of the lessons of the first five years of the university's existence and alter course for the long haul.

1.13   In conclusion, we would like to say that, having immersed ourselves for the last three months in these matters of university government, we feel we have some idea of the hard, devoted work put in by the Principal and the small group of early pioneers. We do not wish in any sense to belittle that effort. We think, however, that an opportunity was missed of pioneering new methods of university government in a new university, that old (too old) wine was poured into a new bottle. Perhaps we should now take seriously to heart what the University Grants Committee had to say in their 1964 Report: "... we should have welcomed in the statutes of the new universities some greater changes in the system of university government".

Notes

Chapter 1

1. G. S. Osborne (1968), *Change in Scottish Education*, London, Longmans, p. 9.
2. S. S. Laurie (1886), *Lectures on the Rise and early Constitution of Universities*, London, Kegan Paul, Trench & Co, p. 9.
3. Ibid., p. 12.
4. Ibid., p. 13.
5. Ibid., p. 21.
6. Ibid, quoted on p. 27.
7. Ibid., p. 33.
8. Ibid., p. 33–4.
9. Alexander Morgan (1927), *Rise and Progress of Scottish Education*, Edinburgh, Oliver & Boyd, p. 5.
10. Ibid., p. 7. John Edgar (1893), *History of Early Scottish Education*, James Thin, Edinburgh, p. 12, says of Columba, "this famous Christian teacher", that "from his boyhood he showed a great devotion to study". He stresses that: "There was a strange vitality and reproductive power in these Scotic monasteries. From them went forth bands of earnest missionaries, even as far as Central Europe."
11. Ibid., p. 41.
12. Ibid., p. 59. Rashdall (see note 26 of Ch. 2), Vol. 2, p. 324, says "It is not only in its curriculum – in the wide range and the regular succession of subjects prescribed to its students – that the Scottish university preserves to this day the impress of the Middle Ages. Here alone perhaps in Europe were the bulk of the students in the arts faculty, till very recently, boys of about the same age as the artists of medieval Paris or Oxford. The average age is still below that of most universities. Here alone does the ancient chancellorship – no longer held by a bishop – survive side by side with the rectorship. Above all, here alone do the students .. elect the head of a university. These Scottish rectorial elections, now used as the means of paying a trien-

nial homage to some distinguished public man, reproduce more both of the outward mechanism and the ancient spirit of medieval student life than any feature of the more venerable, but also in some respects far more altered, constitutions of Oxford and Cambridge [written in 1895].

13. The Council of Valence in 855 described his heterodox views as "pultes Scotorum" (Scots porridge). He also had a distinctly pawky sense of humour. Charles the Bald having asked him "Quod distat inter sottum et Scottum?", Erigena replied, "Mensa tantum." (What's the difference between a sot and a Scot? Only the table.)

14. Ibid., p. 99.

15. Ibid., p. 104.

16. Ibid., p. 161. Quoted from Savigny, *Geschichte des Römischen Rechts*.

17. Ibid., p. 161.

18. Peter Scott (1984), *The Crisis of the University*, London, Croom Helm.

19. Laurie, op. cit., p. 187.

20. Ibid., p. 188.

Chapter 2

1. John Kerr (1910), *Scottish Education: School and University from Early Times to 1908*, Cambridge University Press, p. 28.

2. Ibid., p. 34.

3. *Times Education Supplement for Scotland (TESS)*, March 22, 1968, p. 97.

4. Sir James Irvine, CBE (1942), *The Scottish Universities* (pamphlet), Edinburgh, Oliver & Boyd, p. 8.

5. Ibid., p. 34.

6. Ibid., quoted on p. 147.

7. A. B. Cobban, *Student Revolutions, Ancient and Modern, Times Higher Education Supplement (THES)*, 28 March 1975.

8. Irvine, op. cit., p. 12.

9. Ibid., p. 16.

10. *Time to cut our longer courses, The Scotsman*, 30 October 1991, p. 20.

11. *Academics wary of separate funding, The Scotsman*, 11 December, 1991.

12. S. S. Laurie, op. cit., p. 193.

13. John Kerr, op. cit., p. 113.

14. Morgan, op. cit., quoted on p. 36.

15. Ibid., p. 25.

16. Ibid., p. 34.

17. Hume Brown, *Life of George Buchanan*.

18. Quoted in Morgan, op. cit., p. 36.

19. Sir William Hamilton, *Dissertations*, quoted in Kerr, op. cit., p. 70.

20. Alexander Morgan (1933), *Scottish University Studies (SUS)* Oxford University Press p. 59.

21. Laurie, op. cit., pp. 273–47.
22. Morgan, op. cit., p. 593.
23. H. F. Kearney (1970), *Scholars and Gentlemen: Universities and Society in Pre-industrial Britain, 1500–1700,* London, Faber, p. 154.
24. H. M. Knox (1953), *250 Years of Scottish Education, 1696–1946* Edinburgh, Oliver & Boyd.
25. Morgan, op. cit., p. 1394.
26. Hastings Rashdall (1936), *The Universities of Europe in the Middle Ages, Vol. 2* (Oxford University Press), pp. 322–3.
27. Morgan, op. cit., pp. 72–3.
28. James Scotland (1969), *The History of Scottish Education,* 2 vols, London, University of London Press.
29. Both quotations from Morgan, *Rise and Progress of Scottish Education,* pp. 50–53.
30. V. H. H. Green (1969), *The Universities,* Harmondsworth, Pelican, pp. 77–92.
31. Ronald G. Cant, 'The Universities' in R. H. Campbell and Andrew Skinner, eds (1983), *The Origins and Nature of the Scottish Enlightenment,* John Donald p. 45.
32. Ibid., p. 55.
33. Ibid., p. 59.
34. R. H. Campbell, 'The Enlightenment and the Economy', in *The Origins and Nature of the Scottish Enlightenment,* p. 15.
35. Andrew McPherson, *Selections and Survivals: A Sociology of the Ancient Scottish Universities* in *Knowledge, Education and Cultural Change,* Richard Brown, ed. (1974), p. 167.
36. Ibid., p. 168.
37. Ibid., Note 25, p. 190.
38. Ibid., p. 169.
39. D. J. Withrington 'Education and Society in the eighteenth Century' in *Scotland in the Age of Enlightenment* (1970), eds N. T. Phillipson and R. Mitcheson, Edinburgh, EUP, p. 172.
40. From his evidence given to the 1826 Commission on the Universities and Colleges of Scotland.
41. Lyon Playfair (1876), quoted in Green, op. cit., p. 118

Chapter 3

1. Quoted in H. F. Kearney (1970), *Scholars and Gentlemen: Universities and Society in Pre-industrial Britain, 1500–1700,* London, Faber.
2. Ibid., p. 24.
3. Ibid., p. 27.
4. Ibid., p. 30.
5. Ibid., p. 129.
6. Ibid., p. 129. This is a reference by the author to a paper by Hugh Trevor-Roper, *Scotland and the Puritan Revolution.*
7. Ibid., p. 149.

8. Ibid., p. 169.
9. Green, op. cit., p. 16.
10. Ibid., p. 50.
11. Ibid., p. 47.
12. Sir Charles Grant Robertson (1930 & 1944), *The British Universities*.
13. A. H. Halsey, 'Oxford's Power Game', in *THES*, 6 January 1984.
14. Brian Simon, *Studies in Higher Education*, Vol. 8 No. 1 (1983).
15. Laurie, op. cit., p. 233.
16. Michael Sanderson, 'Fire and Crucible of Social Change – Universities in the nineteenth Century 1850–1914', *THES*, 28 February 1975.
17. Green, op. cit., p. 50.
18. Ibid., pp. 51–2.
19. Dr. Colin Radford, Reader in Philosophy at the University of Kent, *THES*, 9 September 1983.
20. Edward Copleston (1810), *A Reply to the Calumnies of the Edinburgh Review against Oxford*.
21. William Whewell (1837), *On the Principles of English University Education*.
22. R. L. Edgworth (1810), *Essays on Professional Education*.
23. Sidney Smith (1810), in the *Edinburgh Review*.
24. Edward Copleston, in the *Quarterly Review*.
25. C. A. Bristed (1852), *Five Years in an English University*, New York.
26. Mark Pattison (1668,) *Suggestions on Academical Organization*.
27. 1876, *Address on Education*.
28. See note 39, Chapter 2.
29. For this whole debate, see Sanderson, op. cit.
30. Sheldon Rothblatt (1968), *Revolution of the Dons*, London, Faber & Faber, p. 20.
31. Albert Mansbridge (1923), *The Older Universities of England*, quoted in Rothblatt p. 31.
32. Brian Simon, *Studies in the History of Education 1780–1870*, London.
33. Rothblatt, op. cit., p. 48.
34. Ibid., pp. 183–4.
35. Ibid., p. 199.
36. *University Education and Business: A report by a committee appointed by the Cambridge University Appointments Board*, 1946 pp. 20–1, 41, 45.
37. Jasper Rose and John Ziman (1964), *Camford Observed*, London, Gollancz, p. 13.
38. Ibid., p. 35.
39. Ibid., p. 40.
40. Ibid., p. 104.
41. Ibid., p. 129.
42. Ibid., p. 127.
43. Ibid., p. 221.
44. A. H. Halsey and Trow (1971), *The British Academics*, London, Faber & Faber.

Faber & Faber.
45. W. B. Gallie (1960), *A. D. Lindsay and the Keele Experiment*
     London, Chatto & Windus, p. 66.
46. Macdonald Daly and Colin Troup, 'Oxford no' come back again',
     THES, 6 January 1989.
47. Readers of Sir Walter Scott may remember a similar, though fictional,
     encounter in England some 250 years earlier between Jeanie Deans, the
     simple, loyal and courageous heroine of *The Heart of Midlothian* and
     the Scottish wife of a York innkeeper: "The hostess, as we have said,
     was her countrywoman, and the eagerness with which Scottish people
     meet, communicate, and, to the extent of their power, assist each other,
     although it is often objected to us as a prejudice and narrowness of
     sentiment, seems, on the contrary, to arise from a most justifiable and
     honourable feeling of patriotism, combined with a conviction, which,
     if undeserved, would long since have been confuted by experience,
     that the habits and principles of the nation are a sort of guarantee for
     the character of the individual. At any rate, if the extensive influence
     of this national partiality be considered as an additional tie, binding
     man to man, and calling forth the good offices of such as can render
     them to the countryman who happens to need them, we think it must
     be found to exceed, as an active and efficient motive to generosity, that
     more impartial and wider principle of general benevolence, which we
     have sometimes seen pleaded as an excuse for assisting no individual
     whatsoever." Everyman Edition (1956), pp. 298.

Chapter 4
1.   See Chapter 3, note 44.
2.   L. J. Saunders (1950), *Scottish Democracy 1815–1840*, Edinburgh,
     Oliver & Boyd, p. 309.
3.   Quoted in Paul H. Scott (1991), *Towards Independence*, Edinburgh,
     Polygon, p. 83.
4.   Saunders, op. cit., p. 310.
5.   Osborne, op. cit., p. 10.
6.   1826 Universities (Scotland) Commission: Edinburgh University, evi-
     dence of Francis Jeffrey, p. 393.
7.   Quoted in Saunders, op. cit., p. 357.
8.   Ibid., p. 359.
9.   R. E. Bell, for example. A proudly self-proclaimed Englishman, he
     was for long editor of the *Scottish Educational Review*. Also Walter
     Humes, R. D. Anderson.
10. A. F. McPherson. See Chapter 2, note 35.
11. See note 6. Universities Commission General Report.
12. Published in 1892. Name of author unknown. The reference
     to easier and faster communication with England is echoed in
     Michael Lynch (1991) *Scotland: A New History*, London, Century,
     p. 357.
13. Henry Cockburn, *Memorials of his Time*, Chicago, 1974.
14. L. J. Saunders, op. cit., p. 364.

15. H. J. Hanham (1969), *Scottish Nationalism*, London, Faber & Faber See also Lynch, op. cit., p. 357.

16. Professor J. S. Blackie (1855), *On the Advancement of Learning in Scotland*, Edinburgh. (Quoted in George Elder Davie (1961) *The Democratic Intellect*, Edinburgh University Press, p. 43.) See also the *Edinburgh Review*, Vol. 107, pp. 90–1: "The Indian Civil Service was thrown open to competition, and, at the very first trial, those candidates who had been educated in Scotland failed egregiously. Small wonder then that the alternative that was placed before the people of Scotland, either of renouncing for their children the highest and most lucrative branch of the coveted service, or of improving their educational institutions, should have given little cause for hesitation."

    There are only two things wrong with this statement. The alternative was not, of course, 'placed before the people of Scotland'. It was placed before the professional upper middle class, a very small but very powerful section of the population. Secondly, the use of the word 'improving' very much begs the question.

17. This handicapping of young Scots still continues today by the direct comparison, at Scottish university admissions boards, of specialized A-levels and the broader Scottish Highers. *Plus ça change ...*

18. *The Edinburgh Review*, Vol. 107, pp. 99–100.

19. Osborne, op. cit., p. 5.

20. See Chapter 2, note 40.

21. See note 12 above.

22. It is often said that there are recurring fashions in education. It would be equally true to say that there are stubborn long-term trends. It will not have escaped the reader's notice that, in early 1992, the Howie Report recommended that the Scottish secondary school course be extended from five to six years for university entrance. This was jumped on, even before publication, by such luminaries of the English higher education scene as Sir Christopher Ball (student, fellow and college provost at Oxford) and Dr John Ashworth (Director of the London School of Economics and former adviser to Mrs Thatcher) to propose that the traditional Scottish four-year honours course be reduced to three as in the universities of England – which are quite unique in this respect.

23. Editorial comment in J. C. Shairp (1856), *The Wants of the Scots Universities and Some of the Remedies*, Edinburgh.

24. Knox, op. cit., p. 94.

25. Ibid., p. 163.

26. A. F. McPherson, *Selections and Survivals: a Sociology of the Ancient Scottish Universities*, in R. Brown, ed. (1973), *Knowledge, Education and Cultural Change: Papers in the Sociology of Education*, London.

27. Walter M. Humes and H. Paterson, eds (1983), *Scottish Culture and Scottish Education*, Edinburgh, John Donaldson, p. 117.

28. *TESS*, 12 January 1973, A. F. McPherson, *Nobody Wants an Ordinary Degree Nowadays*.

29. See note 21 above.

30. See note 16 above.
31. Quoted in J. David Hoeveler Jun. (1981), *James McCosh and the Scottish Intellectual Tradition: from Glasgow to Princeton*, Princeton University Press, p. 40.
32. See note 21 above.
33. James McCosh (1875), *The Scottish Philosophy*, Georg Olms, Hildesheim 1966 (Copy of London edition of 1875), p. 62.
34. Osborne, op. cit., p. 4
35. Knox, op. cit., p. 242.
36. Sir Fred Clark (1948), *Freedom in the Educated Society*.

Chapter 5
1. J. David Hoeveler Jnr. (1981), *James McCosh and the Scottish Intellectual Tradition*, Princeton University Press, p. x.
2. Lynch, op. cit., p. 354.
3. *THES*, 31 July 1981. In a review of Hoeveler's book T. D. Campbell says: "Professor Hoeveler convincingly presents McCosh as an exemplar of the enormous impact of Scottish philosophy and educational practices on the intellectual culture of American society in the late nineteenth century and on the foundation of North American university education."
4. Hoeveler, op. cit., p. 4.
5. McCosh, op. cit.
6. William C. Rives, *The Life and Times of Madison*. Reprint of 1859–68 edition by Little, Brown & Co. of Boston, Mass.
7. Carl Sagan (1977), *The Dragons of Eden: Speculations on the Evolution of Human Intelligence*, Hodder & Stoughton, p. 183.
8. McCosh, op. cit., p. 190.
9. Ibid., p. 232.
10. T. D. Campbell review: "The objectives for which McCosh strove at Princeton included the introduction of a partially elective system covering a wide range of curricular choice including physics, chemistry, psychology, political science, history and modern languages, the encouragement of graduate study and original research in these areas, and the increase and geographical broadening of the student enrolment, all of which had to be supported by an extensive building programme . McCosh saw the college in personal and pastoral terms and sought to avoid the detachment of teachers from their young students. Much of his influence was due to the inspiration of his infectious intellectual enthusiasms in the classroom."
11. Ibid., p. 240.
12. Ibid., p. 247.
13. Ibid., p. 249.
14. Ibid.: "The uniting theme of McCosh's life was his commitment to *the Scottish philosophy*. His best-known work is *The Scottish Philosophy from Hutcheson to Hamilton* (1875), in which he traces the development of the *common sense* philosophy, which opposed both radical

empiricism and pure idealism by vindicating the reality of the external world and the objectivity of moral principles through the analysis of human experience. Those aspects of the Scottish philosophy which McCosh championed were its dogged realism, its rootedness in the evidence of consciousness and its defence of the autonomy of the moral and spiritual world. This is the philosophy of Thomas Reid rather than David Hume whose unwarranted scepticism McCosh regarded as an aberration, as mistaken at one extreme as Kantian idealism at the other. McCosh's own work is devoted to the thesis that observation of the material world and introspection of human mental and emotional operations are sufficient to establish the existence of matter, the reality of causal power, the bindingness of moral obligation."

15.   Ibid.: "McCosh's religious objectives do not seem to have weakened the rigour of his scholarship . where choices had to be made between the domain of science and that of religion he does not appear to have used the latter to exclude the former. This is well illustrated by his willingness to accommodate and defend evolutionary theory against the biblical fundamentalists. A true polymath, McCosh indulged in amateur botanical and biological studies. Under the influence of the pre-Darwinian evolutionists such as Robert Chalmers, McCosh published a collaborative work, *Typical Forms and Special Ends in Creation (1855)*, a morphological study which drew attention to organic patterns recurring in different species and might have gained more attention had it not been overtaken by the publication of the *Origin of Species*."

16.   Thomas Reid (1785), *Essays on the Intellectual Powers of Man*.

17.   *THES*, 1 October 1990. Letter from Dugald Murdoch, Department of Philosophy, University of Stockholm.

18.   Martin Trow, *American Higher Education – past, present and future* in *Studies in Higher Education* (SHE), Vol. 14, No. 1, 1989.

19.   Ibid.

20.   Saul Bellow (1953), *The Adventures of Augie March*, Penguin, 1966, p. 148.

21.   James Scotland (1969), *The History of Scottish Education*, 2 vols, London, University of London Press.

22.   These quotations are taken from chapter 5 of Michael Allen (1988), *The Goals of Universities*, Society for Research into Higher Education (SRHE) and the Open University.

23.   Graeme C. Moodie, *Debates about Higher Education Quality in Britain and the USA*, SHE, Vol. 14 1989.

24.   McConnell, Berdahl and Fay (1973), *The British and American Transformations*, University of California at Berkeley.

25.   All quotations in this section are taken from Robin S. Harris (1976), *A History of Higher Education in Canada 1663–1960*, Toronto, the University of Toronto Press, pp. 32–3.

26.   P. H. Partridge, 'Anderson as Educator', in D. Z. Phillips Ed. (1980), *Education and Inquiry: John Anderson*, Blackwell.

27.   Ibid.

27. Ibid.
28. John Burnet (1929), *Essays and Addresses*, London, Macmillan.
29. J. Mackie, 'Anderson's Theory of Education', in Phillips, op. cit.,
     p. 11.
30. Ibid.
31. Ibid., p. 143. This paper was published in 1935.
32. Ian Carter, *Dust-up over Kiwi Polish*, THES, 26 May 1989.
33. Ibid.
34. Ibid.

Chapter 6
 1. W. B. Gallie, op. cit.
 2. Ibid., pp. 24–5.
 3. In his paper *Philosophy as the Criticism of Standards*.
 4. A. D. Lindsay, *The Modern Democratic State*.
 5. Quoted in an article on Newman, Pattison and Jowett by A. H. Halsey
     in the *THES*, 15 March 1974.
 6. *THES*, 16 November 1990: Harold Perkin, 'The Last Virgin Births:
     England's new universities': "The dream of the new universities was
     to shake English higher education out of its narrow, specialised, elitist
     academic rut; *to provide a broader foundation for later specializa-
     tion* both for academics and professionals in a more rapidly changing
     world; to educate a new generation of students drawn from both sexes
     and a wider, more democratic swathe of society; to strengthen the
     bond between teaching and research, and to introduce new disciplines
     and linkages more closely geared to surrounding industry, govern-
     ment and social life; to restore the sense of community on a full-time
     integrated campus; to make the universities the focus of intellectual
     and cultural life in their areas; and to make their mark in the wider
     world by networking with foreign scholars and by research in and for
     developing countries." (our italics.)
 7. Gallie, op. cit., p. 77.
 8. Ibid., pp. 92–3.
 9. John Nichol (1888), *Scotch University Reform*, Glasgow, James
     Maclehose & Sons p. 21.
10. Gallie, op. cit., p. 108
11. David Daiches, ed. (1964), *The Idea of a New University: an experi-
     ment in Sussex*, London, Andre Deutsch.
12. J. P. Corbett, 'Opening the Mind' in Daiches, op. cit., p. 26.
13. E. G. Edwards (1982), *Higher Education for Everyone*, Spokesman
     p. 150.
14. Daiches, op. cit., p. 28.
15. Ibid., p. 32.
16. Asa Briggs, 'Drawing a New Map of Learning' in Daiches, op. cit.
17. This fact in itself is incontrovertible evidence of the anglicization of
     Scotland's universities, since they had done without honours degrees
     for centuries and were compelled, as we have seen in Chapter 4, to
     accept them by Acts of Parliament in the late nineteenth century after

their invention at Oxford. The claim by some authors that it was because they corresponded better to the needs of Scottish society in the late Victorian period is severely undermined by Professor Briggs' call for more critical study of them by intellectual and social historians.

18. Perkin (op. cit.) says there was a backlash within the decade. The new universities were seen as a retreat to an unreal world of academic isolation, "a rural idyll far from the madding crowd." In Perkin's view this backlash represents an "anti-intellectual strain in the English – not the Welsh or the Scots – which sees education not as an open road to advancement for everyone but as the reinforcement of class privilege and discrimination." A sort of inverted *Jude the Obscure* syndrome. The new universities could not solve the problems of British higher education. "They are embedded in English culture, in the whole attitude to higher education, and in the English class system. Snobbery and hierarchy pervade the whole of education and frustrate the democratic movement towards meritocracy, which the establishment pays lip service to but perpetuates in practice. The system is as elitist as ever, with Oxford and Cambridge, still dominated by students from the independent schools, at the top, and the polys and local colleges at the bottom. And that reinforces the narrowly specialized curriculum, which pigeonholes students and handicaps them in adapting to new opportunities and careers. So the new universities' dream of a new map of learning has not been realized. What we need in the 1990s is not just more new universities but *the one dream that matters, the renewal of British higher education as a whole* (our italics).

19. *TESS*, 2 January 1970.

20. There had been a somewhat similar reaction from students at Sussex. According to a *THES* leader of 16 February 1973, entitled *New Look for Sussex Arts/Science Scheme*, "Students resented their time was being wasted in a woolly gesture to bridging C. P. Snow's two cultures. What has been discovered is that, however desirable, it is not possible to introduce arts and social science undergraduates to scientific method in any rigorous way when their last brush with science was very likely studying the development of the tadpole for O-level biology. *Years of specialization cannot be eroded and the ignorance of a major part of human knowledge compensated for in a course of seminars, however well planned.* The situation is not the university's fault. It is the legacy of a school curriculum which is still tied to preparing people for entry to specialist courses" (our italics).

21. Sir Kenneth Alexander, 'Higher Education – A Personal View' in *Scottish Educational Review*, Vol. 20, No. 2, November 1988, p. 77.

22. Ibid.

23. Edwards, op. cit.

24. Ibid., p. 12.

25. Ibid., p. 58 This is the same meritocratic phenomenon as when, according to Rothblatt, entry to Oxford and Cambridge was opened to competitive examination.

26. Ibid., p. 17.

27. Ibid., p. 19.
28. Ibid., p. 46.
29. Ibid., p. 21.
30. Ibid., p. 22.
31. Ibid., p. 160.
32. Ibid., p. 51.
33. Ibid., p. 163.
34. Ibid., p. 91.
35. Quoted in Edwards, op. cit., p. 32.
36. Ibid., p. 114.
37. Ibid., p. 172.
38. Ibid., p. 173.
39. Justification is provided for this strong claim by George Bereday (1973), *Universities for All*, San Francisco, Jossey-Bass, p. 35: "We are faced with a fact that might seem astonishing at first sight: with a given selection system, represented by set academic standards and examinations in each generation, an increasing proportion of the population succeeds in clearing each academic hurdle. The explosion of numbers has occurred and will continue *in spite of*, or at least without relation to, scholastic selection . . . The reasons, discovered by the North American countries, seem to lie in the historical development of literacy. The story of European university enrolment today is the sequel to the expansion of elementary education yesterday. Perhaps the time has come to lay down the axiom that *literacy, and hence the capacity for success in schools, is cumulative over the generations.* When literacy is limited, school enrolment can be limited. Once the circle of simple literacy schools is widened, the widening of the circles of higher schools must inevitably follow. The first generation illiterate produces a literate second generation, a third generation capable of traditional secondary education, and a fourth generation capable of higher education. Enough of today's intellectuals are the great-grandsons of ploughmen to make this simple historical truth self-evident."
40. Ibid., p. 135.
41. Ibid., p. 136. Actually Adam Smith was Professor of Moral Philosophy at Glasgow. He only started on the *Wealth of Nations* when he became tutor to the son of the Duke of Buccleuch, possibly to allay the boredom inherent in such a post, as a letter to David Hume seems to imply.
42. Ibid., p. 137.
43. The *THES* of 3 February 1984 contains an article entitled 'New Foundations for a General Approach', by Alan Wilson, Professor of Urban and Regional Geography at the University of Leeds, which demonstrates the need for a return to a general approach in higher education. Professor Wilson says that when faced with first-year students who had taken different geography A-level syllabuses with little in common he used to argue that he would have preferred them to have A-levels in English, philosophy and maths. "Then we could start from

scratch with the appropriate tools and equipment." Now, however, he wonders whether it is possible to define an "enabling" syllabus which provides a foundation for the study of particular disciplines. He would call it a "Foundation syllabus", based on methodological disciplines, offering tools which could be applied to other disciplines with "substantive system" interests, physics, economics, psychology, or whatever. He criticises the way in which English, philosophy and maths are taught: the first concentrates too much on literature and reading and not enough on writing skills; the second has abdicated from the central concerns of the rest of us; and too much of mathematics is either narrowly 'applied' or exaltedly pure.

Wilson would wish to see an interdisciplinary degree and gives an outline framework of it. There should be three types of courses:

1) *Foundation*, catering for appropriate basic skills in literacy, numeracy, mathematics, computing and philosophy;

2) *General Systems*, teaching how to handle concepts which transcend particular disciplines: evolutionary processes, the study of structure;

3) *Substantive Systems*, that is the objects of study of disciplines.

There would be many optional routes and any particular student's scheme would straddle the sciences, the human and social sciences, the arts. Part of a compulsory foundation course would be to develop an understanding of how knowledge in the different areas can be similar or different in character. The graduates would be of more use to industry, with more widely applicable skills and more experience of problem-solving. Wilson thinks that the biggest advantage of all would be that graduates would have connections to the arts, the human and social sciences, and the sciences. "Scientists would be aware of the social contest in which they work; fewer would be naive about sociology and politics."

The resemblance between this scheme and Stirling's *Approaches and Methods* is obvious, as is also the generalising approach so dear to the Scottish universities in the eighteenth and nineteenth centuries.

44. Ibid., p. 185.
45. Ibid., p. 184.
46. Ibid., p. 187.
47. Ibid., p. 147.
48. Ibid., p. 148.
49. Marcos Terena, organiser of the native village gathering at UNCED in Rio de Janeiro, June 1992. Quoted in *The Scotsman* of 13 May 1992 p. 13.

Chapter 7
1. I. F. Stone, *The Trial of Socrates*, London, Carse.
2. Robert M. Pirsig (1974), *Zen and the Art of Motorcycle Maintenance*, London, Corgi, p. 102.

3. Arnold S. Nash (1945), *The University and the Modern World*, SCM Press, p. 1.
4. Ibid., See *Preface*.
5. Charles Singer (1941), *A Short History of Science*, Oxford. Quoted in Nash op. cit..
6. Lancelot Hogben (1939), *Dangerous Thoughts*, London, p. 242.
7. Nash, op. cit., p. 50.
8. Laurie, op. cit, p. 54
9. Ibid., p. 120.
10. Ibid., p. 122.
11. Ibid., p. 122.
12. Ibid., p. 92.
13. Quoted in Laurie, op. cit., p. 233.
14. Nash, op. cit., p. 66.
15. R. H. Tawney (1929), *Religion and the Rise of Capitalism*, London, p. 39.
16. Clark Kerr (1966), *The Uses of the University*, Cambridge, Mass., Harvard University Press.
17. Jonathon Ree, 'Philosophy as an Academic Discipline', in SHE, Vol. 3, No. 1, March 1978.
18. Sir William Hamilton (1853), *Discussions*, 2nd edition, London.
19. Roy Edgley, 'Plato to Nato', THES, 28 November 1975.
20. Letter in *Scotland on Sunday*, January 1989. Kelman is referring to a proposal to shut down the philosophy department at Strathclyde University.
21. Edgley, op. cit.
22. Peter Abbs, 'Signs on the Way to Understanding' in THES, 10 November 1989.
23. At the United Nations Conference on Environment and Development, known as the Earth Summit, held in Brazil in June 1992.
24. Abbs, op. cit.
25. Ibid.
26. A. R. Rodger, 'Aims of Education and the Influence of Positivism', in SHE, Vol. 3, No. 1, May 1971.
27. In debate with F. C. Copleston in Pai and Myers eds (1967), *Philosophic Problems and Education*, Phildelphia, Penn., Lippincott.
28. Rodger, op. cit.,
29. Rodger, op. cit.,
30. Peter Scott. From a paper entitled *Ideologies of the University* in Gunnar Bergendal ed. (1983), *Knowledge and Higher Education*.
31. Roy Niblett, in a review of *The Closing of the American Mind*, by Allan Bloom (1987), in SHE, Vol. 14, No. 2, 1989.
32. Alfred North Whitehead (1927), *Science and the Modern World*, Cambridge University Press, p. 25.
33. Ibid., p. 25.
34. Ibid., p. 26.
35. Ibid., p. 27.
36. Ibid., p. 63.

37. Ibid., p. 65.

38. Ibid., p. 83.

39. Ibid., p. 84.

40. Ibid., p. 86.

41. Ibid., p. 204.

42. Ibid., p. 225.

43. Op. cit.

44. The population problem was not even one of the main items on the agenda of the Earth Summit. See note 16.

45. Arthur Peacocke, ed. (1985), *Reductionism in Academic Disciplines*, Guildford SRHE and NFER–Nelson, p. 3.

46. In an article in *THES*, 9 August 1991, Douglas Kell and G. Richey Welch deal with the tension between reductionism and complexity facing biologists, and particularly with the problem of "hierarchical reductionism". They illustrate the problem with a quotation from Richard Dawkins: "The biologist tries to explain the workings, and comings into existence, of complex things in terms of simpler things. He can regard his task as done when he has arrived at entities so simple that they can be safely handed over to the physicists." This strategy, they say, assumes that living systems are arranged hierarchically, thus: molecules>macromolecules>organelles>cells> tissues>organisms>populations>socio-ecosystems. This "downward causation" is strongly questioned. One must distinguish between the fruitful method of reductionism and the philosophy of reductionism. In moving from level to level there is always a 'residue' that requires a new hypothesis for its solution. The authors quote Sir Karl Popper on this: "Not only is philosophical reductionism a mistake, but the belief that the method of reduction can achieve complete reductions is, it seems, mistaken too. We live, it appears, in a world of 'emergent' evolution; of problems whose solutions, if they are solved, beget new and deeper problems."

   Thus the greatest concern in the contest between biological reductionism and holism is the transition between the hierarchical levels. In an analytical approach there is always a point at which reductionism fails – where the crucial concepts of "irreversibility" and "hierarchical constraints" come into play. Our scientific heritage is to reduce in order to understand. Yet physicists have still to come to grips with the synthetic aspect of understanding. "Analysis is not the reverse of synthesis. If we 'reduce' what is uniquely found in nature, we cannot expect to put the pieces together again, even with the help of 'all the King's horses and all the King's men'."

47. Steven Rose, *The Roots and Social Foundations of Biological Reductionism* in Peacocke, op. cit.

48. Ibid., p. 31.

49. Ibid., p. 38.

50. Other examples of the genre are Robert Ardrey's, *The Territorial Imperative* and Desmond Morris, *The Naked Ape*.

51. Mary Midgley, *Reduction and the Manufacture of Demons* in Peacocke op. cit., p. 47.
52. Ibid., p. 48.
53. Ibid., p. 48
54. Sinclair Goodlad, *Administrative Reductionism*, in Peacocke, op. cit. p. 144.
55. This is particularly harmful for Scottish students since their Highers are broader and less specialized than English A-levels. No allowance is made for this by admissions officers, so that Scottish candidates for entry to university are gravely disadvantaged, both at entry – if they do succeed in getting in – and later. This is stated in a report *School to Higher Education: Bridging the Gap* (May 1991), prepared by the Centre for Learning and Instruction of the University of Edinburgh. The report says it is clear that A-level students are the majority in many courses and that this is "creating a learning environment inimical to students with Highers alone."

Chapter 8
1. Nash, op. cit., p. 9.
2. Ronald Barnett (1990), *The Idea of Higher Education*, Chap. 1 pp. 3–4.
3. R. B. Cottrell *et al.* (1938), *Human Affairs*, London.
4. H. Lawson and L. Appignanesi, eds (1989), *Dismantling Truth*, London, Weidenfeld & Nicholson. Quoted in Barnet, op. cit.
5. Barnett, op. cit., p. 35.
6. Quoted in Barnet, op. cit., p. 35.
7. Ibid p. 36.
8. Ibid, pp. 41–2.
9. *THES*, 20 January 1989.
10. *THES*, 17 February 1989.
11. Feyerabend (1978), *Against Method* and (1982) *Science in a Free Society*, London, Verso.
12. T. S. Kuhn (1970), *The Structure of Scientific Revolutions*, University of Chicago Press and London, Verso.
13. J. Lyotard (1984) *The Postmodern Condition*, Manchester University Press.
14. J. Habermas (1978), *Knowledge and Human Interests*, London, Heinemann.
15. Barnett, op. cit., p. 42
16. Habermas, op. cit.
17. Barnet, op. cit.
18. Allan Bloom (1987), *The Closing of the American Mind*, New York, Simon & Schuster, p. 22.
19. Ibid., p. 337.
20. Ibid., p. 293.
21. Ibid., p. 312.
22. I cannot resist sharing with the reader a gem from Bloom's text:

    "Alexander Koyré, the historian of science, said his appreciation of America was great when, at Chicago, a student spoke in a paper of Mr. Aristotle."

23. Ibid., p. 336.
24. Ibid., p. 357.
25. Michael Polanyi (1958), *Personal Knowledge – Towards a Post-Critical Philosophy*, London, Routledge & Kegan Paul.
26. Quoted in M. Reeves (1988),*The Crisis in Higher Education*, Milton Keynes, Open University Press.
27. We may judge from this the enormous damage done to countries like Scotland, whose native culture has for centuries been, and is still being, dominated and destroyed by external penetration and takeover.
28. Iris Murdoch (i970), *The Sovereignty of Good*, London, Routledge & Kegan Paul; quoted in Reeves op. cit., p. 18.
29. Quoted in Reeves, op. cit., p. 30.
30. Both quotes from Reeves, op. cit., p. 31.
31. Donald Kennedy, President of Stanford University, *Creating a Perfect Match* in *THES*, 17 December 1982. Taken from Kennedy's University of Oregon Fall Convocation Address.
32. Nash, op. cit.
33. Ibid., pp. 76–77.
34. *Scotland on Sunday, Spectrum*, p. 35, Sue Innes, *The Danger when there's Nothing left to Say.*
35. J. K. Galbraith (1992), *The Culture of Contentment.*
36. Allan Bloom, op. cit., p. 169.
37. Alasdair MacIntyre (1981), *After Virtue – a study in moral theory*, London, Duckworth.
38. Patrick Nuttgens (1988), *What Should we Teach and How should we Teach it – Aims and Purposes of Higher Education*, Aldershot, Wildwood.
39. Nuttgens is another of these excellent English writers on higher education – like A. H. Halsey or Ronald Barnet – who tend to ignore Scotland's contribution. It would be quite untrue to say that higher education in Scotland had disliked and feared technology for the last 150 years. It was, after all, the Scottish universities which produced most of the men who made the Industrial Revolution.
40. Nuttgens, op. cit.

Chapter 9
1. Published in 1957.
2. Macmurray (1957), *The Self as Agent*, London, Faber p. 21.
3. Ibid., p. 29.
4. Ibid.
5. Ibid., p. 73.
6. Ibid., p. 118.
7. MacIntyre, op. cit., p. 77.
8. Ibid., p. 83.

9. Ibid., p. 112.
10. Ibid., p. 79.
11. Ibid., p. 146.
12. Ibid., p. 211.
13. Ibid., p. 222.
14. Ibid., p. 241.
15. Alasdair MacIntyre (1988), *Whose Justice? Which Rationality?*, London, Duckworth p. 174.
16. Laurance James Saunders (1950), *Scottish Democracy 1815–1840* (Edinburgh, Oliver & Boyd), speaks of the influence of the Mechanics' Institute at Haddington which was founded in 1823. He quotes Samuel Smiles' *Autobiography* (1905): "These lectures were well attended by the leading mechanics of the town. I remember three of them who worked as carpenters. They made carts, ploughs and agricultural implements. Two of these men made money enough during the summer to pay for their class instruction at Edinburgh University during the winter. One became the minister of a presbyterian congregation at Blackburn; another became master of a large public school at Hull; and the third, who remained a mechanic, rose higher than the others. His name was Andrew Lamb, General Manager of the P & O Steamship Company."
17. Or, as the Justice-Clerk, Lord Braxfield, put it at the trial of Thomas Muir in 1793: "A Government in every country should be like a Corporation, and in the country it is made up of the landed interest, which alone has the right to be represented." Quoted in Lynch, op. cit., p. 386.
18. *Scotland on Sunday Magazine*, 18 August 1991. In an article entitled 'Days of Heaven' the poet Iain Crichton Smith quotes Warden Philip Newell of the Iona Community: "In the Celtic Church Mary is not seen as the High Queen of Heaven, but as the barefooted country girl. The Celts had a sense of Heaven and Earth as being inescapably bonded together. The Earth was shot through with the presence of God. There was *no spirit/matter divide*." (our italics).
19. John Purser (1992), *Scotland's Music*, Edinburgh, Mainstream
20. In setting up the Scotch College at the University of Paris in 1325, David, Bishop of Moray, referred to the "innumerable swarm of our youthful countrymen who at present infest every part of the Continent." James Lorimer says, "There was scarcely a university on the Continent where Scotchmen did not hold professorial chairs during the 16th century." Dr Irving, in his *Lives of Scottish Writers*, mentions no less than 33 names of countrymen who during this time were professors in France, Germany and Holland.
21. Alexander Broadie (1990), *The Tradition of Scottish Philosophy*, Edinburgh, Polygon.
22. *Scotland on Sunday Summit City Supplement*, December 1992. In an article entitled 'An Intricate Past of Scots, Rats and Lice', Christopher Harvie says: "Recently, Professor Alex Broadie of Glasgow has shown how Scots philosophies of this generation (the generation of John

Mair and Buchanan) had created a 'common sense' tradition well in
advance of Hutcheson and Reid in the eighteenth century."
23. In a review of David McCrone's *Understanding Scotland: The
Sociology of a Stateless Nation* in the *Glasgow Herald* of 11 June
1992, Alan Bold says, "Thomas Reid, for whom a tree was a tree was
a tree and reality was mind-independent."
24. *Cencrastus*, No. 25, Spring 1987. In an article entitled *The Continuity of Scottish Philosophy*, Alexander Broadie asks how the Scottish
Enlightenment could have happened in a small poor country far from
Europe's cultural centres. Such a glorious flourish could not have
come from nothing; in fact it had great cultural and philosophical
antecedents in the Scottish Renaissance of the sixteenth century, as he
shows in his book. For example Mair and Lokert were concerned to
defend the theory of epistemological realism, as did Reid in the eighteenth century. So Mair and Reid were discussing the same problems
and providing the same solutions. Broadie concludes that the Scots
are a nation of philosophers, and that this trait "may surface again."
In my view it already has in the persons of Macmurray, MacIntyre
and others.

Chapter 10
1. Henry Thomas Buckle (1861), *On Scotland and the Scotch Intellect*,
Reprinted 1970, University of Chicago Press.
2. Ibid., p. xviii. Editor's introduction.
3. Ibid., p. xxviii.
4. Ibid.
5. See Nigel Grant (1982), *The Crisis of Scottish Education*, Saltire Society Pamphlet, passim.
6. Davie, op. cit., p. 321
7. Quoted in introduction to Buckle, op. cit.
8. Ibid.
9. David Hume (1789), *History of England*, London, Vol. vi, pp. 194–5.
10. John Mackinnon Robertson (1895), *Buckle and his Critics: a Study
in Sociology*, London. Quoted in introduction to Buckle, op, cit.
11. Buckle, op. cit., pp. 26–63 passim. This last point is strongly
reinforced by remarks which Buckle makes on p. 241; "In no other
Protestant country have they (the clergy) exercised such control over
the universities; not only the doctrines taught, but also the mode of
teaching them, being, in Scotland, placed under the supervision of the
Church." The double standards are blatant.
12. Ibid., pp. 138–141. I find it astonishing that a number of contemporary historians of Scottish education, particularly higher education,
can maintain, in the face of such damning evidence, that Scottish education was not subjected to a sustained campaign of anglicization.
13. Ibid., p. 154.
14. Ibid., p. 160. One wonders what Buckle would have made of James

McCosh, an evangelical who walked out with Chalmers in 1843 but took Darwinism in his stride in a way the Church of England found impossible.

15. Ibid., p. 242.
16. Ibid., p. 252.
17. Ibid., p. 284.
18. Ibid., p. 297: Thomas Reid, *Inquiry into the Human Mind*, pp 232–3.
19. Ibid., p. 298: Thomas Reid, *Essays*, Vol. ii, p. 218.
20. Ibid., p. 298: Reid *Essays*, Vol. iii, p. 375.
21. Ibid., p. 317.
22. Ibid., p. 318.
23. Ibid., p. 320.
24. Ibid., p. 341.
25. Ibid., p. 361.
26. Ibid., p. 362.
27. David Daiches, ed. (1981), *A Companion to Scottish Culture*, London.
28. Ibid.
29. The same concern that drove Albert Einstein and Bertrand Russell to write to President Truman warning him of the awful dangers of nuclear weapons, whereas an Oppenheimer was transfixed in horrified immobility. It was also Einstein who demonstrated the validity of the Scottish epistemological approach: "The supreme task is to arrive at the universal elementary laws from which the cosmos can be built up by pure deduction. There is no logical path to these laws; only intuition, resting on sympathetic understanding of experience, can reach them." He even uses the same vocabulary as eighteenth century philosophers like Adam Smith.
30. This rings very true for Scots in the 1990s. For more than a decade Scots have been ruled from London by a government which is in a small minority in Scotland. Indeed in four general elections that minority fell to 11 seats out of 72, causing a historian to end his book with the following two sentences just before the fourth general election in April 1992: "Yet if Scotland manages again to evade some form of Home Rule it will be a remarkable escape story. As Oscar Wilde said of the death of Little Nell, the historian would need a heart of stone not to laugh." (Lynch, op. cit., p. 449) As we know, he was wrong. The same minority government was returned. Yet throughout the decade Scottish culture flourished almost as richly as in the eighteenth century: in painting, in poetry, in music, traditional, classical and popular, where there had never been more activity in composition; in the theatre, in the novel, etc. The number and size of annual cultural festivals that take place in Edinburgh and Glasgow is quite astonishing for such a small country.
31. Our universities have now been taken over in personnel terms since all of them have a large majority of English teaching, research and administrative staff. At least four of them have a majority of English students as well. In one I know student politics and the student radio are run by English students. It is a truly deplorable

situation for the self-confidence, even the self-respect, of the Scottish students.

32. David Daiches (1977), *Scotland and the Union*, London, p. 172.
33. Ibid., p. 195.
34. 'The Scottish Universities – Defects and Remedies', *North British Review*, Vol. 28, February–May 1858, p. 377.
35. A. F. McPherson, "Nobody Wants an Ordinary Degree". *TESS*, 12 January 1973.
36. A Senior Chief Inspector, quoted in A. F. McPherson & G. Atherton *"Graduate Teachers in Scotland"* in *Scottish Education Studies*, 2.1 pp 35–55.
37. James Bridie and M. McLaren (1949), *A Small Stir – Letters on the English*, London, p. 50.
38. An HMSCI, speaking to the Kilbrandon Commission on the Constitution in 1969.
39. See Chapter 9, Note 68.
40. Some day a book will have to be written about the innovatory talents of the Scots in so many areas, from warfare, through diplomacy and trade to mechanical inventions, in addition to philosophy, science and university teaching.
41. Lorimer. op. cit., p. 37.
42. Ibid., p. 38.
43. Ibid., p. 78.
44. See J. Derrick McClure's review of Nigel Grant's *The Crisis of Scottish Education* in SER, Vol. 14, No. 2, November 1982.
45. See note 34 above, *North British Review*, p. 379
46. Ibid., p. 380.
47. Ibid., pp. 384–5.
48. Ibid., p. 388.
49. Ibid., p. 390.
50. Ibid., p. 392.
51. *Scotch University Reform* (1888), being a reprint, with Prefatory note, of a paper *Scotch Universities, their Friends and Foes*, published in the Fortnightly Review, five years earlier. Glasgow, James Maclehose & Sons, pp. 3 & 4.
52. Ibid., p. 5.
53. Ibid., p. 6.
54. Ibid., pp. 11–15 sqq. The internal quotes are from a paper by another writer, but he gives no reference.
55. Ibid., p. 18.
56. Ibid., p. 17.
57. Ibid., p. 22

Chapter 11
1. John Clarke, ed. (1919), *Problems of National Education*, London, Preface p. xx.
2. Ibid., p. 313.

3. Ibid., p. 314.
4. Ibid., p. 316.
5. Ibid., p. 317.
6. Ibid., p. 319.
7. Ibid., pp. 321–2. I make no apology for the lengthy quotations. Most readers can have no inkling of what these classes were like, though this writer did get some faint idea in 1st Ordinary English at Edinburgh in 1942.
8. Ibid., p. 327.
9. Ibid., p. 326.
10. Ibid., p. 334.
11. Ibid., p. 340.
12. Ibid., p. 350.
13. Ibid., p. 356.
14. Ibid., p. 357.
15. Ibid., p. 361.
16. *Cencrastus*, Spring 1987.
17. *TESS*, 17 February 1984.
18. *Cencrastus*, Spring 1990. Bell speaks of the "remarkable national commitment to principles of contest mobility, to the keeping open for as long as possible and for as many people as possible the chance of self-advancement and self-fulfillment through formal education." He adds that this idea came from the Reformers (it may well go back much further than that) and "dominated Scottish arrangements till the very end of the nineteenth century", and the universities "long kept open house."
19. *Edinburgh Review*, No. 83, 1990, 'The Threat to Scottish Education' pp. 35–37.
20. Craig Beveridge and Ronald Turnbull (1989), *The Eclipse of Scottish Culture*, Edinburgh, Polygon, pp. 77–9.
21. Ibid., John Burnet, *The Classics in School and University*.
22. Ibid., p. 189.
23. John Burnet (1917), *Higher Education and the War*, London, Macmillan.
24. Ibid., p. 40.
25. Ibid., p. 45.
26. Ibid., p. 47.
27. Ibid., p. 50.
28. In John Burnet (1929), *Essays and Addresses*, London, Chatto & Windus.
29. Ibid., p. 240.
30. Ibid., p. 241.
31. Op. cit., p. 35, *Form and Matter in Classical Teaching*.
32. Ibid., p. 37.
33. Op. cit., p. 124, *Humanism in Education*.
34. Ibid., p. 119.
35. Burnet, *Higher Education and the War*, p. 67.
36. Ibid., p. 164.

37. *Revue Internationale de l'Enseignement*, liii, p. 384. Quoted in Burnet HEW, p. 169.
38. Ibid., p. 182.
39. *Educational Review*, Vol. xxxix, p. 408. Quoted in HEW, p. 212.
40. Ibid., p. 214.
41. *THES*, 29 July 1983: A leader entitled *The Scottish Experience* has some interesting things to say on this question in a modern context. Up to the time of Robbins the English and Scottish systems were clearly on a convergent course, but since the 1960s there has been a sharp reversal of trend, especially in the West, that is Glasgow and Strathclyde universities. Others kept to the English pattern. In the West the age at entry had fallen and general degrees had held their own. *The effect seems to have been to increase access to higher education in Strathclyde*. This, says the leader, could be the first dim outline of a pattern of higher education that could become more general throughout Britain. That, alas, was not to be, but the leader's reasoning seems valid. "Adding a year at the beginning rather than at the end of degree courses could stimulate access, reduce the overload of knowledge, invigorate the practice of general education – and be realistic within the context of scarce resources. On the other hand, leaving the normal age of entry (i.e. 18 in England) might undermine its role as a socializing and maturing process. Yet why should the demarcation between secondary and higher education be fixed forever at the age of 18? The historical example of Scotland and perhaps the present example of Strathclyde region suggest that it is possible to organize an excellent university system on the basis of a quite different relationship with the schools and further education.
42. Ibid., p. 218.
43. Ibid., p. 222. A. F. McPherson (see note 48 below) says that the fundamental objection to the 1889 reforms was not so much that they pushed a basic education for all down into the secondary schools, but that they "dethroned philosophy from its position. In the universities philosophy became just one among many subjects that might be taken. But, worse still, the teaching of philosophy was separated from the final steps of general education. The result is that the ordinary MA Course lacks any unifying element."
44. Ibid., p. 228.
45. Ibid., p. 227.
46. Ibid., p. 235.
47. Ibid., p. 237.
48. These details are taken from A. F. McPherson (1972), *The Generally Educated Scot: An Old Ideal in a Changing University Structure* in A. F. McPherson, D. Swift and D. Bernstein, *Eighteen-plus: The Final Selection E 282 Units 15–17*, Open University, Bletchley, pp. 5–32.
49. Ibid.
50. Isobel Lindsay, 'Scotland's Migratory Traditions', in *Radical Scotland*, No. 37, Feb-March 1989.

51. Andrew Lockhart Walker, 'The Democratic Intellect under Threat',
     in *Radical Scotland*, No. 41, Oct/Nov 1989.
52. McPherson, op. cit.
53. Ibid.
54. Ronald Barret, Patrick Nuttgens, M. Reeves, Peter Scott.
55. McPherson, op. cit.
56. J. M. Barrie (1894), *An Edinburgh Eleven*, London, Hodder &
     Stoughton.

Chapter 12

 1. *TESS*, 5 February 1971.
 2. *THES*, 8 June 1984. In an article entitled *Looking for a new Vision*
     Kenneth Lawson, who is a defender of empiricism, nonetheless says
     that there is a "sense of dissatisfaction with the empirical approach
     which at its narrowest has been described as 'number-crunching' or
     'pebble-counting'." His fear is that the hugely successful empirical
     scientific approach has led to an "explosion of knowledge" but also
     to a "disintegrating process of Western culture, and this in turn is
     leading to a "more subjective, experiential approach" which cannot
     be tested, so that we could "end up with dogma and mystical belief.
     We depart from the empirical tradition, therefore, at great cost."
         THES 6 April 1973. Speaking in a House of Lords debate, Lord
     Robbins said: "It is the organization of teaching and standards in
     the universities which are most in need of drastic revision. It is the
     continued prevalence of extreme honours specialization in the English
     universities which is at the root of what I venture to call the sickness
     in our middle range and higher education."
 3. *TESS*, 16 September 1966.
 4. *THES*, 12 July 1985.
 5. *THES*, 21 December 1973. In his regular column on higher education
     A. H. Halsey gives the answer of two leading writers on the subject;
     "Weber put his emphasis on the demand of a modern economy for
     highly trained specialist manpower, the advance of bureaucracy in all
     forms of social organization, and the 'proletarianization' of the uni-
     versity's research worker and teacher …Veblen too saw the scholar as
     a member of the thwarted class. In his analysis of the power structure
     of the higher learning in America, he emphasised the function of the
     university as itself a business enterprise in competition with other uni-
     versities, bureaucratically organized under its president or 'captain of
     erudition' in pursuit of the aims of 'notoriety, prestige and advertising
     in all its branches and bearings' at the expense of scholarship and to
     the accompaniment of a vast competitive waste of resources." (The
     prescience of these two gentlemen is quite uncanny.)
         Halsey goes on: "The subsequent literature constitutes a huge rami-
     fication on these basic themes. Higher education is now big business
     and big politics and the university is illuminated as an intellectual
     reflection of the economic and political drama of our day." His own

view of all this is: "I would assert that the civilizing mission of the university in the capitalist world is bound to bring it into conflict with the values of business and commerce. To be true to itself, the university in such a society must always struggle to maintain the distinction between value and price."

6. Spoken at a public meeting, *TESS*, 22 September 1966.
7. *TESS*, 21 October 1966.
8. *TESS*, 31 March 1969.
9. Ibid.
10. *TESS*, 25 November 1966.
11. *THES*, 12 July 1985.
12. *The Scotsman*, 14 July 1992.
13. *THES*, 16 October 1981.
14. *THES*, 5 October 1973. John Morrison, the President of Wolfson College, Cambridge, says that five realizations have come to him from 20 years in academic life: 1) The overriding concern of Oxbridge is to provide an annual supply of first-class performers, i.e. future dons. The rest are also-rans. This is known as the 'maintenance of standards' and it is applied to largely the wrong people; 2) So boys and girls must be made 'subject-minded' at the earliest possible age (15) by concentrating on a narrow area of study, thus becoming a suitable input for the "don production-line", though only 10% will ever use the specialist knowledge in their future careers; 3) This might have been all right when only 4000 people went annually into the professions, but it is ridiculous now that numbers are very much greater; 4) This intense specialization at school, supposedly to prepare pupils for university, in fact often spoils them for it. "I could not bear doing the Tudors for the fourth time." Often, too, the teachers use the lecture notes of the course the students are going to follow. "Why were they not provided with a much broader basis of interest at school?" asks Morrison; 5) His last 'realization' is the very trivial and flimsy grounds for the original choice on which "subject-mindedness" is then based.

Morrison's conclusions are that

1) "A broad school curriculum stretching across the spectrum of human knowledge would be a much better basis for a university course than the present pattern;" and

2) "The traditional aim of the university course to get people to research level after an Honours degree is inappropriate in a situation where 90% will not use specialist knowledge in subsequent careers. It should be replaced by the aim to produce men and women with lively and critical minds and the flexibility of outlook and potential required in the multifarious employments now open to graduates."

Such conclusions from a man in such a post at Cambridge after 20 years of academic life are damning. Yet it is the Scottish university traditions which are being eliminated, not those of Oxford and Cambridge.

15. Lord Robbins, *Higher Education Revisited*.
16. *TESS*, 28 December 1973.

17. *TESS*, 28 December 1973.
18. *THES*, 18 May 1990.
19. *THES*, 16 November 1990.
20. *THES*, 2 February 1990.
21. *TESS*, 5 July 1968.
22. *TESS*, 7 January 1966
23. *TESS*, 21 January 1966.
24. *TESS*, 15 November 1968.
25. The writer knew personally a young American engineer who was an excellent viola player and had studied physics, maths, French, music and philosophy at his liberal arts college in the Middle West.
26. *TESS*, 11 February 1966.
27. *TESS*, 21 July 1967.
28. Foreword to *Words and Numbers*, F. R. Bradbury ed. (1969), Edinburgh University Press.
29. *TESS*, 13 October 1967.
30. *TESS*, 20 June 1975.
31. *THES*, 20 July 1990.
32. *TESS*, 9 November 1973.
33. *TESS*, 25 December 1970.
34. The figures are now much worse. In 1989 there were 14,000 fewer graduates working in Scotland than in 1983, as mentioned earlier.
35. *TESS*, 20 June 1975.
36. *THES*, October 1973. Author Tim Robinson.
37. In Sir Christopher Ball and Heather Eggins, eds (1989), *Higher Education into the 1990s*, SRHE & Open University.
38. *THES*, 3 September 1982. In an article entitled *Specialty of the Day*.
39. Peter Scott, 'Pluralism in Diversity', *THES*, 31 August 1990.
40. *THES*, 13 July 1990.
41. J. P. B. Lovell, 'Crossing the Divide – earth science for arts students at the University of Edinburgh', in SER, Vol. 3, No. 2, October 1978.
42. *THES*, 20 July 1990.
43. *TESS*, July 1970.
44. George B. Jeffery (1950), *The Unity of Knowledge*, Cambridge University Press, pp. 47–8.
45. Ibid., p. 52.
46. Ibid., p. 53.
47. Ibid., pp. 54–5.
48. Ibid., p. 56.
49. Ortega y Gasset (1946), *The Mission of the University*, London Kegan Paul.
50. Or, as George Steiner put it: "It is a Socrates, a Mozart, a Gauss or a Galileo who, in some degree, compensate for man. It is they who, on fragile occasion, redeem the murderous imbecile mess we dignify with the name of history." *THES*, 6 March 1981, 'America as the Archive of Eden'.
51. *THES*, 2 December 1988. 'The Past in Clearer Light, a Beacon on our Future'.

52. Jacques Barzun (1969), *The American University*, Oxford University Press, p. 18.
53. Ibid., p. 203.
54. Ibid., p. 62.
55. Ibid., p. 69.
56. Ibid., p. 210.
57. Ibid., p. 213.
58. Ibid., p. 216.
59. Ibid., p. 221.
60. Ibid., p. 223.
61. Ibid., p. 229.
62. Ibid., p. 230.

Chapter 13
1. R. E. Bell, *The Growth of the Modern University*, in Hooper ed. (1971), *The Curriculum: Context, Design and Development*, Edinburgh, Oliver & Boyd.
2. Robert Anderson, 'A Higher and Wider Road', in THES 3 February 1989.
3. *Scotsman Weekend*, 27 October 1990. In a review, 'Dim views from the upper circle', of Noel Annan's, *Our Age: Portrait of a Generation*, Owen Dudley Edwards says: "His book is important in showing the world which came so strongly to dominate our university horizons after 1945, but it is so deficient in accuracy and so parochial in its emphases that its chief value seems to consist in unintentionally showing up the limitations of that world. His mention of Scottish education, in particular, is little more than condescending drivel. His mingling of intellectual assurance and indifference of scholarship has the value of indicating the poverty of the pottage for which Scottish universities surrendered so much of their birthright.".
4. Professor J. F. Allen, Professor Emeritus of Physics and Astronomy, University of St. Andrews, in a letter to the THES, 12 February 1988.
5. In 'Victorian Values', a review of R. D. Anderson's book *Education and Opportunity in Victorian Scotland – Schools and Universities*, Oxford University Press.
6. See Ch. 4, p. 60.
7. See Ch. 4, p. 66.
8. In W. Humes and H. Paterson, eds (1983), *Science, Religion and Education: A Study in Cultural Interaction*, Edinburgh, John Donald, p. 115.
9. I am reminded of one of Robert Louis Stevenson's barbs: "Beware of your sham impartialists, wolves in sheep's clothing, simpering honestly as they suppress."
10. *Modern Scotland* (1980), London.
11. It is interesting to compare D. J. Withrington's views on this with those of Hume's, in *Towards a National System 1867–72: the last years in the struggle for a Scottish Education Act* in SER, Vol. iv,

No 2, November 1972. Following the second report of the Argyll Commission on Scottish education in 1867 everyone expected legislation would come quickly. "Yet not till 1872, " says Withrington, "was Scottish legislation passed. Why did Parliament legislate for England first? And why was the Scottish Act, when it did come, so distinctively different from the Argyll proposals of five years earlier?" He adds that it was simply not true that the 1872 Act was based on Argyll, whose aim was schooling for all children, and asks why the new national Board of Education was set up in Edinburgh. His answer is that "The Commissioners were probably attempting to soften the London control of Scottish education which was exercised by the Privy Council and had raised a good deal of objection; and also to remove fears, especially those of schoolmasters, that an extended state system would only make it simpler for the Privy Council to infiltrate English principles and English preconceptions." Everything that has happened since, SED or no SOED, has shown how right the schoolmasters were.

12. THES, 23 November 1990. A leader entitled *Scotland's Opportunity* has a view on this: "The repatriation of the Scottish universities is generally seen as a national cause, a devolutionary demand. At best this is only half true. Rather it is a reform deeply consistent with the original intentions of the Treaty of Union which guaranteed Scotland the independence of its historic institutions in perpetuity within a new and more hopeful political nation. The present arrangements for the Scottish universities, therefore, are an anomaly in terms of that original union – as well as being increasingly problematical for the universities themselves and damaging to the prospects of creating a higher education system worthy of Scotland, whatever its future political condition."

13. From I. B. Macfarlane of Stirling University, in *The Scotsman*, 20 September 1974.

14. *TESS*, 31 January 1975.

15. Letter from Bruce Lenman, lecturer in Scottish history at St. Andrews, in *The Scotsman*, 20 September 1974.

16. In *The Scotsman*, 11 September 1974.

17. *TESS*, 4 January 1974.

18. *TESS*, 12 June 1981.

19. *TESS*, 15 July 1977.

20. *TESS*, 5 November 1976.

21. *TESS*, 3 April 1981.

22. *TESS*, 29 August 1975

23. *TESS*, 10 September 1976.

24. *TESS*, 16 January 1976.

25. *TESS*, 26 January 1973.

26. *TESS*, 10 December 1971.

27. *TESS*, 8 February 1974.

28. *TESS*, 22 February 1974.

29. So persuasive is Bell's siren-song that even Peter Scott, editor of that excellent higher education journal *The Times Higher Education Sup-*

plement, had the following to say, in its issue of 3 August 1984, in the first of a series of articles entitled *Towards a Common Culture 1 – There'll always be an England*: "A few would argue that Scotland and Wales have also been incorporated dishonestly in a British State dominated by the English and their native traditions suppressed. But the failure of these nationalisms to attract majority support and their lack of rancour seem to demonstrate the opposite conclusion: that our national culture, whether English or British, is a broad church that can easily embrace such separate traditions within the wide territory of 'us'." That such a perceptive writer as Peter Scott should fail to see that this 'embrace' is in fact a 'kiss of death' for Scotland's separate and philosophically different educational tradition – of which the *THES* has on a number of occasions spoken so eloquently – shows how far down the road of total absorption we have gone.

30. In a *Saltire* pamphlet *The Crisis in Scottish Education*, 1982 Edinburgh.
31. In a review of the pamphlet in *Scottish Educational Studies*, Vol. iv, No. 2, November 1982.
32. Grant, op. cit., pp. 6–7.
33. Ibid., p. 12.
34. Ibid., p. 21.
35. Ibid., p. 23.
36. Ibid., pp. 26–7.
37. Ibid., p. 29.
38. Ibid., p. 30.
39. Ibid., p. 35.

Chapter 14
1. *TESS*, 3 February 1984.
2. *TESS*, 9 December 1977. In May 1989 Jack Dale, higher education secretary of the EIS, said: "If we had a properly constituted Scottish Committee – not just the Scottish committee of the Universities Funding Council – than there would be a case for saying 'Let's construct a system of higher education for Scotland in the next century.' But deals between Principals and the Government would not be acceptable."
3. Nigel Grant (1976), *Scottish Universities – The Case for Devolution.*
4. *TESS*, 3 February 1967.
5. *TESS* report 24 May 1968.
6. *THES*, 22 August 1975. The report was contained in a student booklet entitled *Student Opinions.*
7. *Scotland on Sunday*, 'Scots Students Shun Capital', 12 January 1992.
8. *THES*, 20 July 1990.
9. May 1991. Centre for Research on Learning and Instruction, University of Edinburgh.
10. "That anglicization of the student populations of Scottish universities has reached catastrophic proportions – not only in St. Andrews and

Stirling, but in Edinburgh, one hub of our Enlightenment – is now generally acknowledged." This quote is taken from an article by Angus Calder, entitled *Autonomy and Scottish Culture* in *Cencrastus*, No. 34.

11. John Marshall, *The Oxford Experiment*, *THES*, 2 May 1980.

12. *Radical Scotland*, No. 26 April–May 1987, pp. 13–16.

13. If the author of these lines may be permitted to quote personal, and therefore purely anecdotal, evidence, I remember that a month or two after beginning his Mechanical Engineering course at the University of Edinburgh in 1987, my son, not an intolerant young man, rang me up to ask me with a note of exasperation in his voice, "Where do all the yahs come from?", and to complain mildly at the great difference in standards of living between Scots students and English public school boys and girls. He also mentioned graffiti wars. Any bad feeling that may develop is not the result of 'nationalism' but of the unthinking policies of university leaders, and they would bear full responsibility.

14. Peter Burnhill, Cathy Garner and Andrew McPherson in *The Education Scotsman*, 31 January and 7 February 1989.

15. Writing in *Chapman*, 35–36, 1983.

16. *The Scotsman*, 15 July 1992. From P. H. Scott.

17. At a conference in Glasgow towards the end of 1992 I listened to a leading figure in the metropolitan gallery and museum world, who chaired the conference, declaring publicly at a meeting that Glasgow had good museums and galleries because it had no history!

18. *THES*, 29 January 1988.

19. *THES*, 29 January 1988: *Rhythms of a Nation*; 21 October 1988: *Ane Old Song*; 19 April 1991: *The Herald of Devolution*; 4 October 1991: *Scotland's Strays Come Home*.

20. *TESS*, 24 May 1991.

21. *The Scotsman*, 3 December 1992. An editorial, *Matching ends to ways and means*, says: "Similar policy issues dog the increased allocation for education. This is the first year that Mr. Lang has enjoyed responsibility for Scottish universities, but the figures offer little sign that devolved responsibility is going to equate with devolved policy authority. After a period in which student intake has risen rapidly, the brakes appear to be going on, while recruitment to further education rises – exactly in line with policy south of the border. That might be arguably be no bad thing, but it must revive old doubts about the real worth of administrative devolution."

22. *The Scotsman*, 10 July 1992.

23. Ibid.

24. *The Scotsman*, 30 November 1992. This fear was confirmed by Sir David Smith, Edinburgh's Principal, at a graduation ceremony, who warned that his staff and students were facing an unequal struggle to maintain quality "in spite of the 50% rise in student numbers over the past four years." Staff had greater workloads, taught larger classes, were producing more research "under poorer working conditions, with gloomier career prospects and with much more impenetrable

bureaucratic jungles" than he had ever done as a university lecturer, and were consequently suffering an increase in stress-related illness and were spending less time with their families. It was richly ironic that because of the concern from external bodies about quality, the staff were forced to spend a great deal of time on detailed assessments, which then adversely affected the quality of teaching and research they could achieve. "To prepare for a recent visit from quality auditors, more than 200 people were involved in producing documentation weighing well over a hundredweight. It cost a total of eight man-years in staff time and £3,500 in photocopying."

25. *The Scotsman*, 11 December 1991.

26. *The Scotsman, Education section*, 23 October 1991.

27. *The Scotsman*, 18 November 1992. An article entitled *Anger over new levels of funding* shows that this is no empty threat by quoting the Education Secretary John Patten as saying that he was asking the English Funding Council "to advise me on what action it can take to deter any trend towards longer courses." The article warns that the new Scottish Higher Education Council will be under pressure to follow Mr. Patten's leads.

28. *Scotland on Sunday*, 29 January 1989. 'Why Universities are living in Fear'.

29. Ibid.

30. *The Scotsman*,16 January 1989. 'Scotland's Qualified Failure'.

31. *The Scotsman*, 6 July 1992. 'Graduates chase work with degree of pessimism'.

32. *The Scotsman*, 20 July 1992. 'Principal attacks policy on pay rises'.

33. *THES*, 14 October 1988. A leader states the Chilver principle: "Courses of higher education should be available to all those who value them so highly that they are prepared to commit resources to them." It comments: "The implication is that financial commitment is a more appropriate test of eligibility than academic merit whether defined in terms of 'ability and attainment' or 'ability to benefit'."
THES, 17 November 1989. The above pearl of wisdom was put even more bluntly and cynically by Sir Christopher Ball, then Chairman of the NAB: " The demand for higher education is becoming so buoyant that rising costs, in the form of full-cost fees and reductions in the real value of student grants are unlikely to dampen student demand." The strategy therefore, since public funds were limited, was to charge private fees and set up bursaries for the needy.

34. *The Scotsman*, 30 June 1992. 'Call for the universities to make sacrifices'.

35. *THES*, 6 May 1988. Sir John Burnett, formerly Principal of the University of Edinburgh, said that, "At best policy for higher education seems to be a wish to obtain more and more for less and less, and this had been expressed in terms applicable and appropriate to industry or commerce without any serious consideration of whether such language, much less such concepts, could be applied to higher education."
THES 17 November 1989. Similarly, Dr. Ronald Barnet, chairman of

the Higher Education Foundation's Higher Education Group, speaks (*Responsiveness and Fulfilment: The value of higher education in the modern world*) of the new vocabulary emerging in higher education: enterprise skills, transferable skills, student competencies, education for capability, etc. This approach was "fundamentally damaging": "Attempting to found a curriculum purely on the technical and instrumental requirements of graduates can only serve to limit the student experience ... a higher education course aimed purely at competence or enterprise or capability cannot be a genuine course of higher education. Higher education comes to take on the form of a technique, going through the motions without a clear understanding of what it is about, and why. Courses must not be surrendered to 'a narrow instrumentalism'. To do justice to the values of higher education, evaluation cannot be confined to numerical performance indicators, but must find ways of assessing the character of the internal life of institutions, especially the quality of the student experience."

36. *TESS*, 5 July 1968.
37. *The Scotsman*, 5 July 1992. 'Student book famine makes grim reading'.
38. *The Scotsman*, 1 July 1992. 'Measuring success by degrees'
39. *The Scotsman*, 1 February 1989. 'Paying the price of a classroom revolution'.
40. See note 24 above.
41. This is what John McFall MP, Labour's Scottish education spokesman, called a "pile 'em high, teach 'em cheap" policy in *The Scotsman* of 5 November 1992. The newspaper also reported action by the AUT and NUS in Scotland "calling for an independent pay review body for lecturers, and an increase in cash for student finances and university facilities." Significantly, they launched an *Action for Quality* campaign and, unsurprisingly, Sir David Smith, Edinburgh University's Principal, announced his retirement 20 months early.
42. *Scotland on Sunday*, 28 June 1992. 'Gag rectors and I'll tell tales out of court'.
43. Not to mention an Albert Einstein whose school report read: "Unsuccessful, unsociable and permanently adrift in foolish dreams".
44. *The Scotsman*, 27 January 1989: 'From Yes Minister to No Minister'.

Chapter 15
1. At a conference on *The Scottish Gift*, *TESS*, 4 November 1977.
2. Patrick Nuttgens (1988), *What Should we Teach and how Should we Teach it – Aims and Purposes of Higher Education*, Aldershot, Wildwood, p. 102.
3. Douglas Dunn (1992), *Scotland: An Anthology*, Fontana, Preface. An English correspondent of *Scotland on Sunday* 30 August 1992, said in a letter: "A well-known fact is that of all the emigrants entering the New World the Scottish people have been the most resourceful and successful."

4. Alfred North Whitehead, *The Aims of Education*, Cambridge, Cambridge University Press, pp. 138–40.

5. Peter Scott (1979), *What Future for Higher Education?*, Fabian Tract, p. 7.

6. Ibid., p. 16 "Disciplines have become so specialist that it has become increasingly difficult to talk across disciplines – with very damaging effects, as nearly all the great issues facing mankind, intellectual as well as practical, do not fall into the neat compartments designed by professional scholars."

7. *THES*, 25 December 1981. Already eleven years ago the editor was saying that "the 'knowledge' society often has an unhappy tendency to become an authoritarian society", and that "knowledge has become a more loyal servant of power almost everywhere".

8. Clark Kerr op. cit.

9. T. Becher and M. Kogan (1980), *Process and Structure in Higher Education*, London.

10. Martin Trow (1973), *Problems in the Transition from Elite to Mass Higher Education*, Carnegie Commission on Higher Education, Berkeley, p. 2.

11. Norman Birnbaum, *Students, Professors and Philosopher-Kings*, in Carl Kaysen, ed., (1973), *Content and Context*, New York.

12. Peter Scott (1984), *The Crisis of the University*, London, Croom Helm.

13. Here is Auguste Comte's original definition a century and a half ago: "The positive sciences and the scientific method that their practice demands were destined to furnish the sole and permanent foundation for all subsequent ideas and knowledge."

14. *THES*, 25 December 1981. In an editorial entitled *Knowledge and Morality* the editor has this to say: "To suggest that knowledge is never evil but only the use to which man puts it is to make a distinction that is intellectually and practically without significance. The really important moral questions concern the setting and managing of the social system's priorities for the pursuit of knowledge. So ultimately the scholar or scientist cannot ignore the ethical implications of his scholarship or his research. The unhappiness of the world and the radicalism of new knowledge both forbid such narrowness. This means that scholars and scientists should accept the legitimacy of moral and even ethico-political questions and be engaged with others in searching for answers. To try to evade such questions altogether by appealing to an agnostic and amoral ideology of knowledge is to diminish both the social importance and the intellectual vitality of the modern university."

15. Review of Peter Scott's book in *Studies in Higher Education*, Vol. 10, No. 1, 1985.

16. Peter Scott, op. cit., p. 113.

17. "A thing is right when it tends to preserve the integrity, stability and beauty of the biotic community. It is wrong when it tends other-

wise." Aldo Leopold, *A Sand County Almanac*, New York, Oxford University Press, 1949.

18. Ibid., p. 260.
19. Peter Scott, *Towards a Common Culture IV*, *THES*, 24 August 1984.
20. Ibid.
21. Peter Scott, *Knowledge, Culture and the Modern University*, *THES*, 18, August 1989.
22. Ibid.
23. Peter Scott, *THES*, 1 September 1989.
24. In *Studies in Higher Education* Vol. 15 No. 2 pp. 189–92, a publication of the *Council for Academic Autonomy* entitled *The State and Higher Education* says: "Gone is the old idea of self-regulatory communities of scholars and teachers, devoted to the common cause of the pursuit of knowledge. Instead we have a government conception of academic institutions as 'cartels of knowledge', units of production with a managerial elite and a workforce of intellectual producers whose labour will be increasingly casualised in the interests of 'managerial flexibility' and value for money. This goes together with a profound cultural shift in society over the last ten years, the devaluing of humanist values, the primacy of 'making it' or 'loadsamoney' values, the elevation of entrepreneurial values into an ideology." The authors also say that university academics have failed to assert strongly and publicly their function of intellectual and moral leadership. "The intellectual and linguistic vacuum that was the result has been filled by the values and terminology of the market-place. Such is the bankruptcy of university leadership and the loss of faith and confidence amongst lecturers that we find resistance difficult, and now, with some exceptions, we pay lip-service to the primacy of the market."
25. Ibid., M. E. Tasker and R. E. Packham, *Freedom, Funding and the Future of the Universities*, pp. 181–88.
26. In a review of R. Barnet's *The Idea of Higher Education* in *Studies in Higher Education*, Vol. 16, No. 2, 199.
27. Bernard Crick, *Society's servants and the State's uneasy conscience*, *THES*, 10 March 1989.
28. Quoted in Nuttgens, op. cit.
29. Sir Charles Grant Robertson (1930 & 1944), *The British Universities*, London.
30. William Birch (1988), *The Challenge to Higher Education*, SRHE & OU, p. 3.
31. Op. cit., p. 102.
32. E. Shils (1984), *The Academic Ethic*, University of California Press (Quoted in Birch, op. cit., pp. 29 and 37).
33. A. N. Whitehead (1932), *The Aims of Education*. Quoted in Birch op. cit.
34. J. O'Toole (1977), *Work, Learning and the American Future*, San Francisco Jossey-Bass (Quoted in Birch, op. cit., p. 41).
35. Clark Kerr, op. cit., p. 114.
36. Ibid., p. 87.

37. Ibid., p. 101.
38. *THES*, 21 December 1990. In an article entitled *Teaching's Renewed Role in Evolution of Learning*, Ernest Boyer quotes Michael Severn, President of Columbia University: "Columbia will establish 10 endowed chairs for outstanding teachers. In America today the great teacher is an endangered species. Great research and great teaching fuel each other ... we must acknowledge that great universities like ours are at risk of tilting in favour of research at the expense of teaching. And we must not let that happen."

Stanford University President Donald Kennedy has called for more contact between faculty and students: "It is time for us to reaffirm that education – that is teaching in all its forms – is the primary task of higher education."

The Carnegie Fund Report *Scholarship Reconsidered* says that "the time has come to move beyond the tired old 'teaching versus research' debate and give the honourable term 'scholarship' a broader, more capacious meaning, one that brings legitimacy to the full scope of academic work. Surely scholarship means engaging in original research. But the work of the scholar also means stepping back from one's investigation, looking for connections, building bridges between theory and practice, and communicating one's knowledge effectively to students."

Chapter 16
1. *TESS*, 6 February 1976.
2. *TESS*, 15 January 1971.
3. Brian Morton, *Auld Testament*: *A Profile of George Elder Davie*, *Cencrastus*, 5 September 1986.
4. A modern example is the present Labour Shadow Chancellor Gordon Brown, who, Christopher Harvie says, "turned up at Edinburgh University at an absurdly early age, ended up with a First Class Honours degree and the Rectorship of the university." *The Boys from the North* in *THES*, 28th October 1988.
5. Delivered before the University of Dundee on 30 November 1972.
6. See Chapter 2.
7. *TESS*, 13 July 1973.
8. 'The Long and Winding Road', *TESS*, 14 January 1977.
9. During one of the vicissitudes of her journey to London to save her sister's life, Jeanie Deans – the heroine of Sir Walter Scott's *The Heart of Mid-Lothian* is asked by an old lady whether she can read the Bible, and replies: "I hope sae, madam," said Jeanie, surprised at the question; "my father wad hae wanted mony a thing, ere I had wanted *that* schuling." The action of the novel takes place in the early part of the eighteenth century.
10. One of the most striking examples of this Scottish habit of linking education with life was the lectures on Marxist economics by the schoolteacher and militant Marxist leader John Maclean during and after the First World War. The *THES* of 15 April 1983 contains an article

on him by R. Bennett which says: "By stressing that this 'independent' education was a means whereby the underlying factors shaping the lives and livelihoods of Scottish workers could be understood and therefore possibly changed, Maclean triggered off an enormous and deeply motivated desire for learning. Classes spread throughout the Clyde, Lanarkshire and the West. In the summer Maclean toured throughout Scotland and the south. This capacity to respond to demand and evoke motivation led to Maclean's legendary Sunday economics classes in Bath Street, Glasgow, becoming the biggest of their kind in the world. The linking of the content to the realities of his audiences' working lives and their place in the production process was an important element in Maclean's success. Classes were taken to the point of production itself, mines, engineering and ship-building yards. Maclean had great success in linking content, approach, method and venue to achieve unequalled responses. His touchstone was 'relevance'."

11.   'Within these Ivory Walls', Colin Radford, *THES*, 9 September 1983.
12.   *TESS*, 24 March 1966.
13.   'Faith, Hope and School', Donald Withrington, *TESS*, 4 November 1977.
14.   *TESS*, 8 July 1983.
15.   *THES*, Leader, 24 February 1989.
16.   *THES*, Leader, 'Metaphysical Scotland', 10 October 1986.
17.   Roughly the same idea is expressed in rather different language by John Sessions in *Observer Scotland* 28 January 1990: "The way I think", he says, "is more Scottish than English. In England there is a short-circuit between the brain and the groin, while in Scotland there is an awareness of the soul and the spirit. There is a tradition of discursive wrestling for truth: that eighteenth century Enlightenment thing." He is, of course, speaking of his performance as a sort of intellectual stand-up comic. It is striking that what Robert Louis Stevenson called "a strong Scotch accent of the mind" is present in such comedians as Sessions, Robbie Coltrane and Gregor Fisher, all well educated and all with a philosophical tinge to their humour.
18.   Rory Watson, *Seminars in the Glen of Silence*, *Cencrastus*, No. 25.
19.   Susan Manning, *Scotland and America. National Literatures? National Languages?*, *Cencrastus* No. 32.
20.   Rory Watson, op. cit.
21.   *TESS*, 13 March 1970.
22.   *TESS*, 7 January 1975
23.   *TESS*, 7 January 1977. J. Stuart McClure has some interesting things to say about this in the *Scottish Educational Review*, Vol. 6, No. 2 1981. He considers that universities should be "centres of critical and informed comment on the changing state of civilization." This includes helping people to recognize their hidden assumptions, confronting them with choices betwen courses of action which involve different sets of values. There must be a recognition that decisions may have to be made between levels of profundity as well as between quantities of

evidence. This is existential learning: memorisation and 'hard work' are not enough. There is a connection between cognitive awareness, existential concern and actually doing things. It is important that higher education should "expand the moral imagination", but action is also necessary. So is the crossing of disciplinary boundaries, for specialist knowledge nearly always has consequences outside its own province – hence the limitations of concentrating solely on specialism. Coping in the real world also means recognizing human and moral problems. "The surgeon, the economist, the business manager, all need an education which increases the range of their awareness while not reducing their specialist skills." Students need to be encouraged to work out the differences in standards people use in their public and private lives; and to feel profoundly the need for a philosophy of life of their own. A highly departmentalized form of higher education, almost all of whose emphasis is on specialisms and the production of professional expertise, carries the danger of giving its students a reduced and limited concept of knowledge itself. "Where is the knowledge we have lost in information?" McClure asks.

24. *THES*, 27 July 1990.
25. *THES*, 7 February 1978.
26. In a speech the retiring Principal of the University of Edinburgh, Sir John Burnett, described Mr. Baker's educational reform bill as "this most philistine of documents which disposed of the humanities in a mere three lines, and the message comes through, loud and clear, that the worth of the subject is to be measured by the tangible benefits it confers on the individual and the nation."
27. *THES*, 25 January 1991.
28. *THES*, 3 February 1984.
29. *THES*, 1 January 1981.
30. *THES*, 23 March 1984. 'Adding a degree of subtlety'.
31. *TESS*, 15 July 1966.
32. *TESS*, 28 July 1967. Letter from Andrew Munro.
33. *TESS*, 21 August 1970. 'First steps in philosophy', Alastair Shanks.
34. *TESS*, 1 & 8 October 1971. 'Unique Opportunity of Scottish Sixth' and 'Fundamentals for Tutorial Groups'.
35. Particularly neatly described by the late John Smith, QC, MP, then leader of the Labour Party, when speaking of his studies at Glasgow University. He first took an Arts degree, then studied law. Of this he said: "They educated you first and then went on to train you." Quoted by Charles Kennedy, *The Scotsman*, 31 August 1992.
36. *TESS*, 4 December 1970. 'The Idea of a University'.
37. It is fascinating to observe the similarities in the thought of John Macmurray and Patrick Geddes. They were both opposed to dualism, the holistic ideas of Geddes taking shape in his unities of body-mind-spirit and folk-place-work. He said: "Education is not merely by and for the sake of thought; it is in a still higher degree by and for the sake of action." That might have been written by Macmurray. Geddes also said, apropos of his famous Summer Meetings, that their highest

principle was to seek "to fit the student for some of the higher activities of life by letting him actually share them. He is invited to become
not a mere passive auditor, a receptacle for such tidbits of knowledge
as may be tossed to him, but an active collaborator in all that we
are carrying on here." Another dictum which Macmurray must have
enjoyed: "If we have any dogma, it is to teach a utilitarianism which
treats life and culture as a whole and which may sometimes find the
Beautiful more useful than the Useful."

38. George Steiner makes a similar remark: "It has been said that Oxford
     and Cambridge own land whereas American universities own loyal-
     ties," in *America as the Archive of Eden, THES*, 6 March 1981.
39. Philip Boardman (1978), *The Worlds of Patrick Geddes*, Routledge
     & Kegan Paul.
40. Derek Bok (1982), *Beyond the Ivory Tower*, Harvard University Press
     p. 117.
41. *The Ecologist*,Vol 18, No. 4/5, 1988 pp. 121–2.
42. *Education set to move into radical decade, Entrepreneurial approach*
     A 'special feature' in *The Scotsman*, 19 August 1992 pp. 12–13.

Chapter 17
 1. Richard H. Grove, *Origins of Western Environmentalism* in *Scientific
     American*, July 1992, p. 22–7.
 2. Ibid., p. 25.
 3. The following is taken from a speech by William Gaillard, Director of
     the UN International Drug Control Programme, at the 36th Congress
     on Alcohol and Drug Dependency, Glasgow, 16–21 August 1992:
     "1992 has been the year of the Earth Summit, the year of ecology. In
     the battle that we are fighting against drug abuse, we cannot overlook
     the cultural aspects of the problem and they are closely related to
     our attitude towards the environment. Drugs and pollution constitute
     the down side of industrial development and the consumer society.
     They are the bitter fruits of our frantic search for profit *and the loss
     of our reference points*. They reflect the anomie of the situation, the
     destruction of age-old equilibria but without new ones in their place.
     If pollution and industrial waste destroy nature or drugs cloud our
     minds, *the relationship between man and the universe is undermined*.
     Since drug abuse is never the root cause of the ills that plague the
     world but only the symptom that often rings the alarm bell that the
     international community should heed, I feel it is our duty to point
     out clearly, to the powers that be, the urgency of beginning to give
     an answer to the multiple problems that beset the world. UNDCP has
     formulated two main objectives in its long-term strategy; one is social
     reconstruction, *the other is cultural change*. Both are obviously inti-
     mately linked, structurally intertwined. And both depend on a world-
     wide effort that must involve the international community at large,
     that is the United Nations, the governments and the non-governmental
     organizations. The threat of drug abuse must compel us to confront

the North-South development issues, the unequal terms of trade, the increasing inadequacies of social policy, urban decay, *the crisis of the education systems*, poverty and marginality" (all italics are ours).

4. As Freya Matthews (1991), puts it: "We are, then, a cosmologically dispossessed culture, a culture clinging to a bankrupt world view which prescribes a cramped, materialistic individualism, the consequences of which we are presently reaping. We need cosmological rehabilitation." *The Ecological Self*, London, Routledge, p. 48.

5. Quotations from *The Ecologist*, op. cit., p. 162.

6. *The Scotsman*, 17 July 1992.

7. *THES*, 18 January 1991.

8. A single issue of the *Scotsman*, picked at random, shows that William Gaillard's warnings are not exaggerated and that Edinburgh's welcome environmental initiative is arriving – that is, if it succeeds – in the nick of time. The issue for 14 November 1992 carries the following articles related to our theme:

   UK wastes 10 billion of energy a year: "British industry adds to global warming by wasting 10 billion worth of energy a year," says Scottish Office industry minister, Allan Stewart.

   Harris Quarry Plan Attacked: Scottish National Heritage is unhappy at the possibility of environmental destruction and pollution of the sea by the proposed giant coastal quarry on the southern tip of Harris.

   Dolphins Row Looms: Greenpeace gets ready to protect Britain's largest colony of bottle-nosed dolphins from oil exploration in the Moray Firth.

   Study to Show Water Pollution: The Scottish *Wildlife Trust* has appointed a research officer to look at the damage caused to Scotland's freshwater lochs by pollution from industry, agriculture, and sewage. This follows the ban on eating trout caught in Loch Leven because of dangerous algal blooms caused by pollution.

   Ozone levels fall to lowest for decades: says the UN's World Meteorological Organization.

   Meantime, on p. 13 there is an article entitled *University collections that should be treasured, not traded*: says the Curator of Edinburgh University's Collections, in the continuing controversy over the sale of an art masterpiece; while in a double-page spread on pp. 8 and 9, Heriot-Watt University regales the reader, in dreadful advertising speak, with proud claims that, like the new universities of Paisley, etc., Heriot Watt places the emphasis "very much on the technological and the vocational" and boasts of its "intense focus on the real world – something that is not always shared by the more ancient seats of learning." Just to make sure the reader has not missed that important point, the article repeats it: "Heriot-Watt's commitment to achievement in the areas of technology and business give it a distinct practical slant which homes in on the real world of today and on future achievements." But just in case this looks rather too unintellectual, we get: "Theory is not ignored, but it always takes second place to the practicalities of the real world." And, of course, "the university is consistently a key player in Europe-wide initiatives."

I am grateful to *The Scotsman* for an issue which perfectly illustrates my central theme. The Scottish universities, as at present led, are cognitively maladjusted. They are part of the disease that afflicts Western civilization and must, for all our sakes, make the breakthrough to a new – albeit ancient – view of the university's role in society.

9. It is of the utmost importance to note how civilizations we have castigated as savage and ignorant, and all but wiped out, have handled these problems of man's relationship with the rest of creation with great intelligence and sophistication. Freya Matthews (op. cit., p. 139) says: "Although the cultural dimension of a society is abstract and symbolic, there is a sense in which a culture may be ecologically informed with elements of its environment. For instance, the peculiar quality or essence of certain American Indian or Australian aboriginal cultures reflects the relation of the societies in question to specific beings or elements of their respective ecosystems. These cultures may be essentially buffalo or kangaroo cultures, let us say, physically, technologically and spiritually centred on these particular animal species. Typically, the dependence of such societies on their local ecosystem is mutual – their interaction with their environment contributes to the stability of the ecosystem. The role of such cultures, with their pointedly value-laden belief systems, is precisely to generate such interaction – to channel social action in ecologically sustainable and beneficial directions. Despite its abstractness, then, a culture may act as a naturally selected instrument of Nature, or participant in the local ecosystem. The society which practises such a culture, tied to a particular region and a particular set of ecological relations, may thus qualify as a self-sustaining system – since it successfully perpetuates its own social structures by means of its belief-system – and this as a holistic subsystem of the local ecology."

10. *THES*, 6 April 1990.

11. *THES*, 14 September 1990.

12. *The Scotsman*, 22 November 1991.

13. *THES*, 5 October 1990.

14. *The Makar, Marx and the Messianic, The Scotsman* 11 August 1992, p. 2.

15. 'The New Classics', *TESS*, 21 May 1982.

16. *THES*, 20 December 1991.

17. *The Scotsman*, 7 May 1992.

18. *THES* , 3 January 1992.

19. *The Scotsman, Call for long-term green agenda from Earth Summit*, 26 May 1992.

20. *The Ecologist*, Vol. 22, No. 4, July/August 1992, p. 122.

21. *THES*, 26 January 1990. *Uncovering Emeralds: Max Nicholson on the greening of human ethics.*

22. Somewhere, probably in *L'Esprit Sauvage*, Claude Levi-Strauss, the great structural anthropologist, speaks of a walk in the jungle with

an Amazonian Indian who, in space of a few miles, showed him well over one hundred plants, named them and described the medicinal and/or culinary value of each one.

23. There was fine television programme with David Attenborough on the hunter-killer operations of chimpanzees, entitled *Too Close for Comfort*. See also William's Boyd's *Brazzaville Beach*, 1991, Penguin.

24. Or indeed an old ethic whose creators we have all but wiped out. In his poem *My Heart Soars*, Chief Dan George, an Indian from British Columbia, writes: "Take care, or soon our ears will strain/In vain to hear the Creator's song;" and "When I pray/ I pray for all living things/ When I thank/I thank for everything." Our students would, I am sure react with delight to seminars conducted by Chief Dan George and other Indian writers, thinkers and artists, for it is the aboriginals who possess ecological wisdom.

25. John Passmore (1974), *Man's Responsibility for Nature: Ecological Problems and Western Traditions*, London, Duckworth.

26. Ibid p. 177.

27. Ibid p. 184.

28. *THES*, 11 January 1974, *Philosopher of Biology for the 'new age of mechanism'*.

29. Daniel Bell (1976), *The Coming of Post-Industrial Society*, Harmondsworth, Penguin, p. 480.

30. Lawrence E. Johnson (1991), *A Morally Deep World*, Cambridge University Press, p. 239.

31. *THES*, 23 November 1990.

32. The English writer, John Fowles, compares the human race to a "ravenous, self-destroying horde of rats, that has been multiplying like an uncontrolled virus." Gerald Durrell, the wild-life specialist, put the same point even more explosively – and live – at the end of a TV programme entitled *The Last Show on Earth*: "What do their silly little boundaries matter? Or their stupid religions? If there's no planet!"

33. In a British Association address reported in *TESS*, 11 September 1970.

34. *Student debt threatens long courses* by Steve Briggs, Education Correspondent, *Scotland on Sunday*, 30 August 1992.

35. *THES*, 17 February 1989. Support for breadth and depth (and therefore length) of education comes from a much earlier English writer, John Case, who, in his *Apologia Academiarum* (1596), said that learned men were "the eyes of the state" and universities were "the training-ground for learned men, the abode of the wise, the soul of the world and the surest anchor of the state." Case replies to the charge that the universities are too impractical and theoretical by riposting that the best professional men are those who come to their profession after a prior study of its theory and who have had a university training in philosophy in its widest sense. The *THES* describes Case as the voice of a sane and articulate conservatism.

36. Geoffrey Squires (1990), *The Undergraduate Curriculum*, SRHE & OU, p. 151.

37. *Scotland on Sunday*, 23 August 1992. In two reports, *Pupils Lose*

Higher Ground and *Student debts threaten long courses*, in the 30 August issue, the paper's education correspondent says "Scotland's renown as a highly-educated nation is under threat." He shows that Scottish students are reducing the number of Highers they sit in order to get better grades to compete with A-level candidates from South of the Border, thus defeating the object of the Highers, which is breadth. (It is interesting, incidentally, that he quite openly equates 'highly-educated' with breadth, at least by implication.) The system of student loans is hitting Scottish students so hard that many of the most able are opting out of Honours in favour of the three-year Ordinary degree, but of course in its post-1892 degraded form.

Envoi
1. Entitled 'Mad Market', *TESS*, p. 213 October 1967.
2. *TESS*, 8 July 1988.
3. A rare example of such "confusions of identity" was provided by the third of three TV programmes on the *Tribes of Europe*, which dealt with Scotland, in October 1992. A group of such expatriate Scots from the USA, with the name *MacLean* printed on the front of their baseball caps, were attending the clan gathering at Torosay Castle on the Isle of Mull. They were overwhelmed – one very nice young woman wept openly – as they were regaled with tales of the clan by the clan chief in a typical Oxbridge accent, he being resident in London and working in the City. Sir Fitzroy MacLean was there, looking like something out of a Raeburn painting, and sounding very unScottish. Meantime a TV reporter was being driven over the moors and having it explained to him that most of the houses on the island were holiday or retirement homes belonging to 'incomers'. He spoke to only one occupant, a nice lady from the north of England, who was sad about what was happening to the island. Finally, there was a visit to one of Glasgow's giant housing schemes, where some very foul-tongued ladies cursed the English for what they were doing to Scotland. I do wish they had been introduced to the nice young American woman; her expression would have been something to see.
4. Tom Nairn, *The Three Dreams of Scottish Nationalism* in Karl Miller, ed. (1970), *Memoirs of a Modern Scotland*, London, Faber & Faber, pp. 52–3.
5. It was given powerful expression on 12 December 1992, during the EC Summit Meeting in Edinburgh, when between 30 and 40 thousand people marched peacefully and colourfully through Edinburgh on a bitterly cold but sunny day to demonstrate their unabated desire for self-determination in the form of a Scottish Parliament.
6. Typically, the last sentence of an article detailing Scotland's close connections with Europe, entitled *Putting Scotland on the Map*, by Murray Pittock, runs as follows; "Whatever emerges from the current debates on the EC's political future, it is to be hoped that Scotland can once again offer something distinctive, not to European wars, but

the European mind." In a Eurosummit supplement to *Scotland on Sunday*, 31 August 1992.

7. *Hansard*, 24 November 1932.
8. *The Scotsman*, 27 May 1991.
9. *THES*,10 October 1986. An editorial says that to escape this authoritarian behaviour of the SED in the 1920s "the universities resisted and escaped into the gentler hands of the UGC south of the border", and that this was "a symbolic arrangement of crucial cultural significance." For "a price has been paid. First, they have cut themselves off from their older populist roots. Second, they have been persuaded to *embrace a utilitarian and positivistic interpretation of knowledge that is at odds with the idealism of the old Scottish common sense philosophy*. Finally, of course, they have had to admit that their contributions to science and scholarship must be mediated through a British tradition inevitably dominated by the different intellectual culture of England" (our italics).
10. Angus Calder, op. cit., 5.
11. *Glasgow Herald*, 24 October 1990. In an article entitled *The subtle erosion of a nation's identity*, Ian Bell traces the diminution of Scottish national individuality from the anglocentric tendency of the Treaty of Union to the globalising influence of modern communications. In particular he speaks of the universities, saying that in drafting proposals for student loans no-one seemed to care that "they were writing a death sentence for the four-year Scottish degree"; and that "they seemed equally unconcerned that such a drastic change would impinge on the secondary education with its broadly-based curriculum." With greater relevance to Fry's last point he also says: "It is bad enough . . that universities are run on a UK-wide basis which allows little scope for any recognition of a Scottish dimension. But since these institutions have participated in – have perhaps even encouraged – the anglicization of the Scottish middle class, *their negative effect on the Scottish identity is profound. Edinburgh University, to take one example, is a favourite of English students whose preponderance does much to make the place cosmopolitan but little to protect its Scottishness.*" Our universities "are, as their opposition to devolution showed during the 70s, severely anglicised. The idea that they should be contributing to the preservation of a Scottish identity would bemuse most of our academics." Understandably, it should be added, since most of them are English.

Bell shows that the same process is going on in Scots law, despite the fact that under the Treaty of Union it was one of the reserved national institutions; and that, quoting Professor Walker in a standard text on the legal system, the greatest threat to Scots law "springs from facile acceptance of English books and judgments, acceptance of English legal training as of value in Scotland. *Unwillingness and inability to search far back for a true principle consistent with the development of the native law.*" Bell calls this "little more than assimilation" and show that it has been going on since the union of parliaments because it carries rewards. "The Union of the Parliaments was followed by a mania for anglicisation among the Scottish bourgeoisie, many of whom submitted to English education and elocution classes in an effort to become proper North Britons and to participate in England's mercantile success. Others found that political patronage flowed only through London and were happy to become lobby fodder controlled by the likes of Henry Dundas. *The Scottish Enlightenment, for all its intellectual glory, was similarly the triumph of anglicization.*" Bell notes that today large numbers of English people are coming into Scotland and that this "modern invasion has seen a virtual take-over of Scottish cultural institutions by southerners, most of whom are highly competent but few of whom are comfortable with talk of Scottish identity." He concludes: "There is a considerable irony in the fact that Scotland is once again asserting itself in politics and culture just as its social institutions are coming under renewed pressure. *What price nationhood after the sinews of the nation have withered?* " (our italics).

12. Sir Walter Scott, *The Letters of Malachi Malagrowther*. The second letter, published on 1 March 1826, the year in which the long campaign to 'English' the Scottish universities began.

13. *The Scotsman*, 16 November 1992.

14. *Democracy or Tribalism? Scottish political culture and the chances of autonomy* in *Cencrastus*, No. 34. This remark has surely been overtaken by events. The identity is well on the way to recovery. It is political behaviour, particularly that of the Labour Party in Scotland, that needs to change.

15. An apt contemporary illustration of this was given by Colin Young, retiring first director of the National Film School at Beaconsfield. A very obvious Scot, who had spent 17 years of his life at UCLA, he said that he had always approached his work and his life from general principles rather than trying to work on the basis of individual events, and that his training as a filmmaker and teacher had been in philosophy. BBC2, *Edinburgh Nights*, 2 September 1992.

16. These social theories and attitudes, as they operate in society, are well reflected in what Tom Clarke MP, newly appointed as Labour's Shadow Secretary of State for Scotland, had to say about his country: "What I love about Scotland – the casual decencies of people, the friendliness and the fairness, the lack of snobbery, that delightful sense of always being included in the communities you meet."

17. Reporting on a conference at Edinburgh University in *The Scotsman*, 22 November 1989, Owen Dudley Edwards, Reader in History at Edinburgh, had this to say: "The debate on universities in the London-Oxbridge triangle, among its many limitations, is clearly being carried on without reference to Scotland, and even the least Scottish-minded among our university personnel must realize that they must think in Scottish terms or be counted out." One of the speakers at the conference, the well-known Glasgow poet Edwin Morgan, said he took early retirement from Glasgow in 1980 because of his colleagues'

hostility to devolution and insistence on universities standing apart from the growing Scottish national consciousness. There were signs that Scottish universities were changing, but they still had to show clearly what side they were on in the debate on Scottish identity. It would be disastrous if, in an attempt to join English universities, they continued to jettison their primary obligations to the esteem of their own public, where loyalty to the universities was much stronger than "in the much more anti-intellectual English society."

18. *Glasgow Herald*, 24 October 1990. In an article entitled *While the debate goes on, the assimilative forces gain ground'*, the editor, Arnold Kemp, concludes: "The political and economic debate must confront the questions of wealth and national income. They are not as difficult to resolve, with goodwill, as Mr. Rifkind suggests. *But the assimilative forces eating away at the Scottish identity cannot be as easily placated.*" (our italics).

19. *TESS*, 17 December 1976. In an article entitled *Wanted: a national council on Scottish Education*, George Foulkes, the Labour MP has this to say:

"I start off from the premise that the Assembly would have in its Executive a minister with responsibility for education, who would be reporting regularly to the education committee consisting of elected members of the Assembly. In itself this would give an emphasis to education that has never existed before.

I envisage that over a period of years all the various institutions of higher education in Scotland could come to work more closely together, and we would see the development of an allembracing system of higher education in which there was greater coming and going of students between institutions and acknowledgement of the reciprocity of courses and degrees. This could be achieved without losing the integrity of the organizational structure and academic freedom of individual institutions by a policy of mutual cooperation and trust and recognition of the unique contribution each had to make."

20. Isobel Lindsay, *Scotland's Migratory Traditions*, *Radical Scotland*, No. 37, February/March 1989.

21. Robert Louis Stevenson (1904), *Vailima Letters*, 4th Edition, London, Methuen & Co., pp. 361–3.

22. S. S. Laurie, op. cit., p. 144.

Bibliography

The Times Education Supplement for Scotland
The Times Higher Education Supplement
Addison, W. I. (1901) *The Snell Exhibitioners from the University of Glasgow to Balliol College Oxford*
Allen, Michael (1988) *The Goals of Universities* SHRE & OU
Anderson, John, ed. D. Z. Phillips (1980) *Education and Enquiry* Oxford, Blackwell
Anderson, R. D. (1983) *Education and Opportunity in Victorian Scotland Schools and Universities* OUP
Ashby, Eric (1958) *Technology and the Academics* London, Macmillan
Ashby, Eric (1974) *Adapting Universities to a Technological Society* San Francisco London, Jossey-bass
Ball, C. & H. Eggins (1989) *Higher Education into the 1990s New dimensions* SRHE & OU
Barnet, Ronald (1990) *The Idea of Higher Education* SRHE & OU
Barrie, J. M. (1894) *An Edinburgh, Eleven* London, Hodder & Stoughton
Barzun, J. (1968) *The American University: How it runs; Where it is going* New York, Harper & Row
Becher, T. & M. Kogan (1980) *Process and Structure in Higher Education* London, Heinemann
Becher, T. Ed. (1987) *British Higher Education* London, Allen & Unwin
– (1989) *Academic Tribes and Territories* SRHE & OU
Bell, D. (1976) *The Coming of the Post-Industrial Society* Harmondsworth Penguin
Bell, R. E. *Home Rule and the Scottish Universities* in Wolfe, J. N. (1969) *Government and Nationalism in Scotland* Edinburgh & Chicago
Bell, R. E. *The Growth of the Modern University* in R. Hooper, ed. (1971) *The Curriculum: Content, Design and Development* Edinburgh, Oliver & Boyd
Bell, R. E. & N. Grant (1977) *A Mythology of British Education* London, Allen & Unwin
Benda, Julien (1990) *La Trahison des Clercs* Paris, Grasset

Beveridge C. & R. Turnbull (1982) *Inferiorism* in *Cencrastus* No 8

Beveridge C. & R. Turnbull (1989) *The Eclipse of Scottish Culture* Edinburgh, Polygon

Bibby, C. (1959) *T. H. Huxley: scientist, humanist and educator* London, Chatto

Bibby, C. (1971) *T. H. Huxley on Education* CUP

Birch, William (1988) *The Challenge to Higher Education: Reconciling responsibilities to scholarship and society* SHRE & OU

Birch, Wm. (1988) *Towards a Model for Problem-based Learning* SHE Vol 3 No 1

Birnbaum, N. (1973) *Students, Professors and Philosopher-Kings* in Carl Kaysen, ed. *Context and Content* New York

Black, R. C. (1850) *Some considerations on the educational system of the Scottish universities as compared with those of England* Edinburgh, W. P. Kennedy

Blackett, P. M. S. (1964) *The Universities and the Nation's Crises* in *Advancement of Science* 20 pp 379–89

Blackie, J. S. (1855) *On the Advancement of Learning in Scotland* Edinburgh

Blackie, J. S. (1868) *On Education Political Tracts* No 11 Edmonstone & Douglas

Block, F. & M. R. Somers *Beyond the Economic Fallacy: The Holistic Social Science of Karl Polanyi* in Scokpol, T. (1984) *Vision and Method in Historical Sociology* Cambridge

Bloom, Allan (1987) *The Closing of the American Mind* New York, Simon & Schuster

Boak, G. & H. Lantz (1970) *The Universities and Research* John Wiley & Co

Boardman, P. (1978) *The Worlds of Patrick Geddes* London, Routledge & Kegan Paul

Bok, Derek (1982) *Beyond the Ivory Tower* Cambridge Mass., Harvard University Press

Bok, Serek (1986) *Higher Learning* Cambridge Mass. & London, Harvard University Press

Bradbury, F. R. (1969) *Words and Numbers: a student's guide to intellectual methods* Edinburgh, EUP

Bridie, J. & M. McLaren (1949) *A Small Stir: Letters on the English* London

Broadie, A. (1990) *The Tradition of Scottish Philosophy* Edinburgh, Polygon

Brown, P. H. (1890) *George Buchanan, Humanist and Reformer, a biography* Edinburgh, David Douglas

Brown R., ed. (1973) *Knowledge, Education and Cultural Change: Papers in the Sociology of Education* London, Tavistock Publications

Brubacher, J. S. (1978) *On the Philosophy of Higher Education* San Francisco & London, Jossey-Bass

Buckle, H. T. (1861) *In Scotland and the Scotch Intellect* Reprinted 1970 by the University of Chicago Press

Burnett, James (1779-99) *Ancient Metaphysics or the Science of Universals*
    6 vols
Burnet, John (1917) *Higher Education and the War* London, Macmillan
Burnet, John (1929) *Essays and Addresses* London, Chatto & Windus
Callahan, D. & S. Bok, eds (1980) *Ethics Teaching in Higher Education*
    New York, Plenum Press
Cameron, J. M. (1978) *On the Idea of a University* Toronto University Press
Campbell, R. H. & A. Skinner (1982) *The Origins and Nature of the
    Scottish Enlightenment* Edinburgh, John Donald
Cant, R. G. *The Scottish Universities and Scottish Society in the 18th
    Century* in T. Besterman ed (1967) *Studies on Voltaire and the 18th
    Century*
Carlyle, T. (1829) *Signs of the Times* Edinburgh, Review
Carter, C. (1980) *Higher Education for the Future* Oxford, Blackwell
Chaplin, Maud (1978) *Philosophies of Higher Education, historical and
    contemporary* in A. S. Knowles *The International Encyclopedia of
    Higher Education* London, Jossey-Bass
Chastaing, M. (1954) *Reid, la philosophie du sens commun et le problème
    de la connaissance d'autrui* in *Revue philosophique CXLIV*
Checklamd, S. G. (1975) *A History of Scottish Banking* Glasgow, Collins
Clark, B. (1984) *The Higher Education System* University of California
    Press
Clarke, J., ed (1919) *Problems of National Education by Twelve Scottish
    Educationists* London, Macmillan
Collier, G. et al. (1974) *Values and Moral Development in Higher
    Education* London, Croom Helm
Cornford, P. (1977) *John Macmurray: A Neglected Philosopher* in *Radical
    Philosophy 16*
Cousin, V. (1857) *La Philosophie Écossaise* 3rd Edn. Paris.
Cousin, V. (1977) *Défense de l'université et de la philosophie* Paris Solin
Craigie, J. (1970) *A Bibliography of Scottish Education before 1872*
    SCRE
Culler, A. D. (1955) *The Imperial Intellect: a study of Newman's
    educational ideal* New Haven Conn., Yale University Press
Daiches, D. (1964) *The Paradox of Scottish Culture* OUP
Daiches, D. (1964) *The Idea of a New University: an experiment in Sussex*
    London, André Deutsch
Daiches, D. (1977) *Scotland and the Union* London, J. Murray
Daiches, D. Ed. (1979) *Andrew Fletcher of Saltoun: Selected political
    writings and speeches* Edinburgh, Scottish Academic Press
Daiches, D., ed. (1981) *A Companion to Scottish Culture* London, Edward
    Arnold
Davie, G. E. (1953) *The Scotch Metaphysics* D. Litt Edinburgh
Davie. G. E. (1964) *The Democratic Intellect* Edinburgh, EUP
Davie, G. E. (1967) *Hume, Reid and the Passion for Ideas* in George Bruce,
    ed. *Edinburgh in the Age of Reason*
Davie, G. E. (1973) *The Social Significance of the Scottish Philosophy of
    Common Sense* (The Dow Lecture) Edinburgh, T. A. Constable

Davie, G. E. (1989) *The Crisis of the Democratic Intellect* Edinburgh Polygon

Dixon, K. (1972) *Philosophy of Education and the Curriculum* Oxford Pergamon

Dunn, D . (1992) *Scotland: An Anthology* London Fontana

Durkan, J. & J. Kirk (1977) *The University of Glasgow 1451-1577* University of Glasgow Press

Edwards, E. G. (1982) *Higher Education for Everyone* Nottingham, Spokesman

Edinburgh University Quatercentenary Conference (1984) *Universities, Society and the Future*

Ferguson, Adam (1768) *An Essay on the History of Civil Society* Edinburgh

Feyerabend, P (1978) *Against Method* London Verso

Feyerabend, P. (1982) *Science in a Free Society* London Verso

Galbraith, J. K. (1992) *The Culture of Contentment* London Sinclair-Stevenson

Gallie, W. B. (1960) *A New University: A. D. Lindsay and the Keele experiment* London, Chatto & Windus

Gasset, Ortega y (1932) *The Revolt of the Masses* London

Gasset, Ortega y (1946) *The Mission of the University* Translated by H. L. Norstrand London

Geddes, P. (1890) *Scottish University Needs and Aims* Dundee

Gouldner, A. (1979) *The Future of Intellectuals and the Rise of the New Class* London Macmillan

Green, V. H. H. (1969) *The Universities* Pelican

Grant, N. (1982) *The Crisis in Scottish Education* Edinburgh Saltire Pamphlet

Grant, N. & A. Main(1976) *Scottish Universities the case for devolution* Edinburgh The Authors

Grierson, H. J. C. (1936) *The University and a Liberal Education* London Oliver & Boyd

Grierson, H. J. C. (1919) *The Scottish Universities* in J. Clarke, ed. *Problems of National Education* London

Grieve, C. M. (1926) *Contemporary Scottish Studies* London Parsons

Gutman, A. (1987) *Democratic Education* Princeton University

Habermas, J. (1978) *Knowledge and Human Interests* London Heinemann

Halsey, A. H. (1971) *The British Academics* London Faber

Hanham, J. H. (1969) *Scottish Nationalism* London Faber

Harris, R. S. (1976) *A History of Higher Education in Canada 1663–1960* Toronto TUP

Harvard University Report (1945, *General Education in a Free Society*

Harvie, C. (1977) *Scotland and Nationalism: Scottish Society and Politics 1707–1797* London Allen & Unwin

Harvie, C. (1981) *No Gods and Precious Few Heroes* London Arnold

Harvie, C. (1992) *Europe and the Scottish Nation* Edinburgh Scottish Centre for Economic and Social Research

Hechter, M. (1975) *Internal Colonialism* London Routledge & Kegan Paul

Hechter, M. (1983) *Internal Colonialism Revisited* in E. A. Tiryakian &
    R. Rogowski Eds. *Western Nationalism: Theory, Methodology and
    Comparative Framework* London Allen & Unwin
Hetherington, H. J. W. (1930) *The History and Significance of the Modern
    Universities* in H. Martin, ed. *The Life of a Modern University*
    London S. C. M. Press
Hirst, P. H. (1965) *Liberal Education and the Nature of Knowledge* in
    R. D. Archambault, ed. *Philosophical Analysis and Education* Henley
    Routledge & Kegan Paul
Hoeveler, J. D. (1981) *James McCosh and the Scottish Intellectual Tradition*
    Princeton University Press
Horn, D. B. (1967) *A Short History of the University of Edinburgh
    1556–1889* EUP
Houston, R. (1985) *Scottish Literacy and the Scottish Identity 1600–1800*
    CUP
Humes, W. (1980) *Alexander Bain and the Development of Educational
    Theory* in J. V. Smith & D. Hamilton, eds. *The Meritocratic Intellect*
    Aberdeen University Press
Humes, W. & H. Paterson, eds (1982) *Scottish Culture and Scottish
    Education* Edinburgh John Donald
Hutchins, R. (1962) *The Higher Learning in America* Storr Lectures 1936.
    Yale University Press
Huxley, T. H. (1894–1908) *Collected Essays Vol 3* London Macmillan
Iliffe, A. H. (1966) *The Foundation Year at the University of Keele
    Sociological Review* Monograph No. 12
Jacob, F. (1970) *La Logique du Vivant* Paris Gallimard
Jardine, G. (1825) *Outlines of philosophical education, illustrated by the
    method of teaching the logic class in the University of Glasgow*
    Glasgow Oliver & Boyd   .
Jaspers, K. (1960) *The Idea of a University* London Peter Owen
Jebb, R. (1901) *The University Extension Movement* in R. D. Roberts, ed.
    Education in the 19th Century CUP
Jeffrey, R. W. (1950) *The Unity of Knowledge* CUP
Kearney, H. F. (1970) *Scholars and Gentlemen: Universities and Society in
    Pre-industrial Britain, 1500–1700* London Faber & Faber
Kellas, J. G. (1980) *Modern Scotland* London Allen & Unwin
Keniston, K. (1972) *Human and Social Benefits* in *Universal Higher
    Education: Costs, Benefits, Options* Washington D.C. American
    Council on Education
Kerr, C. (1966) *The Uses of the University* Cambridge Mass. Harvard
    University Press
Kerr, J. (1910) *Scottish Education: School and University from Early Times
    to 1908* CUP
Kilgour, A. (1857) *University Reform, Letters to the Rt. Hon. the Earl of
    Aberdeen, on the Constitution and Government of the Universities*
    Aberdeen Smith
Kilgour, A. (1857) *The Scottish Universities and What to Reform in Them*
    Sutherland & Knox

Kitchen, P. (1975) *A Most Unsettling Person: An Introduction to the Ideas and Life of Patrick Geddes* London, Gollancz

Knox, H. M. (1953) *250 Years of Scottish Education 1696–1946* Oliver & Boyd

Knox, J. (1905) *The History of the Reformation in Scotland and the Book of Discipline*, ed. C. Lennox, London, Andrew Melrose

Kogan, M. and D. Kogan (1983) *The Attack on Higher Education* London, Kogan Page

Kotschig, W. (1932) *The University in a Changing World* OUP

Kuhn, T. S. (1970) *The Structure of Scientific Revolutions* University of Chicago Press & Verso

Laurie, S. (1889) *The University and Scottish University Reforms* Edinburgh, James Thin

Laurie, S. S. (1903) *Studies in the History of Educational Opinion* CUP

Lawson, H. & L. Appignanesi, eds (1989) *Dismantling Truth* London -p p Weidenfeld & Nicholson

Leavis, F. R. (1948) *Education and a University* 2nd ed. London, Chatto & Windus

Lewis, I. (1984) *The Student Experience of Higher Education* London, Croom Helm

Linklater, E. (1968) *The Survival of Scotland* London, Heinemann

Lorimer, J. (1854) *Scottish Universities, Past, Present and Possible* Edinburgh, W. P. Kennedy

Lyell, C. (1827) *State of the Universities Quarterly Review XXXVI*

Lyons, L. (1984) *The Idea of a University: Newman to Robbins* in *Universities, Society and the Future* Edinburgh, EUP

Mackay, D. J. (1885) *University Reform in Scotland* Rectorial Address at the University of St. Andrews 30 January 1885 London, P. S. King & Son

Mackintosh, M. (1962) *Education in Scotland, Yesterday and Today* Glasgow Robert Gibson & Sons

MacIntyre, A. (1981) *After Virtue: a study in moral theory* London, Duckworth

MacIntyre, A. (1988) *Whose Justice? Which Rationality?* London, Duckworth

Macmurray, J. (1932 *Symposium: What is Philosophy?* Proceedings of the Aristotelian Society, Supplementary Vol 11

Macmurray, J. (1944) *The Functions of a University, Political Quarterly* 15

Macmurray, J. (1957) *The Self as Agent* London, Faber & Faber

Macmurray, J. (1957) *Persons in Relation* London, Faber & Faber

Marwick, W. H. *Early Adult Education in Edinburgh Journal of Adult Education 5 1930–32 pp 389–404*

Marwick, W. H. *Mechanics' Institutes in Scotland Journal of Adult Education 6, 1932–34 pp. 292--09*

Matthews, F. (1991) *The Ecological Self* London, Routledge & Kegan Paul

McConnell, Berdahl & Fay (1973) *The British and American Transformations* University of California at Berkeley

McCosh, J. (1860) *The Intuitions of the Human Mind Inductively Investigated* London J. Murray

McCosh, J. (1866) *An Examination of Mr. J. S. Mill's Philosophy* London Macmillan

McCosh, J. (1875) *The Scottish Philosophy from Hutcheson to Hamilton* London Macmillan

McPherson, A. F . (1972) *The Generally-Educated Scot: An Old Ideal in a Changing University Structure* in A. F. McPherson, D. Swift and B. Bernstein *Eighteen plus: The Final Selection E282 units 15-17* Bletchley, the Open University

McPherson, A. F. (1973) *Selections and Survivals: A Sociology of the Ancient Scottish Universities* in R. Brown, ed. *Knowledge, Education and Cultural Change*: Papers in the Sociology of Education

McPherson, A. F. & G. R. Neave (1976) *The Scottish Sixth: A Sociological Evaluation of Sixth Year Studies and the Changing Relationship between School and University in Scotland* Windsor NFER

Mill. J. S. (1926) *A Speech on the Universities Journal of Adult Education 1926* pp 138–144

Miller, K., ed. (1970) *Memoirs of a Modern Scotland* London Faber

Minogue, K. (1973) *The Concept of a University* London Weidenfeld & Nicholson

Moberly, W. H. (1949) *The Crisis in the University* London SCM Press

Moberly, W. H. (1950) *Universities Ancient and Modern* A Ludwig Mond Lecture Manchester MUP

Monod, Jacques (1971) *Le Hasard et la Nécessité* Translated by Austyn Wainhouse *Chance and Necessity* New York Knopf

Morgan, A. (1927) *The Rise and Progress of Scottish Education* Edinburgh Oliver & Boyd

Morgan, A. (1933) *Scottish University Studies* London OUP

Morton, J. N. (1889) *An analysis of the Universities (Scotland) Act 1889 with the Act itself, the Act of 1858 and an index* Edinburgh Blackwood

Muirhead, J. H. (1899) *A Liberal Education an address* Birmingham

Murdoch, I. (1970) *The Sovereignty of Good* London Routledge & Kegan Paul

Nairn, T. (1970) *The Three Dreams of Scottish Nationalism* in K. Miller Ed. *Memoirs of a Modern Scotland*

Nash, Arnold S. (1945) *The University and the Modern World* SCM Press

Newman, J. H. (1976) *The Idea of a University* Ed. with introduction and notes by I. T. Ker, Oxford Clarendon Press

Niblett, W. R. (1963) *Oxbridge and Redbrick: the debt and the interest* in P. Halmos, ed. *The Sociological Review Monograph No 7: Sociological Studies in British University Education* Keele

Nuttgens, P. (1988) *What should we teach, and how should we teach it? Aims and Purposes of Higher Education* Aldershot Wildwood

Osborne, G. S. (1968) *Change in Scottish Education* London Longman

Pai, Y. & J. T. Myers (1967) *Philosophic Problems and Education* Philadelphia, Lippincott

Passmore, J. (1974) *Man's Responsibility for Nature: Ecological Problems and Western Traditions* London, Duckworth

Peacocke, A., ed. (1985) *Reductionism in Academic Disciplines* Guildford SRHE & NFER Nelson

Pedley, R. (1977) *Towards the Comprehensive University* London, Macmillan

Perkin, H. (1983) *Higher Education as an Historical System* Paper presented to a conference in Los Angeles

Phillipson, N., ed. (1984) *Universities, Society and the Future* (Edinburgh, University Quatercentenary Conference) EUP

Pippard, A. B. (1968) *Outline of a Proposal for Reorganising University Education Swann Report* London, HMSO

Pippard, A. B. et al (1970) *University Developments in the 1970s* in *Nature* 228 pp 813-815 London

Pippard, A. B. (1972) *The Structure of a Morally Committed University* in J. Lawlor *Higher Education: Patterns of Change in the 1970s* London, Routledge & Kegan Paul

Pippard, A. B. (1982) *The Curriculum of Higher Education* in D. Bligh, ed. *Professionalism and Flexibility in Learning* Leverhulme programme of study into the future of higher education Guildford SRHE

Playfair, L. (1873) *Universities in their Relation to Professional Education* Edinburgh, Edmondstone & Douglas

Plumb, J. H. (1964) *The Crisis in the Humanities* Harmondsworth Penguin

Polanyi, K. (1957) *The Great Transformation* Beacon Press

Polanyi, K. (1962) *The Republic of Science* Minerva 1, 59

Ponting, C. (1991) *A Green History of the World* London, Sinclair-Stevenson

Powell, J. P. (1966, 1971) *Universities and University Education: A Select Bibliography* Slough NFER

Quarterly Review (1827) *State of the Universities* 36 pp. 216-68

Rashdall, H. (1936) *The Universities of Europe in the Middle Ages* F. M. Pavicke & A. B. Emden eds 3 vols Oxford, OUP

Reeves, M. (1988) *The Crisis in Higher Education* Milton Keynes Open University Press

Reid, T. (1785) *Essays on the Intellectual Powers of Man*

Reid, T. (1872) *The Works of Thomas Reid*, ed. Sir William Hamilton 2 vols. 7th edn Edinburgh

Rives, W. C. (1970) *History of the Life and Times of James Madison* New York Books for Libraries Press 3 vols. Reprint of 1859–1868 ed. by Little, Brown & Co of Boston

Robbins, L. C. (1966) *The University and the Modern World* London, Macmillan

Robertson, C. G. (1924) *Humanism and Science* in Robertson et al *Humanism and Technology and other Essays* Oxford, OUP

Robertson, C. G. (1930 & 1944) *The British Universities* London, Methuen

Robertson, J. *Climate of Dissatisfaction Tess 28 March 1969* Principal author of the Scottish Advisory Council's Report on Secondary Education in 1947

Robbins, Lord (1980) *Higher Education Revisited* London, Macmillan
Rose, S., ed. (1982) *Against Biological Determinism* London, Allison
    & Busby
Rose, S. et al (1984) *Not in Our Genes* Harmondsworth Penguin
Rose, S. (1986) *A Vision out of Focus THES*
Rothblatt, S. (1968) *Revolution of the Dons* London, Faber & Faber
Rudolph, F. (1962) *The American College and University* New York, Alfred
    A. Knopf
Sanderson, Michael (1972) *The Universities and British Industry
    1850–1976* London, Routledge & Kegan Paul
Sanderson, Michael, ed. (1975) *The Universities in the the 19th Century*
    London, Methuen & Co
Saunders, L. J. (1950) *Scottish Democracy 1815–1840: The Social and
    Intellectual Background* Edinburgh, Oliver & Boyd
Schon, D. A. (1984) *The Reflective Practitioner* London, Smith
Scott, P. (1979) *What Future for Higher Education?* London, Fabian Society
Scott, P. (1984) *The Crisis of the University* London, Croom Helm
Shairp, J. C. (1856) *The Wants of the Scottish Universities and Some of the
    Remedies* Edinburgh
Shapin, S. (1981) *Science* in David Daiches, ed. *A Companion to Scottish
    Culture* London
Shils, E. (1984) *The Academic Ethic* Chicago U of C Press
Silver, H. (1970) *The History of British Universities 1800–1969 a
    bibliography* London, SRHE
Silver, H. & J. Brennan (1988) *A Liberal Vocationalism* London, Methuen
Simon, B. (1965) *Education and the Labour Movement 1870–1920*
    London, Lawrence & Wishart
Singer, C. (1941) *A Short History of Science to the 19th Century* Oxford,
    Clarendon Press
Sloman, A. (1964) *A University in the Making* BBC
Smith, A. (1805) *An Inquiry into the Nature and Causes of the Wealth of
    Nations* New ed. Glasgow, J & J Scrymgeour
Smout, T. C. (1969) *History of the Scottish People* London, Collins
Snow, C. (1964 & 1978) *The Two Cultures and a Second Look* CUP
Sparrow, J. (1967) *Mark Pattison and the Idea of a University* Clark
    Lectures at Cambridge, CUP
Squires, G. (1976) *Breadth and Depth: a study of curricula* Group for
    Research and Innovation in Higher Education 7
Squires, G. (1990) *First Degree: the undergraduate curriculum* SRHE & OU
Steiner, G. (1980) *Archives of Eden* in *Salmagundi* Saratoga Springs NY
Stevenson, R. L. (1904) *Vailima Letters* 4th Edn London, Methuen & Co
Stone, I. F. (1988) *The Trial of Socrates* London, Carse
Trow, M. (1973) *Problems in the Transition from Elite to Mass Higher
    Education* Carnegie Commission on Higher Education Berkely
Truscott, B. (1943) *Redbrick University* London, Faber
Veblen, T. (1918) *The Higher Learning in America* New York
Wenley, R. M. (1895) *The University Extension Movement in Scotland*
    Glasgow, Robert Maclehose

Whewell, W. (1837) *On the Principles of English University Education* London

Whitehead, A. N. (1927) *Science and the Modern World* Cambridge, CUP

Whitehead, A. N. (1929) *The Aims of Education* London, Williams & Norgate

Wilson, E. O. (1975) *Sociobiology* Harvard University Press

Wilson, G. (1855) *What is Technology?* An inaugural lecture delivered in the University of Edinburgh. Edinburgh, Sutherland & Knox

Wilson, J. D. (1981) *Student Learning in Higher Education* London, Croom Helm

Wolfe, J. N., ed. (1969) *Government and Nationalism* Edinburgh, EUP

Index